Roadside Silhouettes

1 MOURNING DOVE
2 HOUSE SPARROW
3 GRACKLE
4 STARLING
5 COWBIRD
6 RED-WINGED BLACKBIRD
7 KINGFISHER
8 BLUE JAY
9 MOCKINGBIRD
10 SONG SPARROW
11 SHRIKE
12 FLICKER
13 BLUEBIRD
14 NIGHTHAWK
15 ROBIN
16 KILLDEER
17 PHEASANT
18 PURPLE MARTIN
19 BARN SWALLOW
20 CLIFF SWALLOW
21 KESTREL
22 CARDINAL
23 MEADOWLARK
24 KINGBIRD
25 HORNED LARK
26 PHOEBE
27 BOBWHITE
28 CROW

A Field Guide
to the Birds of Texas
and Adjacent States

THE PETERSON FIELD GUIDE SERIES ®

A Field Guide to the
Birds of Texas
and Adjacent States

Roger Tory Peterson

Illustrations by
Roger Tory Peterson

Sponsored by
the Texas Parks and Wildlife Department,
the National Audubon Society,
the National Wildlife Federation,
and the Roger Tory Peterson Institute

HOUGHTON MIFFLIN COMPANY   BOSTON   NEW YORK

For information about this and other Houghton Mifflin
trade and reference books and multimedia products, visit
The Bookstore at Houghton Mifflin on the World Wide Web
at http://www.hmco.com/trade/ .

PETERSON FIELD GUIDES and PETERSON FIELD GUIDE SERIES
are registered trademarks of Houghton Mifflin Company.

Library of Congress catalog card number: 59-9110

ISBN: 0-395-08087-8
ISBN 0-395-92138-4 (pbk.)

First printing February 1960
for the Texas Fish and Game Commission

Printed in the United States of America

VB 30 29 28 27 26 25 24 23 22

Preface

TEXAS, as everyone knows, is vast. So vast that it can boast a greater variety of birds than any other state in the Union. In its mid-sections, East meets West, faunally, and people who live near its center line (Fort Worth, Dallas, Waco, Austin, San Antonio, and Brownsville) have long had to carry two bird books, one in each side pocket — my eastern *Field Guide to the Birds* and its companion volume, *A Field Guide to Western Birds*. Or, if they use Richard Pough's excellent Audubon Bird Guides, three books.

When I was asked by the Texas Game and Fish Commission to prepare a special Field Guide for Texas, I suspected that this secession from the national Field Guides was due to the too frequent irritation of looking things up in the wrong book. However, I was assured that the motive was more idealistic. This project was visualized as part of a larger plan of publication, in which stock would be taken of the wildlife resources of Texas — its birds, mammals, fish, and other wildlife — so that they might be more wisely administered. Equally important was the educational objective, that people throughout the state might be made more aware of their wildlife heritage, the better to enjoy and conserve it. Recognition is the first principle, the ability to name things.

In 1934 my first eastern Field Guide was written. It was designed so that live birds could be run down by their field marks without resorting to the anatomical differences and measurements that the old-time collector used. The "Peterson System," as it is called, is based on patternistic drawings that indicate the key field marks with arrows. These and the comparisons between similar species are the core of the system. This practical method has enjoyed universal acceptance not only in this country but also in Europe, where Field Guides now exist in 10 languages.

This new book on Texas birds represents 25 years of evolution wherein the system has been considerably modified and improved. Although the same birds are also figured in either the eastern or western Field Guides or in both, the discussion of their status and distribution in Texas is a new contribution.

Acknowledgments

I can truly say the Field Guides have been written not only for the bird students of America but *by* them. I shall not list again the 200 or more correspondents, collaborators, and critics who helped me with the basic guides and their revisions, nor the mass of ornithological literature that was digested in their preparation,

v

but I must acknowledge the many Texas sources that made the present adaptation possible.

Basic regional checklists consulted were: The A.O.U. *Check-list of North American Birds*, 5th edition (1957); *The Birds of Texas, an Annotated Check-list* (J. K. Strecker, 1912); *Check-list of the Birds of Texas* (Col. L. R. Wolfe, 1956); *Principal Game Birds and Mammals of Texas* (Texas Game, Fish and Oyster Commission, 1945); *Field Checklist of the Birds of the Panhandle of Texas* (1955); *Field Check-list of Birds of the Southern Plains Area* (1956; Andrews, Crane, Ector, Glasscock, Howard, Martin, Midland, Reagan, and Upton Cos.); *Field Check-list of the Upper Gulf Coast Area of Texas* (Austin, Brazoria, Calhoun, Chambers, Colorado, Fort Bend, Galveston, Harris, Jackson, Jefferson, Matagorda, Orange, Victoria, Waller, and Wharton Cos.); *Checklist of the Birds of the Central Coast of Texas* (by Hagar and Packard, 1956; Aransas, Bee, Jim Wells, Kleberg, Nueces, Refugio, and San Patricio Cos.); *Bird Check-list of Southeast Texas* (Miner, 1946); *Checklist of Bird Species of the Rio Grande Delta Region of Texas* (I. Davis, 1955).

A number of county checklists were examined, some of which have been published on field cards and some on mimeographed sheets. Others were unpublished or were in preliminary form. The single counties covered in this way were: Bell, Bexar, Brewster, Coleman, Dallas, Denton, Guadalupe, Howard, Hunt, Kendall, Maverick, McLennan, Midland, Kerr, Smith, Tarrant, and Travis Counties. Additional lists covering more restricted areas included: Aransas National Wildlife Refuge, Austin, Balmorhea and Lower Limpia Canyon (preliminary), Big Bend National Park, Dallas, Davis Mountains (preliminary), Del Rio (preliminary), El Paso, Fort Worth, Guadalupe Mountains region, Hagerman and Tishomingo National Wildlife Refuge, Laguna Atascosa National Wildlife Refuge, Pecos River Valley (preliminary), Santa Ana National Wildlife Refuge, Waco and Wink (Winkler Co., preliminary).

In addition to the above checklists the following periodicals were combed for pertinent data: *The Auk, The Wilson Bulletin, The Condor, Audubon Field Notes* (including the *Christmas Census*), *The Gulf Coast Migrant*, the *Texas Ornithological Society Newsletter*, and *The Phalarope*. George Lowery's *Louisiana Birds* proved most useful in understanding more clearly the status of birds that approach the limits of their ranges near the Texas-Louisiana border. After organizing all the above material a check was made of the files of the United States Fish and Wildlife Service in Washington for any significant unpublished records.

A first draft of the ranges was then circulated to more than 30 key people throughout the state for their comments and additions. Each collaborator had things to add or to modify, and contributed valuable information. Perhaps the most thorough fine-toothed comb among my critics was Edgar Kincaid of Austin, who in addition to perusing the ranges also gave the entire manuscript a going-over. He was invaluable in his knowledge of the Texas ornithological literature and in his personal acquaintance with observers throughout the state. Because of this wide familiarity he was able to advise me which checklists should be used with caution and which records were "unsanitary."

I am very grateful to Fred Webster of Austin, regional editor for south Texas in the *Audubon Field Notes*, who with his usual care combed the recent files of *Audubon Field Notes* for significant records. Colonel L. R. Wolfe, of Kerrville, with his knowledge of the Edwards Plateau and the entire state, also gave valued counsel. Others who examined the range manuscripts critically with a special eye to their regions and to whom I owe a special debt of gratitude are: Lena McBee and Mary Belle Keefer (El Paso); Mrs. J. D. Acord and J. H. and Betty Bailey (Panhandle); John Galley, Mrs. J. W. LeSassier, Frances Williams, and Walter Ammon (Southern Plains, West Texas); Warren Pulich, Kent and Roddy Rylander, and Jerry Stillwell (north Texas); Howard McCarley, B. B. Watson and O. C. Sheffield (east Texas); Dr. Keith Dixon and Dr. William Davis (central Texas); J. M. Heiser, Jr., Arlie McKay, Frank Watson, and George and Stephen Williams (upper coast); Dr. Clarence Cottam, Mrs. A. H. Geiselbrecht and Mrs. Connie Hagar (central coast); Irby Davis, Luther Goldman, and Dr. Pauline James (Rio Grande delta).

Mr. A. S. Jackson and Mr. P. B. Uzzell of the Texas Game and Fish Commission have kindly furnished information on the status of exotic game birds introduced in various parts of the state. I am also much indebted to Dr. John W. Aldrich for kindly granting access to the records of the U.S. Fish and Wildlife Service.

Many others answered inquiries, sent information, or in other ways helped with the preparation of this book: Carl H. Aiken II, Dr. Richard O. Albert, Robert P. Allen, Dr. Dean Amadon, Thomas Burleigh, C. W. Christian, Amy Clampitt, Margaret H. Eaton, Philip Dumont, Mrs. Marcus Durham, Eugene Eisenmann, Guy Emerson, Carrie Holcomb, Mrs. E. H. Johnson, C. E. Kiblinger, Mrs. R. LeRoy, William L. McCart, Charles McNeese, Mrs. M. O'Neill, Barbara Peterson, Mrs. Bruce Reid, William Schultz, Alexander Sprunt III, H. W. Stevenson, Dr. Alexander Wetmore, Harold Williams, and Armond Yramategui.

For specimen material I am indebted to the American Museum of Natural History in New York, the Smithsonian Institution in Washington, and the Peabody Museum in New Haven.

Finally, I would like to express appreciation to the Texas Game and Fish Commission, the University of Texas Press, and Houghton Mifflin Company, and especially those who wrestled with the problems of actual publication: Morton Baker, Katharine Bernard, Paul Brooks, Everett T. Dawson, Howard Dodgen, Helen Phillips, Lovell Thompson, Benjamin Tilghman, and Frank Wardlaw.

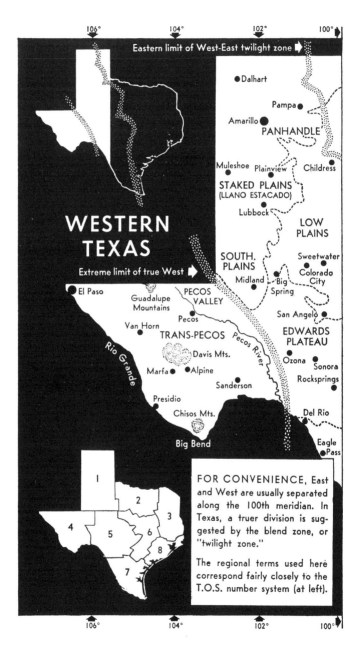

106°   104°   102°   100°

Eastern limit of West-East twilight zone ➡

●Dalhart

Pampa ●

Amarillo ●

PANHANDLE

Muleshoe ●   Plainview   ● Childress

STAKED PLAINS
(LLANO ESTACADO)

Lubbock ●

LOW PLAINS

WESTERN TEXAS

Extreme limit of true West ➡

SOUTH. PLAINS

Sweetwater ●

Colorado City ●

Midland ●   Big Spring ●

PECOS VALLEY

El Paso ●

Guadalupe Mountains

Pecos ●

Van Horn ●

TRANS-PECOS

Pecos River

San Angelo ●

EDWARDS PLATEAU

Davis Mts.

Marfa ● ● Alpine

Rio Grande

Sanderson ●

Ozona ●   Sonora ●

Rocksprings ●

Presidio ●

Chisos Mts.

Del Rio ●

Big Bend

Eagle ● Pass

1

2

3

4   5   6

8

7

FOR CONVENIENCE, East and West are usually separated along the 100th meridian. In Texas, a truer division is suggested by the blend zone, or "twilight zone."

The regional terms used here correspond fairly closely to the T.O.S. number system (at left).

106°   104°   102°   100°

Introduction:
Texas, the No. 1 Bird State

TEXAS, in keeping with its reputation for bigness, can boast the largest avifauna of any of the 50 states. More than 540 species have been recorded, not including several extinct species. (California runs a poor second with roughly 80 fewer species.) This is three-quarters of all the species known to occur between Mexico and the Canadian border and very nearly as many as have been listed for all Europe west of the iron curtain.

According to Dr. H. C. Oberholser, the leading authority on Texas birds, the number exceeds 800 if one includes the subspecies. But subspecies are hardly in the province of a field guide such as this. They belong in a more technical work, such as the one Dr. Oberholser has labored on for so many years. Every serious ornithologist hopes that this monumental work, now being edited, soon will see publication.

Nearly 800 miles from top to bottom or from east to west and covering some 267,000 square miles, Texas can claim diversity by virtue of size alone, but even more significant than size in determining its rich avifauna is the state's location on the continent. East meets West, biologically, along the 100th meridian, and North meets South, especially along the Rio Grande, where birds from the northern plains meet Mexican types. Altitudes range from sea level along the Gulf to 8000 feet in the Trans-Pecos; rainfall varies from a wet 50+ inches on the Louisiana border to less than 10 inches in the extreme west.

A large percentage of those North American birds that spend the winter in the tropics pass through Texas on their migrations, greatly augmenting a large winter and a large resident population. Truly Texas is the state above all others that offers the most lively "birding," a factor that is now luring many binocular-toting tourists from the rest of the United States.

Three hundred and eighty miles of coast, with long barrier beaches, include the longest island for its width in the world (Padre Island) and constitute an area tenanted throughout the year by myriads of shorebirds, gulls, terns, pelicans, and other coastal birds. These sandy strips guard great salt lagoons and coastal marshes that harbor some of the finest waterfowl concentrations on the continent. The Aransas National Wildlife Refuge is famous for its relict flock of Whooping Cranes (which Dr. Clarence Cottam states is worth not less than a million dollars a year to the state of Texas, through tourist trade alone). Farther down the coast, at Laguna Atascosa, great flocks of Redheads and other ducks spend the winter. Many islands, such as Green Island, Lydia Ann Island, and the Second Chain of Islands, swarm with nesting colonial water birds, among them such spectacular long-legged waders as Spoonbills and Reddish Egrets.

Perhaps the most noted bird mecca in Texas is Rockport, made famous by Connie Hagar, who with her husband Jack Hagar operates the Rockport Cottages, which are often filled to capacity with bird watchers — especially during spring migration. The best time is in April or early May, when "northers" sometimes pin down great numbers of migrants along the Gulf. Over 400 species have been recorded at Rockport. The new Welder Refuge, operated by Dr. Clarence Cottam at nearby Sinton, now rivals Rockport's fame. Do not miss it.

The belt of coastal prairie, 30 to 50 miles wide, has few trees, except where rivers dissect it. These rich river groves give great variety to a region where bird life would otherwise be mainly represented by grassland species.

East Texas is heavily forested, partly with pines and partly with deciduous woods, from the Louisiana border westward roughly to 95°W or 96°W. South of this forested area is the coastal prairie. Many birds — the Wood Thrush, Kentucky Warbler, Acadian Flycatcher, etc. — breed in this eastern Texas forested area but are seen only as migrants in the wide coastal belt. Several Eastern species, such as the Red-cockaded Woodpecker and Brown-headed Nuthatch, are found in Texas only in the pine forests of this part of the state, while in the swampy streambottoms Swainson's and Prothonotary Warblers nest and occasionally even Swallow-tailed Kites may be seen.

Farther inland lies the Blackland Prairie area, a belt running from San Antonio to the central-northern part of the state. Here, along the line that includes San Antonio, Austin, Waco, Dallas, and Fort Worth, is the western limit for many Eastern birds and the eastern limit for some Western species.

Southern Texas, covered with great stretches of mesquite and other brush, has its own specialities, but its most exciting section is the lower Rio Grande Valley, where a number of Mexican birds have established their only outposts on North American soil. The Santa Ana National Wildlife Refuge is by far the largest sample of the original Rio Grande woodland left, and here Green Jays, Chachalacas, Kiskadees, Red-billed Pigeons, Black-headed Orioles, Olive-backed Warblers, and Tropical Kingbirds can be counted on.

The Edwards Plateau, an area of low hills, cedar, and scrub oak in the west-central part of the state, boasts the only bird that nests exclusively in Texas, the Golden-cheeked Warbler. The Black-capped Vireo of the oak scrub and the Cave Swallow, found in about 16 limestone caves, are also specialities of this interesting area (now being denuded of much of its cedar).

The Panhandle is an area of vast grassy plains, cut by a few deep canyons and valleys. For a change of diet from Horned Larks and other grassland birds, birders of Amarillo frequently go to Palo Duro Canyon, south of the city. There in the broken country in this great geological gash and in the groves along the river may be found a surprising variety, and it is here that unusual birds from the West as well as stragglers from the East are frequently noted. The Staked Plain, or Llano Estacado, is a short-grass plain that occupies most of the northern and western parts of the Panhandle and extends southward to merge imperceptibly into the Edwards Plateau and the Pecos River Valley in the west. Innumerable "wet-weather" lakes and water impoundments attract many migrant waterfowl and shorebirds. At Muleshoe National Wildlife Refuge, close to the border of New Mexico, flocks of thousands of Sandhill Cranes make a spectacular display in migration and in winter.

Although quite a few Western species may be found as far east as central Texas, the Pecos River is the classic dividing line between East and West. Beyond this point many Eastern species drop out and Western birds take over. The Trans-Pecos is a varied area of desert and mountains and in the higher reaches of these mountains may be found many birds that reside nowhere else in Texas. Each mountain range has a somewhat different bird life. In the high canyons of the Chisos Mountains in Big Bend National Park, Painted Redstarts, Blue-throated Hummingbirds, Mexican Jays, Colima Warblers, and many other specialities of the Mexican mountains reach their northeastern outpost; while in the fir groves on the crests of the Guadalupe Mountains certain Rocky Mountain species attain their southern limit. There are still new discoveries to be made in the mountains of the Trans-Pecos, as indeed there are in many sections of west Texas.

El Paso, situated on the Rio Grande at the extreme western tip of the state, has its own group of specialties, like the Mexican Duck, Lucy's Warbler, and Lawrence's Goldfinch, but the main attraction is the river, which acts as a highway for traveling birds.

I have catalogued only briefly some of the main bird regions of Texas. I would strongly urge the birder who has a desire to explore the state to obtain a copy of *A Guide to Bird Finding West of the Mississippi* (1953) by Dr. Olin Sewall Pettingill. In this Baedeker of bird localities, Dr. Pettingill devotes nearly 60 pages to Texas. In a very thorough manner he covers every portion of the state, names the outstanding places, gives explicit directions for getting to them, and lists the special birds to be looked for. He also gives a very useful coverage of New Mexico, Oklahoma, Arkansas, and Louisiana, which share with Texas a very similar avifauna.

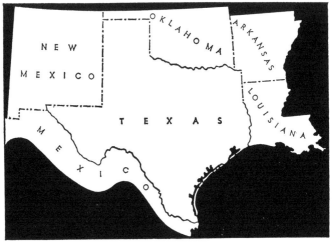

The major area where this book is useful

THE four states, shown above, which surround Texas, and also the immediately adjacent parts of Mexico, share virtually the same avifauna with Texas, and therefore most bird watchers throughout this region prefer to use this Field Guide, although the well-equipped birder may own the eastern and western Field Guides as well.

Although Texas has by far the largest list (more than 540), both New Mexico and Oklahoma can now boast 400, Louisiana is not far behind with 395, and the Arkansas list stands at 310.

Only 4 species on the Oklahoma list have never been recorded in Texas. These all are accidental (Iceland Gull, Glaucous-winged Gull, White-winged Crossbill, and White-winged Junco).

Six species of accidentals on the Louisiana list have not been recorded in Texas (Red-footed Booby, Ancient Murrelet, Smooth-billed Ani, Wheatear, Black-whiskered Vireo, and Snow Bunting).

Seventeen species on the New Mexico list have never been recorded in Texas. As they are found mostly in the western part of the state, some commonly, the birder west of the Rio Grande will prefer to use the *Field Guide to Western Birds*.

Contents

Illustrations

How to Use This Book

VETERANS who have watched birds for years will know how to use this book. Beginners, however, should spend a few moments becoming familiar, in a general way, with the illustrations: ducks, it will be seen, do not resemble loons; gulls are readily distinguishable from terns. The needle-like bills of the warblers immediately differentiate them from the seed-cracking bills of the sparrows. Birds that could be confused are here grouped together when easy comparison is possible. Thus, when a bird has been seen the observer can turn to the picture most resembling it and feel confident that he has reduced the possibilities to the few species in its own group.

In most instances the pictures and their legend pages tell the story without help from the main text. The short arrows point to the most outstanding field marks, briefly explained on the page opposite. In every case it is well to check identifications by referring to the text. The plates give visual field marks; the text gives aids such as manner of flight, range, season, preferred habitat, etc., not visually portrayable, and under a separate heading discusses the birds that might be confused with a given species.

It is hoped that besides helping the beginner who can scarcely tell a gull from a duck this guide will be useful to the advanced student in recognizing the unusual. The *accidentals*, species recorded in Texas five times or less, are briefly treated in Appendix I. For illustrations of these stragglers and a more thorough discussion consult either *A Field Guide to the Birds* or *A Field Guide to Western Birds*. A field guide to Mexican birds is in preparation.

One need only to take a trip with one of the experts — someone like Edgar Kincaid of Austin, Luther Goldman of San Benito, Irby Davis of Harlingen, or Connie Hagar of Rockport — to realize the possibility of identifying almost any Texas bird, with amazing certainty, at the snap of a finger. Most of the "rare finds" are made by people who are alive to the possibilities and know just what field marks to look for. It is the discovery of rarities that gives birding all the elements of a sport. When we become more proficient we may attempt to list as many birds as we can in a day, totting them up on the widely used small white checklists. The "big day" or "century run," taken at the peak of the spring migration, is the apogee of this sort of thing. In fact the biggest "big day" ever recorded in the U.S. — that is, the largest list of birds ever made in one day *by one party* — was tallied by Connie Hagar and C. D. Brown at Rockport. Their staggering total was 204 species listed between dawn and dusk.

Many people who are mildly interested in birds are afraid to pursue the subject because, as they sometimes express it, they "can hardly tell a robin from a sparrow." Others, perhaps, have shied away from unfamiliar terminology. Such people do themselves needless injustice. The enjoyment of birds depends neither upon intensive study nor academic qualifications. Those who claim to be hardly able to distinguish a robin from a sparrow certainly recognize a gull, a duck, goose, or swan, an owl, pelican, and many others of the various families. They are, in fact, already quite a long way on the road to knowing the birds.

We are concerned in Texas with 487 basic species. All these are given full treatment in this book. An additional 55 species plus 2 hybrids have been noted in the state fewer than 5 times: these are described briefly in Appendix I, "Accidentals." This makes a total of 542 species and 2 hybrids on the Texas list up to 1960, not including those that have become extinct and those that no longer visit the state. Nor does this include subspecies.

Subspecies: Subspecies have no definite entity, but merely represent subdivisions within the geographic range of a species. They are races, usually determined by morphological characteristics such as slight differences in measurements, shades of color, etc. These subdivisions, generally discernible only by comparison of museum series, are seldom apparent in the field and should not concern the field observer. To illustrate, the Mockingbirds of west Texas (*Mimus polyglottos leucopterus*) differ very slightly from those in the eastern half of the state (*M. p. polyglottos*), and are given a different subspecific name. No one but an expert comparing specimens would detect the difference.

So forget about subspecies. It is a challenge, however, to be able to identify some of the more well-marked races. In this book subspecies are ignored unless field distinctions are fairly obvious. There are not many such inclusions (a case in point is the Canada Goose, whose races differ greatly in size). Advanced students, using skins in a good museum, might work out ways of telling others, but a too thorough treatment in these pages would lead to many errors in the field.

Make This Guide a Personal Thing: It is gratifying to see a *Field Guide* marked on every page, for I know it has been well used. Although the covers are waterproofed, I have seen copies with homemade oilcloth jackets; others are jacketed in close-fitting plastic envelopes, obtainable in bookstores. I have seen copies reorganized and rebound to suit the owner's taste; local checklists, and even illustrations from other books, have been bound in. Many have been tabbed with index tabs on the margins, or fitted with flaps or envelopes to hold daily checklists. In this book I have included a checklist, to be used in making up a "life list," so that the owner need not mark up the index.

The Illustrations: The plates and line cuts throughout the text are intended as diagrams, arranged for quick, easy comparison of the species most resembling each other. As they are not intended to be pictures or portraits, modeling of form and feathering is often subordinated to simple contour and pattern. Some birds are better adapted than others to this simplified handling, hence the variation in treatment. Even color is sometimes unnecessary, if not indeed confusing. In many of the water birds that we seldom see at close range this is especially true; therefore many of the diagrams are carried out in black and white. With most small birds, however, color is quite essential.

Range (Where found): The area covered by this book is basically Texas. However, it will be virtually as useful to birders in the adjacent states. In order that the user may have an over-all concept of each bird's distribution, I have under the heading "Where found" first given a brief outline of the bird's general range and then, under the subheading "Texas," described how it fits into the Texas picture. The Texas Ornithological Society has adopted a plan that divides the state into 8 sections. I prefer to use names rather than the 1 to 8 system, but in general my named areas, listed below, conform fairly closely to the T.O.S. break-down (see maps).

Panhandle: The northwestern block of counties almost making a square in the upper part of Region 1.

Staked Plain: The Llano Estacado, covering the northern and western parts of the Panhandle and extending south, to merge imperceptibly with the Edwards Plateau near Midland. I have used the colloquial Texan form, "Staked Plains."

North Texas (Region 2): A block bordering the Red River on the north, the southward extension of the Panhandle on the west, the east Texas forests on the east, and south to a line just short of Coleman and Waco.

East Texas (Region 3): The eastern block of counties (excluding the coastal plain); dominated by woodlands.

Trans-Pecos (Region 4): The area west of the Pecos River in western Texas. "Extreme w. Texas" means the El Paso area.

Southern Plains: Roughly from the southern part of the Panhandle south through Midland to the edge of the Pecos Valley and the Edwards Plateau.

Edwards Plateau (Region 5): The west-central part of the state — east of the Pecos; an area of low hills and cedar brakes.

Central Texas (Region 6): Really east-central — the area between the Edwards Plateau and the coastal prairie and east Texas.

South Texas (Region 7): The region south of the Edwards Plateau; extending south of a line drawn from Maverick County on the Rio Grande to Refugio County on the central coast.

Central coast (included in Region 7): That part of the coast centering around Rockport and Corpus Christi.

EASTERN AND MIDDLE TEXAS

MANY eastern birds find their western limits along a line joining Fort Worth, Austin, and Brownsville, somewhat east of the "twilight zone."

Eastern limit of West-East twilight zone

LOW PLAINS

Wichita Falls
Sherman
Gainesville
Bonham
Red River
Paris
Texarkana
Mt. Pleasant

NORTH TEXAS

Denton
Sulphur Springs
Breckenridge
Fort Worth
Dallas
Tyler
Marshall
Abilene
Athens
Hillsboro
Corsicana
Coleman
Rusk
Brownwood
Waco
Palestine
Nacogdoches
Crockett
Lufkin

CENTRAL TEXAS

EAST TEXAS

Brady
Llano
Bryan
Conroe
Orange
EDWARDS PLATEAU
Austin
Brenham
Beaumont
Kerrville
Bastrop
Port Arthur
San Marcos
Houston
Seguin
Gonzales
UPPER COASTAL PLAIN
San Antonio
Galveston
Uvalde
Bay City
Victoria
Crystal City
Rockport
Upper Coast
SOUTH TEXAS
Sinton
Corpus Christi
Alice
Central Coast
Kingsville
Laredo
Rio Grande
LOWER RIO GRANDE VALLEY
Norias
Rio Grande City
McAllen
Raymondville
Harlingen
Lower Coast
Brownsville

The T.O.S. numbered regions

1
2
3
4
5
6
7
8

Upper coast (Region 8): The counties near the coast from the Louisiana border south and west to Port Lavaca and Victoria.

Lower Rio Grande Valley or Delta: A somewhat elastic term. The ornithologist defines it as the southern tip of Texas south of a line drawn from Rio Grande City to Raymondville.

Eastern Texas in the broader sense may be bounded by a line drawn from Gainesville and Fort Worth to Brownsville, skirting the Edwards Plateau through Austin and San Antonio. This is the western limit for many Eastern birds.

Inasmuch as Texans know the locations of cities and towns in their state but often have only a hazy knowledge of most of the counties (there are 254), generally I have outlined the range of a species by mentioning the nearest good-sized towns or cities (within 20 miles) rather than the counties.

When indicating the abundance of various species, some of the local Texas checklists have used a system of numbers from 1 to 7, or some variant of that system. For example: 1 — Abundant; 2 — Common; 3 — Fairly Common; 4 — Uncommon; 5 — Rare; 6 — Very Rare; 7 — No Recent Record. Since a bird common in one county may be rare in the next, usually I have not indicated abundance; that is more adequately covered by the local checklists. I do mention relative frequency in some instances and therefore I must define my terms (I have not used the number system):

Abundant: 100–500 or more may be seen in a day

Common: Familiar; 5–100 may be seen in a good day

Uncommon: Less than 5 in a day; less than 25 in a year

Rare: 1–5 in a year but probably regular

Irregular: Not every year, but may occur in numbers

Casual (or *Occasional*): On the local level this means only 1 or 2 records in a decade, but the bird might be expected to reappear. When referring to the state as a whole it means more than 5 records but less than 15.

Accidental: On the local level this means 1 record; the bird might not reasonably be expected again. On the state level, accidental means 5 records or less.

Resident: The same thing as *permanent resident;* the bird is found throughout the year. *Migrant* means a bird in passage, a bird whose stay is brief in spring or fall while en route between its summer and winter homes. The terms *summers* and *winters* are self-evident, but the dates (Mar.–Oct., etc.) may include the migration period when many birds are not yet established on their summering or wintering grounds. These seasonal dates may not represent the exact situation in any one locality. Extreme dates for the southern tip of Texas may vary many days, or even weeks, from those of the northern parts of the state.

Habitat: One looks for Meadowlarks in meadows, Wood Thrushes in woods. Therefore, those of the field-glass fraternity, out in early morning to run up a list, do not remain in one kind of place. They do not stay all day in the woods. After a while they investigate a field or explore a pond or a marsh. The experienced bird watcher can look at a woodland, a piece of brush, a prairie, or a swamp and can predict almost exactly what he will find there.

In this book each bird's preferred environment is indicated briefly under the heading "Habitat," but do not be surprised if your bird is not always where it is supposed to be, particularly in migration. At coastal concentration points like Rockport, birds in passage will often be found in an untypical environment.

Nest: Nest location and nest form are noted very briefly (but only if the species breeds in Texas). Only the merest mention of egg numbers and appearance is given. There is not room in a guide of these dimensions to go into the more subtle distinctions between the nests and eggs of various species. That would be a book in itself. The main reason for including these data at all is not to aid the observer in recognizing an unattended nest, but to alert him as to where he might look for a suspected nest.

Local Checklists: Many of the local bird clubs have published their own checklists. Some are mimeographed on large sheets; others are printed on cards small enough to be slipped into the pocket or inserted into the *Field Guide*. These cards are available in quantity and are usually used for keeping the daily tally. Most of them have a great deal of abbreviated information on local status.

I shall not list the checklists available, or the clubs, because new ones appear. If you do not have contact with a local club, my suggestion, should you be a Texan, is that you get in touch with the Texas Ornithological Society. This fine organization, which acts as a parent body and liaison to the local bird clubs, publishes a monthly newsletter, holds field trips, and has a three-day annual meeting.

Voice: We make our first identification of a species, as a rule, by sight. Then we become familiar with its song or notes. A "sizzling trill" or a "bubbling warble" conveys but a wretched idea of the voice of any particular bird. Though inadequate descriptions, they do help to fix a note or song in our minds. Word syllabifications in most books vary greatly, according to the author's interpretation. There are a few species whose voices we often hear long before we become acquainted with the bird in life. Who has known the Chuck-will's-widow, the Poor-will, or the Pauraque before hearing their cries at night? And there are those few — such as the small flycatchers — far more readily recognized by voice than by appearance.

In learning bird voices (and some experts do 90 per cent of their field work by ear), there is no substitute for the actual sounds. Authors often attempt to fit songs into syllables, words, and phrases. Musical notations, comparative descriptions, and even ingenious systems of symbols have been employed. But since the advent of tape recording, these older techniques have been eclipsed.

Use *A Field Guide to Bird Songs* in conjunction with this book. It is an album containing the most comprehensive collection of sound recordings yet attempted, the calls and songs of 305 North American land and water birds — a fairly large percentage of all the species found in Texas. Three 12-inch LP records, prepared under the direction of Dr. Peter Paul Kellogg and Dr. Arthur A. Allen of the Laboratory of Ornithology, Cornell University, and Dr. William W. H. Gunn, have been arranged to accompany, page by page, *A Field Guide to Western Birds*, second edition. These records can also be used satisfactorily with *A Field Guide to the Birds of Texas*, but the page numbers are different.

To prepare yourself for your field trips, play the records; read each description in this book for an analysis. Play the records repeatedly and compare similar songs. Repetition is the key to learning bird voices. Remember, however, that there are "song dialects" and birds in your locality may not always sing precisely as those on the record do. However, the quality will be the same and the general effect will be recognizable.

Identification by Elimination: Identification by elimination is important in field work. For example, five brown thrushes migrate through Texas. In east Texas one remains to nest, the Wood Thrush. The student there, knowing this, does not bother about the other four in the summertime, once having ascertained the bird to be a thrush. Similarly, in winter any thrush could be called, with almost complete certainty, the Hermit Thrush.

Suppose that a thrush is in the field of our glass with its back turned. It has no hint of rusty color anywhere. We know, then, that it is not a Veery, a Wood Thrush, or a Hermit Thrush. The bird faces about; it has grayish cheeks and a dim eye-ring. By experience, or consultation of the text, we know that Swainson's Thrush has a conspicuous eye-ring and buffy cheeks. Our bird, then, must be a Gray-cheek. It is almost as helpful to know what a bird could not be as what it might be.

Caution in Sight Records: One should always use caution in making identifications, especially where rarities are concerned. Not long ago some ornithologists would not accept sight records unless they were made along the barrel of a shotgun. Today it is difficult for the average person to secure collecting privileges; moreover, rarities may show up in parks, sanctuaries, or on municipal property, where collecting is out of the question. There is no good reason why we should not trust our eyes — at least after we have a good basic knowledge of the commoner species. In the case of a very rare bird, the rule is that two qualified observers should see it to make the record valid.

Photography, especially color photography, both in movies and stills, is becoming increasingly useful in substantiating state records. The first record of the Purple Sandpiper for Texas and the first record of the Varied Thrush were authenticated in this way.

A majority (two-thirds) of the plates in this Texas version of the Field Guide were new when the book first appeared. Some of these were since used in the second edition of the western Field Guide. The other plates are identical with those already published in the eastern Field Guide. Several species shown in these latter plates have occurred in Texas only as accidentals; and the inclusion of two species, the Arctic Tern and the Common (European) Teal, has been justified on even more slender grounds. There has been at least one sight record of the Arctic Tern in Texas — certainly very questionable — and therefore the portrait of this bird is included as an educational item. The European Teal, never actually recorded in Texas, is included because, in the opinion of the author, some sharp field observer will someday turn one up among the numerous flocks of Green-winged Teal.

The comparative numbers of species in various bird families — their world numbers, North American numbers, and Texas numbers — will interest many students. The world numbers follow the appraisal of Ernst Mayr and Dean Amadon (*American Museum Novitates* for Apr. 2, 1951). The North American figures are based on the A.O.U. *Check-list*, 5th edition. It will be seen that the Texas list lays claim to a large percentage of all North American birds.

The names of all birds are those officially designated by the A.O.U. *Check-list* committee. To prevent confusion, when the names differ from those in earlier editions of the eastern or western Field Guides, I have given the previous official names in parentheses. If a name within the parentheses appears in quotes, the name has never been official (sanctioned by the A.O.U.) but has attained wide popular use either because of its adoption in Richard Pough's Audubon Bird Guides or because of very widespread gunners' use. I have not gone beyond this point by listing other unofficial vernacular names; their perpetuation in most instances would serve no useful purpose.

Checklist

KEEP your "Life List" up to date by checking the birds you have seen.

......COMMON LOON
......RED-THROATED LOON
......RED-NECKED GREBE
......HORNED GREBE
......EARED GREBE
......LEAST GREBE
......WESTERN GREBE
......PIED-BILLED GREBE
......SOOTY SHEARWATER
......AUDUBON'S SHEARWATER
......WHITE-T. TROPIC-BIRD
......WHITE PELICAN
......BROWN PELICAN
......BLUE-FACED BOOBY
......GANNET
......D.-CRESTED CORMORANT
......OLIVACEOUS CORMORANT
......ANHINGA
......MAG. FRIGATE-BIRD
......GREAT WHITE HERON
......GREAT BLUE HERON
......GREEN HERON
......LITTLE BLUE HERON
......CATTLE EGRET
......REDDISH EGRET
......COMMON EGRET
......SNOWY EGRET
......LOUISIANA HERON
......BLACK-C. NIGHT HERON
......YELLOW-C. NIGHT HERON
......LEAST BITTERN
......AMERICAN BITTERN
......WOOD IBIS
......GLOSSY IBIS
......WHITE-FACED IBIS
......WHITE IBIS
......ROSEATE SPOONBILL
......WHISTLING SWAN
......CANADA GOOSE
......BRANT
......WHITE-FRONTED GOOSE
......SNOW GOOSE
......BLUE GOOSE
......ROSS' GOOSE
......BLACK-BELLIED TREE DUCK
......FULVOUS TREE DUCK
......MALLARD
......MEXICAN DUCK

......BLACK DUCK
......MOTTLED DUCK
......GADWALL
......PINTAIL
......GREEN-WINGED TEAL
......BLUE-WINGED TEAL
......CINNAMON TEAL
......EUROPEAN WIDGEON
......AMERICAN WIDGEON
......SHOVELER
......WOOD DUCK
......REDHEAD
......RING-NECKED DUCK
......CANVASBACK
......GREATER SCAUP
......LESSER SCAUP
......COMMON GOLDENEYE
......BUFFLEHEAD
......OLDSQUAW
......WHITE-WINGED SCOTER
......SURF SCOTER
......COMMON SCOTER
......RUDDY DUCK
......MASKED DUCK
......HOODED MERGANSER
......COMMON MERGANSER
......R.-BREASTED MERGANSER
......TURKEY VULTURE
......BLACK VULTURE
......WHITE-TAILED KITE
......SWALLOW-TAILED KITE
......MISSISSIPPI KITE
......GOSHAWK
......SHARP-SHINNED HAWK
......COOPER'S HAWK
......RED-TAILED HAWK
......HARLAN'S HAWK
......RED-SHOULDERED HAWK
......BROAD-WINGED HAWK
......SWAINSON'S HAWK
......ZONE-TAILED HAWK
......WHITE-TAILED HAWK
......ROUGH-LEGGED HAWK
......FERRUGINOUS HAWK
......GRAY HAWK
......HARRIS' HAWK
......BLACK HAWK
......GOLDEN EAGLE

.....BALD EAGLE
.....MARSH HAWK
.....OSPREY
.....CARACARA
.....PRAIRIE FALCON
.....PEREGRINE FALCON
.....APLOMADO FALCON
.....PIGEON HAWK
.....SPARROW HAWK
.....CHACHALACA
.....GR. PRAIRIE CHICKEN
.....LESSER PRAIRIE CHICKEN
.....BOBWHITE
.....SCALED QUAIL
.....GAMBEL'S QUAIL
.....HARLEQUIN QUAIL
.....RING-NECKED PHEASANT
.....CHUKAR
.....COTURNIX
.....TURKEY
.....WHOOPING CRANE
.....SANDHILL CRANE
.....LIMPKIN
.....KING RAIL
.....CLAPPER RAIL
.....VIRGINIA RAIL
.....SORA
.....YELLOW RAIL
.....BLACK RAIL
.....PURPLE GALLINULE
.....COMMON GALLINULE
.....AMERICAN COOT
.....JACANA
.....AM. OYSTERCATCHER
.....SEMIPALMATED PLOVER
.....PIPING PLOVER
.....SNOWY PLOVER
.....WILSON'S PLOVER
.....KILLDEER
.....MOUNTAIN PLOVER
.....AMERICAN GOLDEN PLOVER
.....BLACK-BELLIED PLOVER
.....RUDDY TURNSTONE
.....AMERICAN WOODCOCK
.....COMMON SNIPE
.....LONG-BILLED CURLEW
.....WHIMBREL
.....UPLAND PLOVER
.....SPOTTED SANDPIPER
.....SOLITARY SANDPIPER
.....WILLET
.....GREATER YELLOWLEGS
.....LESSER YELLOWLEGS
.....KNOT
.....PECTORAL SANDPIPER
.....WHITE-RUMPED SANDPIPER
.....BAIRD'S SANDPIPER
.....LEAST SANDPIPER
.....DUNLIN
.....SHORT-BILLED DOWITCHER
.....LONG-BILLED DOWITCHER

.....STILT SANDPIPER
.....SEMIPALMATED SANDPIPER
.....WESTERN SANDPIPER
.....BUFF-BREASTED SANDPIPER
.....MARBLED GODWIT
.....HUDSONIAN GODWIT
.....SANDERLING
.....AMERICAN AVOCET
.....BLACK-NECKED STILT
.....RED PHALAROPE
.....WILSON'S PHALAROPE
.....NORTHERN PHALAROPE
.....POMARINE JAEGER
.....HERRING GULL
.....CALIFORNIA GULL
.....RING-BILLED GULL
.....LAUGHING GULL
.....FRANKLIN'S GULL
.....BONAPARTE'S GULL
.....GULL-BILLED TERN
.....FORSTER'S TERN
.....COMMON TERN
.....ROSEATE TERN
.....SOOTY TERN
.....LEAST TERN
.....ROYAL TERN
.....SANDWICH TERN
.....CASPIAN TERN
.....BLACK TERN
.....BLACK SKIMMER
.....BAND-TAILED PIGEON
.....RED-BILLED PIGEON
.....ROCK DOVE
.....WHITE-WINGED DOVE
.....MOURNING DOVE
.....GROUND DOVE
.....INCA DOVE
.....WHITE-FRONTED DOVE
.....YELLOW-BILLED CUCKOO
.....BLACK-BILLED CUCKOO
.....ROADRUNNER
.....GROOVE-BILLED ANI
.....BARN OWL
.....SCREECH OWL
.....FLAMMULATED OWL
.....GREAT HORNED OWL
.....SNOWY OWL
.....FERRUGINOUS OWL
.....ELF OWL
.....BURROWING OWL
.....BARRED OWL
.....SPOTTED OWL
.....LONG-EARED OWL
.....SHORT-EARED OWL
.....SAW-WHET OWL
.....CHUCK-WILL'S-WIDOW
.....WHIP-POOR-WILL
.....POOR-WILL
.....PAURAQUE
.....COMMON NIGHTHAWK
.....LESSER NIGHTHAWK

.....CHIMNEY SWIFT
.....WHITE-THROATED SWIFT
.....LUCIFER HUMMINGBIRD
.....RUBY-THR. HUMMINGBIRD
.....BLACK-CH. HUMMINGBIRD
.....BROAD-T. HUMMINGBIRD
.....RUFOUS HUMMINGBIRD
.....RIVOLI'S HUMMINGBIRD
.....BLUE-THR. HUMMINGBIRD
.....BUFF-B. HUMMINGBIRD
.....BROAD-B. HUMMINGBIRD
.....BELTED KINGFISHER
.....RINGED KINGFISHER
.....GREEN KINGFISHER
.....YELLOW-SHAFTED FLICKER
.....RED-SHAFTED FLICKER
.....PILEATED WOODPECKER
.....RED-BELLIED WOODPECKER
.....GOLDEN-FR. WOODPECKER
.....RED-HEADED WOODPECKER
.....ACORN WOODPECKER
.....LEWIS' WOODPECKER
.....YELLOW-B. SAPSUCKER
.....WILLIAMSON'S SAPSUCKER
.....HAIRY WOODPECKER
.....DOWNY WOODPECKER
.....LADDER-B. WOODPECKER
.....RED-COCK. WOODPECKER
.....ROSE-THROATED BECARD
.....EASTERN KINGBIRD
.....TROPICAL KINGBIRD
.....WESTERN KINGBIRD
.....CASSIN'S KINGBIRD
.....SCISSOR-T. FLYCATCHER
.....KISKADEE FLYCATCHER
.....GREAT CRESTED FLYC.
.....WIED'S CRESTED FLYC.
.....ASH-THROATED FLYC.
.....EASTERN PHOEBE
.....BLACK PHOEBE
.....SAY'S PHOEBE
.....YELLOW-BELLIED FLYC.
.....ACADIAN FLYCATCHER
.....TRAILL'S FLYCATCHER
.....LEAST FLYCATCHER
.....HAMMOND'S FLYCATCHER
.....DUSKY FLYCATCHER
.....GRAY FLYCATCHER
.....WESTERN FLYCATCHER
.....EASTERN WOOD PEWEE
.....WESTERN WOOD PEWEE
.....OLIVE-SIDED FLYCATCHER
.....VERMILION FLYCATCHER
.....BEARDLESS FLYCATCHER
.....HORNED LARK
.....VIOLET-GREEN SWALLOW
.....TREE SWALLOW
.....BANK SWALLOW
.....ROUGH-WINGED SWALLOW
.....BARN SWALLOW
.....CLIFF SWALLOW

.....CAVE SWALLOW
.....PURPLE MARTIN
.....BLUE JAY
.....STELLER'S JAY
.....SCRUB JAY
.....MEXICAN JAY
.....GREEN JAY
.....BLACK-BILLED MAGPIE
.....COMMON RAVEN
.....WHITE-NECKED RAVEN
.....COMMON CROW
.....FISH CROW
.....PIÑON JAY
.....BLACK-CAPPED CHICKADEE
.....CAROLINA CHICKADEE
.....MOUNTAIN CHICKADEE
.....TUFTED TITMOUSE
.....BLACK-CRESTED TITMOUSE
.....PLAIN TITMOUSE
.....VERDIN
.....COMMON BUSHTIT
.....BLACK-EARED BUSHTIT
.....WHITE-BR. NUTHATCH
.....RED-BR. NUTHATCH
.....BROWN-H. NUTHATCH
.....PIGMY NUTHATCH
.....BROWN CREEPER
.....HOUSE WREN
.....WINTER WREN
.....BEWICK'S WREN
.....CAROLINA WREN
.....CACTUS WREN
.....LONG-BILLED MARSH WREN
.....SHORT-B. MARSH WREN
.....CAÑON WREN
.....ROCK WREN
.....MOCKINGBIRD
.....CATBIRD
.....BROWN THRASHER
.....LONG-BILLED THRASHER
.....CURVE-BILLED THRASHER
.....CRISSAL THRASHER
.....SAGE THRASHER
.....ROBIN
.....WOOD THRUSH
.....HERMIT THRUSH
.....SWAINSON'S THRUSH
.....GRAY-CHEEKED THRUSH
.....VEERY
.....EASTERN BLUEBIRD
.....WESTERN BLUEBIRD
.....MOUNTAIN BLUEBIRD
.....TOWNSEND'S SOLITAIRE
.....BLUE-GRAY GNATCATCHER
.....BLACK-T. GNATCATCHER
.....GOLDEN-CR. KINGLET
.....RUBY-CROWNED KINGLET
.....WATER PIPIT
.....SPRAGUE'S PIPIT
.....BOHEMIAN WAXWING
.....CEDAR WAXWING

......PHAINOPEPLA
......NORTHERN SHRIKE
......LOGGERHEAD SHRIKE
......STARLING
......BLACK-CAPPED VIREO
......WHITE-EYED VIREO
......HUTTON'S VIREO
......BELL'S VIREO
......GRAY VIREO
......YELLOW-THROATED VIREO
......SOLITARY VIREO
......YELLOW-GREEN VIREO
......RED-EYED VIREO
......PHILADELPHIA VIREO
......WARBLING VIREO
......BLACK-AND-W. WARBLER
......PROTHONOTARY WARBLER
......SWAINSON'S WARBLER
......WORM-EATING WARBLER
......GOLDEN-W. WARBLER
......BLUE-WINGED WARBLER
......TENNESSEE WARBLER
......ORANGE-CR. WARBLER
......NASHVILLE WARBLER
......VIRGINIA'S WARBLER
......COLIMA WARBLER
......LUCY'S WARBLER
......PARULA WARBLER
......OLIVE-BACKED WARBLER
......YELLOW WARBLER
......MAGNOLIA WARBLER
......CAPE MAY WARBLER
......BLACK-THR. BLUE WARBLER
......MYRTLE WARBLER
......AUDUBON'S WARBLER
......B.-THR. GRAY WARBLER
......TOWNSEND'S WARBLER
......B.-THR. GREEN WARBLER
......GOLDEN-CH WARBLER
......CERULEAN WARBLER
......BLACKBURNIAN WARBLER
......YELLOW-THR. WARBLER
......GRACE'S WARBLER
......CHESTNUT-SIDED WARBLER
......BAY-BREASTED WARBLER
......BLACKPOLL WARBLER
......PINE WARBLER
......PRAIRIE WARBLER
......PALM WARBLER
......OVENBIRD
......NORTHERN WATERTHRUSH
......LOUISIANA WATERTHRUSH
......KENTUCKY WARBLER
......CONNECTICUT WARBLER
......MOURNING WARBLER
......MacGILLIVRAY'S WARBLER
......YELLOWTHROAT
......YELLOW-BREASTED CHAT
......HOODED WARBLER
......WILSON'S WARBLER
......CANADA WARBLER

......AMERICAN REDSTART
......PAINTED REDSTART
......HOUSE SPARROW
......BOBOLINK
......EASTERN MEADOWLARK
......WESTERN MEADOWLARK
......YELLOW-H. BLACKBIRD
......REDWINGED BLACKBIRD
......ORCHARD ORIOLE
......BLACK-HEADED ORIOLE
......HOODED ORIOLE
......LICHTENSTEIN'S ORIOLE
......SCOTT'S ORIOLE
......BALTIMORE ORIOLE
......BULLOCK'S ORIOLE
......RUSTY BLACKBIRD
......BREWER'S BLACKBIRD
......BOAT-TAILED GRACKLE
......COMMON GRACKLE
......BROWN-HEADED COWBIRD
......BRONZED COWBIRD
......WESTERN TANAGER
......SCARLET TANAGER
......HEPATIC TANAGER
......SUMMER TANAGER
..X..CARDINAL
......PYRRHULOXIA
......ROSE-BREASTED GROSBEAK
......BLACK-HEADED GROSBEAK
......BLUE GROSBEAK
......INDIGO BUNTING
......LAZULI BUNTING
......VARIED BUNTING
......PAINTED BUNTING
......DICKCISSEL
......EVENING GROSBEAK
......PURPLE FINCH
......CASSIN'S FINCH
......HOUSE FINCH
......W.-COLLARED SEEDEATER
......PINE SISKIN
..X..AMERICAN GOLDFINCH
......LESSER GOLDFINCH
......LAWRENCE'S GOLDFINCH
......RED CROSSBILL
......OLIVE SPARROW
......GREEN-TAILED TOWHEE
......RUFOUS-SIDED TOWHEE
......BROWN TOWHEE
......LARK BUNTING
......SAVANNAH SPARROW
......GRASSHOPPER SPARROW
......BAIRD'S SPARROW
......LE CONTE'S SPARROW
......HENSLOW'S SPARROW
......SHARP-TAILED SPARROW
......SEASIDE SPARROW
......VESPER SPARROW
......LARK SPARROW
......RUFOUS-CR. SPARROW
......BACHMAN'S SPARROW

Checklist of Texas Accidentals

IT IS extremely unlikely that you will see any of these species in Texas. These are the ones that have been recorded less than 5 times in the state. Some have never been supported by an actual specimen. The Eskimo Curlew, once common, would now be accidental. A few borderline birds (5 or 6 records each) are included in the previous list. See the Appendixes for a brief discussion of the following species.

```
......ARCTIC LOON
......HARCOURT'S PETREL
......WILSON'S PETREL
......BROWN BOOBY
......RED-FOOTED BOOBY
......SCARLET IBIS
......AMERICAN FLAMINGO
......BLACK BRANT
......BARROW'S GOLDENEYE
......HARLEQUIN DUCK
......SURFBIRD
......ESKIMO CURLEW
......PURPLE SANDPIPER
......SHARP-TAILED SANDPIPER
......CURLEW SANDPIPER
......RUFF; REEVE
......PARASITIC JAEGER
......GLAUCOUS GULL
......GR. BLACK BACKED GULL
......LESSER B.-BACKED GULL
......BLACK-LEGGED KITTIWAKE
......SABINE'S GULL
......ELEGANT TERN
......NODDY TERN
......RUDDY GROUND DOVE
......PYGMY OWL
......BLACK SWIFT
......VAUX'S SWIFT
......COSTA'S HUMMINGBIRD
......ANNA'S HUMMINGBIRD
......ALLEN'S HUMMINGBIRD
```

```
......CALLIOPE HUMMINGBIRD
......RIEFFER'S HUMMINGBIRD
......W.-EARED HUMMINGBIRD
......COPPERY-TAILED TROGON
......GRAY KINGBIRD
......FORK-TAILED FLYCATCHER
......SULPHUR-B. FLYCATCHER
......OLIVACEOUS FLYCATCHER
......COUES' FLYCATCHER
......GRAY-BREASTED MARTIN
......CLARK'S NUTCRACKER
......BRIDLED TITMOUSE
......DIPPER
......BENDIRE'S THRASHER
......CLAY-COLORED ROBIN
......VARIED THRUSH
......BREWSTER'S WARBLER
......LAWRENCE'S WARBLER
......BACHMAN'S WARBLER
......HERMIT WARBLER
......GROUND-CHAT
......RED-FACED WARBLER
......GOLDEN-CR. WARBLER
......PINE GROSBEAK
......COMMON REDPOLL
......GOLDEN-CR. SPARROW
..†...............................
..†...............................
.†................................
.†................................
```

A Field Guide
to the Birds of Texas
and Adjacent States

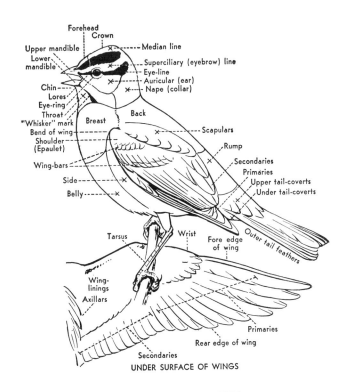

UNDER SURFACE OF WINGS

TOPOGRAPHY OF A BIRD

Showing the terms used in this book

Loons: Gaviidae

OPEN-WATER swimming birds with pointed, daggerlike bills. Larger than most ducks, longer-bodied, thicker-necked than grebes. Float low in water. Can dive to 200 feet. Seldom on land; unable to stand upright. Food: Fish (mostly non-game), other small aquatic animals. N. parts of N. Hemisphere. No. of species: World, 4; N. America, 4; Texas, 2 (plus 1 accidental).

COMMON LOON *Gavia immer* 28–36   p. 4
Field marks: Size of a small goose. A large, long-bodied, low-swimming bird with a dagger-shaped bill; sometimes swims with only head and neck above water. May dive or merely submerge; thrashes along surface when taking off. In flight appears like a big merganser but with broad webbed feet projecting rudder-like beyond stubby tail; downward droop of neck and feet gives a sagging silhouette. Wingbeats slower than those of any duck. *Breeding plumage:* Head and neck glossy black with white collar; back checkered with black and white; underparts white. *Winter:* Mostly grayish; top of head, back of neck, and back dark gray; cheek, throat, and underparts white. Immatures are often puzzlingly blotched with black and white.
Similar species: (1) See Red-throated Loon. (2) Immature cormorants are often mistaken for loons, but have thinner necks, longer tails. They swim with the hook-tipped bill pointed slightly upward and fly with the neck above horizontal. (3) Mergansers in silhouette also slightly resemble loons.
Voice: Usually silent in Texas; occasionally weird yodeling calls, quavering laughter; also a ringing *ha-oo-oo.*
Where found: Alaska, Canada, n. U.S., Greenland, Iceland. Winters south along coasts. **Texas:** *Migrant* over much of state. *Winters* (Oct.–May) along coast; occasional inland. Rare south of Corpus Christi. *Habitat:* Open water; lakes, bays, Gulf.

RED-THROATED LOON *Gavia stellata* 24–27   p. 4
Field marks: Smaller than Common Loon; near size of Common Merganser. *Breeding plumage:* Gray head, unpatterned back and rufous throat-patch. *Winter:* Mainly grayish above and white beneath, like Common Loon, but back *spotted* with white, giving a paler appearance; head paler, less contrast; profile more snaky. The sharp bill, *distinctly upturned,* is the key mark.
Similar species: (1) Common Loon is larger; bill more robust, *straight.* See (2) Western Grebe and (3) Red-necked Grebe.

Voice: Usually silent. In Arctic a repeated *kwuk;* a thin wail. **Where found:** Arctic. Winters south along N. Pacific and N. Atlantic Coasts. **Texas:** Casual (Nov.–Apr.) along coast. Accidental inland to Dallas, Denton. *Habitat:* Open water.

Grebes: Podicipedidae

GREBES are highly aquatic; expert divers but labored flyers (with drooping neck). Distinguished from ducks by the usually pointed bill, thin neck, tailless appearance. Feet *lobed* (flaps along toes). Sometimes grebes submerge slowly instead of diving. Helpless on land; skitter on water when taking wing. Most young grebes have striped heads. All United States species except Pied-bill have white wing-patches. Food: Small fish, crustaceans, tadpoles, aquatic insects; they also eat *feathers* (reason unknown). Nearly cosmopolitan. No. of species: World, 20; N. America, 6; Texas, 6.

RED-NECKED GREBE *Podiceps grisegena* 18–20
(Holboell's Grebe) p. 4
  Field marks: Much larger than other grebes, except Western. *Breeding plumage:* Body gray; neck rufous; *cheeks whitish;* crown black (slightly tufted); bill *yellowish. Winter:* Grayish; top of head darker; *vertical white crescent-shaped mark* on side of gray head (often absent in first-year birds).
  Similar species: In winter plumage, Red-necked Grebe separated from (1) Horned and (2) Eared Grebes by larger size, heavier head and neck, large dull yellow bill, and more uniform gray coloration; from (3) winter loons by grayer face and neck, dull yellow bill, shorter body. (4) See also Western Grebe.
  Voice: Usually silent. On nesting grounds, wails and trills.
  Where found: Alaska, Canada, n. U.S., n. Eurasia. Winters south to s. U.S., n. Africa. **Texas:** Occasional visitor (Nov.–Feb.); reports few but widely scattered throughout state. *Habitat:* Open water, lakes, Gulf.

HORNED GREBE *Podiceps auritus* 12–15 p. 4
  Field marks: A small compact ducklike bird with a small pointed bill, white wing-patch (usually concealed). *Breeding plumage:* Head black, with conspicuous *buff-colored ear-tufts;* neck and flanks *rufous. Winter:* Contrastingly patterned. Top of head, line down back of neck, and back dark gray; underparts, neck, cheeks clear white. Dark cap ends sharply at *eye level.*
  Similar species: See Eared Grebe.
  Voice: Usually silent. When nesting, trills, croaks, shrieks.
  Where found: Alaska, Canada, n. Eurasia. Winters south to

s. U.S., Mediterranean. **Texas:** Rare *transient* in most areas. *Winters* (Oct.–Apr.) principally along coast (occasionally to Rio Grande delta). *Habitat:* Lakes, bays, Gulf.

EARED GREBE *Podiceps caspicus* 12–14 p. 4
Field marks: A small thin-necked diving bird, dark above, light below. *Breeding plumage: Crested* black head and golden ear-tufts. Horned Grebe in breeding plumage also has golden ear-tufts. Eared Grebe can always be told by its *helmet-like crown and black neck* (Horned Grebe, chestnut). *Winter:* Very similar to Horned Grebe. Forehead more abruptly vertical from bill; dark gray on head and neck *extending below eye level and less clearly defined,* giving a "dirtier" look; almost invariably a suffused whitish patch on side of head just behind ear (see plate). Neck of Eared Grebe more slender; bill *slimmer, appears slightly upturned.* On water, stern seems to ride higher.
Voice: On nesting ponds a mellow *poo-eep;* froglike peeping.
Where found: W. N. America and Old World. Winters south to n. S. America. **Texas:** *Migrant* throughout; rare eastward. *Winters* (Oct.–May) inland on ice-free waters and along coast. *Breeds* rarely and very locally from Panhandle to cent. Texas. *Habitat:* Ponds, lakes, marshes, bays, Gulf. **Nest:** A platform anchored to reeds or floating in shallow water. Eggs (4–5) whitish, stained.

LEAST GREBE *Podiceps dominicus* 10
(Mexican Grebe) p. 4
Field marks: A very small dark slaty grebe, smaller than the similarly shaped Pied-billed Grebe, with *white wing-patches* (often concealed), a slender *black* pointed bill and conspicuous *golden eyes.* In winter, throat is white.
Voice: A ringing *beep* or *pete;* a chatter or trill (P. James).
Where found: Tropical America. **Texas:** *Resident* in s. Texas north to Eagle Pass, San Antonio, Refugio, Rockport. In winter also to Houston (rare). Casual Big Bend, Austin; accidental Panhandle. *Habitat:* Fresh-water ponds, resacas. **Nest:** A semi-floating raft in shallow water or anchored to emergent vegetation. Eggs (4–6) buffy, brown-stained.

WESTERN GREBE *Aechmophorus occidentalis* 22–29 p. 4
Field marks: A very large grebe with an extremely long slender neck. In any plumage, all *black and white* except for the slightly upturned *light yellow bill.* Top of head, line on back of neck, and back black; cheeks, neck, and underparts white.
Similar species: (1) Winter Red-necked Grebe is dingy, gray-looking, not clean-cut; has *two* white areas on each wing (Western, one). (2) Loons are shorter-necked, have solid dark wings.
Voice: A shrill whistle suggesting Osprey. A rolling croak.

GREBES AND LOONS

HORNED GREBE   p. 2
Summer: Buffy "ears"; rufous neck.
Winter: Black and white pattern, thin dark bill.

EARED GREBE   p. 3
Summer: Buffy "ears"; black neck.
Winter: Like Horned Grebe; grayer neck, upturned bill,
dark cap to below eye.

PIED-BILLED GREBE   p. 6
Rounded bill, white under tail-coverts.
Summer: Black bill-ring, black throat.
Winter (not shown): Lacks black on throat and bill.
Juvenal: Striped face.

LEAST GREBE   p. 3
Very small, dark; small dark bill, yellow eye. In winter,
throat is whitish.

WESTERN GREBE   p. 3
Black upper parts, long white neck.

RED-NECKED GREBE   p. 2
Summer: Reddish neck, white chin and cheek.
Winter: Grayish neck, yellowish bill.

RED-THROATED LOON   p. 1
Summer: Gray head; rusty throat.
Winter: Pale color; slender upturned bill.

ARCTIC LOON   p. 268
Accidental in Texas.
Summer: Gray crown; back spots in patches.
Winter: Bill slender, but not upturned.

COMMON LOON   p. 1
Summer: Black head, all-checkered back.
Winter: Dark back; stout, straight bill.

Loons in flight are hunch-backed and
gangly, with a slight downward sweep
to the neck and the feet projecting
behind the scanty tail.

HORNED GREBE

Summer   Winter

EARED GREBE

Summer   Winter

PIED-BILLED GREBE

Summer   Juvenal

LEAST GREBE

Summer   Winter

WESTERN GREBE

RED-NECKED GREBE

Summer   Winter

RED-THROATED LOON

Summer   Winter

ARCTIC LOON

Summer   Winter

COMMON LOON

Summer   Winter

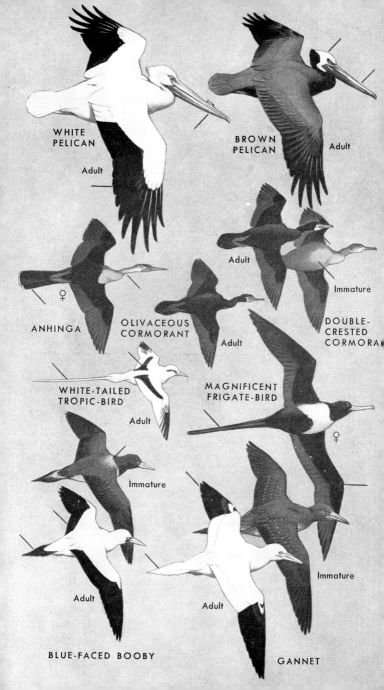

WHITE
PELICAN

Adult

BROWN
PELICAN

Adult

ANHINGA

♀

OLIVACEOUS
CORMORANT

Adult

Adult

Immature

DOUBLE-
CRESTED
CORMORA

WHITE-TAILED
TROPIC-BIRD

Adult

MAGNIFICENT
FRIGATE-BIRD

♀

Immature

Adult

Immature

BLUE-FACED BOOBY

Adult

GANNET

Plate 2   5

PELICANS, CORMORANTS, AND RELATIVES

WHITE PELICAN   p. 8
    Huge; white with black in wings; long yellow bill.

BROWN PELICAN   p. 8
    Large, dark; long bill. Immature has dark head.

ANHINGA   p. 11
    Serpentine neck, long fan-shaped tail.
    Female has light chest and neck; male black.

DOUBLE-CRESTED CORMORANT   p. 10
    Adult: Black body, orange-yellow throat-pouch.
    Immature: Pale breast, blending into dark belly; dark above.

OLIVACEOUS CORMORANT   p. 10
    Smaller than Double-crested. See text.
    Narrow white border on throat-pouch in breeding season.

WHITE-TAILED TROPIC-BIRD   p. 7
    White; black patches; extremely long tail feathers.

MAGNIFICENT FRIGATE-BIRD   p. 15
    Very long, black, angled wings. Tail deeply forked; usually
    folded in long point. Male has all-black body. Immature
    has white head and underparts.

BLUE-FACED BOOBY   p. 9
    Adult: Black on rear edge of wing; pointed *black* tail.
    Immature: Dark; whitish patch on upper back.

GANNET   p. 9
    Adult: White; black wing-ends; pointed *white* tail.
    Immature: Brown; pointed tail.

Double-crested   Olivaceous

HEADS OF CORMORANTS

Where found: W. Canada, w. U.S., and w. Mexico (Lake Chapala). Winters south to Mexico. **Texas:** Rare *migrant* through w. Texas and Panhandle; casual winter visitor in cent. and coastal Texas. *Habitat:* Open water; lakes, bays, Gulf.

PIED-BILLED GREBE *Podilymbus podiceps* 12–15   p. 4
Field marks: A small, blunt-shaped, "chicken-billed" diver of small ponds and fresh marshes. May ride with stern high, showing white under tail-coverts. Dives with a forward leap or may slowly submerge. *Breeding plumage:* Gray-brown, darkest on top of head and back; black throat-patch and *black ring* around *thick* whitish bill. *Winter:* Browner, without throat-patch and bill mark; bill darker. Young have striped heads.
Similar species: Horned, Eared, and Least Grebes have slender bills. Pied-bill has no white wing-patches as have others.
Voice: A cuckoo-like *cow-cow-cow-cow-cow-cow-cowm-cowm*, etc.
Where found: Most of N., Cent., and S. America. Migrates from colder areas. **Texas:** *Migrant* through much of state. *Winters* inland on ice-free waters and along coast. *Breeds* locally, west to El Paso, east to Louisiana, and north to Red River, perhaps most commonly in s. parts of state. *Habitat:* Fresh ponds, lakes, creeks, marshes; also salt water in winter. **Nest:** A semi-floating raft in reedy pond or marsh. Eggs (5–8) whitish, brown-stained.

Shearwaters: Procellariidae

GULL-LIKE birds of the open sea. Their flight, several flaps and a glide, banking on long stiff wings just above the waves, is distinctive. A shearwater's wings are proportionately narrower than a gull's; the tail is smaller, not so fanlike. In the hand, distinguished by tube-like external nostrils. Food: Plankton; also animal fat, refuse thrown from ships. No. of species: World, 33; N. America, 18; Texas, 2.

SOOTY SHEARWATER *Puffinus griseus* 16–18
Field marks: A gull-like sea bird (size of Laughing Gull) that *looks all black* at a distance; glides and tilts over the waves on narrow rigid wings. Uniformly dusky except undersurface of wings, which show pale or whitish areas. Thin black bill.
Similar species: (1) Young Laughing Gull has white rump. (2) Dark jaegers (very rare) show white at base of flight feathers.
Voice: Silent at sea.
Where found: Breeds in S. Hemisphere; ranges to N. Hemisphere. **Texas:** Rare or casual in Gulf (Apr.–June). Reported Port Aransas, Rockport (several), Padre I. *Habitat:* Open seas.

SOOTY SHEARWATER (left). AUDUBON'S SHEARWATER (right).

AUDUBON'S SHEARWATER *Puffinus lherminieri* 12
Field marks: A very small gull-like bird much smaller than Laughing Gull; black above, white below, with black cap and thin black bill. The flight (rapid flaps and a glide), skimming the waves on narrow rigid wings, is distinctive.
Similar species: See (1) Sooty Tern; (2) Black Skimmer.
Voice: Silent at sea.
Where found: Breeds on tropical islands in Atlantic, Pacific, and Indian Oceans; ranges widely. **Texas:** Casual visitor along coast; recorded Sabine Pass, Brazos I., Rockport, Port Aransas, mouth of Rio Grande. *Habitat:* Open seas.

Tropic-birds: Phaethontidae

ALTHOUGH related to pelicans and cormorants, tropic-birds resemble large terns with greatly elongated central tail feathers. Ternlike, they dive headfirst. Food: Chiefly squids. They live mainly in tropic seas, nesting on rocky or coral islands. No. of species: World, 3; N. America, 2; Texas, 1.

WHITE-TAILED TROPIC-BIRD *Phaethon lepturus* 32
(Yellow-billed Tropic-bird) p. 5
Field marks: Near size of Ring-billed Gull; white, with black shoulder-patches and two *extremely long central tail feathers* (19 in.). Bill orange-red or yellow; bold black mark through eye. Young birds lack the long tail feathers; are narrowly barred

above. Except when nesting Tropic-birds spend their lives at sea, flying with strong pigeon-like flight.
Similar species: Terns have *forked* tails. See Royal Tern.
Voice: A harsh, ternlike scream. Also *tik-et, tik-et* (K. Plath).
Where found: West Indies and elsewhere in tropical oceans; ranges widely. **Texas:** Casual (June–Dec.) off coast. Reported Matagorda I., Sabine, Cove, Rockport. *Habitat:* Open seas.

Pelicans: Pelecanidae

PELICANS are huge water birds with long flat bills and tremendous throat-pouches. They swim buoyantly and fly in orderly lines, drawing their heads back on their shoulders. They alternate several flaps with a short sail, each bird flapping and sailing in rhythm, taking its cue from the bird ahead. Food: Fish (chiefly non-game). Tropical and warm temperate zones. No. of species: World, 6; N. America, 2; Texas, 2.

WHITE PELICAN   *Pelecanus erythrorhynchos*   55–70   p. 5
  Field marks: Huge; wingspread 9 ft. White with black primaries and a great yellow throat-pouch. Flies with head hunched back on shoulders, and long flat bill resting on curved neck. Flocks fly in lines, often circle at a great height. Swims buoyantly. Scoops up fish while swimming, does not plunge like Brown Pelican.
  Similar species: (1) Swans have no black in wings. (2) Wood Ibis and (3) very rare Whooping Crane have black primaries but fly with necks extended and long legs trailing. (4) Snow Goose is much smaller; noisy in flight.
  Voice: Adults virtually silent (in colony, a low groan). Young birds utter whining grunts.
  Where found: Chiefly w. N. America. Winters from s. U.S. to Guatemala. **Texas:** Irregular *migrant* (Mar.–June, July–Nov.) throughout; often seen traveling in flocks. *Resident* along Gulf and in Delta, breeding only in one colony in Laguna Madre. *Habitat:* Lakes, salt bays, beaches. **Nest:** On ground on island; in colony. Eggs (2–3) whitish, brown-stained.

BROWN PELICAN   *Pelecanus occidentalis*   45–54   p. 5
  Field marks: Spread 6½ ft. A ponderous dark water bird; adult with much white about head and neck; immature has dark head, whitish underparts. Often perches on posts, boats. Flies with head hunched back on shoulders and long flat bill resting on breast. Bulk, great bill, and flight (a few flaps and a sail) indicate a pelican; dusky color and habit of *plunging* bill first from the air proclaim it this species. Lines of Pelicans often scale very close to water, almost touching it with wing-tips.

Voice: Adults silent (rarely, a low croak). Nestlings noisy. **Where found:** Coasts of s. U.S. to S. America. **Texas:** *Resident* along coast, breeds locally. Casual inland to n. Texas, Panhandle, Midland. *Habitat:* Salt bays, Gulf. **Nest:** Usually on ground in colony on island. Eggs (2–3) whitish, stained.

Boobies and Gannets: Sulidae

LARGE sea birds with large, pointed bills, pointed tails; shaped like fat cigars. They fish by spectacular plunges, sometimes from 100 feet in the air. Gannets are cold-water birds of the North Atlantic and the oceans near South Africa and Australia; boobies inhabit tropical seas. No. of species: World, 9; N. America, 5; Texas, 2 (plus 2 accidentals).

BLUE-FACED BOOBY *Sula dactylatra* 27   p. 5
   Field marks: Large *snow-white* birds with extensive *black primaries* wheeling in circles over the sea may be either Gannets or this species. Blue-faced Boobies are a bit larger than Herring Gulls, with much longer necks and larger bills, and *pointed*, not fan-shaped, *black* tails. They fly with strong beats and glides. Plunge Brown-Pelican-like into the waves (White Pelicans do not plunge). *Immature:* Dusky brown with white underparts, whitish patch on upper back, and whitish rump.
   Similar species: (1) Gannet is larger, has *white* tail and black toward ends of wings only (Blue-faced Booby has black on *entire rear edge of wing*). (2) The accidental Brown Booby (adult) resembles immature Blue-faced but is more clean-cut; solid dark above without light patches on upper back, rump.
   Voice: Silent at sea.
   Where found: Breeds locally on islands in tropical Atlantic, Pacific, and Indian Oceans; ranges widely. **Texas:** Occasional, perhaps regular, off coast (Apr.–Dec.). Reported Rockport (several), Freeport, Matagorda Bay, Galveston, Padre I., Port Isabel, and off mouth of Rio Grande. *Habitat:* Offshore waters.

GANNET *Morus bassanus* 35–40   p. 5
   Field marks: Gannets are large white sea birds with black primaries; nearly twice the size of Herring Gull, with much larger necks, larger pointed bills (often pointed toward water), and pointed, not fan-shaped, tails. See under Blue-faced Booby (above). Young birds are dusky all over, but actions and pointed "cigar shape" identify them. Changing young have a piebald look; boldly splotched with brown and white.
   Similar species: Blue-faced Booby (smaller, black tail, more black on wing), is slightly more frequent off Gulf Coast. Gannet is more likely in winter.

Voice: Silent at sea. In colony, a harsh *arrah;* a groan.
Where found: N. Atlantic coasts. Winters south to Gulf of Mexico and Mediterranean. **Texas:** Casual winter straggler (perhaps regular) along coast. Reported Jefferson Co., Galveston, Rockport. *Habitat:* Offshore coastal waters.

Cormorants: Phalacrocoracidae

LARGE, blackish, slender-billed water birds. Often confused with loons, but tail longer, bill hook-tipped. In flight, wing action is more rapid and axis of body and neck is tilted upward slightly (loon's neck droops). Young birds are browner, with a pale or whitish breast. Flocks fly in line or wedge formation very much like geese but they are *silent.* Cormorants often perch in *upright position* on buoys or posts with neck in an S; sometimes strike a "spread eagle" pose. Swimming, they lie low like loons, but with necks more erect and snakelike, and bills tilted upward *at an angle.* Food: Fish (chiefly non-game). Nearly cosmopolitan. No. of species: World, 30; N. America, 6; Texas, 2.

DOUBLE-CRESTED CORMORANT
Phalacrocorax auritus 30–35   p. 5
Field marks: See discussion above. This has been said to be the common winter cormorant on the Texas coast and the one most likely to be seen inland, but these are debatable points. Its size, luster, and orange-yellow throat-pouch are helpful marks.
Similar species: See Olivaceous Cormorant.
Voice: Usually silent; in colony, low grunts, croaks.
Where found: Most of N. America. Winters south to British Honduras. **Texas:** *Migrant* (Mar.–May, Sept.–Nov.) in most of state; in *winter* most numerous on coast. *Resident* in e. and cent. Texas (rare in summer); breeds very locally (Wilbarger Co., Baylor Co., etc.). *Habitat:* Lakes, rivers, Gulf. **Nest:** A mass of sticks; in tree or bush; in colony. Eggs (3–4) pale blue, chalky.

OLIVACEOUS CORMORANT   *Phalacrocorax olivaceus* 25
(Mexican Cormorant)   p. 5
Field marks: Similar to Double-crest, but looks slimmer and very much smaller (when birds are together, which is not often); thinner-billed and dingier both in plumage and in color of throat-pouch. At very close range feathers have a purplish rather than greenish sheen. In breeding season pouch is edged by a *narrow border of white.*
Similar species: Distinguishing Olivaceous from Double-crested Cormorant when the two are not together is one of the *real problems* of Texas field ornithology.
Voice: Low grunts.

Where found: Texas, Louisiana to s. S. America. **Texas:** *Resident* along coast and short distance inland, breeding locally. Large colony as far inland as Falcon Dam (lower Rio Grande). Uncommon inland to Eagle Pass, San Antonio, Austin (has nested), Dallas, Denton, Lake Texhoma. *Habitat:* Lakes, rivers, Gulf. **Nest:** A mass of sticks in bush or tree over water or on ground on island; in colony. Eggs (4–5) pale blue, chalky.

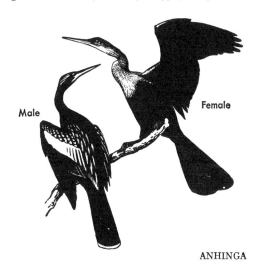

Male

Female

ANHINGA

Darters (Anhingas): Anhingidae

SIMILAR TO cormorants, but much more slender, tail much larger, longer. Bill sharp-pointed, not hook-tipped. Food: Fish (mostly non-game), other aquatic life. Some authorities recognize 4 species in the tropical and warm temperate zones of the world, and others lump them into one species.

ANHINGA *Anhinga anhinga* 34
(Water-turkey) p. 5
Field marks: The Water-turkey, Snakebird, or Anhinga, as it is variously called, is like a very slender cormorant with a snakier neck, *sharp-pointed* bill. It is blackish, with large silvery patches on the forepart of the wings, a long tail, and a long, serpentine neck. Females have pale buffy breasts, males black. Immature birds are brownish. In flight it progresses with alternate flapping and sailing, the slender neck extended,

SKIMMER AND GULLS

BLACK SKIMMER   p. 119
Adult: Black upper parts; long, unequal red bill.
Immature: Smaller, browner, with skimmer bill.

HERRING GULL   p. 111
Adult: Gray mantle, black wing-tips, flesh legs.
First winter: Relatively uniform brown.
Second winter: Whiter, with tail broadly dark.

CALIFORNIA GULL (not illustrated)   p. 111
Adult: Differs from Herring Gull by greenish legs; from
Ring-billed Gull by red or red and black spot on lower
mandible. See text.

RING-BILLED GULL   p. 114
Adult: Like small Herring Gull; black ring on bill; legs
yellowish or greenish.
Immature: Narrow black tailband.

FRANKLIN'S GULL*   p. 114
Adult: "Windows" separating black on wing from gray.
First winter: Like Laughing Gull but breast and forehead
whiter (young Laughing at a later stage can be almost
identical).

LAUGHING GULL*   p. 114
Adult: Small size; dark wings with white border.
First winter: Small, dark gull; white rump.

BONAPARTE'S GULL*   p. 115
Adult: Wedge of white in primaries.
Immature: Black cheek-spot, narrow tailband.

* In winter adult Franklin's, Laughing, and Bonaparte's Gulls lose
the black heads. The wing patterns remain the same.

BLACK SKIMMER

Adult

Imm.

HERRING
Adult
Spring

HERRING
Second Winter

HERRING
First Winter

**RING-
BILLED**

Adult
Spring

Imm.

FRANKLIN'S

Adult
Spring

First
Winter

LAUGHING

Adult
Spring

First
Winter

Adult
Spring

BONAPARTE'S

Imm.

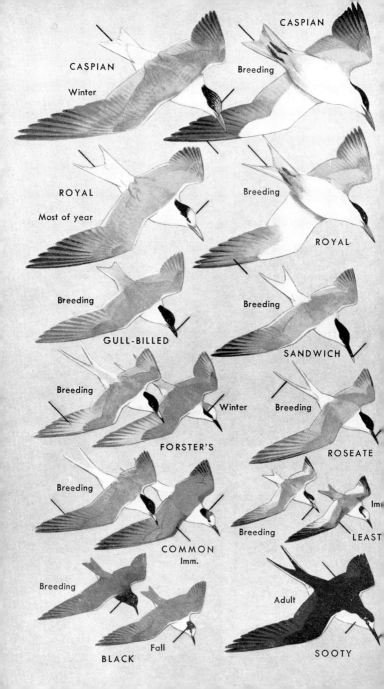

CASPIAN
Winter

CASPIAN
Breeding

ROYAL
Most of year

Breeding

ROYAL

Breeding

GULL-BILLED

Breeding

SANDWICH

Breeding

Winter

Breeding

FORSTER'S

ROSEATE

Breeding

Breeding

Im

COMMON
Imm.

LEAST

Breeding

Adult

Fall

BLACK

SOOTY

Plate 4   13

TERNS

Terns are more slender, narrower of wing, and more graceful in flight than gulls. Bills are more slender, sharply pointed; tails forked. Most terns are whitish, with black caps. Foreheads become white in winter.

CASPIAN TERN   p. 118
  Much black on underside of primaries; tail slightly forked.
  Winter: Forehead streaked.

ROYAL TERN   p. 118
  Primaries relatively light below; tail deeply forked.
  Most of year: Forehead white.

GULL-BILLED TERN   p. 116
  Stout gull-like black bill.

SANDWICH (CABOT'S) TERN   p. 118
  Slender black bill, yellow tip.

FORSTER'S TERN   p. 116
  Breeding: Pale primaries, orange bill.
  Winter adult: Black patch through eye and ear only.

ROSEATE TERN   p. 117
  Breeding: Very pale; long tail feathers, blackish bill.

COMMON TERN   p. 116
  Breeding: Dusky primaries, orange-red bill.
  Immature: Black patch extends around nape; dusky shoulder-patch.
  Winter adult (not shown): Head pattern similar to immature's.

LEAST TERN   p. 117
  Breeding: Small size, yellow bill.
  Immature: Small size, black fore edge of wing.

BLACK TERN   p. 119
  Breeding: Black body.
  Fall: Pied head, dark back, gray tail.

SOOTY TERN   p. 117
  Adult: Black above, white below; thin black bill.

the long tail spread fanwise. Often soars high overhead. Perches like a cormorant, in upright posture or "spread eagle," but neck much snakier, head smaller. Dives from surface or submerges; sometimes swims with only head and neck above water.

Similar species: The pale-breasted females suggest immature cormorants, but cormorants do not have light wing-patches. Anhinga's tail is much longer, suggesting name Water-turkey.

Voice: Low guttural grunts. Usually silent.

Where found: S. U.S. south to Argentina. Partial migrant. **Texas:** *Summers* (Mar.–Oct.) in e. and s.-cent. Texas; west to Waco, New Braunfels, San Antonio; south to coast. *Breeds* locally in small colonies or with herons. Wanders rarely to n. Texas (Dallas, Fort Worth, Denton, Panhandle); west casually to Edwards Plateau. *Winters* in s. tip of state and sparingly near coast. *Habitat:* Fresh swamps, lakes, rivers. **Nest:** A platform of sticks in tree or bush in swamp. Eggs (3–5) pale blue, chalky, stained.

Immature

Female

Male

MAGNIFICENT
FRIGATE-BIRD

Frigate-birds: Fregatidae

TROPICAL sea birds with a greater wing expanse (7½ ft.) in proportion to body weight (3½ lb.) than any other birds in the world. Although sea birds, they normally cannot swim or rise from the water. They swoop from the air to snatch food without wetting a feather. They also rob boobies, gulls, terns of their fish. No. of species: World, 5; N. America, 1; Texas, 1.

MAGNIFICENT FRIGATE-BIRD *Fregata magnificens* 40
(Man-o'-War Bird)   p. 5
  Field marks: Spread 7½ ft. "Man-o'-Wars," long-winged black birds, with scissor-like tails (usually folded in a long point), soar with an ease that gulls cannot match. Their extremely long, angled wings seem to have a hump in middle. Bill long and hooked. They do not swim, often perch. *Male:* Black, with inflatable orange throat-pouch. *Female:* White breast. *Immature:* (most frequent) Head and underparts white.
  Similar species: See Swallow-tailed Kite (not really similar).
  Voice: Voiceless at sea. A gurgling note during courtship.
  Where found: Gulf of Mexico, tropical Atlantic and e. Pacific Oceans. **Texas:** Summer *transient* along coast (Apr.–Sept.); casual in winter. *Habitat:* Oceanic coasts, islands.

Herons and Bitterns: Ardeidae

LARGE wading birds with long necks, long legs, and pointed daggerlike bills. In sustained flight, heads are tucked back on shoulders in an S; long legs trail behind; wingbeats slow and "bowed." At rest, neck may be erect or "pulled in." Subject to post-breeding wanderings. Food: Fish (mostly non-game), frogs, aquatic life; sometimes mice. Nearly cosmopolitan. No. of species: World, 59; N. America, 14; Texas, 13.

GREAT WHITE HERON *Ardea occidentalis* 49–52   p. 28
  Field marks: Size and build of Great Blue Heron. Pure white with yellow beak and *greenish-yellow legs*, the latter infallibly separating it from the smaller Common Egret, which has black legs. Breeding adult has white crest plumes.
  Voice: Similar to Great Blue Heron's.
  Where found: Florida Keys, Cuba, Yucatan. **Texas:** Casual (reported Sabine River, Rockport four times, Laguna Madre, Green I.). *Habitat:* Salt-water bays.

GREAT BLUE HERON *Ardea herodias* 42–52   p. 28
  Field marks: This lean bird, often miscalled "crane," stands 4 feet tall, and is the largest heron normally found in Texas. Its long legs, long neck, dagger-shaped bill, and, in flight, folded neck and trailing legs mark it as a heron. Great size (spread 6 ft.) and blue-gray color, whiter about head and neck (in adults), identify it as this species. Often stands motionless with neck erect, or head sunk between shoulders.
  Similar species: See Sandhill Crane.

Voice: Deep, harsh croaks: *frahnk, frahnk, frawnk.*
Where found: Most of N. America. Winters south to n. S. America. **Texas:** *Resident* throughout most sections, nesting very locally. *Habitat:* Marshes, swamps, ricefields, rivers, shores. **Nest:** A platform of sticks in bush or tree in swamp or on island; usually in colony; occasionally away from water. Sometimes on duck blind. Eggs (3–6) blue.

GREEN HERON *Butorides virescens* 16–22 p. 21
Field marks: A small heron with comparatively short legs. Looks quite dark and crow-like, but flies with slower, more arched, wingbeats. Stretches neck, elevates shaggy crest, and jerks tail when alarmed. Legs orange (breeding) or greenish yellow. Neck deep chestnut. Young birds have streaked necks. **Similar species:** See adult Little Blue Heron.
Voice: A series of *kucks* or a loud *skyow* or *skewk.*
Where found: E. Canada to Colombia. Winters mainly south of U.S. **Texas:** *Summers* (Mar.–Oct.) throughout most of state, commoner eastward, nesting locally. *Winters* rarely at El Paso and s. Texas. *Habitat:* Ponds, lakes, marshes, rivers, shores. **Nest:** A flimsy stick platform in tree or bush (not always near water); singly or in small scattered groups. Eggs (3–6) bluish.

LITTLE BLUE HERON *Florida caerulea* 20–29 p. 28
Field marks: A medium-sized, slender heron. *Adult:* Slaty blue with dark maroon neck (blackish at a distance); legs dark. *Immature:* Snowy white; legs dull *greenish;* bill *bluish* tipped with black. White birds changing to adulthood are boldly patched with dark.
Similar species: (1) Green Heron is smaller, with much shorter *yellowish* or *orange* legs. (2) Young Snowy Egrets are frequently suspected of being young Little Blues because of a stripe of yellowish up the posterior side of the legs visible as the bird walks away. Note the all-black bill. (3) See Reddish Egret.
Voice: Low clucking notes; a hoarse croak.
Where found: E. U.S. south to Peru, Argentina. Migratory in U.S. **Texas:** *Summers* (Mar.–Oct.) in e., cent., and coastal parts; less frequent westward (fairly common in white plumage at El Paso); wanders irregularly (late summer) to n. Texas and Panhandle. *Winters* chiefly near coast. *Breeds* locally in fresh-water swamps, mostly in e. and s. sections. *Habitat:* Marshes, swamps, ricefields, mudflats, shores. **Nest:** A platform of sticks in bush or tree; in colony. Eggs (3–5) bluish.

CATTLE EGRET *Bubulcus ibis* 20 p. 28
Field marks: A small white heron that associates with grazing cattle. Slightly smaller, stockier, and thicker-necked than Snowy Egret. When breeding, shows *buff* on crown, breast, and

back but looks quite white at a distance. Little or no buff in winter. Throat appears "stuffed with cotton." Bill yellow, but may be orange-pink at nesting time. Legs coral-pink (when nesting), yellow, greenish, or blackish (immature).
Similar species: (1) Snowy Egret is more slender, has slim black bill, black legs, yellow feet. (2) Common Egret (long yellow bill, black legs) is much larger, longer-necked. (3) Young Little Blue has bluish bill, longer neck.
Voice: A variety of croaking notes in breeding season.
Where found: Colonizer of Old World origin (via S. America). First reported in U.S. in 1952; rapidly spreading; reached **Texas** in 1955, bred by 1958 and should eventually become common in coastal and perhaps other parts of state. *Habitat:* Cow pastures, fields, marshes. **Nest:** A platform of sticks in bush or tree; in colony often with Snowy Egrets. Eggs (3–5) bluish.

REDDISH EGRET *Dichromanassa rufescens* 29   p. 28
  Field marks: A medium-sized heron, neutral gray, with a rusty-brown head and neck, a *flesh-colored, black-tipped bill,* and bluish legs. It is loose-feathered and its neck is quite shaggy. There is a scarcer white phase. Occasional white birds have some dark feathers. Young birds less than two years old have all-black bills and dark olive legs, making recognition more uncertain. When feeding, often lurches about and seems quite drunk.
  Similar species: (1) Adult Little Blue Heron is darker, with bill *pale bluish* at base. (2) White phase of Reddish Egret appears like Common Egret but shorter and stouter; legs blue. By far the best field mark for adults in either plumage is the *flesh-colored* black-tipped bill.
  Voice: A low croak or squawk.
  Where found: Gulf States, West Indies, and Mexico. **Texas:** *Resident* along coast (rare in winter on upper coast). Fall straggler to n. Texas. *Breeds* locally on coastal islands east to Galveston. *Habitat:* Shores, lagoons, salt marshes. **Nest:** A platform of sticks in bush or on ground on island; in colony. Eggs (3–5) bluish.

COMMON EGRET *Casmerodius albus* 37–40
(American Egret)   p. 28
  Field marks: A large slender heron, snowy white with black legs and feet; *yellow bill. Straight* plumes on back when breeding.
  Similar species: (1) Snowy Egret and (2) immature Little Blue are much smaller and have *black or blackish bills.* (3) Cattle Egret (yellow bill) is much smaller, stockier, and may have yellow, greenish, or pinkish legs (immature may have black legs).
  Voice: A low, hoarse croak. Also a *cuk, cuk, cuk.*
  Where found: N. U.S. south to Strait of Magellan; also warmer

parts of Old World. Partially migratory. **Texas:** *Resident* in e. and s. Texas, wandering irregularly in summer to n. Texas, Panhandle, and west to El Paso. *Breeds* locally, mainly near coast. *Habitat:* Marshes, ricefields, ponds, shores. **Nest:** A platform of sticks in tree in swamp or in bush on island; in colony. Eggs (3–5) blue.

SNOWY EGRET *Leucophoyx thula* 20–27 p. 28
Field marks: A rather small white heron with a *slender black bill*, black legs, and *yellow feet* ("golden slippers"). *Curved* plumes on back when breeding. Often shuffles feet so as to stir up food. Young Snowies have a yellowish stripe up back of leg and may appear yellow-legged when walking away.
Similar species: (1) Common Egret is much larger, has a *yellow* bill, *black* feet. (2) Cattle Egret has a *yellow* (sometimes pink) bill. (3) See immature Little Blue.
Voice: A low croak; in colony, a bubbling *wulla-wulla-wulla*.
Where found: N. U.S. to Chile, Argentina. Partially migratory. **Texas:** Wanders widely (Mar.–Nov.) throughout state. *Winters* (in reduced numbers) near coast. *Breeds* locally in coastal lowlands and in e. and s. parts of state, also in extreme w. Texas. *Habitat:* Marshes, swamps, ricefields, shores. **Nest:** A platform of sticks in bush or tree in swamp or on island; in colony. Eggs (3–5) blue.

LOUISIANA HERON *Hydranassa tricolor* 26
("Tricolored Heron") p. 28
Field marks: A very slender, snaky, rather small *dark* heron with a clear *white belly* and white rump. The contrasting white belly is the key mark in any plumage.
Similar species: (1) Occasional Little Blues changing from white to blue might be dark-winged and white-bellied, but they would also show white feathers elsewhere. (2) See young White Ibis.
Voice: In colony, croaking notes, squawks.
Where found: New Jersey south to Brazil. Partially migratory. **Texas:** *Resident* mainly along coast (inland to Eagle Lake), breeding locally. Irregular summer visitor to cent. and n. Texas (Tyler, Denton, Dallas, Fort Worth, Coleman); casually west to El Paso. *Habitat:* Marshes, swamps, ricefields, lagoons, shores. **Nests:** A platform of sticks in bush or small tree in swamp or on island; in colony. Eggs (3–5) bluish.

BLACK-CROWNED NIGHT HERON
Nycticorax nycticorax 23–28 p. 21
Field marks: A stocky, short-billed, short-legged heron. Usually sits hunched and inactive by day; flies to feed at dusk. *Adult:* Pale gray or white below; black back, gray wings, black cap, red eyes, yellowish legs. When breeding, acquires two long

white head plumes, pink legs. *Immature:* Brown, spotted and streaked with white.

Similar species: (1) Immature resembles American Bittern (which see). (2) See also Yellow-crowned Night Heron.

Voice: A flat *quok!* or *quark!*, most often heard in evening.

Where found: Canada south to s. S. America. Partial migrant. **Texas:** *Summers* (Mar.–Oct.) in most sections; breeding locally. *Winters* near coast, a few inland. *Habitat:* Marshes, swamps, shores. **Nest:** A platform of sticks, usually in bush or tree in swamp or on island; in colony. Eggs (3–6) blue-green.

YELLOW-CROWNED NIGHT HERON

Nyctanassa violacea 22–28   p. 21

Field marks: *Adult:* A stocky gray heron with a *black and white head.* Yellow on crown seldom noticeable. *Immature:* See below.

Similar species: Adult Black-crowned Night Heron has more contrast; black above and white below. Immatures are very similar; Black-crown is browner with larger spotting. Yellow-crown is darker and more finely speckled; its bill is slightly stouter, its legs longer and yellower. In flight, *the entire foot and a short space of leg* extend beyond the tail.

Voice: *Quak,* higher-pitched than note of Black-crown.

Where found: Ne. U.S. south to Peru, Brazil. Partial migrant. **Texas:** *Summer visitor* (Mar.–Oct.) in e. two-thirds of Texas (west to Edwards Plateau, s. Staked Plains, and Panhandle), breeding locally. *Winters* locally along coast, casually inland. *Habitat:* Swamps, marshes, shores. **Nest:** A platform of sticks, in bush or tree in swamp or grove; alone or in small group. Eggs (3–6) bluish green.

LEAST BITTERN *Ixobrychus exilis* 11–14   p. 21

Field marks: The secretive midget of the heron family, near the size of a Meadowlark, but body much thinner. Usually flushes close at hand from the marsh, flies a short distance and drops in again. The *large buff wing-patches,* black back, small size identify it.

Similar species: (1) Rails lack the buff wing-patches and are without much pattern. (2) Beginners sometimes mistake Green Heron (dark wings) for Least Bittern. Green Heron often perches in trees. (3) See American Bittern.

Voice: "Song," a low rapid *coo-coo-coo-coo* heard in the marsh (cuckoo-like, but not in long series).

Where found: Nw. U.S., se. Canada south to S. America. Winters mostly south of U.S. **Texas:** *Summers* (Mar.–Oct.) in e. half (Red River to Brownsville); locally in Panhandle and at El Paso. *Winters* in Delta; rarely El Paso. *Habitat:* Fresh and brackish marshes, swamps. **Nest:** A flimsy platform among reeds, growth; not in colony. Eggs (3–6) bluish white.

HEADS OF TERNS

The bills of terns are the key feature in their recognition. All terns in breeding season have black caps. By late summer they begin to get the white foreheads typical of winter plumage.

BLACK TERN   p. 119
> *Breeding:* Black head.
> *Winter:* "Pied" head (see text).

LEAST TERN   p. 117
> *Breeding:* Yellow bill, white forehead-patch.
> *Immature:* Small size (see text).

FORSTER'S TERN   p. 116
> *Breeding:* Orange bill, black tip (see text).
> *Winter:* Black eye-patch; light or gray nape.

COMMON TERN   p. 116
> *Breeding:* Orange-red bill, black tip (see text).
> *Winter:* Black patch from eye *around nape.*

ROSEATE TERN   p. 117
> *Breeding:* Bill mostly black.
> *Variant:* Some have much red (see text).

ARCTIC TERN
> No authentic Texas record. Sight records very question-
> able.
> *Breeding:* Bill blood-red; no black tip.
> *Caution:* Some late-summer Common Terns may lack
> black tip.

SANDWICH (CABOT'S) TERN   p. 118
> *Breeding:* Bill black with yellow tip.

GULL-BILLED TERN   p. 116
> *Breeding:* Bill gull-like, stout and black.
> *Immature:* Very gull-like (see text).

ROYAL TERN   p. 118
> *Most of year:* Orange bill, white forehead, tufted crest.
> *Spring:* Similar, with solid black cap.

CASPIAN TERN   p. 118
> *Winter:* Scarlet bill, streaked forehead.
> *Spring:* Scarlet bill, less crest than Royal.

Winter

Summer

BLACK

Immature

Summer

LEAST

Winter

Summer

FORSTER'S

Winter

Summer

COMMON

Variant

Summer

ROSEATE

Summer

ARCTIC

Immature

Summer

GULL-BILLED

Summer

CABOT'S

Winter

ROYAL

Summer

Winter

CASPIAN

Summer

YELLOW-
NIGHT
CROWNED
HERON

Adult

Adult

BLACK-CROWNED
NIGHT HERON

GREEN HERON

Immature

Adult

LEAST
BITTERM

Immature

Immature

AMERICAN
BITTERN

YELLOW-CROWNED
NIGHT HERON

BLACK-CROWNED
NIGHT HERON

WHITE IBIS

Immature

GLOSSY IBIS

LIMPKIN

Adult

WHITE IBIS

WOOD IBIS

Plate 6   21

LONG-LEGGED WADING BIRDS

YELLOW-CROWNED NIGHT HERON   p. 19
Adult: Gray body, black head, light crown.
Immature: Like Black-crown but slatier, more finely speckled, legs longer.

BLACK-CROWNED NIGHT HERON   p. 18
Adult: White breast, black back, black crown.
Immature: Brown, large spots on back.

GREEN HERON   p. 16
Small, dark; short yellowish legs (orange when breeding).

LEAST BITTERN   p. 19
Tiny; back and crown black, wings buff.

AMERICAN BITTERN   p. 22
Tawny; black neck mark; bill pointed up.

WHITE IBIS   p. 24
Adult: Red face, decurved bill.
Immature: Decurved bill, white belly, white rump.

GLOSSY IBIS   p. 23
Perhaps only casual in Texas. Dark body, decurved bill.

WHITE-FACED IBIS   p. 24
The common dark ibis in Texas. White face-patch only in breeding plumage. Most of year virtually indistinguishable from Glossy Ibis.

LIMPKIN   p. 82
Casual in Texas. Spotted; decurved bill.

WOOD IBIS or WOOD STORK   p. 22
Naked gray head, large black wing areas.

Comparison of heads of White-faced Ibis in breeding plumage (upper) and Glossy Ibis (lower).

AMERICAN BITTERN *Botaurus lentiginosus* 23–34   p. 21
  Field marks: In crossing a marsh we flush this large, stocky brown bird. In flight the blackish outer wing contrasts with the streaked buffy brown of the rest of the bird. Discovered, it often stands rigid, pointing bill skyward; shows a black stripe on each side of neck. Rarely ever perches in trees.
  Similar species: (1) Young Night Heron is not as rich a brown and lacks blackish outer wing. Silhouetted in flight, the faster wingbeats and less curved wings are the Bittern's marks; its bill is held more horizontal. (2) Least Bittern is tiny, contrastingly patterned with buff and black.
  Voice: The "pumping," or spring song is a slow, deep *oong-ka-choonk–oong-ka-choonk–oong-ka-choonk*, etc. Distorted by distance, only the *ka* may be audible and sounds like a mallet driving a stake. Flushing note, *kok-kok-kok*.
  Where found: Canada south to Gulf States. Winters south to Panama. **Texas:** *Migrant* (Mar.–May, Sept.–Nov.) in most sections. *Winters* along coast and sparingly inland (rarely north to Dallas). *Summers* across n. half of state from e. Texas to El Paso (rare), breeding very locally. *Habitat:* Marshes, swamps. **Nest:** A platform of dead stalks among marsh plants; not in colony. Eggs (4–7) olive.

Storks and Wood Ibises: Ciconiidae

LARGE, long-legged, heron-like birds with long straight bills. Flight slow and deliberate, with neck extended and slightly drooped. Gait a sedate walk. Food: Frogs, crustaceans, lizards, insects, rodents. Tropical and temperate regions of world. No. of species: World, 17; N. America, 1; Texas, 1.

WOOD IBIS or WOOD STORK
Mycteria americana 34–47   p. 21
  Field marks: Spread 5½ ft. A very large white stork with a *dark, naked* head and *extensive black wing-areas* and black tail. Bill long, thick at base and *decurved.* Young birds are dingier with a lighter head and neck. When feeding, keeps head down. Flies by alternate flapping and sailing. Often soars in flocks at a great height, then resembling White Pelican (which also soars) except for its black tail, long legs.
  Similar species: (1) White herons in flight retract neck, have no black in wings. See (2) White Ibis, (3) Whooping Crane.
  Voice: A hoarse croak; usually silent. Young noisy in colony.
  Where found: S. U.S. south to Argentina. **Texas:** Irregular *visitor* along coast (June–Nov.) wandering occasionally in late

WHITE IBIS AND WOOD IBIS

Note the great amount of black in the Wood Ibis.

summer to cent. and n. Texas (Dallas, Fort Worth, Denton); casual El Paso. Bred in Chambers Co. (Elm Grove) in 1930; also unconfirmed rumors of breeding in Harris and Refugio Cos. *Habitat:* Swamps, marshes, ponds. **Nest:** A platform of sticks in tree in swamp; in colony. Eggs (2–3) white, chalky.

Ibises and Spoonbills: Threskiornithidae

IBISES are long-legged marsh birds with long decurved bills similar to those of curlews. The name alone describes the spoonbill. Ibises and spoonbills travel in V-shaped flocks or lines and bunched formations; unlike herons, they fly with necks outstretched. Food: Small crustaceans, insects, leeches, small fish, etc. Tropical and warm temperate regions. No. of species: World, 28; N. America, 5; Texas, 4 (plus 1 accidental).

GLOSSY IBIS *Plegadis falcinellus* 22–25   p. 21
    Field marks: Very similar to White-faced Ibis but breeding birds lack the narrow white patch on the face as well as the reddish lores. Many Glossy Ibises show a narrow strip of whitish or bluish skin between bill and eye and are thus mistaken for the White-face, but in the latter the white goes *in behind eye*

and under chin. Problem is complicated because White-faced Ibis in fall, winter, and early spring lacks white face.

Voice: Similar to that of White-faced Ibis.

Where found: E. U.S., West Indies, s. Eurasia, Africa, Australia, etc. Probably only a casual straggler to e. part of Texas coast. Undoubtedly most records are of White-faced Ibis.

WHITE-FACED IBIS *Plegadis chihi* 22–25
(White-faced Glossy Ibis)   p. 21

Field marks: A medium-sized marsh wader with a long, decurved bill; deep purplish chestnut; at a distance appears quite black, like a large black curlew. At close range in breeding plumage shows a white border about base of bill. Flies in lines with necks outstretched, with quicker wingbeats than herons, alternately flapping and gliding. Immature, and also adult in non-breeding plumage are duller, lack white face. Winter adults have some white speckling about head.

Voice: A guttural *ka-onk*, repeated; a low *kruk, kruk.*

Where found: S. U.S. south to Argentina, Chile. Winters north to sw. U.S. **Texas:** *Resident* along coast, breeding locally; has bred as far inland as San Antonio. Wanders to n. Texas (Fort Worth, Dallas, Denton); transient in Panhandle (uncommon) and w. parts (formerly abundant at El Paso). *Habitat:* Marshes, ricefields, swamps. **Nest:** Cuplike, of old reeds in marsh, or of sticks in bushes; in colony. Eggs (3–4) pale blue.

WHITE IBIS *Eudocimus albus* 22–27   pp. 21, 23

Field marks: Few sights are as impressive as long streamers of White Ibis drifting over a marsh, flying with necks outstretched, alternately flapping and gliding. Sometimes they circle in big flocks. They are medium-sized white wading birds with red legs, *red faces,* and long decurved bills. Tips of wings (four outer primaries) *black.* Young birds are dark grayish brown with white bellies and show conspicuous *white rumps.*

Similar species: (1) White herons have no black on wing-tips. (2) Wood Ibis is very much larger; black areas on wings are much more extensive. (3) Young Glossy Ibis differs from young White Ibis by uniformly dark appearance.

Voice: Occasional grunting sounds. Normally silent.

Where found: Se. U.S. south to Peru. **Texas:** *Resident* along coast, breeding locally. In summer, occasionally to e., cent., and n. Texas (Tyler, Waco, Fort Worth, Gainesville). *Habitat:* Marshes, swamps, ricefields. **Nest:** A stick platform in tree in swamp or on island; in colony. Eggs (3–5) blotched.

ROSEATE SPOONBILL *Ajaia ajaja* 32   p. 28

Field marks: A *pink* wading bird with a flat *spoonlike* bill. Adults are *bright pink* with blood-red "drip" along shoulders,

orange tail. Head naked, greenish gray. Immature birds are whitish, acquiring pink as they mature. During feeding, bill swung rapidly from side to side. In flight bird often glides between wing-strokes; neck is extended like that of ibis.
Similar species: See Flamingo and Scarlet Ibis (p. 269).
Voice: About nesting colony, a low grunting croak.
Where found: Gulf States to Chile, Argentina. **Texas:** *Resident* (rare in winter) along coast. Straggler inland to Dallas, Fort Worth. Accidental Panhandle. *Breeds* locally along cent. and e. coast; occasionally inland (Eagle Lake, Bay City). *Habitat:* Marshes, lagoons, mudflats. **Nest:** Platform of sticks in bush or tree; in colony on island or in swamp. Eggs (1–4) white.

Swans, Geese, and Ducks: Anatidae

THE BEST-KNOWN family of water birds. Divided by the A.O.U. *Check-list* into several subfamilies. These are discussed separately. Food: Very diverse; mainly aquatic plants and animal life; also roots, grass, seeds, insects, etc. Cosmopolitan. No. of species: World, 145; N. America, 62; Texas, 39 (plus 3 accidentals).

Swans: Cygninae

HUGE, WHITE swimming birds larger and with much longer, more slender necks than geese; like some geese, they migrate in lines or V-shaped flocks. Young are brownish white.

WHISTLING SWAN *Olor columbianus* 48–55 pp. 32, 33
Field marks: A huge white swimming bird, larger and with a much longer neck than any goose. Feeds by "tipping-up." The completely white wings devoid of black and the extremely long neck distinguish it from other large white swimming birds (Snow Goose, White Pelican). A small yellow spot at the base of the *black bill* can be seen at very close range (sometimes absent). Young birds are quite dingy, with dull pinkish bills.
Similar species: (1) Mute Swan (park variety) has *orange bill* with black knob; floats with more curve in neck. (2) See also Trumpeter Swan (p. 277).
Voice: High-pitched cooing notes, less harsh than honking of geese; a musical, loud *woo-ho, woo-woo, woo-hoo*
Where found: Arctic America. Winters in U.S. **Texas:** Rare winter visitor (coast and inland, from Rio Grande delta to n. and w. Texas, Panhandle). Formerly more frequent. *Habitat:* Lakes, bays.

Geese: Anserinae

LARGE waterfowl; larger, heavier-bodied, and longer-necked than ducks; bills thick at base. Noisy in flight; some species fly in diagonal lines or V-formation. Unlike ducks, *sexes look alike* at all seasons. They are more terrestrial, feeding mainly on land, and may be looked for in grassy marshes, grain or stubble fields, but sometimes also "upend" in water. Gregarious outside breeding season. See cormorants.

CANADA GOOSE *Branta canadensis* 23–42   pp. 32, 33
Field marks: A gray-brown goose with black head and neck or "stocking" that contrasts strikingly with the light-colored breast. The most characteristic mark is the white patch or "chin strap" that runs on to the side of the head. Bill and legs black. People in many sections are very familiar with the long strings of these geese passing high overhead in V-formation. Canada Geese vary greatly in size from the typical large ones, the largest of Texas geese (35–42), to Mallard-sized birds (23–25), which are the smallest. Ten races are currently recognized by the A.O.U. *Check-list* (1957), at least four of which winter in Texas. Although there is variation and a clinal blend in size it is possible to compare certain races in the field.

B. c. moffitti (Western Canada Goose) and *B. c. interior* (Interior Canada Goose) both winter in Texas. They are large forms (35–42), not safely separable in the field.

B. c. parvipes (Lesser Canada Goose). Medium-sized, about size of Snow and White-fronted Geese (25–34).

B. c. hutchinsii (Richardson's Canada Goose). Very small. Not much larger than a Mallard (25); stubby bill, short neck. **Voice:** The large forms when traveling have a musical honking or barking *ka-ronk* or *ka-lunk* (second syllable higher). The medium-sized "Lesser" Canada Goose has a higher-pitched *lo-ank, lo-ank, a-lank, a-lank.* The tiny "Richardson's" Canada Goose is still higher-pitched — yelping rather than barking.
Where found: Alaska, Canada, n. U.S. Winters to Mexico and Gulf States. **Texas:** *Migrant* throughout. *Winters* (Sept.-Apr.) along coast; locally inland. *Habitat:* Lakes, bays, marshes, prairies, fields.

BRANT *Branta bernicla* 23–29   pp. 32, 33
Field marks: A small black-necked goose not much larger than a Mallard. Has a white "stern," conspicuous when it "upends"; and a fleck of white on side of neck (absent in immature).
Similar species: Resembles Canada Goose somewhat, but much smaller and shorter-necked than most races. Foreparts of Brant are black, *to the waterline:* Canada Goose's breast shows light

above the water. Brant has much more white on the sides and its white rear is very conspicuous. Canada Goose has a large chin strap of white. *Caution:* Hunters often use the term "brant" for various other geese.

Voice: A throaty *cr-r-r-ruk* or *krr-onk, krrr-onk.*

Where found: Arctic Canada, arctic Eurasia. Winters along U.S. and European coasts. **Texas:** Casual visitor coastwise (Oct.–Apr.).

WHITE-FRONTED GOOSE *Anser albifrons* 27–30 pp. 32, 33
Field marks: Near size of Snow Goose. *Adult:* Gray-brown with a pink bill, white patch *on front of face*, and irregular *black bars* on belly (variable); white crescent on rump. Legs bright *orange* or *yellow. Immature:* Dusky with pale bill, *yellow* or *orange* feet; otherwise without distinctive marks of adult. No other Texas goose has yellow or orange legs.
Similar species: (1) Canada Goose shows contrast of black "stocking" and light chest. Overhead, more uniform color of White-front is at once apparent. (2) Immature Blue Goose is also dusky but has dusky feet and a blackish bill.
Voice: *Kah-lah-a-luck,* high-pitched "tooling"; *kow-lyow* or *lyo-lyok.*
Where found: Arctic. Winters south to Mexico, Gulf States, n. Africa, India. **Texas:** *Migrates* through most of state except Trans-Pecos (casual El Paso). *Winters* chiefly along coast (Oct.–Apr.). *Habitat:* Marshes, prairies, fields, lakes, bays.

SNOW GOOSE *Chen hyperborea* 23–30
("White Brant") pp. 32, 33
Field marks: A *white* goose, smaller than the large Canada, with *black wing-tips.* Often rust-stained on head. Young duskier, with dark bills, but recognizable as Snow Geese.
Similar species: Swans have *no black* in wings, are much larger, have longer necks, and a more elegant shape. At a great distance Snow Goose and White Pelican might be confused.
Voice: Loud, nasal, resonant *whouk* or *kaahk,* uttered singly, twice, rarely three times. A conversational *zung-ung-ung.*
Where found: Ne. Siberia, arctic America. Winters south to Mexico, Gulf coast, Japan. **Texas:** *Migrant* throughout. *Winters* (Sept.–Apr.) mainly along coast. *Habitat:* Marshes, prairies, ponds, bays.

BLUE GOOSE *Chen caerulescens* 25–30
("Blue Brant") pp. 32, 33
Field marks: A dark goose, smaller than the large Canada, with a *white head and neck.* Face often stained with rusty. Normally associates with Snow Geese. Intermediates with white breasts, dark backs are frequent. Some authorities

LONG-LEGGED WADING BIRDS

LOUISIANA HERON p. 18
Dark; white belly.

LITTLE BLUE HERON p. 16
Adult: Dark body, slender dark legs, bluish bill.
Immature: White body; dark bill and feet.

REDDISH EGRET p. 17
Dark phase: Dark; flesh-colored bill.
White phase: White; flesh-colored bill.

SNOWY EGRET p. 18
Small; black bill, yellow feet.

CATTLE EGRET p. 16
Small; yellow bill; yellow, greenish, pink, or black legs.
Associates with cattle.

COMMON EGRET p. 17
Large; yellow bill, dark legs.

GREAT WHITE HERON p. 15
Casual in Texas. Large; white, with yellowish legs.

GREAT BLUE HERON p. 15
Large; blue-gray.

SANDHILL CRANE p. 79
Gray; red forehead; tufted rear.
Immature birds washed with brown.

WHOOPING CRANE p. 79
White; red forehead, black primaries.
Immature birds washed with rusty.

ROSEATE SPOONBILL p. 24
Pink wings, spatulate bill.
Immature birds whitish.

Herons (including egrets and bitterns) fly with their necks folded; cranes and all other long-legged waders, with their necks extended.

LOUISIANA
HERON

Adult

LITTLE
BLUE
HERON

Dark Phase

REDDISH
EGRET

Immature

SNOWY
EGRET

Adult

CATTLE
EGRET

LITTLE
BLUE
HERON

White Phase

REDDISH
EGRET

COMMON
EGRET

GREAT
WHITE
HERON

GREAT
BLUE
HERON

Immature

Immature

Adult

Adult

Adult

SANDHILL CRANE

WHOOPING CRANE

ROSEATE SPOONBILL

CLAPPER RAIL

KING RAIL

VIRGINIA RAIL
Adult

Juvenile

Adult

Immature

SORA

YELLOW RAIL

BLACK RAIL

COMMON GALLINULE
Downy Young

COOT
Downy Young

KING RAIL
Downy Young

PURPLE GALLINULE

COMMON GALLINULE

AMERICAN COOT

Plate 8   29

RAILS, GALLINULES, AND COOT

CLAPPER RAIL   p. 83
  Large, gray-brown or gray; salt marshes.

KING RAIL   p. 82
  Large, rusty brown; fresh marshes.
  Downy young: Glossy black, white on bill.

VIRGINIA RAIL   p. 83
  Small; gray cheeks, long bill.
  Juvenal: Blackish.

SORA   p. 83
  Adult: Gray-brown; short yellow bill.
  Immature: Buffy brown; short bill.

YELLOW RAIL   p. 86
  Buffy; striped back, white wing-patch.

BLACK RAIL   p. 86
  Small; slaty with black bill.
  All young rails are black, so do not call them Black Rails.

PURPLE GALLINULE   p. 86
  Pale blue frontal shield, purple neck.

COMMON GALLINULE   p. 87
  Adult: Red bill, white flank-stripe.
  Downy young: Glossy black; red bill.

AMERICAN COOT   p. 87
  Adult: White bill.
  Downy young: Orange-red head.

Coots and gallinules skitter over
the water when taking flight.

consider the Blue Goose merely a color phase of the Snow Goose. *Immature:* Dusky, very similar to immature White-front, but bill and feet *dark;* wings paler, bluish.
Similar species: Young White-front has light bill, yellow legs.
Voice: Exactly like Snow Goose's.
Where found: Arctic Canada. Winters mainly along Gulf of Mexico. **Texas:** *Migrant* through e. half of state (rare west to Panhandle, Muleshoe). *Winters* (Sept.–Apr.) along entire coast. *Habitat:* Marshes, prairies, ponds, bays.

ROSS' GOOSE *Chen rossii* 23   p. 32
  Field marks: Smaller than Snow Goose (near size of Mallard); *decidedly smaller bill*, which at very close range is seen to lack the black "lips" of the larger bird.
  Voice: No loud notes like Snow Goose's; a simple gruntlike *kug,* or weak *kek, kek* or *ke-gak, ke-gak* (J. Moffitt).
  Where found: Nw. Canada; winters mainly in California. **Texas:** Casual winter visitor (birds taken Wharton, Jefferson, Chambers, and Wilbarger Cos., Eagle Lake, Port Isabel).

Tree Ducks: Dendrocygninae

GOOSE-LIKE ducks with long legs and erect necks. Also called "whistling ducks" because of voice.

BLACK-BELLIED TREE DUCK *Dendrocygna autumnalis* 22
("Black-bellied Whistling Duck")   pp. 37, 49
  Field marks: A goose-like duck with long pink legs. Rusty with *black belly*, bright *coral-pink* bill. Very broad *white stripe* near fore edge of wing. Immature has gray bill and legs. Thrusts head and feet down when landing. Frequently sits in trees.
  Similar species: Muscovy Duck (Mexico) is larger, blacker, short-legged, with *squarish* white wing-patch (not stripe); does not whistle. Feral Muscovies are occasionally seen in Texas.
  Voice: A squealing whistle, *pe-che-che-ne.*
  Where found: Tropical America north to s. Texas. Winters south of U.S. **Texas:** *Summer resident* (Apr.–Dec.) in Rio Grande delta; upriver to Rio Grande City; north locally to Corpus Christi; occasionally to San Antonio, Eagle Lake. *Habitat:* Ponds, resacas, marshes, swamps. **Nest:** In tree cavity or in marsh. Eggs (12–16) whitish.

FULVOUS TREE DUCK *Dendrocygna bicolor* 20–21
("Fulvous Whistling Duck," "Mexican Squealer")   pp. 37, 49, 52
  Field marks: This long-legged, gangly goose-like duck does not ordinarily frequent trees. Its *tawny* body, dark back, and broad *creamy stripe* on the side identify it. Sexes similar. Flying, it

looks dark, with blackish underwings and a *white ring* at the tail base. The slightly drooped neck, long legs extending beyond the tail, and slow wingbeats (for a duck) are distinctive. Before bird alights, the "landing gear" is let down.

Similar species: (1) Cinnamon Teal is smaller, not goose-like; it is of a deeper color. (2) See Black-bellied Tree Duck.

Voice: A squealing double-noted whistle, weaker than Black-bellied Tree Duck's, "a weak, whistled *kill-dee*" (E. Kincaid).

Where found: Sw. U.S. south to Cent. America; also S. America, tropical Asia, Madagascar, and E. Africa. **Texas:** *Summers* (Apr.–Oct.) along Texas coast. Rare and irregular in *winter*. Casual in Trans-Pecos. *Habitat:* Marshes, ricefields, ponds.

Nest: A grass-lined saucer in grass or marsh vegetation; rarely in tree cavity. Eggs (12–30) buffy.

Surface-feeding Ducks: Anatinae

DUCKS of this group ("puddle ducks") are characteristic of shallow waters, creeks, ponds, and marshes. They feed by dabbling and "upending" rather than by diving; occasionally feed on land. When frightened, they spring directly into the air instead of pattering before getting under way. They swim as a rule with the tail held off the water. They can dive, but seldom do. Most birds of this group have an iridescent *speculum*, or "*mirror*," a rectangular patch on the hind edge of the wing.

In summer most males molt into a drab plumage known as the "eclipse." This phase is not covered here: first, because most ducks are not in Texas during this period; second, because they look so much like the females of their species as to be identifiable. Before the summer is out they commence a second molt, in which they regain their bright pattern.

Non-breeders may be recorded in Texas in summer.

MALLARD *Anas platyrhynchos* 20–28   pp. 36, 44, 53

Field marks: *Male:* Grayish with *glossy green head, narrow white collar,* purplish-brown breast, and white tail with curled black central feathers ("duck-tail"), yellowish bill, orange feet. *Female:* Mottled; brown with a *whitish tail* and conspicuous white borders *on each side* of the metallic violet-blue speculum. Bill dark, patched with orange, feet orange. In flight, Mallards have a characteristic wing-stroke, slower than in most ducks; the downward sweep is not much below body level.

Similar species: (1) Several other ducks have green-glossed heads, but white neck-ring and ruddy breast mark male Mallard (see Red-breasted Merganser). (2) Mottled Ducks are very similar to female Mallards but show no white borders on metallic wing-patch, or only a very narrow one on hind edge. (3) Female

GEESE AND SWANS

CANADA GOOSE   p. 26
  Black "stocking," white cheek-patch.
  Several races of the Canada Goose, varying in size, visit
  Texas, but separation in the field is not too safe. The
  Richardson's form (*B. c. hutchinsii*) is the small extreme.
  See text.

BRANT*   p. 26
  Black chest and "stocking"; white neck-spot.

WHITE-FRONTED GOOSE   p. 27
  Adult: White at base of bill.
  Immature: Dusky, with pale bill.

BLUE GOOSE   p. 27
  Adult: White head, dark body.
  Immature: Dusky, with dark bill, pale wings.

BLUE–SNOW HYBRID
  Hybrids, looking like Blue Geese with white bellies, etc.,
  are frequent.

SNOW GOOSE   p. 27
  Adult: White with black wing-tips.
  Immature: Similar but duskier, dark bill.

ROSS' GOOSE   p. 30
  Casual in Texas. Smaller than Snow Goose; bill smaller,
  lacking black "lips" or "grinning patch."

WHISTLING SWAN   p. 25
  Black bill, long straight neck.

MUTE SWAN
  Knobbed orange bill, more curved neck.
  The domesticated park swan. See under Whistling Swan,
  p. 25.

* Gunners often call other geese "brant."

CANADA GOOSE (3 forms)

BRANT

WHITE-FRONTED GOOSE

Immature

Adult

BLUE GOOSE

Immature

Adult

BLUE-SNOW HYBRID

SNOW GOOSE

Immature

Adult

ROSS' GOOSE

WHISTLING SWAN

MUTE SWAN

CANADA GOOSE

BRANT

Lower

Upper

WHITE-FRONTED GOOSE

Adult

Immature

BLUE GOOSE

Immature

SNOW GOOSE

Upper

WHISTLING SWAN

BLUE GOOSE

Adult

Upper

Plate 10   33

GEESE AND SWAN

Many geese and swans fly in
line or wedge formation.

CANADA GOOSE   p. 26
    Black "stocking," light chest, white throat-patch.

BRANT*   p. 26
    Small; black "stocking," black chest, black head.

WHITE-FRONTED GOOSE   p. 27
    Adult: Gray neck, black splotches on belly.
    Immature: Dusky; light bill, light feet.

SNOW GOOSE   p. 27
    White body, black wing-tips.

BLUE GOOSE   p. 27
    Adult: Dark body, white head.
    Immature: Dusky; pale wing-linings, dark bill, dark feet.

WHISTLING SWAN   p. 25
    Very long neck; wings with no black.

* Gunners often call various other geese "brant."

Pintails are more streamlined and have a conspicuous white border only on rear edge of dull speculum. Bill of Pintail is gray; that of Mallard usually orange and black. In flight Mallard's wing-linings are whiter.

Voice: *Female* quacks loudly. Male, a quiet *yeeb;* a low *kwek*.
Where found: N. parts of N. Hemisphere. Winters south to Mexico, n. Africa, India. **Texas:** *Migrates and winters* (Sept.– Apr.) throughout. *Summers* at least in n. parts. *Breeds* very locally. *Habitat:* Marshes, swamps, ponds, lakes, bays. **Nest:** A hollow lined with grass and down, usually among reeds or grass, close to water. Eggs (8–15) greenish buff.

MEXICAN DUCK *Anas diazi* 22
(New Mexican Duck)   pp. 36, 44
Field marks: Both sexes very similar to female Mallard. Bill of male like male Mallard's (unmarked yellowish green). Female has spotted bill and is almost indistinguishable from female Mallard. Frequently hybridizes with Mallard.
Similar species: Not as dark as Black Duck; more like Mottled Duck but with a white border on each side of metallic wing-patch. Black and Mottled Ducks do not normally occur in w. Texas.
Voice: Similar to Mallard's.
Where found: New Mexico and extreme w. Texas south to cent. Mexico. **Texas:** *Resident* along Rio Grande from El Paso to Big Bend (occasional). **Nest:** Similar to Mallard's.

BLACK DUCK *Anas rubripes* 21–25
("Black Mallard")   pp. 36, 44, 53
Field marks: The Black Duck in flight may be known by its *very dark coloration* and *flashing white wing-linings*. It is dark sooty brown with a lighter gray-brown head and a metallic violet patch in the wing. Feet may be red or brown; bill yellowish or dull greenish. Sexes similar.
Similar species: Mottled Duck is nearly identical in general pattern but browner, less sooty, approaching color of female Mallard (without whitish tail and double speculum bars).
Voice: Similar to Mallard's.
Where found: E. and cent. N. America. Winters south to Gulf Coast. **Texas:** *Winters* (Oct.–Apr.) sparingly in e. half of Texas and Panhandle, and along coast, perhaps to Rio Grande delta. Status poorly known because of confusion with Mottled Duck. *Habitat:* Lakes, bays, rivers, marshes, mudflats.

MOTTLED DUCK *Anas fulvigula* 20   pp. 36, 44, 53
("Black Mallard," "Summer Black Mallard," "Dusky Duck")
Field marks: Somewhat darker than female Mallard and lacking the dark blotches on the *yellow bill*. General pattern (dark

tail and single white line on rear edge of speculum) like Black Duck, from which it may be told (sometimes with much difficulty) by its tawnier color and pale tan instead of gray-brown head. Sexes similar.
Similar species: Black Duck is a bit more sooty; very similar.
Voice: Similar to Mallard's.
Where found: Gulf States, ne. Mexico. **Texas:** *Resident* along coast. Straggler inland (reported San Antonio, Waco, Mason, Dallas). *Habitat:* Coastal marshes, mudflats, ponds, bays.
Nest: Of grass, lined with down; among sedges and grass or under bush, in or near marsh. Eggs (6–11) buff.

GADWALL   *Anas strepera*   19–21   pp. 36, 44, 53
Field marks: *Male:* A slender gray duck with a *black rump*, a *white speculum or patch* on the *hind* edge of the wing, and a dull reddish patch on the forewing. Flank feathers usually conceal these patches; then the best mark is the jet-black "stern," which contrasts sharply with the gray plumage. Belly white, feet yellow. Male has a more abrupt forehead than similar ducks, darker crown. *Female:* Brown, mottled; *white speculum,* yellow feet, yellow on bill.
Similar species: (1) Female Pintail has obscure speculum, gray feet (not seen when swimming); shows solid-gray bill at close range. (2) Female American Widgeon is more ruddy, with a gray head, light bluish bill. White wing-patch is on *fore edge* of wing. Some young Widgeons show so little white on wing that they might be confused with Gadwall, but they swim with "stern" high in widgeon fashion. (3) See female Mallard.
Voice: Female quacks loudly in falling diminuendo, *kaaak-kaaak-kak-kak-kak.* Male has a low note; also a whistled call.
Where found: S. Alaska, Canada, n. U.S., n. Eurasia. Winters to Mexico, Africa, India. **Texas:** *Migrates, winters* (Sept.–May) throughout. *Summers* rarely; has nested Amarillo. *Habitat:* Ponds, bays, rivers, marshes. Eggs (7–12) whitish.

PINTAIL   *Anas acuta*   26–30
("Sprig")   pp. 36, 44, 53
Field marks: Male Pintails are slender white-breasted ducks with long, slim necks and long, *needle-pointed* tails, quite different in cut from other ducks of ponds and marshes. They show a white patch near the black "stern." A conspicuous *white point* runs from the neck onto the side of the brown head. *Female:* Mottled brown with a slender neck and somewhat pointed tail. In flight, shows one *light border* on rear of wing.
Similar species: (1) Oldsquaw, only other duck with a needle-pointed tail, is not a marsh duck. (2) See female Mallard. (3) Easily confused with females of American Widgeon and Gadwall (see those species).

DUCKS IN FLIGHT
(through the binocular)

Note: Males are analyzed below. Some females are similar.

BLACK DUCK (BLACK MALLARD)   p. 34
Dark body, paler head (see Plate 18).

MOTTLED DUCK (not illustrated)   p. 34
Very similar to Black Duck. Slightly paler. See text.

MEXICAN DUCK   p. 34
Pattern of female Mallard, but bill unmarked. See text.

MALLARD   p. 31
Dark head, two white borders on speculum; neck-ring.

GADWALL   p. 35
White speculum.

PINTAIL (SPRIG)   p. 35
Needle tail, one white border on speculum, neck stripe.

AMERICAN WIDGEON (BALDPATE)   p. 39
Large white shoulder-patch.

SHOVELER (SPOONBILL)   p. 40
Spoon bill, large bluish shoulder-patch.

WOOD DUCK   p. 40
Stocky; long dark tail, white border on dark wing.

BLUE-WINGED TEAL   p. 38
Small; large bluish shoulder-patch.
Females of Blue-winged and Cinnamon Teal are nearly
identical.

CINNAMON TEAL   p. 39
Very dark (mahogany); bluish shoulder-patch.

GREEN-WINGED TEAL   p. 38
Small, dark-winged; green speculum.

HOODED MERGANSER   p. 51
Merganser shape; small wing-patch.

COMMON MERGANSER   p. 51
Merganser shape; white chest, large wing-patch.

RED-BREASTED MERGANSER   p. 54
Merganser shape; dark chest, large wing-patch.

Mergansers fly with bill, head, neck, and
body held in a horizontal line.

Sexes Similar

MEXICAN DUCK

BLACK DUCK

Sexes Similar

MALLARD

♂ GADWALL

PINTAIL

AMERICAN WIDGEON

SHOVELER

CINNAMON TEAL

BLUE-WINGED TEAL

GREEN-WINGED TEAL

WOOD DUCK

COMMON MERGANSER

HOODED MERGANSER

RED-BREASTED MERGANSER

LESSER SCAUP

REDHEAD

RING-NECKED DUCK

CANVASBACK

COMMON GOLDENEYE

BUFFLEHEAD

OLDSQUAW

MASKED DUCK

RUDDY DUCK

BLACK-BELLIED TREE DUCK

Sexes alike

FULVOUS TREE DUCK

Sexes alike

WHITE-WINGED SCOTER

SURF SCOTER

COMMON SCOTER

Plate 12   37

DUCKS IN FLIGHT
(through the binocular)

Note: Males are analyzed below. Some females are similar.

REDHEAD   p. 41
   Gray back, broad gray wing-stripe.

LESSER SCAUP (BLUEBILL)   p. 43
   Broad rear white wing-stripe (see Greater Scaup).

RING-NECKED DUCK   p. 42
   Black back, broad gray wing-stripe.

CANVASBACK   p. 42
   White back, long profile.

COMMON GOLDENEYE (WHISTLER)   p. 46
   Large white wing-squares, short neck, black head.

BUFFLEHEAD (BUTTERBALL)   p. 46
   Small; large wing-patches, white head-patch.

RUDDY DUCK   p. 50
   Small; dark, with white cheeks.

OLDSQUAW   p. 46
   Dark wings, white on body.

MASKED DUCK   p. 50
   Resembles Ruddy, but white patch in wing, black face.

BLACK-BELLIED TREE DUCK   p. 30
   Dark; very broad white patch nearly length of wing.

FULVOUS TREE DUCK   p. 30
   Dark; white ring near rump.

WHITE-WINGED SCOTER   p. 47
   Black body, white wing-patch.

SURF SCOTER   p. 47
   Black body, white head-patches.

COMMON SCOTER   p. 47
   All-black plumage.

Voice: Seldom vocal. Male utters a double-toned whistle, also wheezy teal-like notes. Female has a low *quack*.

Where found: N. parts of N. Hemisphere. Winters south to n. S. America, Africa, India. **Texas:** *Migrates and winters* (Aug.–May) throughout. *Breeds* occasionally in n. Texas (probably elsewhere). *Habitat:* Marshes, prairies, ponds, lakes, rivers, salt bays. **Nest:** A down-lined hollow; may be well concealed in marsh or exposed on prairie. Eggs (6–12) olive-buff.

GREEN-WINGED TEAL

Anas carolinensis   13–15½   pp. 36, 44, 53

Field marks: When ducks fly from the marsh, teal are conspicuous by their small size. If they show no large light-colored wing-patches, they are this species. *Male:* A small compact gray duck with brown head, *white mark* in front of wing and cream-colored patch toward tail. In sunlight, shows an iridescent *green speculum* in wing and green patch on side of head. *Female:* A little speckled duck with iridescent green speculum.

Similar species: Blue-winged Teal (both sexes) have light blue wing-patches. In flight, from below, male Blue-wings show dark bellies; Green-wings, white bellies. Female Green-wings, though smaller, shorter-necked, and shorter-billed are difficult to distinguish unless absence of blue wing-patch is seen.

Voice: Male utters a short whistle, sometimes repeated; also froglike peeping notes. Female has a crisp quack.

Where found: Alaska, Canada, w. and ne. U.S. Winters to Cent. America, West Indies. **Texas:** *Migrates, winters* (Sept.–Apr.) throughout. *Summers* rarely in w. Texas (El Paso); may breed. *Habitat:* Marshes, lakes, ponds, rivers, bays. **Nest:** A down-lined hollow in grass or marsh. Eggs (10–12) whitish.

BLUE-WINGED TEAL   *Anas discors*   15–16   pp. 36, 44, 53

Field marks: A little half-sized marsh duck with a large light-colored patch on the forewing. *Male:* Small, dull-colored, with large *white crescent in front of eye*, and large *chalky-blue patch on forewing*. The blue, at a distance may look whitish. Also a white patch near black tail. Males hold "eclipse" plumage longer than most ducks (often to end of year) and most birds seen in fall lack the white face crescent or show it poorly. They resemble females. *Female:* Brown, mottled, with large blue patch on forewing.

Similar species: (1) Cinnamon Teal also has blue wing-patches, but male can be told by deep mahogany color. (In poor light, this species and autumn male Blue-wing without face-patch both look dark-bodied with pale wing-patches.) (2) Shoveler (big bill) also has pale blue wing-patches. (3) Female Scaup also has white patch before eye. (4) See Green-winged Teal.

Voice: Males utter peeping notes; females, a light quack.

Where found: Canada south to s. U.S. Winters south to S. America. **Texas:** *Migrant* throughout. *Winters* (Aug.–May) along coast and inland to Edwards Plateau and n. Texas. *Breeds* rarely and locally in n. half of state; irregularly south to Galveston, Eagle Lake, Corpus Christi, Kingsville. *Habitat:* Ponds, marshes. **Nest:** A down-lined hollow among grass near water. Eggs (6–12) whitish, buff.

CINNAMON TEAL *Anas cyanoptera* 15½–17 pp. 36, 44, 53
Field marks: *Male:* A small, dark cinnamon-red duck with a large chalky-blue patch on fore edge of wing. *Female:* A small mottled brown duck with a pale blue wing-patch.
Similar species: (1) On wing resembles Blue-winged Teal (female cannot be separated from female Blue-wing except by her associates). (2) Only other small rufous duck is male Ruddy.
Voice: Seldom vocal; male, a low chattering; female, a *quack.*
Where found: Sw. Canada south locally to S. America. Winters from sw. U.S. south. **Texas:** *Migrant* throughout; rare in e. parts. *Winters* (Aug.–May) in s. Texas and along lower coast (sparingly); inland locally, west to El Paso. *Breeds* rarely in w. Texas; has bred San Antonio. *Habitat:* Fresh ponds, marshes. **Nest:** A down-lined hollow in reeds, or grass sometimes away from water. Eggs (10–12) whitish, buff.

EUROPEAN WIDGEON *Mareca penelope* 18–20 p. 53
Field marks: *Male:* A gray widgeon with a *reddish-brown* head and *buffy* crown; breast pinkish. *Female:* Very similar to female American Widgeon, but in good light, head is tinged with *reddish,* whereas that of American is gray. The surest point in the hand is the axillars (feathers in "armpits"), which are dusky in this species, white in the American.
Similar species: (1) Suggests Redhead Duck (which has black chest). (2) Male American Widgeon (Baldpate) is *brown* with a gray head and *white* crown.
Voice: Male, a whistling *whee-oo.* Female, a low purring.
Where found: Iceland, Eurasia. Regular visitor to U.S. **Texas:** Occasional; most frequent in April. Reported Panhandle, Dallas, Cove, Rockport, Corpus Christi, Laguna Atascosa, etc.

AMERICAN WIDGEON *Mareca americana* 18–22
(Baldpate) pp. 36, 44, 53
Field marks: By the shining white crown of the male, beginners learn this bird. In flight, recognized by the large white patch covering *front* of the wing; in other ducks possessing white patches they are placed on the hind edge. (Similarly placed blue patches of Blue-winged Teal, Cinnamon Teal, and Shoveler often appear whitish at a distance.) On water, rides high, picking at the surface like a coot. Often grazes on land. *Male:*

Brownish with gray head, white crown; patch on side of head glossy green, visible in good light; white patch on forewing and white patch near tail; bill pale blue with black tip. *Female:* Ruddy brown with gray head and neck; belly and forewing whitish. *Immatures:* Nondescript; brownish with a paler gray head and neck; white belly contrasts sharply with brown breast. **Similar species:** Female is easily confused with (1) female Gadwall and (2) female Pintail. Gray head contrasting with brown breast is best mark; bill paler, bluish. Has whitish wing-patches similar to male's. (3) See European Widgeon.
Voice: A whistled *whee whee whew* (male). *Qua-ack* (female).
Where found: Alaska, w. Canada, n. U.S. Winters south to Cent. America, West Indies. **Texas:** *Migrates and winters* (Oct.–May) throughout. *Habitat:* Marshes, ponds, lakes, bays.

SHOVELER *Spatula clypeata* 17–20
("Spoonbill")   pp. 36, 44, 53
Field marks: The Shoveler is a small duck, somewhat larger than a teal; best identified by its spoon-shaped bill, which in flight makes the wings seem set far back. Swimming, the bird sits low, with the big bill pointed toward the water. *Male:* Largely black and white; belly and *sides rufous;* head blackish, glossed with green; breast white; pale blue patch on forewing. Orange legs. Seen on the water or overhead, the pattern of the drake is unique, five alternating areas of light and dark: dark, white, dark, white, dark. *Female:* Mottled brownish, with big bill, large pale blue wing-patches, orange legs.
Similar species: Wing pattern suggests Blue-winged Teal.
Voice: Female, a light *quack;* male, a low *took, took, took.*
Where found: Widespread in N. Hemisphere. Winters south to Cent. America, Africa, etc. **Texas:** *Migrant* throughout. *Winters* (Sept.–May) except in Panhandle and other cold sections. *Summers* rarely in n. and cent. parts (south to San Antonio and Fort Bend Co.); has nested occasionally. *Habitat:* Marshes, ponds, lakes, salt bays. **Nest:** A down-lined hollow in grass or sedge. Eggs (10–12) pale olive.

WOOD DUCK *Aix sponsa* 17–20
("Carolina Duck," "Summer Duck")   pp. 36, 44, 52
Field marks: The most highly colored North American duck. Often perches in trees. On the wing, the white belly contrasts strikingly with the dark breast and wings. The long square dark tail, short neck, and angle at which the bill points downward are also good points. *Male:* Crested; bizarre face pattern; rainbow iridescence. Descriptive words fail; the illustration explains it. *Male in "eclipse"* (late summer): Similar to female, but retaining white face-markings and red and white bill of

spring male. *Female:* Dark brown with lighter flanks, white belly, dark crested head, and *white patch surrounding eye.*
Similar species: In flight, female and young American Widgeon suggest female Wood Duck but have pointed tails.
Voice: A distressed *whoo–eek*, shrill and raucous (female); and a finchlike *jeee* with rising inflection (male).
Where found: S. Canada south through much of U.S., Cuba. Winters to Mexico, Cuba. **Texas:** *Resident* locally in e. Texas. Scarce in cent. parts (has nested Austin); has also nested in Panhandle; casual west to El Paso and south to Brownsville. *Habitat:* Wooded swamps, wooded streams, ponds. **Nest:** A bed of down in tree cavity. Eggs (10–15) whitish.

Diving Ducks: Aythyinae

"SEA DUCKS" or "bay ducks" they are also called, but many are found commonly on lakes and rivers and they may breed in marshes. They all dive, whereas surface-feeding ducks rarely dive. The hind toe has a lobe or flap like a little paddle; this the surface-feeders lack. In taking wing they patter along the surface while getting under way (their legs are placed closer to the tail than in surface-feeding ducks). Non-breeders of various species are often recorded in Texas in summer.

REDHEAD *Aythya americana* 18–23 pp. 37, 45, 48
Field marks: *Male:* Gray with a black chest and *round red-brown head;* bill blue with black tip. *Female:* Brownish with a broad *gray wing-stripe* and a *suffused light patch* about base of bill.
Similar species: (1) Male Canvasback is much whiter, with long sloping forehead and black bill in contrast to Redhead's high, abrupt forehead and blue bill. Redhead is shorter, chunkier, much more like Greater Scaup in contour. (2) Scaup on wing has a black and white pattern, in contrast to gray Redhead with its gray wing-stripe. Female Scaup in addition to a *white* wing-stripe has a *well defined* white patch near bill. (3) Other female ducks with broad gray wing-stripes are: Canvasback (larger, paler, with long profile); and Ring-neck (smaller, darker, with white ring on bill and white eye-ring).
Voice: Male, a catlike *meow*, also a deep purr. Female, a high *quack* or *squak*.
Where found: W. Canada and nw. U.S. Winters south to Mexico, West Indies. **Texas:** *Migrant* in all sections. *Winters* (Oct.–May) mainly on coastal bays (especially south of Corpus Christi); locally inland. *Habitat:* Lakes, reservoirs, bays, estuaries.

RING-NECKED DUCK *Aythya collaris*   16–18   pp. 37, 45, 48
   Field marks: *Male:* Like a *black-backed* Scaup. Head, chest, and back black; sides light gray with *conspicuous white mark in front of wing;* bill crossed by two white rings. In flight, the only black-backed duck with a broad *gray* wing-stripe. The dull chestnut ring on the neck is seldom visible. *Female:* Brown, darkest on crown and back; wing-stripe *gray;* indistinct whitish area about base of bill; *white eye-ring and ring on bill;* white belly. The rather triangular head shape is distinctive.
   Similar species: (1) Female Scaup has a well-defined white face "mask," and *white* wing-stripe; lacks white eye-ring and ring on bill. (2) Female Redhead is larger, paler, with less contrast; lacks conspicuous rings about eye and on bill.
   Voice: Similar to Lesser Scaup's.
   Where found: Canada, n. U.S. Winters south to Panama, West Indies. **Texas:** *Migrant* throughout much of state. *Winters* (Oct.–Apr.) along coast; locally inland except in Panhandle. *Habitat:* Lakes, wooded ponds, marsh ponds, rivers, bays.

CANVASBACK *Aythya valisineria*   20–24   pp. 37, 45, 48
   Field marks: *Male:* A very white-looking duck with a *rusty-red head and neck,* black breast, long blackish bill. *Female:* Grayish, with a suggestion of red on head and neck. The *long, sloping head profile* separates either sex from any other species they superficially resemble. In flight, Canvasbacks string out in lines or V-formation. The long head, neck, and bill give a front-heavy look, as if the wings were set far back.
   Similar species: (1) See Redhead. (2) Female mergansers are redheaded but have crests and whitish chests.
   Voice: Male, a low croak; growling notes. Female, a *quack.*
   Where found: Alaska, w. Canada, nw. U.S. Winters south to Mexico, Gulf Coast. **Texas:** *Migrant* throughout. *Winters* (Oct.–May) mainly on coastal bays; also locally inland except in n. Panhandle. *Habitat:* Lakes, bays, lagoons, estuaries.

GREATER SCAUP *Aythya marila*   17½–20
("Big Bluebill," "Big Broadbill")   pp. 45, 48
   Field marks: Similar to the much more numerous Lesser Scaup, but slightly larger; male whiter on flanks; head rounder, glossed with *green.* (Lesser has a less rounded head, glossed in some lights with dull purple.) These differences can be made sure of only nearby in good light. The length of the wing-stripe is the surest way to separate typical individuals of both sexes. The white in the Lesser extends about halfway along the rear edge of the wing; in the Greater it extends considerably farther toward the wing-tip. There are occasional intermediates.

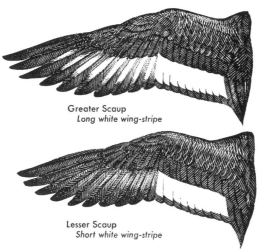

Greater Scaup
Long white wing-stripe

Lesser Scaup
Short white wing-stripe

WINGS OF SCAUPS

Voice: Similar to Lesser Scaup's.
Where found: Alaska, Canada, n. Eurasia. Winters south to Mexico, West Indies, Mediterranean, India. **Texas:** Rare *migrant* in Panhandle and n. Texas south to coast, Brownsville (very rare). Rare transient at Midland, El Paso. *Winters* (Nov.–Mar.) along coast. *Habitat:* Open water; lakes, bays.

LESSER SCAUP *Aythya affinis* 15–18
("Bluebill," "Broadbill") pp. 37, 48
Field marks: *Male:* Scaups on the water appear "black at both ends and white in the middle." The flanks and back are finely barred, but at any distance those parts appear white. The bill is blue; head glossed with dull purple. *Female:* Brown, with a broad white wing-stripe and white "mask" at base of bill. The scaups are our only *common* ducks possessing a broad white stripe (Black-bellied Tree Duck also has broad white stripe).
Similar species: See Greater Scaup.
Voice: Male, a loud *scaup;* also purring notes.
Where found: Alaska, w. Canada. Winters south to n. S. America. **Texas:** *Migrant* throughout. *Winters* (Sept.–May) mainly along coast; locally inland, west to El Paso, north to n. Texas, but not Panhandle. *Habitat:* Ponds, lakes, rivers, bays; open water.

DUCKS OVERHEAD

(as the sportsman often sees them)

Note: Only males are analyzed below.

BLACK DUCK (BLACK MALLARD*)   p. 34
    Very dark body, white wing-linings.

MOTTLED DUCK (not illustrated)   p. 34
    Similar to Black Duck; slightly lighter. See text.

MEXICAN DUCK (not illustrated)   p. 34
    Similar to female Mallard. See text.

GADWALL   p. 35
    White belly, white rear wing-patches.

PINTAIL (SPRIG*)   p. 35
    White breast, thin neck, needle tail.

MALLARD   p. 31
    Dark chest, light belly, white neck-ring.

AMERICAN WIDGEON (BALDPATE*)   p. 39
    White belly, dark pointed tail.

SHOVELER (SPOONBILL*)   p. 40
    Dark belly, white chest; big bill.

WOOD DUCK   p. 40
    White belly, dusky wings, long square tail.

BLUE-WINGED TEAL   p. 38
    Small; dark belly.
    Females of Blue-winged and Cinnamon Teal inseparable.

CINNAMON TEAL   p. 39
    Small; very dark below (deep rufous).

GREEN-WINGED TEAL   p. 38
    Small; light belly, dark head.

HOODED MERGANSER*   p. 51
    Merganser shape; dark bar in wing-linings.

COMMON MERGANSER*   p. 51
    Blackish head, white body, very white wing-linings.

RED-BREASTED MERGANSER*   p. 54
    Merganser shape; dark breastband.

* The sportsman usually calls mergansers "sheldrakes." The names
in parentheses are also common gunners' names.

BLACK DUCK
(Sexes similar)

MALLARD

GADWALL ♂

PINTAIL

AMERICAN
WIDGEON

SHOVELER

CINNAMON
TEAL

BLUE-
WINGED
TEAL

GREEN-WINGED
TEAL

'OOD DUCK

HOODED
MERGANSER

COMMON
MERGANSER

RED-BREASTED
MERGANSER

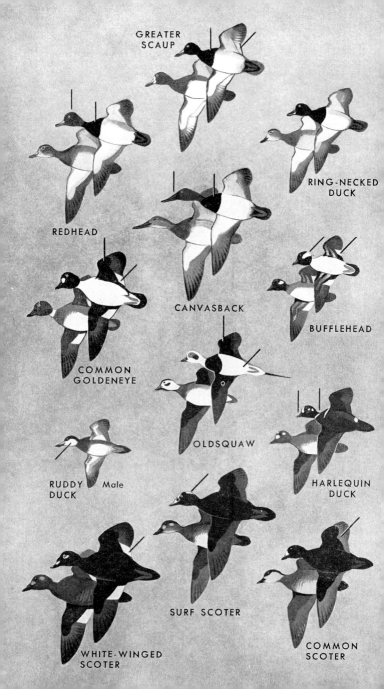

GREATER
SCAUP

RING-NECKED
DUCK

REDHEAD

CANVASBACK

BUFFLEHEAD

COMMON
GOLDENEYE

OLDSQUAW

RUDDY
DUCK   Male

HARLEQUIN
DUCK

WHITE-WINGED
SCOTER

SURF SCOTER

COMMON
SCOTER

Plate 14   45

DUCKS OVERHEAD
(as the sportsman often sees them)

Note: Only males are analyzed below. The first four all have black chests and white wing-linings, and look very much alike.

GREATER SCAUP (BIG BLUEBILL*) p. 42
Black chest, white stripe showing through wing.

REDHEAD p. 41
Black chest, round rufous head.

CANVASBACK p. 42
Black chest, long profile.

RING-NECKED DUCK p. 42
Not surely distinguished from Scaup overhead (except possibly for lack of white rear wing-stripe).

COMMON GOLDENEYE (WHISTLER*) p. 46
Blackish wing-linings, white patches.

BUFFLEHEAD (BUTTERBALL*) p. 46
Resembles small Goldeneye; note head pattern.

OLDSQUAW p. 46
Solid dark wings, white belly.

RUDDY DUCK p. 50
Stubby; white face, dark chest.

HARLEQUIN DUCK p. 269
Accidental in Texas.
Solid dark color, white spots, small bill.

WHITE-WINGED SCOTER* p. 47
Black body, white wing-patch.

SURF SCOTER* p. 47
Black body, white on head.

COMMON SCOTER* p. 47
Black body, silvery flight feathers.

* The three scoters are often called "coots" by sportsmen. The names in parentheses are also common gunners' names.

COMMON GOLDENEYE *Bucephala clangula* 17–23
(American Goldeneye, "Whistler") pp. 37, 45, 48
  Field marks: *Male:* White-looking with a black back and puffy green-glossed head (black at a distance). A large *round white spot* before the eye is the best mark. In flight short-necked; wings show large white patches. Legs orange. *Female:* Gray with a white collar and dark brown head; wings with large square white patches (showing on closed wing). The "singing" of the Goldeneye's wings has earned it the nickname "Whistler."
  Similar species: (1) Scaup at a distance bears a slight resemblance but has a black chest. (2) Male Common Merganser (white-chested) bears a closer resemblance, but is long-lined, low, with an attenuated profile. Look for the face spot on Goldeneye.
  Voice: Courting males have a harsh nasal double note, suggesting *pee-ik* of Nighthawk. Female, a harsh *quack*.
  Where found: Alaska, Canada, n. U.S., n. Eurasia. Winters south to Mexico, Gulf Coast, Mediterranean, n. India. **Texas:** *Winters* (Oct.–Mar.) on rivers, lakes, in e. and n. parts and Panhandle; commoner along coast; south rarely to mouth of Rio Grande. Rare transient El Paso and along Rio Grande. *Habitat:* Lakes, rivers, bays, Gulf.

BUFFLEHEAD *Bucephala albeola* 13–15
("Butterball") pp. 37, 45, 52
  Field marks: One of the smallest ducks. *Male:* Mostly white, with black back; large, puffy head with *great white patch* that extends from eye around back of head; large white wing-patches in flight (suggests small Goldeneye). *Female:* Dark, compact; large head, small bill, *white cheek-spot;* white wing-patch.
  Similar species: See Hooded Merganser. The dark female Bufflehead can be mistaken for a male Hooded Merganser with its crest laid back. Look for the Merganser's spike-like bill. See also winter Ruddy Duck.
  Voice: A hoarse rolling note; also a squeaky call (male). A hoarse *quack* (female).
  Where found: Alaska, w. Canada. Winters south to Mexico, Gulf Coast. **Texas:** *Migrant* in most sections. *Winters* (Oct.–Apr.), along coast (mainly lower coast); locally inland to n. and w. Texas and Panhandle. *Habitat:* Lakes, ponds, rivers, bays.

OLDSQUAW *Clangula hyemalis* ♂ 21, ♀ 17 pp. 37, 45, 49
  Field marks: Oldsquaws are the only sea ducks combining *white on the body and unpatterned dark wings. Male in winter:* Boldly patterned; *long needle-pointed* tail. Head, neck, belly, and scapulars white; breast, back, and wings dusky brown; dark patch on side of face; short bill banded with black and pink. *Male in summer:* Dark with white flanks and belly;

white patch surrounding eye. *Female in winter:* Lacks long, pointed tail feathers. Dark above, white below; head white with black crown and cheek-spot. *Female in summer:* Similar but darker.
Similar species: See Pintail.
Voice: Talkative; musical *onk-a-lik, ow-owdle-ow,* etc.
Where found: Arctic. Winters south on seacoasts, Great Lakes.
Texas: Rare or occasional *winter visitor* (Nov.–May) to Panhandle, n., w.-cent., and coastal Texas. *Habitat:* Open water.

WHITE-WINGED SCOTER
Melanitta deglandi   20–23   pp. 37, 45, 49
Field marks: *Male:* A heavy coal-black duck, easily identified by a squarish white patch on rear edge of wing. When it swims, the wing-patch may be concealed by the flank feathers (wait for it to flap its wings). At close range a tick of white shows just below the eye. Bill orange with black knob. *Female:* Sooty brown with white wing-patch and two light patches on side of head (sometimes obscure; more pronounced in young birds).
Similar species: See Surf and Common Scoters.
Voice: In flight "a bell-like low whistle in a series of six or eight notes" (Kortright). Said to be produced by wings.
Where found: Alaska, w. Canada. Winters south to s. U. S. **Texas:** Occasional visitor to n. Texas (Fort Worth, Dallas, Archer Co.); and coast (south to Laguna Atascosa). *Habitat:* Large lakes, Gulf.

SURF SCOTER   *Melanitta perspicillata*   18–22   pp. 37, 45, 49
Field marks: The "Skunk-head Coot." *Male:* Black, with one or two white patches on crown and back of head. Bill patterned with orange, black, and white. *Female:* Dusky brown with two light spots on side of face (sometimes obscured; more conspicuous on young birds).
Similar species: (1) Female White-wing is similarly marked around head, but has white wing-patches (which often do not show until bird flaps). (2) See Common Scoter.
Voice: Usually silent. A low croak or grunting note.
Where found: Alaska, n. Canada. Winters to s. U. S. **Texas:** Occasional in winter (chiefly coastal). Reported Panhandle, Jefferson Co., San Antonio, Rockport, Laguna Madre.

COMMON SCOTER   *Oidemia nigra*   17–21
(American Scoter)   pp. 37, 45, 49
Field marks: *Male:* The only adult American duck with *entirely* black plumage. This, and the bright yellow-orange knob at the base of the bill ("butter-nose") are diagnostic. *Female:* Sooty; *light cheeks* contrasting with *dark cap*.
Similar species: (1) Coot is blackish but has white bill, white

BAY DUCKS

Diving Ducks (Bay Ducks and Sea Ducks) run and patter along the water when taking flight. Surface-feeding Ducks (Marsh Ducks, Plate 18) spring directly up.

Note: Males of the first five species share a generic similarity, the black chest.

CANVASBACK   p. 42
Male: White body, rusty head, sloping profile.
Female: Grayish; dark chest, sloping profile.

REDHEAD   p. 41
Male: Gray; black chest, round rufous head.
Female: Indistinct face-patch near bill (see text).

RING-NECKED DUCK   p. 42
Male: Black back, white mark before wing.
Female: Eye-ring and ring on bill (see text).

LESSER SCAUP (BLUEBILL)   p. 43
Male: Black chest, black head (purple gloss), blue bill.
Female: Sharp white patch at base of bill.

GREATER SCAUP (BIG BLUEBILL)   p. 42
Male: Like preceding; head rounder (green gloss).
Female: Similar to preceding (see text).

BARROW'S GOLDENEYE   p. 269
Accidental in Texas.
Male: White crescent on face; blacker above than Common Goldeneye.

COMMON GOLDENEYE (WHISTLER)   p. 46
Male: Round white spot before eye.
Female: Gray body, brown head, light collar.

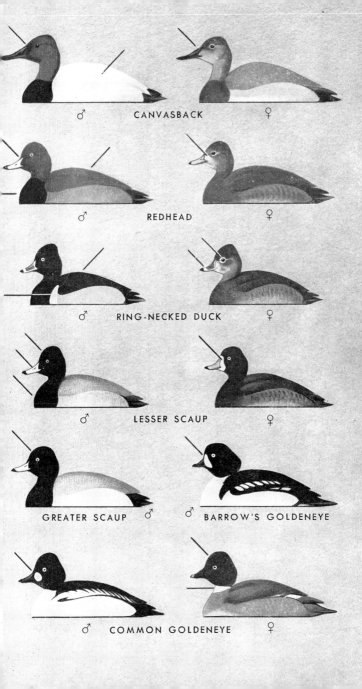

♂ CANVASBACK ♀

♂ REDHEAD ♀

♂ RING-NECKED DUCK ♀

♂ LESSER SCAUP ♀

GREATER SCAUP ♂   ♂ BARROW'S GOLDENEYE

♂ COMMON GOLDENEYE ♀

♂ Summer   OLDSQUAW   Winter ♀
♂ Winter

♂   SURF SCOTER   ♀

♂   WHITE-WINGED SCOTER   ♀

♂   COMMON SCOTER   ♀

BLACK-BELLIED TREE DUCK

♀
♂
MASKED DUCK

FULVOUS TREE DUCK   BLACK-BELLIED TREE DUCK

Plate 16   49

SEA DUCKS, MASKED DUCK, TREE DUCKS

OLDSQUAW   p. 46
    Male in summer: Needle tail, white face-patch.
    Male in winter: Needle tail, pied pattern.
    Female in winter: Dark wings; white face, dark cheek-mark.

SURF SCOTER   p. 47
    Male: Black body, white head-patches.
    Female: Light face-spots, no white in wing.

WHITE-WINGED SCOTER   p. 47
    Male: Black body, white wing-patch.
    Female: Light face-spots, white wing-patch.

COMMON SCOTER   p. 47
    Male: Plumage all black, yellow-orange on bill.
    Female: Dark body, light cheek, dark crown.

MASKED DUCK   p. 50
    Male: Similar to Ruddy Duck, but black face, white wing-patch.
    Female: Similar to female Ruddy, but *two* dark lines on face; white wing-patch.

BLACK-BELLIED TREE DUCK   p. 30
    Black belly, large white wing-patches; pink bill, legs. Sexes similar.

FULVOUS TREE DUCK   p. 30
    Tawny; white side-stripe. Sexes similar.

patch under tail. Gunners often call scoters "coots." (2) Some young male Surf Scoters may lack head-patches and will appear all black. Look for round black spot at base of bill. (3) Females of the other scoters have two light spots on each side of head. (4) Female Common Scoter can be confused with winter Ruddy Duck (which is smaller, paler, and has light chest).

Voice: Melodious cooing notes (male); growls (female).

Where found: Alaska, Iceland, n. Eurasia. Winters south to s. U.S., Mediterranean. **Texas:** Casual (chiefly coastal); reported Panhandle, Galveston Bay, Rockport, lower Laguna Madre.

Ruddy and Masked Ducks: Oxyurinae

SMALL chunky ducks that cannot walk on land. The spiky tail has 18 or 20 feathers.

RUDDY DUCK   *Oxyura jamaicensis*   14–17   pp. 37, 45, 52
  Field marks: A small, chubby duck, unpatterned except for *conspicuous white cheeks*, dark cap. The short wing-stroke gives it a "buzzy" flight. Often cocks its tail vertically, like a wren. It cannot walk. *Male in breeding plumage:* Rusty red with *white cheeks*, black cap, large blue bill. *Male in winter:* Gray with *white cheeks*, dark cap, dull blue bill. *Female:* Similar to winter male, but light cheeks crossed by *dark line*.
  Similar species: See Cinnamon Teal; female Bufflehead.
  Voice: Usually silent. Displaying males, a low chuckling *chuck-uck-uck-uck-ur-r-r*.
  Where found: Canada south locally to Colombia. Migratory. **Texas:** *Migrant* in most areas. *Winters* (Oct.–May) along coast and inland to n. Texas (Tyler, Dallas, Denton, Fort Worth); west to El Paso. Breeds or has bred in w., cent., and s. Texas south to Brownsville. *Habitat:* Ponds, rivers, lakes, bays. **Nest:** A woven basket anchored above water to reeds or marsh plants. Eggs (6–10) whitish.

MASKED DUCK   *Oxyura dominica*   12–14   pp. 37, 49
  Field marks: Similar to Ruddy Duck; smaller. *Male:* Rusty with black marks on back and *black face. Female:* Like small female Ruddy, but with *two* black stripes crossing each side of face instead of one. Both sexes have *white wing-patches* (concealed when swimming). Ruddy has solid dark wings.
  Voice: A hornlike note; also a henlike clucking.
  Where found: Tropical America. **Texas:** Casual visitor to Rio Grande delta. Accidental Alice, cent. coast. *Habitat:* Resacas, ponds.

Mergansers: Merginae

THE THREE mergansers, or fish ducks, have spike-like bills with toothed mandibles for seizing slippery fish. Most species have crests and are long-lined, slender-bodied. They skitter when taking off; flight is swift, direct. In flight, the bill, head, neck, and body are held horizontal, quite unlike other ducks.

HOODED MERGANSER *Lophodytes cucullatus* 16–19
("Hooded Sawbill," "Swamp Sheldrake") pp. 36, 44, 52
 Field marks: *Male:* Black and white; head with vertical *fan-shaped white crest*, which it habitually spreads. Breast white with two vertical black bars in front of wing; wing with white patch; flanks brownish. *Female:* Recognized as a merganser by the narrow, spike-like bill; in flight by the long-drawn appearance, with bill, head, neck, and body in a horizontal line. Known as this species by its small size, dark coloration, *dark head*, bill, and chest, loose tawny crest.
 Similar species: (1) Male Bufflehead is smaller, chubbier, with *white* flanks; flanks of Hooded Merganser are dark and its white crest is outlined with a black border (see female Bufflehead). (2) Other female mergansers are larger, grayer, with rufous heads; red bills. (3) Female Wood Duck is also dark with a crest, but square white wing-patch, spike-like bill, and flight identify the merganser. Both frequent wooded pools.
 Voice: Low grunting or croaking notes.
 Where found: Se. Alaska, Canada, n. U.S. Winters to Mexico, Gulf Coast. **Texas:** Rare *migrant* through e. half of state and in Panhandle. Rare transient El Paso. *Winters* (Nov.–May) rarely, locally, along coast and inland to e. and n. Texas. *Habitat:* Lakes, ponds, bays.

COMMON MERGANSER *Mergus merganser* 22–27
(American Merganser, "Sawbill," "Sheldrake") pp. 36, 44, 52
 Field marks: In line formation, low over the water, the rakish, long-bodied Mergansers follow the winding course of streams. *Male:* Long white body with black back and green-black head; bill and feet red; breast tinged with delicate peach-colored bloom. In flight, the whiteness and the merganser shape (with bill, head, neck, and body all horizontal) identify this species. *Female:* Gray with *crested* rufous head, clean white underparts, and large square white wing-patch. Bill and feet red.
 Similar species: (1) Male Goldeneye resembles Merganser at a distance, but has a white eye-spot, is chubbier, shorter-necked, puffy-headed. (2) Rusty-headed female Mergansers suggest Canvasbacks or Redheads, but those two birds have black chests, no crests. (3) Males may be mistaken for Mallards

MERGANSERS AND OTHER DUCKS

WOOD DUCK   p. 40
  Male: Distinctive face pattern.
  Male in eclipse: Duller, face pattern similar.
  Female: White spot around eye.

BUFFLEHEAD (BUTTERBALL)   p. 46
  Male: Large white head-patch, white sides.
  Female: Small; dark head, white cheek-spot.

HOODED MERGANSER   p. 51
  Male: White crest, dark sides.
  Female: Dark head, tawny crest.

RED-BREASTED MERGANSER   p. 54
  Male: White collar; crest.
  Female: Crested rufous head, *blended* throat and neck.

COMMON MERGANSER   p. 51
  Male: Long whitish body, dark head.
  Female: Crested rufous head, *sharply marked* throat and
  neck.

FULVOUS TREE DUCK   p. 30
  Tawny color, white side-stripe; sexes similar.

RUDDY DUCK   p. 50
  Male in spring: Rufous, white cheeks.
  Male in winter: Gray, white cheeks.
  Female: Light cheek crossed by dark line.
  Note: Ruddy Ducks often cock their tails.

Marsh and	Bay and	Mergansers	Ruddy	Tree
Pond Ducks	Sea Ducks	(Divers)	Duck	Ducks
(Dabblers)	(Divers)		(Diver)	(Dabblers)

POSTURES OF DUCKS ON LAND

Male in eclipse

WOOD DUCK
♂   ♀

BUFFLEHEAD
♂   ♀

HOODED MERGANSER
♂   ♀

RED-BREASTED MERGANSER
♂   ♀

COMMON MERGANSER
♂   ♀

FULVOUS TREE DUCK

♀
♂ Winter
♂ Spring

RUDDY DUCK

MOTTLED DUCK

BLACK DUCK
Sexes similar

GADWALL ♂

MALLARD
♂   ♀

PINTAIL
♂   ♀

EUROPEAN WIDGEON ♂

AMERICAN WIDGEON
♀   ♂

SHOVELER ♀ ♂

BLUE-WINGED TEAL
♀   ♂

GREEN-WINGED TEAL
♂   ♀

COMMON TEAL ♂

CINNAMON TEAL ♂

Plate 18   53

MARSH AND POND DUCKS
(Surface-feeding Ducks)

MOTTLED DUCK (BLACK MALLARD)   p. 34
Dusky-brown body, paler head, yellow bill.
Sexes similar.

BLACK DUCK (BLACK MALLARD)   p. 34
Darker. Often very similar to Mottled Duck.
See text.

GADWALL   p. 35
Male: Gray body, black rear.
Female: White patch (in flight); yellowish bill.

MALLARD   p. 31
Male: Green head, white neck-ring.
Female: Orange on bill, whitish tail.

PINTAIL (SPRIG)   p. 35
Male: Needle tail, neck-stripe.
Female: Gray bill, slim pointed tail.

EUROPEAN WIDGEON   p. 39
Casual in Texas.
Male: Rufous head, buffy crown.
Female: See text.

AMERICAN WIDGEON (BALDPATE)   p. 39
Male: White crown.
Female: Gray head, brown body.

SHOVELER (SPOONBILL)   p. 40
Male: Shovel bill, dark chestnut sides.
Female: Shovel bill.

BLUE-WINGED TEAL   p. 38
Male: White face crescent, blue wing-patch.
Female: Small size, blue wing-patch.

GREEN-WINGED TEAL   p. 38
Male: Vertical white mark on body.
Female: Small size, dark wing.

COMMON (EUROPEAN) TEAL
No authentic Texas record. To be looked for in flocks of
Green-wings.
Male: Horizontal white stripe.
Female: Like female Green-wing.

CINNAMON TEAL   p. 39
Male: Deep rufous; blue wing-patch.
Female: Like female Blue-wing.

(because of green head). (4) See Red-breasted Merganser (females similar).

Voice: A low croak (male); a guttural *karrr* (female).

Where found: Cooler parts of N. Hemisphere. Winters south to Mexico, Gulf Coast, Mediterranean, India. **Texas:** *Migrates and winters* (Oct.–Mar.) locally throughout state. Rare in south. *Habitat:* Rivers, lakes, bays; prefers fresh water.

RED-BREASTED MERGANSER *Mergus serrator* 20–25
("Salt-water Sheldrake") pp. 36, 44, 52

Field marks: *Male:* Rakish; head black glossed with green and *conspicuously crested;* breast at waterline rusty, separated from head by *wide white collar;* bill and feet red. *Female:* Gray with crested dull rufous head and large square white patch on wing; bill and feet reddish.

Similar species: Male Common Merganser is whiter, without collar and breastband effect; lacks crest. Females are very similar but in Red-breast rufous of head is paler, *blending* into whitish of throat and neck. In the Common, the white chin, white chest are sharply defined.

Voice: Usually silent. A hoarse croak; *karrr* (female).

Where found: Cooler parts of N. Hemisphere. Winters to Gulf of Mexico, Mediterranean, etc. **Texas:** Rare *migrant* in Panhandle and through e. half of state. *Winters* (Nov.–May) on coast; rarely inland to n. Texas. *Habitat:* Lakes, bays, Gulf.

American Vultures: Cathartidae

GREAT, blackish eagle-like birds, often seen soaring high in wide circles. Their naked heads are relatively small; at a great distance they may appear almost headless (hawks and eagles have larger heads). They are often called "buzzards." Foods: Mainly carrion. S. Canada to Strait of Magellan. No. of species: World, 6; N. America, 3; Texas, 2.

TURKEY VULTURE *Cathartes aura* 30
("Turkey Buzzard") p. 81

Field marks: Spread 6 ft. Nearly eagle-size, with great two-toned blackish wings (flight feathers noticeably lighter than foreparts). Usually seen soaring, with wings slightly above horizontal (forming dihedral); rocks and tilts unsteadily as it floats along. At close range red head of adult can be seen; young birds have blackish heads.

Similar species: See Black Vulture. Diminutive head and slimmer tail distinguish Turkey Vultures from eagles. Soars with wings above horizontal; eagles soar with flat outstretched wings; Osprey with kink or crook in wings.

Voice: Usually silent. A hiss when cornered; a low grunt.
Where found: S. Canada south to Strait of Magellan. **Texas:** *Breeds* throughout. *Winters* except in Panhandle, Staked Plains, Trans-Pecos. *Habitat:* Usually seen in sky or perched on dead trees, posts, carrion, or on ground. **Nest:** In hollow log, stump, cave, dark ledge, etc. Eggs (1–3) blotched.

BLACK VULTURE *Coragyps atratus* 24
("Black Buzzard")   p. 81
  Field marks: Spread under 5 ft. This big black bird is quickly identified by the short square tail that barely projects beyond the wings and by a whitish patch on each wing toward the tip. Head black. Legs longer and whiter than Turkey Vulture's.
  Similar species: Tail of Turkey Vulture is longer and slimmer. Black Vulture has much less "sail area"; tail is stubby, wings are shorter and wider. It can be spotted at a great distance by its quick, labored flapping — several rapid flaps and a short glide. The Turkey flaps more deliberately, soars more. *Caution:* Young Turkey Vultures have black heads.
  Voice: Usually silent. Hissing and low grunting sounds.
  Where found: Ohio, Maryland to Chile, Argentina. **Texas:** *Resident* throughout much of state; very local in Panhandle; absent in Staked Plains and Trans-Pecos except in s. part of Big Bend. *Habitat:* Same as Turkey Vulture's. **Nest:** In hollow log, stump, broken tree trunk, on ground in thicket or in small cave, ledge. Eggs (1–3) blotched.

Hawks, Kites, Harriers, Eagles: Accipitridae

DIURNAL birds of prey, divided into several subfamilies, which will be treated separately. Much persecuted and misunderstood. Many species are in need of greater protection. Wildlife technicians can prove by food-habit studies that most of these birds are an important cog in the natural balance. Food: Small mammals, birds, reptiles, insects. Cosmopolitan. No. of species: World, 205; N. America, 25; Texas, 21.

Kites: Elaninae and Milvinae

HAWKS of southern distribution, most nearly resembling falcons in shape. Very graceful. Entirely beneficial; becoming scarce.

WHITE-TAILED KITE *Elanus leucurus* 15½   p. 80
  Field marks: Spread 3⅓ ft. This rare whitish species is falcon-shaped, with long, pointed wings and a long tail. Soars and

glides like a small gull; often hovers like Sparrow Hawk. *Adult:* Pale gray with white head, *tail,* and underparts; *large black patch* toward fore edge of wing. No other falcon-like bird in Texas has a white tail. *Immature:* Recognizable, but has rusty breast, brown back, and narrow band near tip of pale tail.
Similar species: See White-tailed Hawk.
Voice: A whistled *kee kee kee,* abrupt or drawn out.
Where found: California, s. Texas south to Chile, Argentina. **Texas:** *Resident* formerly north to cent. Texas. Now restricted to coastal prairie of s. tip (Cameron Co.); rare. Occasional (Apr.–May) along cent. coast; casual farther north. *Habitat:* Open country with scattering of trees. **Nest:** Platform of twigs in tree adjacent to open country. Eggs (4–5) blotched.

SWALLOW-TAILED KITE *Elanoides forficatus* 24   p. 80
Field marks: Spread 4 ft. Shaped like a huge Barn Swallow, this medium-sized hawk flies with swallow-like grace. The black upper parts, white head and underparts, and long, *forked* tail make it a striking, well-marked bird.
Similar species: See immature Magnificent Frigate-bird.
Voice: A shrill, keen *ee-ee-ee* or *pee-pee-pee.*
Where found: Se. U.S. and tropical America. Leaves U.S. in winter. **Texas:** In recent years only an occasional *migrant* (Mar.–May) along coast. *Bred* formerly west to cent. Texas; may breed in corner of e. Texas near coast (no recent records). *Habitat:* River swamps. **Nest:** Moss-lined nest of sticks near top of tall tree. Eggs (1–4) spotted.

BUTEOS
Broad wings
Broad rounded tail
Red-tailed Hawk
Red-shouldered Hawk
Swainson's Hawk
Broad-winged Hawk
Harris' Hawk
Ferruginous Hawk
Rough-legged Hawk
Black Hawk
White-tailed Hawk
Zone-tailed Hawk
Gray Hawk

ACCIPITERS
Long tail
Short, rounded wings
Cooper's Hawk
Sharp-shinned Hawk
Goshawk

FALCONS
Long tail
Long, pointed wings
Sparrow Hawk
Pigeon Hawk
Peregrine Falcon
Prairie Falcon
Aplomado Falcon

SILHOUETTES OF THREE COMMON TYPES OF HAWKS

MISSISSIPPI KITE *Ictinia misisippiensis* 14   p. 80
Field marks: Spread 3 ft. Falcon-shaped; graceful and gray. Dark above, lighter below; head *very pale, almost white;* tail *black.* No other falcon-like hawk has a black unbarred tail. In flight shows from above a *broad pale patch* on rear edge of wing. Immature has heavy brown streakings below but has falcon-like shape and distinctive dark tail (somewhat banded below).
Voice: *Phee-phew* (G. M. Sutton); a clear *kee-ee.*
Where found: Mainly s.-cent. U.S.; winters Cent. and S. America. **Texas:** *Migrant* (Mar.–May, Aug.–Oct.) throughout except in Trans-Pecos; fall straggler at El Paso. *Breeds* locally in Panhandle and n. Texas (formerly south to Lee Co., San Antonio). *Habitat:* Scrub-oak country, wooded creeks, rangeland. **Nest:** Of twigs, sticks in treetop, usually along creek. Eggs (1–3) whitish.

Accipiters, or Bird Hawks: Accipitrinae

LONG-TAILED hawks with short, rounded wings; woodland birds that do not soar in circles high in the air as much as the Buteos. They generally hunt among trees and thickets, using a hedge-hopping technique. The typical flight is several short quick beats and a glide.

GOSHAWK *Accipiter gentilis* 20–26   pp. 61, 80
Field marks: Spread 3½–4 ft. *Adult:* A large, robust hawk, with long tail and rounded wings. Crown and patch behind eye black, *stripe over eye white.* Underparts whitish, finely barred with gray; back blue-gray, paler than back of Cooper's or Sharp-shin. *Immature:* Very much like immature Cooper's, but often larger; usually distinguished by light stripe over eye. Size not always reliable (Cooper's may be almost as large).
Similar species: Cooper's Hawk is crow-sized or smaller; Goshawk is usually considerably larger than Crow. The gray-backed adult Cooper's is reddish below, whereas Goshawk is whitish or *pale gray* below. Flight is much alike — alternate flapping and gliding. Both hunt with agility among trees.
Voice: *Kak, kak, kak,* or *kuk, kuk, kuk;* heavier than Cooper's.
Where found: N. N. America, Eurasia. Periodically migrates southward. **Texas:** Irregular or casual in winter in n. half of state. Reported south to Rockport. *Habitat:* Woodlands.

SHARP-SHINNED HAWK
Accipiter striatus 10–14   pp. 61, 80
Field marks: Spread 2 ft±. A small woodland hawk with a long tail and *short, rounded* wings. Tail notched or square. Flies with several quick beats and a glide. Adult has blue-gray back, rusty-barred breast. Immature is brown, streaked.

Similar species: Two other small hawks, (1) Sparrow and (2) Pigeon Hawks, are *falcons* and have long, pointed (not short rounded) wings. (3) Small male Cooper's is often nearly identical in size and pattern to large female Sharp-shin, but generally Cooper's has *rounded* tail, Sharp-shin *square-tipped* tail (slightly notched when folded). However, Sharp-shin's square-tipped tail can look slightly rounded when spread. Tail shape most reliable when tail is folded.

Voice: Like Cooper's Hawk but shriller, a high *kik, kik, kik,* etc.
Where found: Most of N. America. Migrates from n. sections. **Texas:** *Winters* (Sept.–Apr.) throughout much of state. *Breeds* irregularly and locally in n. half of state. *Habitat:* Woodlands, thickets, groves. **Nest:** A shallow platform of sticks in tree. Eggs (4–5) spotted.

COOPER'S HAWK *Accipiter cooperii* 14–20   pp. 61, 80
Field marks: Spread 2¼–3 ft. A short-winged, long-tailed hawk; not quite so large as a Crow. Adults have blue-gray backs, rusty breasts. Immatures are brown, streaked. Tail *rounded* when folded.

Similar species: (1) The smaller Sharp-shin has a *notched* or *square tail.* Immature Coopers are usually more narrowly streaked below than immature Sharp-shins. (2) See also Goshawk.

Voice: About nest a rapid *kek, kek, kek,* etc.; suggests Flicker.
Where found: S. Canada south to n. Mexico. Migrates from n. sections. **Texas:** *Migrant* throughout. *Winters* (Oct.–May) except in Panhandle. *Breeds* locally and irregularly in nearly every county, south to Brownsville. *Habitat:* Woodlands, brush, sometimes open country. **Nest:** A platform of sticks in tree. Eggs (4–5) white, occasionally spotted.

Buteos, or Buzzard Hawks:
Buteoninae (in part)

LARGE thick-set hawks with broad wings and broad, relatively short rounded tails. They habitually soar in wide circles, high in the air. There is considerable variation within most of the species. Those figured in the plates are the most typical. Young birds may somewhat resemble adults, but in most species are *streaked lengthwise* below.

Black or melanistic phases often occur in birds of this group (Red-tail, Rough-leg, Swainson's, etc.), and one must indeed be an expert to tell some of them apart. In fact, even the seasoned expert gives up on some of the birds he sees.

RED-TAILED HAWK *Buteo jamaicensis* 19–25 pp. 60, 64, 65
Field marks: Spread 4–4½ ft. When this large broad-winged, round-tailed hawk veers in its soaring, the rufous of the upper side of the tail can be seen. From beneath, adults have whitish tails which in strong light overhead might transmit some of the red. Young birds have dark gray tails, which might or might not show banding. Underparts of typical Red-tails are "zoned" (light breast, broad band of streakings across belly). Individuals vary from the whitish *kriderii* race (white tail) and the pale-breasted resident race, *fuertesi* of the Big Bend and s. Texas, to reddish individuals of the race *calurus* (w. Texas), and even dusky melanistic birds. *Black adults usually show red tails*, a point of distinction from other black Buteos. Immatures are often light at base of tail, leading to confusion with Rough-leg and Swainson's.
Similar species: (1) See Harlan's Hawk. (2) Red-shouldered Hawk has a banded tail and is more uniformly patterned below (rufous in adult; striped on both breast and belly in immature); Red-tail is "zoned" (light breast, streaked belly); also chunkier, with wider wings, shorter tail. (3) See also Swainson's Hawk.
Voice: An asthmatic squeal, *keeer–r-r* (slurring downward).
Where found: Alaska, Canada south to Panama. Migrates from n. sections. **Texas:** *Winters* throughout. *Summers* in many sections; rare or absent in some (Rio Grande delta, parts of coast, etc.). *Habitat:* Open country, brush, woodlands, mts.
Nest: A platform of sticks in tall tree, isolated low tree, on cliff, etc. Eggs (2–4) often spotted.

HARLAN'S HAWK *Buteo harlani* 21–22½ pp. 60, 64
Field marks: Spread 4–4½ ft. Until recently this prairie *Buteo* was rated as a race of the Red-tail. Typical birds are black-breasted with *whitish* tails, but light-breasted birds also occur. The whitish or light tail with *black mottling* blending into a broad terminal band is the diagnostic feature.
Similar species: (1) Melanistic Red-tails (adults) show red in tail. (2) *Kriderii* form of Red-tail might be confused with light-colored Harlan's, but is paler above; its white or pale rufous tail has a tendency toward light *barring* near tip (Harlan's is usually *finely mottled*); (3) Black Rough-leg has a somewhat banded (not mottled) tail, is cleaner white on flight feathers below (see plate), and has longer wings and tail. (4) Black Swainson's has less contrast on underwing; it shows a tendency toward dark bands on gray tail.
Voice: Similar to Red-tail's.
Where found: E. Alaska, nw. Canada. Winters south to s. U.S. **Texas:** Rare *winter visitor* (Oct.–Mar.) to e. and cent. Texas, south at least to San Antonio and Corpus Christi. Rare transient in Panhandle. *Habitat:* Same as Red-tail's.

BUTEOS OR BUZZARD HAWKS

 BUTEOS have heavy bodies, short wide tails.

SWAINSON'S HAWK   p. 62
  Dark breastband (adult).

RED-TAILED HAWK   p. 59
  Adult: Rufous tail.
  Immature (and adult): Light chest, streaked belly.

RED-SHOULDERED HAWK   p. 62
  Adult: Rufous shoulders; narrow white tailbands.
  Immature: Streaked on both breast and belly.

ROUGH-LEGGED HAWK   p. 66
  Light phase: Dark belly; white tail with black band.
  Dark phase: Dusky body; see text.

BROAD-WINGED HAWK   p. 62
  Adult: Wide white tailbands.
  Immature: Like immature Red-shoulder, but tail shorter.

HARLAN'S HAWK   p. 59
  Dark body; whitish, mottled tail.

KRIDER'S RED-TAILED HAWK
  Pale body; white or pale rufous tail. See under Red-tailed
  Hawk, p. 59.

SWAINSON'S

Adult

Immature

RED-TAILED

Immature

Adult

Dark Phase

Adult

RED-SHOULDERED

Light Phase

ROUGH-LEGGED

Immature

BROAD-WINGED

Adult

HARLAN'S

KRIDER'S RED-TAIL

COOPER'S
HAWK

Adult

Immature

GOSHAWK

Adult

Immature

HARP-SHINNED
HAWK

Adult

Immature

SPARROW
HAWK
(KESTREL

♂

♀

PIGEON
HAWK
(MERLIN)

♂

♀

Adult

Immature

PEREGRINE
FALCON

MARSH HAWK
(HARRIER)

♂

♀

Plate 20   61

HAWKS

ACCIPITERS (True Hawks)
Small head, short wings, long tail.
Adults, barred breasts; immatures, streaked.

COOPER'S HAWK   p. 58
Crow-sized; rounded tail.

GOSHAWK   p. 57
Adult: Pearly breast, light gray back.
Immature: Large; pronounced eye-stripe.

SHARP-SHINNED HAWK   p. 57
Small; notched or square tail.

FALCONS
Large head, broad shoulders.
Long pointed wings, long tail.

SPARROW HAWK or KESTREL   p. 73
Both sexes: Rufous back, rufous tail.

PIGEON HAWK or MERLIN   p. 72
Male: Small; slaty back, banded gray tail.
Female: Dusky back, banded tail.

PEREGRINE FALCON   p. 72
Adult: Slaty back, light breast, black "mustaches."
Immature: Brown, streaked, typical "mustaches."

HARRIERS
Small head, long body.
Longish wings, long tail.

MARSH HAWK (HARRIER)   p. 69
Male: Pale gray back, white rump.
Female: Brown, with white rump.

RED-SHOULDERED HAWK

Buteo lineatus 18–24   pp. 60, 65

Field marks: Spread, 3–3¾ ft. Recognized as a *Buteo* by ample tail and broad wings; as this species, by heavy dark bands across both sides of tail. Adults have rufous shoulders (not always visible) and pale robin-red underparts. Another mark, not often shared by other Buteos, is a translucent patch or "window" toward wing-tip at base of primaries. Immatures are streaked below, as are most other young hawks. They can be identified by proportions, tailbanding, and, in flight overhead, by the "wing windows," a helpful (but not infallible) mark.

Similar species: (1) Adult Broad-winged Hawk has its white tailbands *as wide* as the black ones. Young Broad-wings have more narrowly barred tails; are frequently called Red-shoulders by hawk watchers. Note the proportions. (2) Adult Cooper's Hawk also has rusty underparts but a very different shape (shorter wings, longer tail). (3) See Red-tailed Hawk.

Voice: A two-syllabled scream, *kee–yar* (dropping inflection).

Where found: Se. Canada south to Mexico. **Texas:** *Resident* locally in e. half of state; occurs west (rarely) to Panhandle, Kerrville, Del Rio; south to Rio Grande delta. *Habitat:* Woodlands, wooded rivers, timbered swamps. **Nest:** A platform of sticks in tall woodland tree. Eggs (2–4) blotched.

BROAD-WINGED HAWK

Buteo platypterus 14–18½   pp. 60, 65

Field marks: Spread 3 ft. The smallest common U.S. *Buteo;* size of a Crow, chunky. The tailbanding of the adult is the best mark — the white bands are *about as wide* as the black. *Immature:* Tailbands more numerous, crowding out the white. The tail then resembles that of Red-shoulder, but bird is of different proportions, with stubbier tail, shorter wings (more like a little Red-tail). Underwing is usually whiter (it is safer to rely on shape). Often migrates in large soaring flocks.

Voice: A high-pitched shrill whistle, suggestive of Wood Pewee; a plaintive *pwee-e-e-e-e-e*, diminishing in force.

Where found: S. Canada south to Gulf States. Winters in Cent. and S. America. **Texas:** *Migrant* (Mar.–May, Sept.–Nov.) through e. half of state; west rarely to Panhandle, s. Staked Plains. Casual in winter on coast. *Breeds* locally in e. Texas, south rarely to Houston and Nueces River. *Habitat:* Woodlands, groves. **Nest:** Of sticks in tree. Eggs (2–3) blotched.

SWAINSON'S HAWK

Buteo swainsoni 19½–22   pp. 60, 64, 65

Field marks: Spread 4 + ft. A *Buteo* of the plains; proportioned like a Red-tail but wings slightly more pointed. When gliding, the wings are held somewhat above horizontal (slightly vulture-like or Marsh-Hawk-like). In typical adults the *wide brown breastband* is the best mark. Overhead, the *unmarked light buffy wing-linings* contrast with the *dark flight feathers*. Tail is gray above often shading to white at base. There are confusing individuals where the dark breastband nearly disappears, and blackish birds, hard to tell from other melanistic Buteos, except by elimination. The underwing, with its dusky flight feathers, is usually a good mark. Gregarious in migration.

Similar species: Red-tail usually has a light chest (Swainson's, dark chest); it also has a belt of streaks on belly. Black Swainson's Hawk lacks the rusty tail of the black Red-tail. It also lacks the clear white primaries and secondaries on under-wing, so distinctive in black Rough-leg.

Voice: A shrill plaintive whistle, *kreeeeeer*.

Where found: W. N. America; winters in Argentina. **Texas:** *Migrant* (Mar.–May; Sept.–Nov.) through all parts (less common eastward), often in large flocks. Does not winter (except very rarely on coast and at El Paso). *Summers* through w. half of state, east to Fort Worth, Waco. Has bred near Houston. *Habitat:* Prairies, rangeland, brush. **Nest:** A platform of sticks in isolated tree, bush, or yucca. Eggs (2–4) often spotted.

ZONE-TAILED HAWK *Buteo albonotatus* 18½–21½ p. 64
Field marks: Spread 4 ft. A dull *black* hawk with somewhat more slender wings than other Buteos. Might be mistaken for Turkey Vulture because of proportions and *two-toned wing effect*. Hawk head and *white tailbands* (pale gray on topside) identify the adult. Immature has narrower tailbanding and a scattering of *small white spots* on its black underparts.

Similar species: Black Hawk is much chunkier, has much broader, more evenly colored wings below (sometimes shows a white spot at base of primaries). Usually has one very broad white band (white on both sides) across tail. Zone-tail has two or three smaller bands but often only the wide one shows, causing confusion. Young Black Hawk has striped *buffy* head and underparts. Black Hawk prefers rivers; Zone-tail is often seen in mountains.

Voice: A squealing whistle, suggesting Red-tail's.

Where found: U.S.–Mexican border south to n. South America. **Texas:** Rare *summer resident* in Trans-Pecos; occasionally east to w. parts of Edwards Plateau. Casual along Rio Grande to Brownsville. *Habitat:* Arid country, rivers, desert mts. **Nest:** A platform of sticks in tall tree or cliff. Eggs (2–3) whitish, usually unmarked.

CARACARA AND BLACK BUTEOS

CARACARA p. 71
White chest, pale patches toward wing-tips.

ROUGH-LEGGED HAWK (dark form) p. 66
Dark body, whitish flight feathers; tail light from below, dark terminal band.

FERRUGINOUS HAWK (dark form) p. 66
Similar to dark form of Rough-leg but pale tail does not have dark banding.

SWAINSON'S HAWK (dark form) p. 62
Wings usually dark throughout, including flight feathers. Tail narrowly banded.

RED-TAILED HAWK (dark form) p. 59
Chunky; tail reddish above, colorless below; variable.

HARLAN'S HAWK p. 59
Shape of Red-tail; tail whitish above, mottled. Not safely distinguishable below from dark form of Red-tail.

WHITE-TAILED HAWK (immature) p. 66
Body patched black and white. Tail white (above and below).

ZONE-TAILED HAWK p. 63
Narrow two-toned wings. Several white tailbands.

HARRIS' HAWK p. 67
Chestnut wing-linings. Very broad white band at base of tail.

BLACK HAWK p. 68
Thick-set black wings; small light spots. Broad white band at mid-tail.

CARACARA

ROUGH-LEGGED
HAWK

Dark form

FERRUGINOUS
HAWK

Dark form

SWAINSON'S
HAWK

Dark form

RED-TAILED
HAWK

Dark form

HARLAN'S
HAWK

WHITE-TAILED
HAWK

Immature

ZONE-TAILED
HAWK

Adult

HARRIS' HAWK

Adult

BLACK HAWK   Adult

OSPREY

ROUGH-LEGGED HAWK

FERRUGINOUS HAWK

WHITE-TAILED HAWK

RED-TAILED HAWK

SWAINSON'S HAWK

RED-SHOULDERED HAWK

BROAD-WINGED HAWK

GRAY HAWK

CARACARA

ROUGH-LEGGED
HAWK

Dark form

FERRUGINOUS
HAWK

Dark form

SWAINSON'S
HAWK

Dark form

RED-TAILED
HAWK

Dark form

HARLAN'S
HAWK

WHITE-TAILED
HAWK

Immature

ZONE-TAILED
HAWK

Adult

HARRIS' HAWK

Adult

BLACK HAWK   Adult

OSPREY

ROUGH-LEGGED HAWK

FERRUGINOUS HAWK

WHITE-TAILED HAWK

RED-TAILED HAWK

SWAINSON'S HAWK

RED-SHOULDERED HAWK

BROAD-WINGED HAWK

GRAY HAWK

Plate 22   65

OSPREY AND BUTEOS

Note: The birds shown opposite are adults.

OSPREY   p. 70
Clear-white belly; black wrist marks.

BUTEOS or **BUZZARD HAWKS** are chunky, with broad wings and broad, rounded tails. They soar and wheel high in the open sky.

ROUGH-LEGGED HAWK   p. 66
Dark belly, black wrist marks. Whitish tail with broad dark terminal band.

FERRUGINOUS HAWK   p. 66
Whitish underparts; dark V formed by legs.

WHITE-TAILED HAWK   p. 66
White underparts; white tail, narrow black band.

RED-TAILED HAWK   p. 59
Light chest, streaked belly. Tail with little or no banding.

SWAINSON'S HAWK   p. 62
Dark breastband, light wing-linings, dark flight feathers.

RED-SHOULDERED HAWK   p. 62
Banded tail (white bands narrow); rusty underparts. Translucent wing "windows" (not infallible).

BROAD-WINGED HAWK   p. 62
Banded tail (white bands wide); rusty underparts.

GRAY HAWK   p. 67
Broadly banded tail; gray-barred underparts.

Both Rough-legged Hawk (left) and Marsh Hawk (right) show some white at the base of the tail when viewed from above. So does Harris' Hawk.

WHITE-TAILED HAWK *Buteo albicaudatus* 23–24
(Sennett's White-tailed Hawk) pp. 64, 65
Field marks: Spread 4 ft. A long-winged, short-tailed *Buteo* with *clear white underparts* and *white tail* with a *black band* near its tip. The upperparts are dark gray, shoulders rusty red. The white tail is the best mark. Does not sit as erect as Red-tail. Immature may be quite blackish below, or may have dark throat, light chest and heavily marked underparts. In flight overhead, it has a whitish tail and blackish wing-linings which contrast with light primaries. The tail may be pale gray, thickly marked with narrow bands.
Similar species: (1) Ferruginous Hawk also has a whitish tail, but it lacks the sharp black band near tip. (2) Rare black Ferruginous Hawk may be confused with young White-tail but has undersurface of primaries and secondaries clear white (not clouded). (3) Black Swainson's has a noticeably barred grayish tail and is more evenly dusky on the underwings (immature White-tail is usually somewhat spotted with white on breast). (4) Black Harlan's has a mottled black terminal band on tail.
Voice: A repeated *ke-ke-ke-ke-ke-ke;* also *cut-a, cut-a,* etc.
Where found: S. Texas south to Patagonia. **Texas:** *Resident* mainly of coastal prairie from Rio Grande delta locally to upper coast; formerly farther inland. *Habitat:* Coastal prairie, brush.
Nest: A bulky platform of sticks in top of yucca, mesquite, scrub oak. Eggs (2–3) usually unmarked.

ROUGH-LEGGED HAWK
Buteo lagopus 20–23½ pp. 60, 64, 65
Field marks: Spread 4½ ft. This big hawk of the open country habitually hovers with beating wings (Sparrow-Hawk-like) in one spot. A *Buteo* by shape; larger, with longer wings and tail than most of the others. Tail *white with a broad black band toward tip.* Normal phase, from below usually has a *black belly* and a conspicious *black patch at "wrist" of wing.* Black Rough-legs are frequent. The latter may lack the large amount of white on the upper tail, but from below usually show much white at the base of the flight feathers.
Similar species: (1) Marsh Hawk has white patch at base of tail, but is slender with slim wings, slim tail. (2) Black Red-tail has rusty on tail, different flight pattern. See also (3) immature Golden Eagle, (4) Ferruginous Hawk, (5) Swainson's Hawk.
Voice: Squealing or mewing whistles.
Where found: Arctic. Winters south to s. U.S., cent. Eurasia.
Texas: Rare *winter visitor* (Oct.–Apr.); of scattered occurrence. Recorded south to Brownsville. *Habitat:* Prairies, marshes.

FERRUGINOUS HAWK *Buteo regalis* 23–24
(Ferruginous Rough-legged Hawk) pp. 64, 65
Field marks: Spread 4½+ ft. A large *Buteo* of the plains, dark

rufous above and whitish below with a *whitish tail*. Head often quite white. A very good mark in typical adults overhead is a dark V formed by the dark feathers on the legs. In flight, shows a light patch on upper wing near tip. (Rough-leg also shows this.) Immatures are dark above and white below without the rufous and without the dark V formed by the legs.

Similar species: (1) *Kriderii* form of Red-tail also has a whitish tail but lacks the ferruginous back and white patches toward wing-tips. (2) Rough-legged Hawk is darker with a broad black tailband. In the scarce dark phase the Ferruginous resembles the black Rough-leg more closely, but is rustier; the long tail is pale, often whitish, without the black band.

Voice: A loud *kree-a;* a harsh *kaah* (A. C. Bent).

Where found: Sw. Canada south to nw. Texas. Winters in sw. U.S., n. Mexico. **Texas:** *Winters* in Panhandle, Staked Plains, and Trans-Pecos; rarely to cent. Texas (Dallas to Brownsville). Rare *transient* (Mar.–May, Sept.–Oct.) at El Paso and along cent. coast. *Breeds* locally in Staked Plains. *Habitat:* Plains, rangeland. **Nest:** A mass of sticks in tree or cliff. Eggs (3–4) blotched.

GRAY HAWK *Buteo nitidus*   16–18
(Mexican Goshawk)   p. 65

Field marks: Spread 3 ft. A small *Buteo*, not a Goshawk. Adults are distinguished by their *Buteo* proportions, gray back, *gray and white barred* underparts, white rump, and *widely banded* black and white tail. (Tailbanding similar to Broad-winged Hawk's.) Young bird has a narrowly barred tail and striped underparts; difficult to separate from young Broadwing, young Swainson's, except perhaps by rustier back.

Voice: A loud plaintive *cree-eer.*

Where found: U.S.–Mexican border south to Brazil. **Texas:** Rare fall and *winter visitor* to Rio Grande delta; possibly has bred. *Habitat:* Wooded bottomlands, mesquite.

HARRIS' HAWK *Parabuteo unicinctus* 19–22   p. 64

Field marks: Spread 3½–3¾ ft. A black *Buteo* with a flashy *white rump* and a *white band* at tip of tail. In good light shows *chestnut-colored areas* on thighs and wings — a mark of distinction from other black or melanistic Buteos. Immature has light, streaked underparts and *rusty shoulders;* might be confused with Red-shouldered Hawk except for more slender proportions, and conspicuous white at base of tail.

Similar species: (1) Male in poor light is frequently confounded with the much chunkier Black Hawk. (2) Immature might also be mistaken for Red-shouldered Hawk (see p. 62), or more likely (3) female and young Marsh Hawk (more slender, do not perch on yucca, etc., and hunt in more open terrain).

Voice: A harsh *karrr.*

Where found: Sw. U.S. south locally to Chile, Argentina.
Texas: *Resident* in s. Texas and Edwards Plateau (local); north
to cent. coast, Austin, Kerrville, Midland; west to Pecos and
Fort Stockton. Strays recorded at El Paso, Panhandle, n. Texas,
and upper coast. *Habitat:* Mesquite, brush, semi-arid country.
Nest: A platform of sticks in yucca, mesquite or low tree. Eggs
(3–5) whitish.

BLACK HAWK *Buteogallus anthracinus* 20–23
(Mexican Black Hawk)   p. 64
Field marks: Spread 4 ft. A black Buteonine Hawk with excep-
tional width of wing, *long* yellow legs. Identified by chunky
shape and broad white *band* crossing middle of tail. A whitish
spot near tip of wing at base of primaries can be seen under
favorable circumstances. Young bird is dark-backed with distinctive streaked *rich buffy* head and underparts; tail narrowly
banded with black and white (about five bands of each).
Similar species: (1) Zone-tailed Hawk bears a superficial
resemblance to Turkey Vulture; Black Hawk to Black Vulture.
(2) See discussion under Zone-tailed Hawk. (3) See also Harris'
Hawk and (4) melanistic Buteos (Swainson's, Red-tail, Harlan's).
Voice: A hoarse squealing whistle; also a harsh *kaaaah.*
Where found: U.S.–Mexican border south to Ecuador. **Texas:**
Very rare visitor to lower Rio Grande Valley (Cameron, Starr,
and Willacy Cos.); has bred. Casual upriver to Big Bend and
El Paso. *Habitat:* Wooded streambottoms. **Nest:** A mass of
sticks in low tree. Eggs (1–3) often spotted.

Eagles: Buteoninae (in part)

EAGLES are recognizable from "buzzard hawks," or Buteos, which
are closely related, by their greater size and proportionately
longer wings. The powerful bill is nearly as long as the head.

GOLDEN EAGLE *Aquila chrysaetos* 30–40   p. 81
Field marks: Spread 6½–7½ ft. Majestic, flat-winged gliding
and soaring flight with occasional wingbeats characterizes the
eagle; its greater size, longer wings set it apart from other large
hawks. *Adult:* Evenly dark below, or with a slight lightening
at base of tail. When the bird wheels, showing the upper
surface, a light wash of gold on the hind neck may be noticed.
Immature: From above and below, typical individuals show a
white flash in the wing at the base of the primaries, and a white
tail with a *broad dark terminal band.* All manner of variation
exists between this easy-to-identify "ring-tailed" plumage and
the less distinctive plumage of the adult.
Similar species: (1) Immature Bald Eagle usually has some

white in wing-linings (not at base of primaries) and often some on body. It often has a tail mottled with white at base, but not a sharply banded tail as exhibited by young Golden. Bald Eagle has bare tarsi (Golden is feathered to toes), a taxonomic character sometimes useful in the field. General contour is different; head and massive bill of Bald Eagle project more; wings are not quite as wide, nor is tail as full. (2) Black Rough-legged Hawk is smaller, has more white under wing.
Voice: Seldom heard; a yelping *kya;* also whistling notes.
Where found: Mountainous regions of N. Hemisphere. Partial migrant. **Texas:** A few *resident* in Panhandle and Trans-Pecos; occasional on Edwards Plateau; most birds are visitors from farther north. Casual straggler east to Dallas, Houston, cent. coast, Brownsville. *Habitat:* Mts., high rangeland. **Nest:** A mass of sticks on cliff or tree. Eggs (2–3) spotted.

BALD EAGLE   *Haliaeetus leucocephalus* 30–31   p. 81
Field marks: Spread 6–7½ ft. Our national bird with its *white head* and *white tail* is "all field mark." Bill of adult, yellow. Immature has dusky head and tail, dark bill. It usually shows some whitish in the wing-linings and often on the breast.
Similar species: Golden Eagle is often confused with immature Bald Eagle (see discussion under that species). Black Buteos (Rough-leg, etc.) are much smaller, with smaller bills.
Voice: A harsh, creaking cackle, *kleek-kik-ik-ik-ik-ik* or a lower *kak-kak-kak.*
Where found: Alaska, Canada, to s. U.S. **Texas:** Rare local *resident* near coast. Formerly bred (may occasionally still do so) along rivers of e. and cent. Texas. *Winter visitor* to n. Texas, Panhandle, Trans-Pecos (casual), Rio Grande delta (rare). *Habitat:* Shores of rivers, lakes, coast. **Nest:** Bulky platform of sticks in tall tree. Eggs (2–3) white.

Harriers: Circinae

HARRIERS have long wings, long tails, and long bodies. Their wings are not as pointed as those of falcons and their flight is more languid and gliding, usually low.

MARSH HAWK   *Circus cyaneus* 18–24   pp. 61, 80
Field marks: Spread 3½–4 ft. The *white rump-patch* is its badge. *Adult males* are pale gray; *females,* streaked brown; young birds, rich russet on underparts. The bird glides buoyantly low over the fields and marshes with wings held slightly above horizontal, suggesting the Turkey Vulture's dihedral. The white rump is always conspicuous. Overhead, the wing-tips of the whitish male have a "dipped in ink" pattern.

Similar species: (1) Rough-leg has white at base of tail, but is much more heavily proportioned. (2) Accipiters (which sometimes appear white-rumped viewed from side) have much shorter wings. (3) See immature Harris' Hawk.

Voice: A weak nasal whistle, *pee, pee, pee*. A lower-pitched *chu-chu-chu;* also *kek* notes about nest.

Where found: Alaska, Canada south to s. U.S.; n. Eurasia. Winters to n. S. America, n. Africa. **Texas:** *Winters* (Sept.–May) throughout. *Summers* locally in n. half of Texas (Panhandle south to Midland, Houston). *Habitat:* Marshes, fields, prairies. **Nest:** A platform of stalks, grass, on ground in shrubby open land or marsh. Eggs (4–6) whitish.

Ospreys: Pandionidae

LARGE fish-eating hawks; resemble small white-breasted eagles. Plunge feet first for fish. Nearly cosmopolitan. No. of species: World, 1; N. America, 1; Texas, 1.

OSPREY *Pandion haliaetus* 21–24   p. 65

Field marks: Spread 4½–6 ft. A large water-frequenting hawk — blackish above and *clear white* below. Head largely white, suggestive of Bald Eagle, but *broad black patch through cheeks*. Flies with a crook in its wings, showing black carpal patches on whitish undersides. The habit of hovering on beating wings, and plunging feet first for fish, is characteristic.

Voice: A series of sharp, cheeping whistles, *cheep, cheep*, or *yewk, yewk*, etc.; sounds annoyed. A frenzied *cheereek!*

Where found: Almost cosmopolitan. Migratory. **Texas:** *Migrant* (Apr.–May, Sept.–Dec.) throughout. *Winters* very rarely along coast. May breed occasionally on Texas coast but this needs verification (bulky nest, usually in isolated tree). *Habitat:* Rivers, lakes, Gulf.

Caracaras and Falcons: Falconidae

CARACARAS are carrion-eating birds with long legs, naked faces. They often associate with vultures. Falcons, on the other hand, are the most streamlined of the hawks. They are known by the combination of long, *pointed* wings, longish tails. The wing-strokes are rapid; the slim wings are built for speed, not sustained soaring. Food: Caracaras eat carrion. Falcons eat birds, rodents, insects. Caracaras are found only in Middle and S. America, whereas falcons are cosmopolitan. No. of species: World, 58; N. America, 8; Texas, 6.

CARACARA

CARACARA *Caracara cheriway* 22
(Audubon's Caracara, "Mexican Eagle") p. 64
Field marks: Spread 4 ft. The "Mexican Eagle" is often seen on fence posts or feeding with vultures, where its *black crest* and red face are its outstanding features. It is a large, long-legged, long-necked, dark hawk. In flight, its underbody presents three alternating areas of light and dark — whitish throat and breast, black belly, and white, dark-tipped tail. *Pale-colored patches* at wing-tips are conspicuous. These are determinative when seen in conjunction with the white breast. Young birds are browner, streaked on breast, not barred.
Similar species: Black Vulture (all-black body) also has white patches near wing-tips.
Voice: Occasionally a high cackling cry (head thrown back).
Where found: Sw. U.S. and Florida south to Peru. **Texas:** *Resident* from Rio Grande delta north along coast to e. Texas; inland rarely to Austin, Waco. Casual straggler to n. Texas, Panhandle, Trans-Pecos. *Habitat:* Prairies, rangeland. **Nest:** A bulky cup in top of yucca or tree. Eggs (2–3) blotched.

PRAIRIE FALCON *Falco mexicanus* 17 p. 80
Field marks: Spread 3½ ft. A pointed-winged hawk, very much like Peregrine Falcon in size and cut of jib, but of a paler sandy or clay-brown color ("like a faded young Peregrine"). Overhead, Prairie Falcon shows *blackish patches* (formed by dark flanks and axillars) in "armpits" where wings join body.
Similar species: (1) Peregrine has stronger face pattern (wide

black "mustaches"), more contrasting back (slaty in adult, brown in immature). (2) Female Sparrow Hawk is smaller, redder.

Voice: A yelping *kik-kik-kik*, etc.; a repeated *kee, kee, kee*.

Where found: Sw. Canada south to s. Mexico. **Texas:** *Resident* in w. Texas, breeding locally (El Paso; perhaps elsewhere in Trans-Pecos; also Panhandle). Occasional visitor through n. and cent. Texas to coast and Brownsville. *Habitat:* Canyons, dry plains, prairies. **Nest:** On bare ledge or niche of cliff. Eggs (3–4) reddish, spotted.

PEREGRINE FALCON *Falco peregrinus* 15–21
(Duck Hawk)   pp. 61, 80

Field marks: Spread 3¾ ft. Recognized as a falcon by its long, pointed wings, narrow tail, and quick, "rowing" wingbeats that are not unlike the flight of a pigeon. Its size, near that of a Crow, and heavy black lobe-shaped "mustaches," identify it as this species. Adults are slaty-backed, barred below. Young birds are dark brown above, heavily striped below.

Similar species: (1) Sparrow Hawk and (2) Pigeon Hawk are smaller, hardly larger than Robin. (3) See Prairie Falcon.

Voice: Usually silent. Around eyrie a repeated *we'chew;* a rapid rasping *cack cack cack*, etc., and a wailing note.

Where found: Nearly cosmopolitan. Migratory. **Texas:** *Migrant* (Apr.–May, Sept.–Oct.) throughout. *Winters* mostly in e. half. Rare *summer resident* west of Pecos River; locally on Edwards Plateau (near bat caves). Has bred Kerr Co. *Habitat:* Open country (mts. to coast). **Nest:** In "scrape" on ledge high on cliff. Eggs (2–4) reddish, spotted.

APLOMADO FALCON *Falco femoralis* 15–18   p. 80

Field marks: Spread 3 ft. A handsome medium-sized falcon now very rare in U.S. Somewhat larger than Sparrow Hawk or a little smaller than Peregrine. Identified by *dark wing-linings* and *black belly* contrasting with white breast. Thighs and under tail-coverts orange-brown. Young birds have a streaked breast, black patch on each flank, and *solid black* wing-linings.

Where found: U.S.–Mexican border south to Patagonia. **Texas:** Very rare local *summer resident* in Big Bend and perhaps elsewhere along Rio Grande. Formerly more widespread. In winter occasionally to Delta. *Habitat:* Arid brushy prairie. **Nest:** A stick platform in yucca or low tree. Eggs (3–4) speckled.

PIGEON HAWK or MERLIN
Falco columbarius 10–13½   pp. 61, 80

Field marks: Spread 2 ft. A small compact falcon, not much longer than a jay. Male, bluish gray above, with broad black bands on a gray tail. Female and young, dusky brown with

banded tails. Both adults and young are boldly streaked below.
Similar species: Suggests a miniature Peregrine. (1) Pointed
wings, falcon wing-action separate it from the little Sharp-
shinned Hawk, which has short rounded wings. (2) Lack of
rufous on tail or back and lack of strong mustaches distinguish
it from the other small falcon, the Sparrow Hawk. Sails less
between strokes; tail shorter.
Voice: Usually silent. At nest a quick chatter, *ki-ki-ki-ki*.
Where found: N. parts of N. Hemisphere. Winters south to n.
S. America, n. Africa. **Texas:** *Migrant* (Mar.–Apr., Sept.–Nov.)
through most sections; less common westward. Infrequent in
winter. *Habitat:* Open country, marshes, prairies, dunes.

SPARROW HAWK or KESTREL
Falco sparverius   9–12   pp. 61, 80
Field marks: Spread 1¾–2 ft. A small swallow-like hawk, size
of a jay. No other *small* hawk has a rufous back or tail. Males
have blue-gray wings. Both sexes have a handsome black
and white face pattern. Habitually *hovers* on rapidly beating
wings, kingfisher-like. Sits fairly erect with an occasional lift or
jerk of tail; perches on telegraph poles, posts, wires.
Similar species: (1) Sharp-shin has rounded wings. Sharp-shin
and (2) Pigeon Hawk have gray or brown backs, gray tails.
Voice: A rapid, high *klee klee klee* or *killy killy killy*.
Where found: Most of N. and S. America. **Texas:** *Winters*
(Sept.–May) throughout. *Breeds* locally in e., n., and w. parts
(not on coast, cent., and s. sections). Has bred at Houston.
Habitat: Open country, farmland. **Nest:** In cavity in isolated
tree, cliff; or on building. Eggs (4–6) buff, spotted.

Guans and Chachalacas: Cracidae

CHICKEN-LIKE birds of woodlands, jungles; long-tailed, strong-
legged. Food: Fruits, seeds, insects. Middle and S. America. No.
of species: World, 38; N. America, 1; Texas, 1.

CHACHALACA   *Ortalis vetula*   20–24   p. 129
Field marks: A large gray-brown bird shaped like a half-grown
Turkey, with a small head and a long rounded, white-tipped tail.
Difficult to observe, a secretive denizen of dense thickets; best
found in morning, when it calls raucously from treetops.
Similar species: See Roadrunner.
Voice: A harsh chicken-like cackle. Spring "song," a raucous
cha'-cha-lac, repeated in chorus from treetops in morning and
evening. Dr. A. A. Allen describes a chorus as *keep'-it-up, keep'-
it-up*, etc., answered by a lower *cut'-it-out, cut'-it-out*.

Where found: S. tip of Texas south to Nicaragua. **Texas:** *Resident* in lower Rio Grande Valley locally from near Falcon Dam to Brownsville; north to Raymondville. *Habitat:* Woodlands, tall brush. **Nest:** Of sticks, leaves, in bush or tree 4–25 ft. from ground. Eggs (3) whitish.

Grouse: Tetraonidae

GROUND-DWELLING, chicken-like birds; larger than quail, and without the long tails of pheasants. Food: Insects, seeds, buds, berries, etc. Mainly northern parts of N. Hemisphere. No. of species: World, 18; N. America, 10; Texas, 2.

GREATER PRAIRIE CHICKEN
Tympanuchus cupido   18   p. 129

Field marks: A large, brown henlike bird of prairies; known by *short, rounded, dark* tail (black in males, barred in females) and, when close, by *heavy barring* on underparts. "Dancing" male inflates orange air-sacs on side of neck; erects blackish neck feathers hornlike over head.

Similar species: See (1) Lesser Prairie Chicken; (2) female Ring-necked Pheasant.

Voice: Males in spring make a hollow "booming" *oo-loo-woo*, suggesting sound made by blowing across opening of bottle.

Where found: Canadian prairies to Texas. **Texas:** *Resident* locally on coastal prairie from Chambers and Jefferson Cos. to Aransas and Refugio Cos. N. Texas population extinct; coastal population declining. *Habitat:* Tall-grass prairie. **Nest:** A grass-lined hollow among grass. Eggs (7–17) olive; spotted.

LESSER PRAIRIE CHICKEN
Tympanuchus pallidicinctus   16   p. 129

Field marks: A small, pale Prairie Chicken; best known by range (below). Gular sacs of male dull red rather than orange.

Voice: Not as rolling or loud as "booming" of Greater Prairie Chicken. Various clucking, cackling, or gobbling notes.

Where found: Local; se. Colorado (rare), w. Kansas (rare), w. Oklahoma, e. New Mexico, and Texas Panhandle. **Texas:** *Resident* locally in Panhandle and Staked Plains; formerly reached Edwards Plateau. *Habitat:* Sandhill country and prairie (bunch grass, sage, oak shinnery). **Nest:** A grass-lined hollow in grass or under bush. Eggs (11–13) buff; dotted.

Quails, Partridges, and Pheasants: Phasianidae

QUAILS and Old World partridges are small, scratching, chicken-like birds, smaller than grouse or pheasants. Pheasants are chicken-sized with long sweeping tails. Food: Insects, seeds, buds, berries. Nearly cosmopolitan. No. of species: World, 165; N. America, 10; Texas, 4 (plus 3 introductions). For other introductions (unsuccessful) see pages 277 ff.

BOBWHITE *Colinus virginianus* 8½–10½   p. 129
Field marks: A small, brown, chicken-like bird, near size of Meadowlark. The male shows a conspicuous white throat and stripe over the eye; in the female these are buffy. Tail short, dark.
Similar species: (1) Distinguished from other quail by its rich brown color; (2) from Woodcock by smaller head, stubby bill, more blustering flight; (3) from Meadowlark in flight by lack of white outer tail feathers.
Voice: A clearly enunciated whistle, *Bob-white!* or *Poor Bob-whoit!* "Covey call," *ka-loi-kee?* answered by *whoil-kee.*
Where found: Cent. and e. U.S. south to Guatemala. **Texas:** *Resident* throughout much of state except Staked Plains and Trans-Pecos (introduced at El Paso). *Habitat:* Farmlands, brushy open country, roadsides, edges. **Nest:** A grass-lined hollow in grass or among brush. Eggs (12–20) white.

SCALED QUAIL *Callipepla squamata* 10–12
("Blue Quail")   p. 129
Field marks: A pale grayish quail of arid country, recognized by the scaly markings on breast and back and a *bushy white crest* or "cotton top." Runs; often reluctant to fly.
Voice: A guinea-hen-like *chek-ah.* (Also interpreted *pay-cos.*)
Where found: Sw. U.S. south to cent. Mexico. **Texas:** *Resident* in Panhandle and Trans-Pecos; east through w. parts of Edwards Plateau; southeast locally to McMullen Co. and lower Rio Grande Valley (Hidalgo Co.). Formerly to cent. Texas and cent. coast. *Habitat:* Grassland, brush, arid country. **Nest:** A grass-lined hollow under bush. Eggs (9–16) speckled.

GAMBEL'S QUAIL *Lophortyx gambelii* 10–11   p. 129
Field marks: A small, plump, grayish chicken-like bird with a *short dark plume curving* forward from crown. Male has an interesting black and white face pattern, a black patch on its buffy belly; striped rusty sides and a rusty crown.
Voice: A loud *kway-er* and a querulous *yuk-kwair'-go.*

Where found: Sw. U.S., nw. Mexico. **Texas:** *Resident* in Trans-Pecos, mostly near El Paso, east sparingly to Big Bend. *Habitat:* Deserts, arid country. **Nest:** On ground. Eggs (10–16) blotched.

HARLEQUIN QUAIL *Cyrtonyx montezumae* 8
(Mearns' Quail)   p. 129

Field marks: A small quail of brushy desert mountains. The oddly striped clown's face, pale bushy crest (not always erected) and speckled body of the male are best shown in the plate. Females are duller, with less obvious facial stripings.

Voice: A soft whinnying or quavering cry; ventriloquial (vaguely suggests Screech Owl's).

Where found: Sw. U.S. south to Oaxaca, Vera Cruz. **Texas:** Rare local *resident* in w. Texas, mostly west of Pecos River. Formerly east to cent. part of Edwards Plateau (still a few?). *Habitat:* Grassy oak canyons, mountain slopes. **Nest:** A grass-lined hollow, arched over; among grass. Eggs (8–14) white.

RING-NECKED PHEASANT
Phasianus colchicus   ♂ 30–36, ♀ 21–25   p. 129

Field mark: A large chicken-like or gamecock-like bird with a *long, sweeping pointed* tail. Male is highly colored and iridescent, with scarlet wattles on face and *white neck-ring* (not always present). Female is mottled brown with a moderately long pointed tail. Runs swiftly; flight strong (take-off noisy).

Similar species: Brown female could be confused with Prairie Chicken but *long pointed tail* is characteristic.

Voice: Crowing male has a loud double squawk, *kork-kok*, followed by brief whir of wing flapping. When flushed, harsh croaks.

Where found: Asia. Introduced widely in N. America and elsewhere. **Texas:** Introduced by Texas Game and Fish Commission into many localities; established locally only in nw. Panhandle (Dallam Co.). *Habitat:* Irrigated land, farmland. **Nest:** A grass-lined hollow among grass. Eggs (6–14) olive.

CHUKAR *Alectoris graeca*   13
(Rock Partridge)   p. 129

Field marks: Like a large pale quail; gray-brown with *bright red* legs and bill; light throat bordered by clean-cut black "necklace." Flanks heavily barred.

Voice: A series of *chuck*'s; a sharp *wheet-u*.

Where found: Asia and e. Europe. Introduced locally in w. U.S. **Texas:** Birds from India released in Moore Co., in 1940. They did not survive. In Sept., 1958, 500 Nevada wild-trapped birds were released in Brewster Co. There is a fair chance of survival.

COTURNIX *Coturnix coturnix* 7
(Migratory Quail)   p. 129
   Field marks: A tiny quail; smaller than Meadowlark. General color sandy, strongly streaked. Male with striped head (light stripe on crown and over eye, blackish stripes on throat). Female has unstreaked throat, closely spotted breast.
   Voice: Liquid *quic, quic-ic* (male); *queep — queep* (female).
   Where found: Eurasia. Birds of Mediterranean or Japanese origin have been widely introduced in w., cent., and n. Texas by Texas Game and Fish Commission. It is too early at this writing to assess results. Reproduction has been recorded.

TURKEY

Turkeys: Meleagrididae

VERY LARGE fowl-like birds; highly iridescent. Males with large tails erected fanwise in display. Food: Berries, acorns, nuts, seeds, insects. E. and s. U.S. and Cent. America. No. of species: World, 2; N. America, 1; Texas, 1.

TURKEY (Wild Turkey) *Meleagris gallopavo* ♂ 48, ♀ 36
   Field marks: A streamlined version of the familiar bronze turkey of the barnyard. Head naked; bluish with red wattles, intensified in male's display. Tail erected fanwise by male; bronzy with buffy tip (rusty or whitish in some strains). Pale

rump and wings; bronzy, iridescent body. Female less colorful.
Voice: "Gobbling" of male identical with domestic Turkey's.
Alarm note, *put-put!*

Where found: Oklahoma, Pennsylvania south to s. Mexico,
Gulf States. **Texas:** Native Turkeys are most numerous in the
Edwards Plateau and coastal prairies and ranches from cent.
coast nearly to the Rio Grande. Texas Game and Fish Commission has restocked Turkeys locally in many other sections
including e., cent., and w. areas and Panhandle. *Habitat:*
Woodlands, thickets, prairie groves, etc. **Nest:** A leaf-lined
depression on ground in thicket or woodland. Eggs (8–15)
buff, dotted.

WHOOPING CRANE
Compare its flight pattern with Wood Ibis and White Pelican.

Cranes: Gruidae

LONG-LEGGED, long-necked stately birds, superficially a little like
large herons; more robust, with long curved tertiary feathers
which curl down over the ends of the wings, giving a tufted
appearance. They also have a shorter bill, and bare red skin
about the face. Migrate in V or line formation. Neck extended in
flight. Blaring trumpet-like calls. Gregarious. Food: Tubers,
seeds, berries, rodents, aquatic life, insects. Nearly world-wide
except S. America and Oceania. No. of species: World, 14; N.
America, 2; Texas, 2.

WHOOPING CRANE *Grus americana* 50 p. 28
  Field marks: Spread 7½ ft. Larger than Sandhill Crane or
  Great Blue Heron. A large *white* crane with a red face. Neck
  outstretched in flight; primary wing feathers *black* (often concealed by curved white tertiary feathers when walking). Young
  are washed with rusty.
  Similar species: (1) Wood Ibis has dark head, decurved bill,
  more black in wing. At a great distance (2) White Pelican and
  (3) Snow Goose may possibly be confused with Whooping Crane
  because of wing pattern. (4) Egrets have no black in wings.
  Voice: A shrill bugle-like trumpeting, *ker-loo! ker-lee-oo!*
  Where found: Perhaps the rarest North American species
  (unless Ivory-billed Woodpecker still exists). The remaining
  flock breeds in w. Canada (Wood Buffalo Park), and migrates
  via the plains to coastal **Texas,** where it winters (Oct.–Apr.) on
  Aransas National Wildlife Refuge. *Habitat:* Wet coastal prairie.

SANDHILL CRANE *Grus canadensis* 40–48 p. 28
  Field marks: Spread 6–7 ft. A long-legged, long-necked gray
  bird with a bald *red* forehead. Some birds are stained with
  rusty. Young birds are brownish without the red forehead.
  On the ground, the tufted appearance of the feathers over the
  tail is a good mark. In flight, the neck is fully *extended*. The
  crane wing motion is distinctive, a smart flick or flap of the
  wings above the body level. (Herons have a bowed downstroke.)
  Often in large flocks. In spring, groups hop, jump, and flap.
  Similar species: Great Blue Heron is often called "crane" but
  is less robust. In sustained flight it carries its neck in a loop
  with the head drawn back to the shoulders.
  Voice: A deep rolling *k-r-r-oo* repeated several times. Some
  notes very suggestive of Canada Goose.
  Where found: Ne. Siberia, Alaska, Canada south to n. U.S.;
  also se. U.S. and Cuba. Winters to Mexico. **Texas:** *Migrant*
  (Mar.–May, Sept.–Dec.) through most sections. *Winters*
  (Nov.–Mar.) widely on coastal prairie and locally along Rio
  Grande and in s. Texas. Locally abundant in winter in Panhandle (Muleshoe Refuge), at salt lakes on Martin–Howard
  county line and elsewhere in s. Staked Plains. *Habitat:* Prairies,
  fields, marshes.

Limpkins: Aramidae

A RELIC of an ancient group of long-legged marsh birds, related to
both cranes and rails. Food: Chiefly fresh-water snails; also frogs,
reptiles, etc. Tropical America. No. of species: World, 1; N.
America, 1; Texas, 1.

ACCIPITERS, FALCONS, KITES, HARRIER

ACCIPITERS have short, rounded wings, long tails. They fly with several rapid beats and a short glide.

COOPER'S HAWK   p. 58
    Near size of Crow; rounded tail.
GOSHAWK   p. 57
    Adult: Very large; pale pearly-gray breast.
    Immature (not shown): See text.
SHARP-SHINNED HAWK   p. 57
    Small; tail square or notched.

FALCONS have long, pointed wings, long tails. Their wing-strokes are strong, rapid but shallow.

PEREGRINE FALCON   p. 72
    Falcon shape; near size of Crow; bold face pattern.
PRAIRIE FALCON   p. 71
    Dark axillars (in "armpits").
APLOMADO FALCON   p. 72
    Black belly, white chest.
PIGEON HAWK or MERLIN   p. 72
    Banded gray tail.
SPARROW HAWK or KESTREL   p. 73
    Banded rufous tail.

KITES are falcon-shaped but are buoyant gliders, not power-fliers.

SWALLOW-TAILED KITE   p. 56
    White below, long forked tail.
WHITE-TAILED KITE   p. 55
    Falcon-shaped, with whitish tail.
MISSISSIPPI KITE   p. 57
    Falcon-shaped, with blackish tail.
    Immature: See text.

HARRIERS are slim, with somewhat rounded wings, long tails and long bodies. They fly low with a vulture-like dihedral and languid flight.

MARSH HAWK (HARRIER)   p. 69
    Male: Whitish, with black wing-tips.
    Female: Harrier shape; brown, streaked.

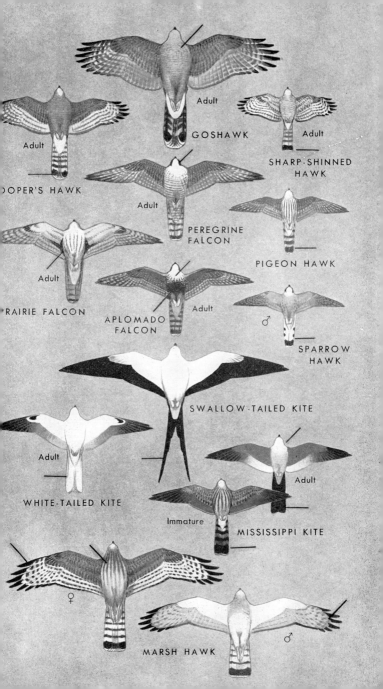

GOSHAWK

Adult

COOPER'S HAWK

Adult

SHARP-SHINNED HAWK

Adult

PEREGRINE FALCON

Adult

PIGEON HAWK

PRAIRIE FALCON

Adult

APLOMADO FALCON

Adult

♂ SPARROW HAWK

SWALLOW-TAILED KITE

WHITE-TAILED KITE

Adult

Adult

Immature

MISSISSIPPI KITE

♀

MARSH HAWK

♂

BALD EAGLE   Adult

BALD EAGLE   Immature

GOLDEN EAGLE   Adult

GOLDEN EAGLE   Immature

BLACK VULTURE

TURKEY VULTURE

Plate 24   81

EAGLES AND VULTURES

BALD EAGLE   p. 69
Adult: White head and white tail.
Immature: Some white in wing-linings.

GOLDEN EAGLE   p. 68
Adult: Almost uniformly dark; wing-linings dark.
Immature: "Ringed" tail; white patch at base of primaries.

BLACK VULTURE   p. 55
Stubby tail, whitish wing-patch.

TURKEY VULTURE   p. 54
Two-toned wings, small head, longish tail.

Where the Bald Eagle, Turkey Vulture, and Osprey
all are found, they can be separated at a great distance by their manner of soaring: the Bald Eagle,
with flat wings; the Turkey Vulture, with a dihedral;
the Osprey, with a kink or crook in its wings.

LIMPKIN *Aramus guarauna* 28   p. 21
   Field marks: A stray, perhaps from Florida swamps. About size of Bittern, but with much longer dark legs, longer neck, and *long, slightly drooping bill* which gives it a slightly ibis-like aspect. No ibis is brown with *white spots and streakings.* Wingbeat has crane-like flick, but legs often dangle, rail-like.
   Similar species: See American Bittern, immature Night Herons, immature White Ibis, and immature White-faced Ibis.
   Voice: A piercing repeated wail, *kree-ow, kra-ow,* etc.
   Where found: S. Georgia, Florida, south locally to Argentina. Casual straggler to e. corner of **Texas** (2 specimens, several others seen in Port Arthur–Beaumont area). One taken at Brownsville, May 23, 1889. *Habitat:* Fresh marshes, swamps.

Rails, Gallinules, and Coots: Rallidae

RAILS are compact, rather chicken-shaped marsh birds of secretive habits and mysterious voices; more often heard than seen. Wings short and rounded; tails short and often cocked. Flight brief and reluctant, with legs dangling. Gallinules and coots swim and therefore resemble ducks except for their smaller heads, forehead shields, and rather chicken-like bills; heads often "pumped" when swimming. Food: Aquatic plants, insects, frogs, crustaceans, mollusks, seeds, buds. Widespread through non-polar regions. No. of species: World, 132; N. America, 11; Texas, 9.

KING RAIL *Rallus elegans* 15–19   p. 29
   Field marks: A large reddish rail with a long, slender bill; twice size of Virginia Rail. Fresh or brackish marshes.
   Similar species: (1) Virginia Rail is size of Meadowlark and has slaty-gray cheeks. (2) Clapper Rail is of similar proportions to King but is grayer and lives only in salt marshes. Birds in typical habitats give no trouble but in borderline areas (brackish salt marshes, where both may be found) it is sometimes difficult to distinguish them.
   Voice: A low, grunting *bup-bup, bup-bup-bup,* etc., or *chuck-chuck-chuck.* Deeper than Virginia Rail's, does not descend scale.
   Where found: Minnesota, Massachusetts south to Cuba, Mexico. Migrant in north. **Texas:** *Summers* locally in e. and cent. Texas; west to Vernon, Fort Worth, San Antonio; south to Port Lavaca and Corpus Christi (rarely). *Winters* in e. Texas and near coast, south (formerly at least) to Brownsville. Rare *migrant* in Panhandle. *Habitat:* Fresh and brackish marshes, ricefields, swamps. **Nest:** A bowl of grass in marsh, sometimes arched over. Eggs (6–16) spotted.

CLAPPER RAIL   *Rallus longirostris*   14–16   p. 29
Field marks: The large gray-brown, tawny-breasted rail of the salt marshes, the "Salt-water Marsh Hen." Henlike appearance, strong legs, thin, slightly decurved bill, and white patch under the short tail identify it. Sometimes swims. Flying, it dangles its long legs.
Similar species: King Rail prefers fresh marshes. It is larger, has blacker stripes on back and flanks, *rusty brown* on wings. Its breast is cinnamon, but Clapper often shows similar warm buff on these parts. (Clapper has gray on cheek.) In fact the two approach each other so closely in some ways that did they not sometimes breed in the same salt-brackish marshes without crossing, they might be suspected of being races of one species.
Voice: A clattering *kek-kek-kek-kek*, etc., or *cha-cha-cha*, etc.
Where found: Coasts of California and e. U.S. south to S. America. **Texas:** *Resident* along coast. *Habitat:* Salt marshes.
Nest: A bowl of grass, arched over, in clump of grass or marsh vegetation. Eggs (8–13) buff, spotted.

VIRGINIA RAIL   *Rallus limicola*   9–10½   p. 29
Field marks: A small rusty-colored rail, with *gray cheeks;* bars on flanks, and a long, slightly decurved reddish bill. The only small rail, near size of Meadowlark, with a *slender* bill. Full-grown young in late summer are sooty black.
Similar species: (1) Sora has short bill. (2) See King Rail.
Voice: *Wak-wak-wak*, etc., descending; also *kidick, kidick*, besides various "kicking" and grunting sounds.
Where found: S. Canada south locally to Strait of Magellan. Migrant. **Texas:** *Migrant* locally in most sections. *Winters* (Oct.–Mar.) mainly along coast. *Summers* occasionally in n. Texas (breeds?). *Habitat:* Fresh and salt marshes.

SORA   *Porzana carolina*   8–9¾   p. 29
Field marks: The adult is a small plump gray-brown rail with a *black patch* on face and throat, and a short, *yellow* bill. Short cocked tail reveals white under coverts. Immature lacks black throat-patch, is buffy brown.
Similar species: (1) The only similarly sized fresh-water rail, the Virginia Rail, has a long, slender bill. (2) Immature Sora can be confused with smaller and rarer Yellow Rail.
Voice: A descending whinny. Also a plaintive whistled *ker-wee* (spring). When stone is tossed into marsh, a sharp *keek*.
Where found: Canada south to se. U.S. Winters to S. America. **Texas:** *Migrant* locally throughout. *Winters* (Sept.–May) along coast and at El Paso; rarely in cent. Texas and Panhandle. *Habitat:* Marshes, fresh and salt; swamps.

LARGE SHOREBIRDS

AMERICAN AVOCET   p. 107
Black and white back pattern, thin upturned bill.

BLACK-NECKED STILT   p. 108
White below; black unpatterned wings.

AMERICAN OYSTERCATCHER   p. 89
White wing-patches, black head, red bill.

HUDSONIAN GODWIT   p. 106
Upturned bill, ringed tail.

MARBLED GODWIT   p. 106
Long upturned bill, tawny-brown color.

WHIMBREL (HUDSONIAN CURLEW)   p. 98
Decurved bill, brownish color, striped crown.

AVOCET

Spring

(Left) BLACK-NECKED STILT

OYSTER-CATCHER

(Left) HUDSONIAN GODWIT

Fall

MARBLED GODWIT

HUDSONIAN CURLEW

SEMIPALMATED PLOVER

SNOWY PLOVER

KILLDEER

Below   BLACK-BELLIED PLOVER (Spring)

Below   AMERICAN GOLDEN PLOVER (Spring)

Below   Above

BLACK-BELLIED PLOVER (Fall)

Above

Below

RUDDY TURNSTONE (Spring)

AMERICAN GOLDEN PLOVER (Fall)

MOUNTAIN PLOVER

Plate 26   85

PLOVERS AND TURNSTONE

SNOWY PLOVER   p. 90
  Pale sand color; white sides of tail.

PIPING PLOVER (not illustrated)   p. 89
  Pale sand color; whitish rump and broad dark patch
  across end of tail.

SEMIPALMATED PLOVER   p. 89
  Mud-brown; dark tail with white borders.

KILLDEER   p. 90
  Tawny-red rump, longish tail.

BLACK-BELLIED PLOVER   p. 94
  Spring: Black breast, white lower belly.
  Fall: Black axillars, white in wing and tail.

AMERICAN GOLDEN PLOVER   p. 94
  Spring: Black from throat to under tail-coverts.
  Fall: Lack of pattern above and below.

RUDDY TURNSTONE   p. 94
  Harlequin pattern.

MOUNTAIN PLOVER   p. 91
  Dark tail-patch. See text.

MOUNTAIN PLOVER
(Breeding plumage)

YELLOW RAIL   *Coturnicops noveboracensis*   6–7½   p. 29
    Field marks: Rare. A small yellowish rail, suggesting a week-old chicken; shows a *white* wing-patch in flight — the only rail so marked. Very short yellow bill. Yellow Rails are so mouse-like that it requires the services of a bird dog to flush them.
    Similar species: Immature Sora might be taken for Yellow Rail but is larger, not so yellow; lacks white wing-patch. Notice back pattern in the plate. See Coturnix (p. 77).
    Voice: Ticking notes often in long series: *tic-tic, tic-tic-tic; tic-tic, tic-tic-tic,* etc. (groups of two and three).
    Where found: Mainly Canada, n. U.S. Winters to s. U.S. **Texas:** Very rare *winter visitor* (Oct.–Apr.) in e. and cent. Texas. Recorded south to Austin, San Antonio, Corpus Christi. Probably overlooked. *Habitat:* Grassy marshes, hayfields.

BLACK RAIL   *Laterallus jamaicensis*   5–6   p. 29
    Field marks: A tiny blackish rail with a *black* bill; about the size of a young Song Sparrow with a bobbed tail. Back speckled with white. Very difficult to glimpse or flush.
    Similar species: All young rails in downy plumage are glossy black (often called Black Rails by the inexperienced).
    Voice: *Kik* notes (male); lighter, more metallic than those of other rails. Also a cuckoo-like *croo-croo-croo-o* (female).
    Where found: Very local. California, Nebraska, ne. U.S. south to S. America. Migrant in n. parts. **Texas:** Extremely rare *migrant,* mainly near coast; probably winters. Recorded Dallas (?), Gainesville, San Angelo, Houston, Rockport, Sinton. Probably overlooked. *Habitat:* Grassy marshes, stubble fields.

PURPLE GALLINULE   *Porphyrula martinica*   12–14   p. 29
    Field marks: One of the most beautiful of all water birds. Swims, wades, and climbs bushes. Size and shape of Common Gallinule but head and underparts deep *purple,* back bronzy green. Bill red tipped with yellow; frontal shield on forehead *light blue;* legs *yellow,* conspicuous in flight. Immature is without bright color; dark above, pale below with white under tail-coverts; *no white side-stripe;* bill dark.
    Similar species: (1) Common Gallinule has *red* frontal shield, greenish legs, white side-stripe. (2) Young Common Gallinule has white line on side. (3) Young American Coot has pale bill; black divides white patch under tail.
    Where found: Se. U.S. south to Argentina. Winters mainly south of U.S. **Texas:** *Summers* (Mar.–Oct.) in e. half of state; west sparingly to Dallas, Austin, San Antonio. Most frequent near coast (winters rarely). Casual in Panhandle. *Habitat:* Fresh swamps, waterlily marshes. **Nest:** A saucer of grass anchored above water in clump of vegetation. Eggs (6–10) spotted.

COMMON GALLINULE *Gallinula chloropus* 12–14½
(Florida Gallinule) p. 29
  Field marks: Gallinules are ducklike marsh-lovers with stout,
rather chicken-like bills, equally at home wading among reeds
or swimming. When swimming, they pump head and neck
(so does Coot). A dark slaty ducklike bird with a *red bill* is
certainly this species. The white feathers under the tail show
prominently and there is a *band of white feathers* on the flanks.
  Similar species: (1) American Coot is stockier, shorter-necked;
has a gray back, *white bill*. (2) See Purple Gallinule.
  Voice: A croaking *kr-r-ruk* repeated, a froglike *kup;* also *kek, kek,
kek* and henlike notes, loud, complaining.
  Where found: S. Canada south to S. America; also Europe,
Asia, Africa. **Texas:** *Summers* in e. half of Texas from Red
River to Brownsville west at least to Vernon, Dallas, Austin,
San Antonio, Uvalde; also at El Paso. *Winters* mainly near
coast and along lower Rio Grande. *Habitat:* Fresh marshes,
swamps, reedy ponds, resacas. **Nest:** A shallow saucer of reeds
usually over water, anchored in reeds or semi-floating. Eggs
(8–14) spotted.

AMERICAN COOT *Fulica americana* 13–16 p. 29
  Field marks: The only slate-gray ducklike bird with a *whitish
bill*. Head and neck blacker than body; divided white patch
under tail. When swimming, pumps neck and small head back
and forth (like gallinule). Gregarious in winter. Dabbles but
also dives expertly. Taking off, it skitters its big lobed feet
("scallops" on toes). In labored flight, white border shows on
rear edge of wing; feet extend beyond tail.
  Similar species: Gallinules are smaller, have smaller heads, red
bills. Coots are more ducklike, resort more to open water and
flock more (sometimes very large concentrations).
  Voice: A grating *kuk-kuk-kuk-kuk;* various cackles, croaks.
  Where found: Canada south to Ecuador. Migrates from n.
sections. **Texas:** *Resident* throughout, summering very locally;
much more abundant in migration and winter. *Habitat:* Ponds,
lakes, marshes, bays. **Nest:** A shallow saucer among reeds or
on raft of dead vegetation; sometimes unconcealed. Eggs
(6–15) speckled.

Jacanas: Jacanidae

SLENDER, long-necked marsh birds with extremely long toes for
walking on floating plants. Called "lily-trotters." Mainly tropical
regions of world. Food: Vegetable matter, invertebrates. No. of
species: World, 7; N. America, 1; Texas, 1.

JACANA: immature (left): adult (right).

JACANA   *Jacana spinosa*   8½
Field marks: Built somewhat like a shorebird, with *extremely long toes*. *Adult:* Head and neck blackish, rest of body deep rusty. The best field marks are the conspicuous yellow *frontal shield* on the forehead and *large pale greenish-yellow wing-patches* (primaries and secondaries). The immature, which occasionally wanders into Texas in autumn, slightly suggests Wilson's Phalarope. It is gray-brown above, with whitish underparts and a broad white stripe over the eye. The extremely long toes, great lemon-yellow wing-patches, and rail-like flight, notes, and habitat distinguish it from any shorebird.
Voice: Cackling cries when bird flies.
Where found: Mexico south to Argentina. **Texas:** Rare visitor to Rio Grande delta; casual elsewhere in s. Texas. Has bred. *Habitat:* Resacas, ponds, marshes. **Nest:** Eggs (4) brown, scrawled; laid on floating vegetation.

Oystercatchers: Haematopodidae

LARGE, spectacular shorebirds with long, laterally flattened, knife-like, chisel-tipped bills. Food: Bivalves, oysters, crabs, marine worms. Widespread on coasts of the world. No. of species: World, 6; N. America, 2; Texas, 1.

AMERICAN OYSTERCATCHER
Haematopus palliatus 17–21   pp. 84, 97

Field marks: A very noisy, thick-set, dark, black-headed shore-bird with white belly, large white wing- and tail-patches. *Large straight red bill,* flattened laterally. Legs pale flesh.

Similar species: See Black Skimmer.

Voice: A piercing *wheep!* or *kleep!* Alarm, a loud *pic, pic, pic.*

Where found: Shores of New Jersey south to Chile, Argentina.
Texas: Local *resident* along coast; most frequent on cent. coast from May to Sept. *Habitat:* Coastal beaches, tidal flats. **Nest:** In scrape on beach or shell bank. Eggs (2–4) spotted.

Plovers and Turnstones: Charadriidae

WADING BIRDS, more compactly built, thicker-necked than sand-pipers, with shorter, pigeon-like bills and larger eyes. Call notes are important in identification. Unlike sandpipers, plovers run in short starts and stops. Food: Insects, crustaceans, marine worms, mollusks, etc. Cosmopolitan. No. of species: World, 63; N. America, 15; Texas, 9 (plus 1 accidental).

SEMIPALMATED PLOVER *Charadrius semipalmatus* 6½–8
("Ringed Plover")   pp. 85, 91, 96

Field marks: A small plump shorebird with a *dark band* across its chest (sometimes incomplete in front); *dark* brown above; half the size of Killdeer. Has plover habit of running a few steps and stopping quite still. Bill may be orange with black tip, or (in winter) all black. Legs orange or yellow.

Similar species: (1) Killdeer is twice as large, its tail is twice as long, and it has *two* black rings across its chest. (2) Piping Plover is similar to Semipalmated in size and pattern but is very much paler. (3) Snowy Plover has *black* legs.

Voice: A plaintive slurred *chi-we,* or *too-li,* second note higher.

Where found: Arctic America. Winters south to S. America.
Texas: *Migrant* (Apr.–May, Aug.–Nov.) in e. half of state, Staked Plains and Panhandle. Casual in Trans-Pecos. Most numerous on coast; some *winter. Habitat:* Beaches, shores, flats.

PIPING PLOVER *Charadrius melodus* 6–7½   pp. 85, 91, 96

Field marks: As pale as a beach flea. In flight, as pale as a winter Sanderling without as bold a wing pattern. Has a more or less complete or incomplete dark ring about neck. Bill yellow with black tip (all black in winter); legs yellow.

Similar species: (1) Semipalmated Plover has back the color of wet sand or mud; that of Piping Plover is pale, like sun-bleached, dry sand. (2) Snowy Plover has *black* legs, darker ear-patch.

Voice: Plaintive whistle; *peep-lo* (first note higher).

Where found: Canada south to Nebraska, Great Lakes, and Virginia. Winters on coasts of s. U.S. **Texas:** *Migrant* (Feb.–June, Aug.–Nov.) along coast; some *winter*. Casual inland (Tyler, Denton, Austin). *Habitat:* Sea beaches, flats.

SNOWY PLOVER *Charadrius alexandrinus* 6   pp. 85, 96
Field marks: Slightly smaller than Semipalmated and Piping Plovers, with a *slim, black bill*, black mark behind eye and *black-ish legs* (the other two have yellow or orange legs). Extremely pale, almost whitish. "Ring" reduced to a dark mark on each side of breast.

Similar species: In winter the stubby bills of most Piping and Semipalmated Plovers are also *all black;* use then the black leg color, the whiter look of the Snowy.

Voice: A fluty whistle, *poo-weet*. In flight a soft *wit-wit*.

Where found: W. U.S. and Gulf States south to Chile; also Europe, Asia, Africa, Australia. Migrant from some areas. **Texas:** *Resident* on Gulf Coast. *Migrates* and *breeds* locally in Panhandle, Staked Plains, and n. Texas. Rare migrant in cent. Texas. *Habitat:* Sand flats, salt flats, sandy beaches of streams, lakes, coast. **Nest:** In depression on open sand or salt flat. Eggs (2–3) buff, spotted.

WILSON'S PLOVER *Charadrius wilsonia* 7–8
("Thick-billed Plover")   p. 96
Field marks: A "ringed" plover, larger than the Semipalmated, Snowy, or Piping Plovers, with a wider breastband and a much longer *heavy, black bill*. Legs *flesh-gray*.

Similar species: (1) Piping and (2) Semipalmated Plovers can be distinguished by size and small bills and also by *yellowish legs*. (3) Snowy Plover has a small bill, *blackish* legs.

Voice: An emphatic whistled *whit!* or *wheet!*

Where found: New Jersey south to S. America. Winters from Gulf Coast, south. **Texas:** *Summers* (Mar.–Oct.) along coast. Casual in winter. Accidental inland. *Habitat:* Open beaches, tidal flats, sandy islands. **Nest:** In scrape or hollow on beach, gravel roadway, or sandy island. Eggs (3) spotted.

KILLDEER *Charadrius vociferus* 9–11   pp. 85, 96
Field marks: The common noisy breeding plover of much of Texas. Larger than the other "ringed" plovers; has *two* black breastbands, instead of one. In flight, displays a *golden-red rump*, longish tail, and white wing-stripe.

Voice: Noisy; a loud insistent *kill-deeah*, repeated; a plaintive *dee-ee* (rising); *dee-dee-dee*, etc. Also a low trill.
Where found: Canada south to cent. Mexico, West Indies. Also Peru. Migrant in north. **Texas:** *Resident* in all parts. *Habitat:* Fields, airports, riverbanks, mudflats, shores. **Nest:** A scrape on bare ground in plowed field, bald spot in pasture, gravel shore, roadway, etc. Eggs (4) spotted.

MOUNTAIN PLOVER *Eupoda montana* 8–9½   p. 85
Field marks: Like a small Killdeer, but with *no breast-rings*. In the breeding season, *white forehead and line over eye*, contrasting with *black* crown. In nondescript winter plumage the bird lacks this, but may be told from the winter-plumaged Golden Plover by its grayer back, devoid of mottling, its *pale legs*, light wing-stripe and dark tailband.
Similar species: Golden Plover (and see above).
Voice: A low whistle; variable.
Where found: High plains of w. U.S., east of Rockies. Winters sw. U.S. and Mexico. **Texas:** *Migrant* (Apr.–May, Aug.–Sept.) through n., w., cent., and s. parts of state. *Winters* irregularly in s.-cent. Texas and more frequently along lower coast. *Summers* locally in Trans-Pecos and Panhandle. *Habitat:* Prairies, fields, plains. **Nest:** A depression among short grass. Eggs (3) olive, spotted.

HEADS OF "RINGED" PLOVERS

SNIPE, SANDPIPERS, AND PHALAROPES

COMMON (WILSON'S) SNIPE   p. 95
Long bill, pointed wings, orange tail, zigzag flight.

AMERICAN WOODCOCK   p. 95
Long bill, rounded wings, dead-leaf color.

DOWITCHER   pp. 103, 104
Snipe bill, white tail and lower back. For identification of
the two dowitchers, see text.

SOLITARY SANDPIPER   p. 100
Dark wings, conspicuous white sides on tail.

LESSER YELLOWLEGS   p. 101
Dark wings, whitish rump and tail.

STILT SANDPIPER   p. 104
Like preceding but legs greenish (see text).

SPOTTED SANDPIPER   p. 99
Identify by very short wing-stroke (giving a stiff, bowed
appearance).

WILSON'S PHALAROPE   p. 109
Fall: Suggests Yellowlegs; smaller, breast whiter, bill needle-
like.

KNOT   p. 101
Fall: Stocky; grayish with light rump. Compare with
Yellowlegs and Dowitcher.

SANDERLING   p. 107
Has most flashing stripe of any small shorebird. Follows
retreating waves like a clockwork toy.

NORTHERN PHALAROPE   p. 109
Fall: Sanderling-like; wing-stripe shorter, bill more needle-
like.

RED PHALAROPE   p. 108
Fall: Sanderling-like; wing-stripe less contrasting; bill
thicker than Northern Phalarope's.

Phalaropes swim on water; spin and dab.

WOODCOCK

WILSON'S
SNIPE

Fall

DOWITCHER

LESSER
YELLOW
LEGS

Fall

STILT
SANDPIPER

SOLITARY
SANDPIPER

Fall

WILSON'S
PHALAROPE

Fall

KNOT

Fall

SPOTTED
SANDPIPER

Fall

Fall

SANDERLING

NORTHERN
PHALAROPE

RED PHALAROPE

LEAST
SANDPIPER

SEMIPALMATED
SANDPIPER

BAIRD'S
SANDPIPER

WHITE-
RUMPED
SANDPIPER

PECTORAL
SANDPIPER

Below

BUFF-
BREASTED
SANDPIPER

Fall

CURLEW
SANDPIPER

PURPLE
SANDPIPER

Fall

RED-BACK
SANDPIPER

UPLAND
PLOVER

WILLET

Plate 28   93

SANDPIPERS

LEAST SANDPIPER*   p. 103
Very small, brown; faint wing-stripe.

SEMIPALMATED SANDPIPER*   p. 105
Larger, grayer; identify by notes (see text).

WESTERN SANDPIPER* **(not illustrated)**   p. 105
Similar; identify by notes (see text).

BAIRD'S SANDPIPER*   p. 102
Still larger, browner, dark rump (see text).

WHITE-RUMPED SANDPIPER*   p. 102
White rump (only "peep" so marked).

PECTORAL SANDPIPER   p. 101
Like double-sized Least Sandpiper. Wing-stripe faint or lacking.

BUFF-BREASTED SANDPIPER   p. 106
Evenly buff below, contrasting with white wing-linings.

CURLEW SANDPIPER   p. 270
Accidental in Texas.
Fall: Suggests Dunlin (Red-backed Sandpiper) but rump *white.*

PURPLE SANDPIPER   p. 270
Accidental in Texas. Slaty color; rock jetties.

DUNLIN (RED-BACKED SANDPIPER)   p. 103
Fall: Gray; larger than "peep," darker than Sanderling.

UPLAND PLOVER   p. 99
Brown; small head, long tail. Often flies like Spotted Sandpiper.

WILLET   p. 100
Large size, flashing wing pattern.

---

* The five small streaked sandpipers are collectively nicknamed "peep."

AMERICAN GOLDEN PLOVER
Pluvialis dominica 10–11 pp. 85, 96

Field marks: A trifle larger than Killdeer. Breeding adults are dark shorebirds, richly spangled with golden spots above; underparts black. A broad white stripe extends over the eye down the side of neck. Young birds and winter adults are brown, darker above than below. They are recognized as plovers by their stocky proportions and short bill; and in flight from the other plovers by their lack of pattern.

Similar species: Black-bellied Plover is larger, pale gray above, and has *white rump and tail* (Golden has brown tail). Blackbelly shows white in wings and a black axillar patch (beneath wings, in "armpits" where they join body); Golden Plovers are smaller, darker, and without pattern.

Voice: A whistled *queedle* or *que-e-e-a* (dropping at end).

Where found: Siberia and arctic America. Winters in S. Hemisphere. **Texas:** *Migrant* (Mar.–May, Aug.–Nov.) both coast and interior. Usually more numerous in spring. *Habitat:* Rangeland, plains, prairies, burned fields, airports, mudflats, shores.

BLACK-BELLIED PLOVER
Squatarola squatarola 10½–13½ pp. 85, 96

Field marks: In breeding dress this large plover, with its black breast and almost whitish back, resembles only the Golden Plover, which is brown-backed. Winter birds and immatures are gray-looking and are recognized as plovers by their stocky proportions and short pigeon-like bills. They have a dejected, hunched posture. In any plumage the *black axillars* ("armpits") under the wing, and the whitish rump and tail, are determinative.

Similar species: See Golden Plover.

Voice: A plaintive slurred whistle, *tlee-u-eee* or *whee-er-eee* (middle note lower).

Where found: Arctic. Winters south to S. Hemisphere. **Texas:** *Migrant* (Mar.–May, Aug.–Dec.) throughout, especially coastwise. Some *winter* on coast. *Habitat:* Beaches, mudflats, marshes.

RUDDY TURNSTONE *Arenaria interpres* 8–9½ pp. 85, 96

Field marks: A squat, robust, orange-legged shorebird with "tortoise shell" plumage. Larger than Spotted Sandpiper. In breeding plumage with its russet-red back and curious black face and breast markings, the bird is very handsome, but when it flies it is even more striking. Its harlequin pattern is best explained by the plate. Young birds and winter adults are duller, but retain enough breast pattern to be recognizable.

Voice: A staccato *tuk-a-tuk* or *kut-a-kut;* also a single *kewk*.

Where found: Arctic and Subarctic. Winters south to S. Hemisphere. **Texas:** *Migrant* (Mar.–May, Aug.–Sept.) along coast.

Many *winter*, especially southward. Casual inland (Dallas, Fort Worth, Denton, Austin, Midland). *Habitat:* Beaches, tidal flats, stone jetties.

Woodcock, Snipe, Sandpipers, etc.: Scolopacidae

A NUMEROUS and varied family of wading birds. Habitat usually seashores and marshes, though some frequent dry open ground and some woodlands. Legs slender, long; bills more slender than those of plovers. Wing-bars, rump and tail patterns are important diagnostically. Chiefly gregarious. Food: Insects, small crustaceans, mollusks, worms, other invertebrates; sometimes seeds, berries. Cosmopolitan. No. of species: World, 77; N. America, 44; Texas, 25 (plus 5 accidentals).

AMERICAN WOODCOCK *Philohela minor* 10–12 pp. 92, 112
   Field marks: A chunky, almost neckless, buffy-brown bird with a "dead-leaf pattern"; near size of a quail, with an *extremely long bill*, large eyes. It is usually flushed from a brushy swamp or thicket, and makes away on a straight course, often producing a whistling sound with its short, *rounded* wings.
   Similar species: Snipe is slimmer, has *pointed* wings, whitish belly; prefers more open terrain and makes off in a *zigzag.*
   Voice: At dusk or on moonlit nights in spring, male utters a low nasal *beezp* (suggests call of Nighthawk). Aerial "song" starts as a chippering trill (made by wings) as bird ascends, and changes at zenith to bubbling warble as bird drops.
   Where found: Se. Canada south to Gulf States. Winters in se. U.S. **Texas:** *Migrant and winter visitor* (Oct.–Feb.) through e. and cent. Texas west to Fort Worth, Austin; south to Corpus Christi, occasionally to the Rio Grande. *Breeds* (rarely) in e. Texas. *Habitat:* Wet thickets, moist woodlands, brushy swamps.
   Nest: A depression on ground in brushy place, edge of thicket or woodland opening. Eggs (4) buff, spotted.

COMMON SNIPE *Capella gallinago* 10½–11½
(Wilson's Snipe)   pp. 92, 112
   Field marks: A tight-sitting marsh wader, larger than a Spotted Sandpiper; brown with a *striped back*, striped head, and an *extremely long, slender bill*. When flushed, it makes off in a *zigzag*, showing a *short orange tail* and uttering a rasping note. Bill pointed downward in flight.
   Similar species: See (1) Woodcock and (2) dowitchers.
   Voice: Nasal, rasping note when flushed.

Plate 29

SHOREBIRDS

SNOWY PLOVER Dark legs, dark ear-patch, *slender* black bill.	p. 90
PIPING PLOVER "Ringed"; color of *dry* sand (pale).	p. 89
SEMIPALMATED PLOVER "Ringed"; color of *wet* sand (dark).	p. 89
WILSON'S PLOVER *Large* black bill.	p. 90
KILLDEER *Two* breast-rings.	p. 90
BLACK-BELLIED PLOVER *Spring:* Black below, pale above. *Fall:* Plover shape; gray.	p. 94
AMERICAN GOLDEN PLOVER *Spring:* Black below, dark above. *Fall:* Plover shape; brown.	p. 94
DUNLIN (RED-BACKED SANDPIPER) *Spring:* Rusty back, black belly.	p. 103
RUDDY TURNSTONE *Spring:* Rusty back; face pattern. *Fall:* Dark breast, orange legs.	p. 94
WILSON'S PHALAROPE *Female in spring:* Dark neck-stripe. *Male in spring:* Paler.	p. 109
NORTHERN PHALAROPE *Female in spring:* Rusty neck, white throat. *Male in spring:* Duller.	p. 109
RED PHALAROPE *Female in spring:* Rusty below, white cheeks. *Male in spring:* Duller.	p. 108

SEMIPALMATED PLOVER

PIPING PLOVER

OWY PLOVER

WILSON'S PLOVER

KILLDEER

Fall

Fall

AMERICAN GOLDEN PLOVER

Spring

BLACK-BELLIED PLOVER

Spring

Spring

ng

DUNLIN

Spring

Fall

RUDDY TURNSTONE

♀

NORTHERN PHALAROPE
Spring

♀

♀

WILSON'S PHALAROPE
Spring

♂

RED PHALAROPE
Spring

AMERICAN
OYSTERCATCHER

Spring

AMERICAN
AVOCET

BLACK–
NECKED
STILT

Spring

HUDSONIAN
GODWIT

Fall

MARBLED GODWIT

LONG–BILLED
CURLEW

WHIMBREL

UPLAND
PLOVER

Plate 30   97

SHOREBIRDS

AMERICAN AVOCET   p. 107
  Upturned bill, black and white back. Pale rusty or pinkish-
  tan neck (spring).

AMERICAN OYSTERCATCHER   p. 89
  Large size, dark head, red bill.

BLACK-NECKED STILT   p. 108
  Black above, white below, red legs.

HUDSONIAN GODWIT   p. 106
  Spring: Upturned bill, rusty breast.
  Fall: Upturned bill, grayish breast.

MARBLED GODWIT   p. 106
  Tawny brown; long upturned bill.

UPLAND PLOVER   p. 99
  Small head, short bill, thin neck, long tail.

LONG-BILLED CURLEW   p. 98
  Very long bill; buffy, no head-stripes.

WHIMBREL (HUDSONIAN CURLEW)   p. 98
  Decurved bill, striped head.

Where found: N. America and n. Eurasia. Winters south to
S. America, Africa. **Texas:** *Winters* (Sept.–Apr.) throughout;
most numerous in migration. *Habitat:* Marshes, swamps, wet
meadows, springs, stream edges.

LONG-BILLED CURLEW

Numenius americanus   20–26   p. 97
Field marks: Bill 5–7. The "Sickle-bill" is much larger than the
Whimbrel, more buffy; lacks contrasting head-striping (i.e.,
dark line through eye, stripes on crown). Overhead, shows
bright cinnamon wing-linings. In many individuals the bill is 7
inches long, twice that of the average Whimbrel; in a few birds
bill lengths approach each other.
Similar species: See (1) Whimbrel, (2) Marbled Godwit.
Voice: A loud *cur-leel* with rising inflection. Also a rapid,
whistled *kli-li-li-li.* "Song," a long, liquid *curleeeeeeeeuuu.*
Where found: Sw. Canada and w. U.S. Winters s. U.S. to
Guatemala. **Texas:** *Migrates and winters* throughout much of
state. Found through nearly every month except June in
Panhandle and locally southward; also on coast, coastal prairies,
and Delta, but *breeds* only in nw. part of Panhandle (Staked
Plains) and possibly on lower coast (needs investigation). Has
nested at Rockport and Houston (once). *Habitat:* Prairies,
rangeland, mudflats, beaches. **Nest:** A depression in grass.
Eggs (4) olive, spotted.

WHIMBREL   *Numenius phaeopus*   15–18

(Hudsonian Curlew)   pp. 84, 97
Field marks: Bill 2¾–4. A large brown shore bird with a long
down-curved bill. The bills of godwits turn up. *Grayer* than
Long-billed Curlew; shorter bill, *striped crown.* In flight,
Whimbrels appear as large as some ducks, and often fly in line
or wedge formation.
Similar species: See Long-billed Curlew (more buffy).
Voice: Five or six short rapid whistles, *whi-whi-whi-whi-whi.*
Where found: Arctic. Winters south to S. America, Africa.
Texas: *Migrant* (Apr.–May, Aug.–Oct.) mainly along coast.
Rare and local in interior and Panhandle. *Winters* occasionally
on coast. *Habitat:* Shores, mudflats, prairies, marshes.

ESKIMO CURLEW   *Numenius borealis*   12–14

Field marks: Bill 1¾–2½, *slightly curved* only. Body not much
more than half the bulk of a Whimbrel. Darker above and on
top of head, the feathers with warm buffy-brown tips. Underparts warm buffy, *appearing lighter* than upper parts. (Whimbrel
appears a uniform dirty grayish brown, with a more conspicuously striped head.) In flight undersurface of wings *conspicuously cinnamon-buff.* Legs *dark greenish,* instead of bluish

gray (Ludlow Griscom). In the hand, has *unbarred* primaries.
Similar species: Young Whimbrel may have a bill almost as short as an Eskimo Curlew's bill. Only a very experienced observer who knows the Whimbrel from A to Z should be taken seriously if he reports an Eskimo Curlew.
Voice: The flight call has been described as a sharp squeak with a squealing quality strongly suggestive of the single note of a Common Tern, but weaker. Other notes are described as soft twittering or whistling in quality (not like Whimbrel).
Where found: Near-extinct. Formerly arctic America, wintered in s. South America. **Texas:** Formerly migrated through prairies of e. and middle Texas. Recent sight records: Galveston, Apr. 20, 1945 (J. M. Heiser, Jr.); Rockport, Apr., 1952 (C. Hagar and D. Snyder); Galveston I., Apr. 5–26, 1959 (Feltner, G. Williams, E. Edwards, and others).

UPLAND PLOVER *Bartramia longicauda* 11–12½ pp. 93, 97
Field marks: A "pigeon-headed," streaked, buffy-brown shorebird, larger than Killdeer but with no really distinctive markings. Habitually perches on fence posts and poles. General brown coloration, rather short bill (shorter than head), comparatively small-headed, thin-necked, long-tailed appearance, and habit of holding wings elevated upon alighting are helpful points. Flies "on tips of wings" like Spotted Sandpiper.
Similar species: Can hardly be confused with any other sandpiper-like bird in the grass country. Curlews and godwits are much larger; Pectoral and Buff-breasted Sandpipers smaller.
Voice: *Kip-ip-ip-ip.* A rolling note in flight. "Song," weird, long-drawn, windlike whistles: *whooooleeeeee, wheeelooooooooooo* (starts with a rattle, ascends; second part descends).
Where found: Mainly Canada and n. U.S. Winters on pampas of S. America. **Texas:** *Migrant* (Mar.–May, July–Oct.) through all parts except Trans-Pecos. *Breeds* rarely and locally in n. Panhandle. *Habitat:* Prairies, fields. **Nest:** A depression among grass. Eggs (4) spotted.

SPOTTED SANDPIPER *Actitis macularia* 7–8 pp. 92, 113
Field marks: Teeters up and down between steps as if too delicately balanced. In breeding plumage the breast is speckled with *large round spots;* many other sandpipers are streaked, but this is the only one with round spots. Young birds and adults in fall and winter lack spotting; they are olive-brown above, whitish below, with a white line over eye. A white mark on side of breast near shoulder is a good aid. The wing-stroke is shallow, quivering, the wings maintaining a stiff, bowed appearance, unlike deeper wing-strokes of other small shorebirds. This and constant teetering are most useful distinctions.
Voice: A clear *peet* or *pee-weet!* or *pee-weet-weet-weet weet.*

Where found: N. Alaska, Canada south to cent. U.S. Winters
south to S. America. **Texas:** *Migrant* (Mar.–May, July–Oct.)
throughout. *Winters* in s. part north to Waco, Kerrville, Del
Rio, and along coast sparingly east to Galveston. *Breeds* in
Panhandle and very locally in n. Texas. *Habitat:* Lake shores,
streamsides, beaches. **Nest:** A grass-lined depression on ground
or under bush. Eggs (4) spotted.

SOLITARY SANDPIPER   *Tringa solitaria*   7½–9   pp. 92, 112
   Field marks: A dark sandpiper, dusky above, whitish below,
   with a white eye-ring. In flight, *dark-winged;* conspicuous *white
   sides of tail,* crossed by bold black bars.
   Similar species: (1) Resembles a small Lesser Yellowlegs; nods
   like one, but has dark rump instead of white, and dark legs
   instead of yellow. (2) Spotted Sandpiper *teeters* more than it
   nods and has a white wing-stripe, which dark-winged Solitary
   lacks. Spotted has a narrow wing-arc; Solitary, a darting,
   almost swallow-like wing-stroke. Both frequent similar places,
   but Solitary strictly avoids salt margins.
   Voice: *Peet!* or *peet-weet-weet!* (higher than Spotted).
   Where found: Alaska, Canada. Winters south to Argentina.
   Texas: *Migrant* (Apr.–May, July–Sept.) throughout. A few
   winter near coast. *Habitat:* Streamsides, wooded swamps, ponds,
   fresh marshes.

WILLET   *Catoptrophorus semipalmatus*   14–17   pp. 93, 112
   Field marks: Its *flashy black and white wing pattern* makes this
   large gray and white wader easy to identify. At rest, when
   banded wings cannot be seen, the bird is rather nondescript;
   gray above, whitish below in fall and winter; somewhat barred
   and spotted below in summer. Legs bluish gray.
   Similar species: Smaller than the brown godwits and curlews; a
   bit larger than Greater Yellowlegs, from which it differs by its
   grayer look, stockier bill, dark legs, and flight pattern.
   Voice: A musical oft-repeated *pill-will-willet* (in breeding
   season); a loud *kay-ee* (second note lower). Also a rapidly
   repeated *kip-kip-kip*, etc. In flight, *whee-wee-wee*.
   Where found: S. Canada south locally to Gulf States and West
   Indies. Winters south to S. America. **Texas:** *Migrant* (Mar.–
   May, July–Nov.) in most sections. *Resident* along coast.
   Habitat: Mudflats, beaches, marshes, pond edges. **Nest:** A
   depression or grassy cup among grass on island, beach edge,
   dune or high spot in marsh. Eggs (3–4) spotted.

GREATER YELLOWLEGS
Totanus melanoleucus   13–15   p. 112
   Field marks: The *bright yellow legs* are the mark of this rather
   large slim sandpiper. Back checkered with gray and white.

Flying, it appears *dark-winged* (no wing-stripes) with a *whitish rump and tail*. Bill long, *slightly upturned*.
Similar species: See Lesser Yellowlegs.
Voice: A 3-syllabled whistle, *whew-whew-whew*, or *dear! dear! dear!* In spring, a fast-repeated *whee-oodle*, etc.
Where found: Alaska, Canada. Winters south to Tierra del Fuego. **Texas:** *Migrant* (Mar.–May, July–Oct.) in most parts of state. *Winters* mainly along coast; locally inland in s. half of state. *Habitat:* Marshes, mudflats, streams, pond margins, shores.

LESSER YELLOWLEGS *Totanus flavipes* 9½–11 pp. 92, 112
    Field marks: Like Greater Yellowlegs but near size of Killdeer; Greater is near size of Willet. The shorter, slimmer bill of the Lesser is perfectly straight; that of the Greater often appears *slightly upturned*. Most easily identified by calls (below).
    Similar species: Fall Stilt Sandpiper and fall Wilson's Phalarope have similar flight pattern.
    Voice: *Yew* or *you-you* (one or two notes); less forceful than clear 3-syllabled *whew-whew-whew* of Greater Yellowlegs.
    Where found: Alaska, Canada. Winters south to Argentina. **Texas:** *Migrant* (Mar.–May, July–Oct.) in most parts. *Winters* mainly along coast; locally inland in s. half of state. *Habitat:* Marshes, mudflats, shores, pond edges, streamsides.

KNOT *Calidris canutus* 10–11   pp. 92, 112, 113
    Field marks: Stocky with a rather short bill; much larger than Spotted Sandpiper. *Spring:* Breast pale robin-red, back mottled gray and black. *Fall:* More nondescript, breast whitish. A dumpy light grayish shorebird with a short bill and a whitish rump. At very close range shows scaly white feather-edgings. Often feeds in densely packed flocks.
    Similar species: (1) Spring Dowitcher, also red-breasted, has a long snipe-like bill (Knot's bill is short, about as long as head). In fall Knot, washed-out gray color, size, and shape are best clues; (2) Sanderlings are smaller and whiter; (3) Dunlins are smaller and darker (both have dark rumps). (4) In flight, Knot's whitish rump does not show so conspicuously as that of yellowlegs, nor does it extend so far up back as in dowitcher.
    Voice: A low *knut;* also a low mellow *tooit-wit* or *wah-quoit*.
    Where found: Arctic. Winters south to S. Hemisphere. **Texas:** *Migrant* (Apr.–May, Aug.–Oct.) along coast. A few winter. Casual inland. *Habitat:* Tidal flats, shores.

PECTORAL SANDPIPER
Erolia melanotos 8–9½   pp. 93, 113
    Field marks: A streaked sandpiper, larger than Spotted; prefers grassy mudflats and marshes. The rusty-brown back is streaked

with black and lined snipe-like with white. The outstanding thing is the heavy breast-streaking which *ends abruptly*, like a bib, against the white belly. Legs yellowish green. Top of head is darker and neck longer than in any other small streaked shorebird. Wing-stripe is faint or lacking.

Similar species: (1) Least Sandpiper is colored similarly, but is half the size. Small Pectorals might be confused with (2) White-rumped or (3) Baird's Sandpipers.

Voice: A reedy *krik, krik* or *trrip-trrip.*

Where found: Ne. Siberia and American Arctic. Winters in s. S. America. **Texas:** *Migrant* (Mar.–May, July–Nov.) through most of state except Trans-Pecos (probably casual there). *Habitat:* Prairie pools, fields, marshes, mudflats.

WHITE-RUMPED SANDPIPER
Erolia fuscicollis   7–8   pp. 93, 113

Field marks: Larger than Semipalmated Sandpiper, smaller than Pectoral. The only *small* streaked sandpiper with a *completely white rump*, conspicuous in flight. In spring it is quite rusty; in the fall, grayer than other "peeps" (small streaked sandpipers).

Similar species: Other small streaked sandpipers have only *sides* of rump white. (1) Similarly sized Baird's Sandpiper does not have the conspicuous back-stripings of this bird in spring plumage. (2) Fall Dunlin is a somewhat similar grayish bird but larger, with a much longer, more decurved bill. If in doubt, make the bird fly and *look for the white rump.*

Voice: A thin mouse-like *jeet*, of similar quality to *jee-jeet* note of Pipit. Like scraping of two flint pebbles.

Where found: Arctic America. Winters in s. South America. **Texas:** *Migrant* (Apr.–June, Aug.–Sept.) through most sections. Casual in winter on coast. *Habitat:* Prairies, shores, mudflats.

BAIRD'S SANDPIPER   *Erolia bairdii*   7–7½   pp. 93, 113

Field marks: A "peep" sandpiper, larger than Semipalmated or Western, and paler, with *buffy head and breast*, rather short bill, and blackish legs.

Similar species: The three smaller "peeps," (1) Least, (2) Semipalmated, and (3) Western, the similarly sized (4) White-rump, and larger (5) Pectoral are more or less *striped* on the back; Baird's has a more *scaly* appearance, and is predominately buff-brown. (6) Buff-breasted Sandpiper is buffy from throat to under tail-coverts, not on breast alone, and has *yellowish*, not blackish legs. (7) Do not confuse with spring and summer Sanderlings, which show much orange-buff or rusty around head and breast (Baird's has only an indistinct wing-stripe).

Voice: Note, *kreep* or *kree.*

Where found: Ne. Siberia and American Arctic. Winters in

Andes. **Texas:** *Migrant* (Apr.–May, Aug.–Oct.) in nearly all sections; most numerous in Panhandle and southward in s. Staked Plains. *Habitat:* Prairie pools, pond margins, mudflats, beaches.

LEAST SANDPIPER *Erolia minutilla* 5–6½   pp. 93, 113
  Field marks: Collectively we call the small sparrow-sized sandpipers "peeps" (Least, Semipalmated, Western, Baird's, White-rump). All have a characteristic streaked, brown pattern. The Least is the smallest. It may be known from the slightly larger Semipalmated and Western Sandpipers by its *yellowish* or *greenish*, instead of blackish legs, browner coloration, *slighter* bill, and more streaked breast. Least Sandpipers ("mud peep") prefer grassy and muddy parts of the marsh flats. Semipalmateds are often called "sand peep." This is an aid, not a rule; they often mix.
  Similar species: See above.
  Voice: A sharp thin *kree-eet*, more drawn out than that of Semipalmated (more of an *ee* sound).
  Where found: Alaska, Canada. Winters south to S. America. **Texas:** *Migrant* (Mar.–May, July–Oct.) throughout. *Winters* mainly along coast and locally inland to ne., n.-cent., and w. Texas. *Habitat:* Mudflats, grassy marshes, prairie pools, shores.

DUNLIN *Erolia alpina* 8–9
(Red-backed Sandpiper)   pp. 93, 96, 113
  Field marks: Slightly larger than Spotted Sandpiper or Sanderling. *Spring plumage:* Rusty-red back; *black patch across belly.* *Winter plumage:* Unpatterned mouse-gray above, with gray suffusion across breast (not clean white as in Sanderling); the best mark is the rather long stout bill, which has a marked *downward droop* at tip. Feeding attitude "hunched up."
  Similar species: No other Texas *sandpiper* has a black belly (but Black-bellied and Golden Plovers and Turnstone have black underparts). In fall or winter, it is grayer than Sanderling.
  Voice: A nasal, rasping *cheezp* or *treezp*.
  Where found: Arctic. Winters south to Gulf Coast, n. Africa, India. **Texas:** *Migrant* through most sections but chiefly coastal; rare in cent. and w. parts. *Winters* (Oct.–May) along coast. *Habitat:* Mudflats, margins, beaches, muddy pools.

SHORT-BILLED DOWITCHER
Limnodromus griseus 11–12   pp. 92, 112
  Field marks: Dowitchers are normally the *only snipe seen on open mudflats.* (However, some people use the term "snipe" for all shorebirds.) In any plumage dowitchers are recognized by the very long straight *snipe-like bill* and *white* lower back, rump, and tail. The white rump extends *up the back* in a long point

(much farther than in other shorebirds with white rumps). In spring plumage the breast is washed with cinnamon-red; in fall, with light gray. Dowitchers feeding suggest sewing machines: rapidly jab long bills perpendicularly into mud.

Similar species: (1) See Long-billed Dowitcher. (2) Common Snipe, the only other bird with similar proportions, is rarely found on open beaches and flats. It has a *dark* rump and tail. **Voice:** A rapid, metallic *tu-tu-tu;* lower than Greater Yellowlegs'. **Where found:** S. Alaska and Canada. Winters south to S. America. **Texas:** *Migrant and winter resident* (Aug.–May) on coast. Less common than Long-billed Dowitcher. Recorded also in n. Texas; probably occurs elsewhere in state. Status needs study. *Habitat:* Beaches, mudflats, shallow ponds.

LONG-BILLED DOWITCHER
Limnodromus scolopaceus 11–12½ pp. 92, 112

Field marks: Dowitchers of two species occur along the Texas coast. Until recently they were regarded as merely races of the same species. Bill measurements of the two overlap, but extreme long-billed birds of this species are easily recognized; the length of the bill (3 in.), by comparison, gives the bird a small-headed appearance. The rusty on the underparts of Long-bills in breeding plumage extends farther down on the belly, often to the under tail-coverts. The sides of the breast are barred rather than spotted; the back is darker, with buffy feather-edgings more restricted. Voices are quite different.

Voice: A single thin *keek*, occasionally trebled. (Short-billed Dowitcher has a trebled *tu-tu-tu*, lower in pitch.) **Where found:** Ne. Siberia, n. Alaska, and nw. Canada. Winters south to Guatemala. **Texas:** *Migrant* (Mar.–May, July–Nov.) throughout much of state. *Winters* on coast. The common dowitcher in Texas. *Habitat:* Mudflats, shallow pools, margins.

STILT SANDPIPER
Micropalama himantopus 7½–9 pp. 92, 112

Field marks: In spring, distinctive; heavily marked beneath with *transverse bars*. Has *rusty cheek-patch*. In fall, not so obvious, gray above, white below; dark-winged and white-rumped (see below). Bill long, tapering; slight droop at tip.

Similar species: (1) Suggests Dowitcher, particularly in fall. Is often found in its company and feeds like it (with rapid perpendicular chopping motion of head and bill) and, like it, often wades up to its belly and submerges its head. Its whiter underparts, shorter bill and longer legs distinguish it. (2) Its flight pattern on the other hand, is like a Lesser Yellowlegs' (dark wings, white rump), but it is smaller, with a white stripe over the eye and *greenish*, not yellow, legs. **Voice:** A single *whu*, like Lesser Yellowlegs; lower, hoarser.

Where found: American Arctic. Winters in S. America. **Texas:** *Migrant* (Apr.–June, July–Oct.) throughout. *Winters* occasionally on coast. *Habitat:* Shallow pools, mudflats, margins.

SEMIPALMATED SANDPIPER

Ereunetes pusillus 5½–6½ pp. 93, 113

Field marks: One of the three common small "peeps." Compared to the Least, it has a *stouter, straighter bill;* usually has *blackish* legs. It is also noticeably larger, grayer above, less streaked on breast (particularly in fall).

Similar species: (1) Least Sandpiper is smaller, browner, thinner-billed, has yellowish legs. (2) See Western Sandpiper.

Voice: Commonest note a simple *cherk* or *cher*. Also *crip*. Less thin and sharp than notes of other "peep."

Where found: American Arctic. Winters s. U.S. south to S. America. **Texas:** *Migrant* (Mar.–May, July–Oct.) through most sections. *Winters* along coast. *Habitat:* Beaches, shores, sandy islands, mudflats.

WESTERN SANDPIPER *Ereunetes mauri* 6–7 pp. 93, 113

Field marks: Hard to distinguish from Semipalmated Sandpiper. It appears a little larger and more coarsely marked. In typical birds the bill is *noticeably longer, thicker at base*, and often droops slightly at tip (profile is more attenuated; that of Semi suggests a ball with a short stick in it). In breeding plumage, rustier on back and crown than Semipalmated. A trace of rusty is often on scapulars in fall, giving a two-toned effect — *rusty against gray.* Many individuals are pale-headed. Legs black;

TYPICAL BILLS
OF "PEEP"

Least

Semipalmated

Western

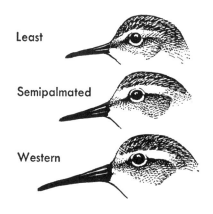

hence no real confusion with smaller Least Sandpiper. Frequently forages in deeper water than other "peep."

Voice: A thin *jeet* or *jee-rp*, thinner than note of Semipalmated — more like squeak of White-rump.

Where found: Coasts of w. and n. Alaska. Winters s. U.S. to S. America. **Texas:** *Migrant* (Mar.–May, Aug.–Nov.) throughout. *Winters* mainly along coast; also in w. Texas. *Habitat:* Shores, mudflats, muddy pools.

BUFF-BREASTED SANDPIPER

Tryngites subruficollis 7½–8½   pp. 93, 113

Field marks: A small, tame buffy shorebird with short bill, light eye-ring, yellowish legs. Looks long-necked, small-headed, like a miniature Upland Plover, and like that bird frequents fields. No other small sandpiper is so evenly buff below (to under tail-coverts). In flight, the buff body contrasts with the underwing, which is *white* with a marbled tip. In spring "display," frequently raises wings, showing white linings.

Similar species: Baird's Sandpiper is buffy only across breast; throat and belly are white; legs are *black*.

Voice: A low, trilled *pr-r-r-reet* (Wetmore). A sharp *tik*.

Where found: American Arctic. Winters in Argentina. **Texas:** *Migrant* (Apr.–May, Aug.–Oct.) in e., cent., and n. Texas; most frequent along coast (especially Rockport). Occasional west to Midland. *Habitat:* Short-grass prairies, fields.

MARBLED GODWIT *Limosa fedoa* 16–20   pp. 84, 97

Field marks: Godwits are large shorebirds with very long, straight or perceptibly *upturned bills*. The rich, mottled *buff-brown* color identifies this species. Wing-linings cinnamon.

Similar species: (1) The bills of curlews turn *down*. (2) Hudsonian Godwit has white in wings and tail.

Voice: An accented *kerrek'* or *terwhit'* (or *godwit'*).

Where found: N. Great Plains. Winters s. U.S. to S. America. **Texas:** *Migrates and winters* (Aug.–May) along coast; rare migrant elsewhere (west to El Paso, north to Panhandle). *Habitat:* Prairies, pools, shores, tidal flats.

HUDSONIAN GODWIT

Limosa haemastica 14–16½   pp. 84, 97

Field marks: The large size (larger than Greater Yellowlegs) and long, straight, or slightly *upturned* bill distinguish this bird as a godwit; the black tail, *ringed broadly with white* at the base, and a white wing-stripe, proclaim it this species. In breeding plumage it is dark reddish-breasted (looks almost black at a distance). In fall, gray-backed, whitish-breasted. Overhead, shows distinctive *blackish underwings*.

Similar species: Marbled Godwit is at all times mottled buffy brown, without wing or tail pattern. Hudsonian Godwit is more likely to suggest a very long-billed Willet.

Voice: "A low *qua qua*" (Wetmore); "a low *ta-it*" (Rowan).

Where found: Arctic America. Winters s. S. America. **Texas:** *Migrant* (Apr.–June, Aug.–Sept.) along coast and in Panhandle and Staked Plains; casual elsewhere. Most frequent in spring. *Habitat:* Ricefields, mudflats, marshes, prairie pools.

SANDERLING *Crocethia alba* 7–8½   pp. 92, 113
    Field marks: Slightly larger than a Spotted Sandpiper. A plump, active sandpiper of the outer beaches, where it chases the retreating waves "like a clockwork toy." It has a *flashing white wing-stripe;* in no other small shorebird does the wing-stripe contrast so boldly or extend so far. Bill and legs stout for a sandpiper; black. In breeding plumage, bright rusty gold about head, back, and breast. In fall and winter the *palest of the sandpipers;* snowy white below; shows a *dark "shoulder."*
    Similar species: Winter Dunlin is darker, has longer bill.
    Voice: A short *twick* or *quit*, distinctive.
    Where found: Arctic. Winters south to S. Hemisphere. **Texas:** *Migrant* (Apr.–June, July–Nov.) locally throughout; west rarely to Panhandle and El Paso; common only on coast, where it *winters. Habitat:* Sandy beaches, tidal flats.

Avocets and Stilts: Recurvirostridae

SLENDER wading birds with very long legs and very slender awl-like bills (bent upward in avocets). Food: Insects, crustaceans, brine shrimp; other small aquatic life. Nearly cosmopolitan. No. of species: World, 7; N. America, 2; Texas, 2.

AMERICAN AVOCET
Recurvirostra americana 16–20   pp. 84, 97
    Field marks: A very large shorebird with a slender *upturned,* somewhat godwit-like bill. This and the striking white and black pattern make it unique. In breeding season the head and neck are pinkish tan; in winter this is replaced with pale gray. Feeds with scythe-like motion of head and bill.
    Voice: A sharp *wheek* or *kleek*, excitedly repeated.
    Where found: Sw. Canada, w. U.S. Winters s. U.S. to Guatemala. **Texas:** *Migrant* (Mar.–May, July–Oct.) throughout. *Winters* along coast. *Breeds* locally in Panhandle, w. Texas and along lower coast (sparingly north to Galveston). *Habitat:* Beaches, flats, shallow lakes, lagoons, prairie ponds. **Nest:** A depression on ground on open dry mudflat; in time of high water may be built up off mud. Eggs (4) buff, spotted.

BLACK-NECKED STILT

Himantopus mexicanus 13½–15½   pp. 84, 97

Field marks: A large, slim wader; black above, white below, with *grotesquely long red legs*. In flight it has black *unpatterned* wings, white rump and underparts, pale tail.

Voice: A sharp yipping, *kyip, kyip, kyip*.

Where found: W. U.S. and Gulf States south to n. S. America. Winters mostly south of U.S. **Texas:** *Summers* (Mar.–Nov.) along coast; locally inland in s. part of state (north to San Antonio); also in w. Texas (San Angelo to El Paso). *Migrant* in Panhandle and very rarely in n. and cent. sections. *Winters* in Rio Grande delta; occasionally elsewhere along coast. *Habitat:* Ricefields, grassy marshes, mudflats, shallow lakes, pools. **Nest:** A scrape on dry mudflat (may be built up during high water), or on hummock in pond or marsh. Eggs (3–4) buff, spotted.

Phalaropes: Phalaropodidae

SMALL sandpiper-like birds with longer necks than most small waders; equally at home wading or swimming. Feet have lobed ("scalloped") toes. When feeding they often spin like tops, rapidly dabbing their thin bills into the roiled water. Females larger and brighter than males. Two species, Northern and Red, are mostly oceanic in migration and rarely visit Texas. Food: Plankton, marine invertebrates, brine shrimp, mosquito larvae, insects, etc. Breed in Arctic and N. American plains; migrate to S. Hemisphere. No. of species: World, 3; N. America, 3; Texas, 3.

RED PHALAROPE

Phalaropus fulicarius 7½–9   pp. 92, 96, 113

Field marks: The swimming habits (suggesting a tiny gull) distinguish it as a phalarope; in breeding plumage (seldom seen), deep *reddish underparts* and *white face* designate it this species. Male is duller but has basic pattern. In fall and winter, blue-gray above, white below; resembles Sanderling but has characteristic "*phalarope-mark*" through eye. At close range, relatively short bill, yellowish toward base, will identify adults (young birds may lack yellow).

Similar species: In winter plumage, Northern Phalarope is very similar but a bit smaller, darker, with a streaked back. Its white wing-stripe contrasts more with rest of wing. Northern has a more *needle-like* black bill.

Voice: Similar to Northern Phalarope's: *whit* or *prip*.

Where found: Arctic. Winters at sea in S. Hemisphere. **Texas:**

Casual. Recorded in n. Texas (Decatur, 2 records, 1895; also Hunt Co.), Panhandle (Armstrong Co.), e. coast (Cove), cent. coast (Rockport), and Rio Grande delta.

WILSON'S PHALAROPE
Steganopus tricolor 8½–10 pp. 92, 96, 112

Field marks: This dainty phalarope is dark-winged (no wing-stripe) with a white rump. In breeding females the broad face and neck-stripe of *black blending into cinnamon* is unique. Males are duller with just a wash of cinnamon on neck and a white spot on hind neck. *Fall plumage:* See below. Swimming and spinning (less often indulged in than by other phalaropes) is conclusive. Most often seen running nervously along margin. **Similar species:** (1) Suggests a Lesser Yellowlegs (dark wings, white rump), particularly in fall. At that season, immaculately white below, with *no breast-streaking;* has a needle-like bill, and greenish or straw-colored (not canary-yellow) legs. Yellowlegs occasionally swim but do not spin and dab. (2) Other phalaropes are shorter-billed, have wing-stripes.
Voice: A grunting note; also a low nasal *wurk.*
Where found: Sw. Canada and w. U.S. Winters in s. S. America. **Texas:** *Migrant* (Apr.–June, July–Oct.) throughout. *Habitat:* Shallow lakes, pools, shores, mudflats.

NORTHERN PHALAROPE
Lobipes lobatus 6½–8 pp. 92, 96, 113

Field marks: Should a "Sanderling" alight upon the water, then it is a phalarope. Breeding females are gray above with a patch of *rufous on the side of the neck* and a white throat. Males are browner, with a similar pattern. In winter plumage both are gray above and white below, with a dark "phalarope-patch" through the eye, needle-like bill.
Similar species: See Red Phalarope.
Voice: A sharp *kit*, or *whit*, similar to note of Sanderling.
Where found: Arctic. Winters at sea in S. Hemisphere. **Texas:** Apparently regular *migrant* in plains of Panhandle south to Midland. Casual elsewhere but recorded from Tyler, Fort Worth, Aransas Refuge (several), Rockport, Rio Grande delta, El Paso. *Habitat:* Open sea, lakes; occasionally pools, shores.

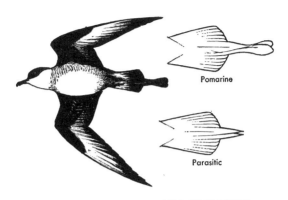

POMARINE JAEGER AND TAILS OF JAEGERS

Jaegers: Stercorariidae

DARK, falcon-like sea birds with narrow, angled wings. Central tail feathers usually elongated, but often broken short. Light, intermediate, and dark-breasted phases, but all show a *flash of white* in wing created by white wing-quills. Juveniles lack tail projections and various species are usually indistinguishable in the field. Piratical, chasing gulls, terns until they disgorge. Food: In Arctic, lemmings, eggs, young birds. At sea, food taken from other birds or from the sea. Seas and coasts of world, breeding near polar regions. No. of species: World, 4; N. America, 4; Texas, 1 (plus 1 accidental).

POMARINE JAEGER   *Stercorarius pomarinus*   20–23
   Field marks: See discussion above. In this species the two long feathers projecting beyond the square-cut tail are *broad and twisted* (in Parasitic Jaeger they are shorter, pointed). Young birds lacking elongated feathers may not be separated with certainty except possibly by size and heavier bill.
   Similar species: See Parasitic Jaeger (p. 270).
   Voice: A harsh, quick *which-you.*
   Where found: Arctic. Winters at sea to S. Hemisphere. **Texas:** Casual straggler to coast; most records in June. Recorded Bolivar Peninsula (3 records), Matagorda I., Archer Co., Loma Alta Lake. Perhaps a regular transient on waters of continental shelf. *Habitat:* Open sea, coastal waters.

Gulls and Terns: Laridae

Gulls: Larinae

LONG-WINGED swimming birds with superb flight. More robust, wider-winged, longer-legged than terns. Bills slightly hooked. They have square or rounded tails; terns, forked. They seldom dive, whereas terns hover above the water, then plunge into it. In gull terminology the word *mantle* means the upper surface of the wings and the broad strip of back separating them. In identifying adult gulls notice particularly (1) feet, (2) bills, and (3) wing-tips. Immature birds are more difficult. Food: Miscellaneous; marine life, plant and animal food, refuse, carrion. Nearly cosmopolitan, favoring coasts. No. of species: World, 43; N. America, 23; Texas, 6 (plus 5 accidentals).

HERRING GULL   *Larus argentatus* 23–26   p. 12
   Field marks: The *large* "seagull." *Adult:* A big gray-mantled gull with *flesh-colored legs.* Wing-tips black with white spots; heavy yellow bill with red spot. *First year:* The common large dusky-brown gull; uniform dark coloration. *Second year:* Whiter. Tail feathers dark, contrasting with whitish rump.
   Similar species: (1) See Ring-billed Gull. (2) Young Laughing Gull is smaller than young Herring; darker with white rump.
   Voice: A loud *kee-ow, kee-ow;* also mewing, squealing notes. A dry *gah-gah-gah* about colonies; *yuk-yuk-yuk-yuckle-yuckle.*
   Where found: Cooler parts of N. Hemisphere. Winters to Cent. America, Africa, India.   **Texas:** *Winters* (Oct.–Apr.) along coast; some non-breeders in summer. Also migrates and winters on large inland waters; west to Panhandle; casual s. Staked Plains. *Habitat:* Beaches, lakes, bays, Gulf, dumps, piers, etc.

CALIFORNIA GULL   *Larus californicus* 20–23   p. 12
   Field marks: *Adult:* Resembles the smaller Ring-billed Gull, which also has *greenish* legs. This species has a *red* or *red and black spot* on the lower mandible, not complete black ring as in Ring-bill. Shows more white in wing-tips. The black on the under wing-tip of the adult is cut straight across "as if dipped in ink." *Young birds* though decidedly smaller than Herring Gull and with similar plumage (without narrow tailband of Ring-bill) are probably not safely identified in the field in Texas.
   Voice: A high-pitched *kyarr;* typical gull vocabulary.
   Where found: W. Canada and nw. U.S. Winters to Guatemala. **Texas:** Rare or casual *winter visitor* (Oct.–May) along coast (regular at Rockport). *Habitat:* Beaches, buoys, bays.

SHOREBIRDS

AMERICAN WOODCOCK   p. 95
Chunky; long bill, barred crown.

COMMON (WILSON'S) SNIPE   p. 95
Long bill, striped crown.

DOWITCHER   pp. 103, 104
Spring: Snipe bill, rusty breast.
Fall: Snipe bill, gray breast.
For distinctions between the two species, **Long-billed Dowitcher** and **Short-billed Dowitcher**, see text.

CURLEW SANDPIPER   p. 270
Accidental in Texas.
Spring: Decurved bill, rufous breast.

KNOT   p. 101
Spring: Chunky; short bill, rusty breast.

STILT SANDPIPER   p. 104
Spring: Barred breast, rusty ear-patch.
Fall: Long greenish legs, white rump, eye-line (see text).

RUFF   p. 270
Accidental in Texas. See text.

WILSON'S PHALAROPE   p. 109
Fall: Needle bill, white breast. See text.

SOLITARY SANDPIPER   p. 100
Dark back, whitish eye-ring, dark legs.

LESSER YELLOWLEGS   p. 101
Yellow legs, slim bill.
Call, a 1- or 2-syllabled *yew* or *you-you.*

GREATER YELLOWLEGS   p. 100
Yellow legs, larger bill.
Call, a clear, 3-syllabled *whew-whew-whew.*

WILLET   p. 100
Gray color, stocky bill, dark legs.

COMMON
SNIPE

Fall

DOWITCHER

Spring

AMERICAN
WOODCOCK

Spring

CURLEW   SANDPIPER

Spring

KNOT

Spring

STILT   SANDPIPER

RUFF

Fall

Fall

WILSON'S
PHALAROPE

Fall

STILT   SANDPIPER

Fall

WILLET

GREATER YELLOWLEGS

SOLITARY
SANDPIPER

LESSER YELLOWLEGS

RED PHALAROPE
Fall

SPOTTED S.
Fall
Spring

PURPLE S.
Winter

NORTHERN PHALAROPE
Fall

DUNLIN
Fall

CURLEW S.
Fall

SANDERLING
Fall

KNOT
Fall

SANDERLING
Spring

WHITE-RUMPED S.
Fall

PECTORAL S.

BUFF-BREASTED S.

WHITE-RUMPED S.
Spring

LEAST S.

BAIRD'S S.

WESTERN S.
Fall

SEMIPALMATED S.
Fall

Plate 32   113

SHOREBIRDS

RING-BILLED GULL *Larus delawarensis* 18–20 p. 12
Field marks: *Adult:* Similar in pattern to Herring Gull; distinguished by smaller size, *black ring* encircling bill, and *yellowish* or *greenish* legs. It is more buoyant and dove-like and shows much more black on *underside* of primaries. *Immature:* Often confused with second-year Herring Gull, which has semblance of ring on tip of its longer bill. Ring-bill's tailband is narrower (a little over 1 in. wide). Leg color is not useful since most young Ring-bills have pinkish or flesh-gray legs.
Similar species: Adult Herring Gull is larger, has flesh-colored legs. In second-year Herring Gull tail terminates in *broad* band (tail feathers dark, contrasting with whitish rump).
Voice: Notes higher-pitched than Herring Gull's.
Where found: Canada, n. U.S. Winters to Mexico, Cuba.
Texas: *Migrates and winters* (Aug.–May) through most sections; casual west of Pecos except at El Paso. Non-breeders summer along coast. *Habitat:* Lakes, bays, Gulf, piers, dumps, plowed fields, etc.

LAUGHING GULL *Larus atricilla* 15½–17 p. 12
Field marks: This strictly coastal gull is a little smaller than the Ring-billed. Distinguished from other small gulls by a *dark mantle* that *blends* into black wing-tips, and a conspicuous white border along trailing edge of wing. In breeding season, *head is blackish;* in winter, white with dark markings. Bill and legs deep red to blackish. The young bird is very dark with a *white rump.* The white border on the rear edge of the wing, the dark breast, and blackish legs are also good marks.
Similar species: On Texas coast can be confused with migrant Franklin's Gull and possibly Bonaparte's. See those species.
Voice: A strident, hysterical *ha-ha-ha-ha-ha-haah-haah-haah;* also *haa-haa-haa* and an abbreviated *ka-ha.*
Where found: Coast from Nova Scotia south to Yucatan, Venezuela; locally in se. California, w. Mexico. Migrant from n. coast. **Texas:** *Resident* on coast. Casual inland; recorded San Antonio, Austin, Dallas, Gainesville, Brewster Co. *Habitat:* Coastal bays, salt marshes, Gulf. **Nest:** A bulky platform of grass in salt marsh or on island; in colony. Eggs (3) spotted.

FRANKLIN'S GULL *Larus pipixcan* 13½–15 p. 12
Field marks: The "Prairie Dove." The best mark is the *white band* separating the black wing-tips from the gray. Overhead, this irregular band is like a "window" transmitting light. In summer the breast has a pale rosy "bloom" (hard to see); the head is black. In fall and winter the head is white, with a dark patch extending from eye around nape. Young birds are small *dark-mantled* gulls with whitish underparts, *white rump*, dark

tailband, and a dusky smudge around back of head.

Similar species: (1) Adult Laughing Gull has dark, *blended* wing-tips; ordinarily, Franklin's and Laughing Gulls come in contact only along the coast (during Franklin's migration). Second-winter Laughing Gulls are so similar to young Franklin's that I do not regard it safe to distinguish them. First-year Laughing Gulls with brown breasts, brown foreheads can be distinguished, however. (2) Inland, the only other black-headed gull is the migrant Bonaparte's. Bonaparte's has a *long triangle of white* on the leading edge of the wing. (3) Ring-billed Gull has *white spots* or "mirrors" within black wing-tips, and pale legs (Franklin's, dark); does not have black head.

Voice: A shrill *kuk-kuk-kuk;* also mewing, laughing cries.

Where found: Prairies of w. Canada and nw. and n.-cent. U.S. Winters mainly Guatemala to Chile. **Texas:** *Migrant* (Mar.–June, Sept.–Dec.) throughout most of state, sometimes in large flocks. Rare in Trans-Pecos. *Habitat:* Prairies.

BONAPARTE'S GULL *Larus philadelphia* 12–14   p. 12
Field marks: The smallest native American gull. Near size of most terns; often acts like one. Identified in flight by a long triangle of white on the leading edge of the wing. In breeding plumage has a blackish head. Legs bright red; bill small, black. In young birds and winter adults the head is white with a conspicuous black spot behind the eye. Immatures have a narrow black band on the tip of the tail.

Voice: A nasal *cheer* or *cherr.*

Where found: Alaska, w. Canada. Winters south to Gulf of Mexico, West Indies. **Texas:** Rare *migrant* in Panhandle, w., n., and e. Texas and along coast. *Winters* (Oct.–Apr.) irregularly on coast. *Habitat:* Lakes, reservoirs, bays, Gulf.

Terns: Sterninae

GULL-LIKE water birds, more streamlined, more maneuverable than gulls. The bill is more slender and sharp-pointed, usually held pointed toward the water. Tail usually forked. Most terns are whitish, with black caps. In winter this cap is imperfect, the black of the forehead being replaced by white. Terns often hover and plunge headfirst into the water. They do not normally swim (gulls do). Food: Small fish (non-game), marine life, large insects. Cosmopolitan. No. of species: World, 39; N. America, 17; Texas, 10 (plus 2 accidentals).

GULL-BILLED TERN

Gelochelidon nilotica   13–14½   pp. 13, 20

Field marks: The stout, almost gull-like *black* bill is the best field mark. Larger and paler than Common or Forster's Tern; tail much less forked; feet black. In winter the black cap is lost, the head is nearly white. Young bird with a short stubby bill looks like a very small gull but has a slightly notched tail. Hawks for insects over land; seldom plunges into water.

Similar species: Sandwich Tern has longer bill, more forked tail.

Voice: A throaty rasping, *za-za-za;* also *kay-weck, kayweck.*

Where found: Breeds locally and wanders widely in many parts of world. **Texas:** *Resident* along coast; breeds locally. Accidental away from coast. *Habitat:* Salt marshes, fields, coastal bays. **Nest:** A scrape, sometimes lined, on sandy or marshy island; in scattered colony. Eggs (2–3) spotted.

FORSTER'S TERN *Sterna forsteri*   14–15   pp. 13, 20

Field marks: This is the small black-capped gull-like bird with the red bill which is so familiar along the coast. *Adult in breeding plumage:* White, with pale gray mantle and tail and a *black cap;* bill *orange-red* with black tip; feet orange-red; tail deeply forked. *Fall and winter plumage:* Similar, but without black cap; instead, a heavy black spot, like an ear cap, on side of head. Feet yellower in some birds; bill blackish.

Similar species: From above, primaries of adult Common Tern are *dusky* (darker than rest of wing); Forster's are *silvery* (lighter than rest of wing). Tail of Common is whiter, contrasting more with back. Bill of Forster's is more orange, less red. In fall, Common Tern has a dark patch around back of head. (Forster's has ear-patch only.) Young Common Tern has dusky patch on forepart of wing (absent in Forster's). Voices quite different.

Voice: A low nasal *za-a-ap* or *kyarr.* Also *kit, kit, kit,* etc.

Where found: W. Canada south to n. Tamaulipas. Winters to Guatemala, Gulf Coast. **Texas:** *Resident* along coast, breeding locally. Uncommon or rare *migrant* inland to n. Texas. Very local in cent. and w. Texas. *Habitat:* Salt marshes, bays, beaches, Gulf; sometimes lakes, rivers. **Nest:** Lined with grass; on salt marsh or marshy island; in colony. Eggs (3–4) buff, spotted.

COMMON TERN *Sterna hirundo*   13–16   pp. 13, 20

Field marks: *Adult in breeding plumage:* White, with light gray mantle and black cap; bill orange-red with black tip; feet orange-red; tail deeply forked. *Immature and winter adult:* Black cap incomplete; instead, a black patch extending from eye around the back of the head. The red bill becomes mostly blackish.

Similar species: See Forster's Tern. Also Roseate Tern.

Voice: A drawling angry *kee-arr* (downward inflection); higher than Forster's hoarse note. Also *kik-kik-kik.*

Where found: Temperate Zone of N. Hemisphere. Winters south to S. Hemisphere. **Texas:** *Migrant* along coast; perhaps inland rarely. *Winters* sparingly along lower coast. Said to have bred very locally from Point Isabel to Galveston (Bird I.). *Habitat:* Beaches, bays, Gulf, lakes. **Nest:** In scrape on sandy island; in colony. Eggs (2–4) spotted.

ROSEATE TERN   *Sterna dougallii*   14–17   pp. 13, 20
Field marks: A rarity, about size of Forster's Tern. *Adult:* White, with a very pale gray mantle, black cap, *black or largely black bill* and red feet; tail *very deeply* forked.
Similar species: The blackish bill sets it apart from Common and Forster's Terns except in fall and winter. Many Roseates have some red at base of bill. Roseate appears even whiter than Forster's (tail is pure white; Forster's, light gray). At rest, the outer tail feathers extend far beyond the wing-tips.
Voice: A rasping *ka-a-ak;* a 2-syllabled *chu-ick* or *cheery.*
Where found: Breeds locally and wanders widely along coasts of Atlantic, Pacific, and Indian Oceans. **Texas:** Very rare or casual transient along coast.

SOOTY TERN   *Sterna fuscata*   15–17   p. 13
Field marks: *The only tern that is black above, white below;* black cap with white forehead; black bill and feet. *Immature:* Dark sooty, above and below; back and wings flecked with white.
Similar species: (1) Black Tern in breeding plumage has black body, gray wings. (2) See Black Skimmer (p 119).
Voice: A nasal *wide-a-wake* or *ker-wacky-wack.*
Where found: Tropical oceans; occasionally blown inland by hurricanes. **Texas:** Formerly bred on coast (Aransas Co., etc.) and still does occasionally. *Breeds* singly or in very small groups with Royal Terns. *Habitat:* Gulf. **Nest:** A scrape on bare ground on sandy coastal island. Eggs (1) spotted.

LEAST TERN   *Sterna albifrons*   8½–9½   pp. 13, 20
Field marks: A *very small* tern with a *yellow* bill. *Adult:* White, with pale gray mantle; white patch on forehead, cutting into black cap; bill and feet *yellow.* *Immature:* Bill darker; dark patch from eye around back of head; large dark area on fore edge of wing. In fall both adults and young have black bills but legs still show some yellow (quite dull). Has quicker wingbeats than other terns; hovers more.
Similar species: (1) Fall Black Tern is larger, darker above, with dark tail. (2) Young Forster's Terns, with rather short tails and yellowish legs, might possibly be mistaken for Least Terns, but are larger and lack dark areas on wings.
Voice: A sharp repeated *kit;* a harsh squealing *zree-eek* or *zeek;* also a rapid *kitti-kitti-kitti.*

Where found: Almost world-wide; local as a breeder. Winters south of U.S. **Texas:** *Summers* (Mar.–Nov.) along coast and very locally in Red River system in n. Texas. Casual transient in cent. Texas and Trans-Pecos. *Habitat:* Beaches, bays, Gulf, lakes, rivers. **Nest:** In scrape on sandy island, beach, or gravel bar; in scattered colony. Eggs (2–3) buff, speckled.

ROYAL TERN *Thalasseus maximus* 18–21   pp. 13, 20
    Field marks: A large tern, near size of Ring-billed Gull, with a large *orange* or *yellow-orange* bill. Tail deeply forked. Although some Royal Terns in spring show a solid black cap, they usually (even in nesting season) have much white on the forehead, the black head feathers forming a sort of bushy crest — standing out from the back of the head.
    Similar species: See Caspian Tern.
    Voice: *Keer,* higher than Caspian's note; also *kaak* or *kak.*
    Where found: Coasts of se. U.S., nw. Mexico, West Indies, and w. Africa. Winters s. U.S. to S. America. **Texas:** *Resident* along coast, breeding locally. *Habitat:* Strictly coastal. **Nest:** Single spotted egg is laid in scrape on bare sand, in dense colonies on islands.

SANDWICH TERN *Thalasseus sandvicensis* 14–16
(Cabot's Tern)   pp. 13, 20
    Field marks: The long black bill with its *yellow tip* identifies the Sandwich Tern. Slightly larger and more slender than Forster's Tern; white with a pale gray mantle and black cap (white forehead acquired during nesting season). Feathers on back of crown elongated, giving a crested appearance; feet black. In young birds, yellow bill-tip is often obscure. Prefers company of Royal Terns.
    Similar species: See Gull-billed Tern.
    Voice: A grating *kirr-ick* (higher than Gull-bill's *kay-weck*).
    Where found: Virginia south to Gulf of Mexico; also Europe. Winters to S. America. **Texas:** *Summers* (Mar.–Sept.) along cent. and lower coast, breeding very locally in small groups often with Royal Terns. Less frequent on upper coast. *Habitat:* Coastal waters, jetties, Gulf. **Nest:** On bare sand on sandy island; in colony. Eggs (1–2) spotted.

CASPIAN TERN *Hydroprogne caspia* 19–23   pp. 13, 20
    Field marks: Almost size of Herring Gull. Distinguished by its black cap, *large red bill,* moderately forked tail.
    Similar species: The great size and large bill set the Caspian apart from all other terns except the slimmer Royal. The Caspian sometimes occurs inland; the Royal never does. Tail of Caspian is forked for only quarter of its length (Royal for fully half). At rest, wings of Caspian extend beyond tail-tip.

Bill of Royal is more slender, *orange* rather than red. Royal has a more *crested* look and usually has a *clear white* forehead; Caspian, even in winter plumage, has a clouded, streaked forehead. Adult Caspians show *much more black* on underside of primaries.

Voice: A hoarse, low *kraa-uh* or *karr;* also repeated *kak*'s.

Where found: Breeds locally, wanders widely around world. **Texas:** *Resident* along coast, breeding locally. Rare *transient* inland to n. Texas, Panhandle. *Habitat:* Coastal waters, lakes.

Nest: In scrape, on sandy island, in colony. Eggs (2–3) spotted.

BLACK TERN *Chlidonias niger* 9–10 pp. 13, 20
Field marks: The only *black-bodied tern. Breeding plumage:* Head and underparts black; back and wings gray; under tail-coverts white. *Immature and autumn:* Head and underparts white; back and wings gray; dark about eye, ear, and back of head; dark patch on side of breast. Mottled changing birds appear in midsummer. Short tail and swooping wingbeats are good points.

Similar species: In fall, more graceful flight, grayer look, small size, and only slightly notched tail distinguish it from Forster's and Common Tern. See Least Tern.

Voice: A sharp *kik, keek,* or *klea.*

Where found: Temperate N. America, Eurasia. Winters south to S. Hemisphere. **Texas:** *Migrant* (Apr.–June, July–Nov.) through most parts. Occasional in winter on coast. *Habitat:* Fresh marshes, lakes, coastal waters.

Skimmers: Rynchopidae

SLIM, short-legged relatives of the gulls and terns; possessing a knife-like red bill with a jutting lower mandible. Food: Small fish, crustaceans. Coasts and rivers of warmer parts of world. No. of species: World, 3; N. America, 1; Texas, 1.

BLACK SKIMMER *Rynchops nigra* 16–20 p. 12
Field marks: The unequal scissor-like bill sets the Skimmer apart. Black above and white below, it is more slender than Ring-billed Gull, with extremely long wings. The bright red bill (tipped with black) is long and flat vertically; the lower mandible juts a third beyond the upper. Young birds are smaller, brownish, streaked, smaller-billed. This coastal species skims low, dipping its lower mandible in the water, knife-like.

Voice: Soft, short, barking notes. Also *kaup, kaup.*

Where found: Massachusetts to Strait of Magellan. Winters from Gulf of Mexico south. **Texas:** *Resident* locally along

coast, occasionally wanders inland a short distance; casual
cent. and n. Texas. *Habitat:* Beaches, salt bays, tidewater.
Nest: In scrape on beach or island; in colony. Eggs (3–4) spotted.

Pigeons and Doves: Columbidae

PLUMP, fast-flying birds with small heads and low crooning voices.
The terms "pigeon" and "dove" are loosely used, but in a general
way "pigeon" refers to the larger species, "dove" to the smaller
ones. Two types occur in Texas; those with fanlike tails (Domestic
Pigeon is the most familiar), and the smaller, brownish type with
rounded or pointed tails (Mourning Dove is characteristic).
Food: Seeds, waste grain, fruits, insects. Nearly cosmopolitan.
No. of species: World, 289; N. America, 15; Texas, 8 (plus 1
accidental).

BAND-TAILED PIGEON　*Columba fasciata*　15½　　　　p. 132
　　Field marks: A heavily built pigeon, with a broad slightly
　　rounded tail. Might be mistaken for Rock Dove (Domestic
　　Pigeon), except for its woodland or mountain habitat and
　　tendency to alight in trees. A pale broad band crosses the end
　　of the tail. At close range, a white crescent is visible on the nape.
　　Legs *yellow.* Bill yellow with dark tip.
　　Similar species: Rock Dove (Domestic Pigeon) has white rump
　　and *black band* across end of tail. Feet *red.* Seldom sits in trees.
　　Voice: A hollow owl-like *oo-whoo* or *whoo-oo-whoo*, repeated.
　　Where found: British Columbia south to Cent. America.
　　Texas: *Resident* locally in mts. of Trans-Pecos (5000–8700 ft.);
　　in *winter* descends to lower levels, more widespread (rarely to
　　Panhandle). *Habitat:* Oak canyons, mt. forests. **Nest:** A flimsy
　　stick platform on horizontal branch. Eggs (1) white.

RED-BILLED PIGEON　*Columba flavirostris*　13　　　　p. 132
　　Field marks: A rather large dark pigeon, with a broad fanlike
　　tail, small red bill. In favorable light shows much deep maroon
　　on foreparts. Distinguished from all other pigeons in the lower
　　Valley by its size and uniform dark appearance.
　　Voice: Cooing similar in quality to that of White-winged Dove
　　but more drawn out: *who who wooooooo*, the long note almost
　　rising to a wail. "Song" of male, "*Ooooooo, up-cup-a-coo,
　　up-cup-a-coo, up-cup-a-coo*" (G. M. Sutton).
　　Where found: S. Texas south to Costa Rica. **Texas:** *Resident*
　　in lower Rio Grande Valley, upriver to Falcon Dam (formerly
　　Eagle Pass); north near coast to Norias. Mostly migratory; rare
　　in winter. *Habitat:* River woodlands, tall brush. **Nest:** A flimsy
　　platform in thicket or low dense tree. Eggs (1) white.

ROCK DOVE or DOMESTIC PIGEON
Columba livia 13 p. 132
Field marks: Feral; in places as self-sustaining as House Sparrow. Typical birds are gray with a *white rump*, two black bars on secondaries and a broad black band at end of tail. Feet red. Domestic birds range from gray to white, tan, blackish varieties.
Voice: Indistinguishable from domestic bird's *oo-roo-coo.*
Where found: Old World origin; now world-wide. **Texas:** Sustains self in wild state about many cities. *Habitat:* Cities, towns.
Nest: Usually on building. Eggs (2) white.

WHITE-WINGED DOVE *Zenaida asiatica* 11–12½ p. 132
Field marks: Like Mourning Dove but heavier; tail *rounded*, tipped with broad white corners. The only dove with a large *white patch* on the wing.
Voice: A harsh cooing, *coo-uh-cuck'-oo;* also, *who cooks for you?* Sounds vaguely like crowing of young rooster.
Where found: Sw. U.S. south to n. Chile. Winters mostly in Cent. America. **Texas:** *Summers* (a few winter) in s. Texas (north to Uvalde, San Antonio, Beeville) and along Rio Grande to El Paso. Casual north to Edwards Plateau, upper coast. Accidental in Panhandle. Nests singly or in colonies. *Habitat:* Woodlands, mesquite, citrus groves, towns. **Nest:** A flimsy twig platform in shade tree, thicket, mesquite. Eggs (2) pale buff.

MOURNING DOVE *Zenaidura macroura* 11–13 p. 132
Field marks: The most widespread wild dove in Texas. A *brown* dove, smaller and slimmer than Domestic Pigeon, with a *pointed*, not rounded, tail bordered with large white spots.
Similar species: White-winged Dove has rounded tail and white wing-patches.
Voice: A hollow mournful *ooah, cooo, cooo, coo.* At a distance only the three *coo*'s are audible.
Where found: Alaska, s. Canada throughout U.S., most of Mexico to Panama. Migratory in north. **Texas:** *Resident* throughout; withdraws somewhat from Panhandle in winter. *Habitat:* Farmlands, ranches, towns, mesquite, woodlands, open country, desert. **Nest:** A flimsy platform of twigs in tree, shrub, cactus, or on ground. Eggs (2) white.

GROUND DOVE *Columbigallina passerina* 6¾ p. 132
Field marks: A very small dove, *not much larger than a sparrow* with a *stubby black tail* and round wings that flash *rufous* in flight. It nods its head as it walks. Feet yellow.
Similar species: See Inca Dove.
Voice: A soft *woo-oo, woo-oo, woo-oo,* repeated monotonously. In distance sounds monosyllabic, *wooo,* with rising inflection.
Where found: S. U.S. south to Costa Rica; also n. S. America.
Texas: *Resident* along coast (rare north of Rockport); inland

at least to Austin and Big Bend. Casual in n. Texas and Panhandle. *Habitat:* Farmlands, dirt and gravel roads, open woodlands, brush. **Nest:** A flimsy platform in vines, cactus, low tree, or on ground. Eggs (2) white.

INCA DOVE *Scardafella inca* 8   p. 132
Field marks: A very small dove with a pale, scaly appearance. May be told from Ground Dove by *comparatively long* square-ended tail (often looks pointed); tail shows white sides when spread. Like Ground Dove, Inca shows rufous in wing in flight. Similar species: Ground Dove's tail is dark and stubby. Ground Dove has black spots on wings; Inca has scaly wings.
Voice: Two notes of nearly even emphasis *ooh-coo.* Heat sufferers interpret it, *"no hope."* Also *"hink-ka-dooo"* (I. Davis). Where found: Sw. U.S. south to nw. Costa Rica. Texas: *Resident* in s. Texas; north along coast locally to Galveston, Houston; north inland to Big Spring, San Angelo, Coleman, Austin, Bryan; also along Rio Grande to El Paso. Spreading. *Habitat:* Towns, gardens, chicken pens, parks, farms. **Nest:** A flimsy twig platform on low limb, sometimes on building. Eggs (2) white.

WHITE-FRONTED DOVE *Leptotila verreauxi* 12   p. 132
Field marks: A large dark-backed, ground-inhabiting dove with a rounded, white-cornered tail. Further distinguished from other similarly sized doves by its *pale underparts,* whitish forehead. In flight, shows reddish underwings.
Similar species: White-winged Dove has white wing-patches.
Voice: A low, soft, ghostly *co-whooooooo,* lower in pitch and softer than the notes of any other dove; at a distance, only the hollow long-drawn *whooooooo* is audible.
Where found: S. Texas south to Argentina. Texas: *Resident* in lower Rio Grande Valley, upriver at least to Rio Grande City. *Habitat:* Shady woodlands, river thickets. **Nest:** A flimsy platform of sticks in low tree or bush. Eggs (2) pale buff.

Cuckoos, Roadrunners, and Anis: Cuculidae

BIRDS OF this family are slender, long-tailed; two toes forward, two behind. Cuckoos are slim, sinuous-looking; a little longer than Robin, dull olive-brown above and whitish below. Roadrunners are large streaked cuckoos that travel on the ground. Anis are loose-jointed and slender, coal-black with deep, high-ridged bills. Food: Caterpillars, other insects. Anis may eat seeds, fruits; Roadrunners eat insects, reptiles, etc. Nearly all warm and temperate parts of world. No. of species: World, 128; N. America, 7; Texas, 4.

YELLOW-BILLED CUCKOO
Coccyzus americanus   11–12½   p. 133
Field marks: Known as a cuckoo by the slim look and its color, dull brown above, white below; as this species by *rufous* in wings, *large white spots* at tips of black tail feathers, and, at close range, *yellow* lower mandible on its slightly curved bill. In flight, sinuous look and flash of rufous in wings are best marks.
Similar species: Black-billed Cuckoo is duller, has very small tail-spots, black lower mandible, no rufous in wings.
Voice: Song, a rapid throaty *ka ka ka ka ka ka ka ka ka ka ka ka ka kow kow kowlp kowlp kowlp kowlp* (retarded toward end).
Where found: S. Canada south to Mexico, West Indies. Winters in S. America. **Texas:** *Summers* (Apr.–Nov.) throughout. *Habitat:* Woodlands, mesquite, thickets, farms. **Nest:** A frail platform of twigs in bush or small tree. Eggs (2–4) blue-green.

BLACK-BILLED CUCKOO
Coccyzus erythropthalmus   11–12   p. 133
Field marks: Brown above, white below; bill *black;* narrow *red* eye-ring. No rufous in wing; only small tail-spots (seen best on underside of tail).
Similar species: See Yellow-billed Cuckoo.
Voice: A fast rhythmic *cu cu cu, cucucu, cucucu, cucucu, cucucu,* etc. The grouped rhythm (three or four) is distinctive. Sometimes a series of single *kuk*'s, softer and without retarded ending of Yellow-bill. Sometimes sings at night.
Where found: S. Canada south to Nebraska, Arkansas, S. Carolina. Winters in n. S. America. **Texas:** *Migrant* (Apr.–May, Sept.–Oct.) through e. and cent. Texas; west to Fort Worth, Austin, Del Rio (rare), Panhandle. *Habitat:* Wood edges, groves, thickets.

ROADRUNNER   *Geococcyx californianus*   20–24   p. 133
Field marks: The cuckoo that runs (tracks show two toes forward, two backward). Unique; slender, heavily streaked, with a long maneuverable, white-tipped tail, shaggy crest, strong legs. In flight the short rounded wings display a white crescent.
Voice: Six to eight dove-like *coo*'s descending in pitch (last note about pitch of Mourning Dove). Also a clattering noise made by rolling mandibles together.
Where found: Sw. U.S. south to cent. Mexico. **Texas:** *Resident* in every section; less frequent in e. parts. *Habitat:* Deserts, brush and open country with scattered cover. **Nest:** Of sticks hidden in bush or low tree. Eggs (3–5) white.

GROOVE-BILLED ANI *Crotophaga sulcirostris* 12½   p. 133
Field marks: A coal-black cuckoo-like bird, with a loose-jointed tail, short wings (weak flight), and a deep bill with a *high, curved ridge.* Bill shape gives the bird a puffin-like profile.
Similar species: Except for the bill and strange appearance, the bird might be mistaken at first for a Boat-tailed Grackle.
Voice: A repeated *pee-oh*, or *tee-ho*, first note higher and thin, second guttural; also cuckoo-like calls and wailing notes.
Where found: S. Texas to Peru. **Texas:** *Resident* (but mostly migratory) in lower Rio Grande Valley; casual north along coast to Galveston Bay and along Rio Grande to Big Bend. *Habitat:* Thick brushy country. **Nest:** A bulky mass of dead twigs lined with green leaves in thick bush or low tree. Often communal, used by more than one female. Eggs (3–4 each female) pale bluish.

Owls: Tytonidae and Strigidae

LARGELY nocturnal birds of prey, with large heads, flattened faces forming "facial disks," and large forward-facing eyes. Hooked bills, powerful claws and usually feathered feet. Flight noiseless, mothlike. Some species have conspicuous feather-tufts, or "horns." Sexes similar, but females larger. Food: Mainly rodents, birds, large insects. Cosmopolitan. No. of species: World, 134; N. America, 18; Texas, 13 (plus 1 accidental).

BARN OWL *Tyto alba* 15–20   p. 128
Field marks: A long-legged, knock-kneed, pale, monkey-faced owl. *Dark eyes*, no ear-tufts. The only owl with a *white* heart-shaped face. Distinguished in flight as an owl by the large head and light, mothlike flight; as this species, by the unstreaked whitish or pale cinnamon underparts (ghostly at night) and golden-buff or rusty upper plumage.
Similar species: Short-eared Owl (marshes) is streaked, has darker face and underparts, yellow eyes, shorter legs.
Voice: An eerie rasping hiss or snore: *kschh!*
Where found: Nearly cosmopolitan; in New World from s. Canada to Tierra del Fuego. **Texas:** *Resident* throughout except in mountains. *Habitat:* Woodlands, ranches, farms, towns, canyons. **Nest:** On litter of fur pellets in barn, belfry, hollow tree, cave, hole in bank. Eggs (5–11) white.

SCREECH OWL *Otus asio* 8–10   p. 128
Field marks: The only common *small* Texas owl with ear-tufts. Two color phases occur: red-brown and gray, no relation to age or sex. No other Texas owl is as bright a red or as gray a gray.

In the western half of the state only gray birds occur. Young
birds in summer lack conspicuous "ears."
Similar species: See Long-eared Owl.
Voice: A mournful whinny, or wail, tremulous, running down
the scale. Also a soft tremulo given on a single pitch.
Where found: Se. Alaska, s. Canada south to cent. Mexico.
Texas: *Resident* locally throughout. *Habitat:* Woodlands, farm
groves, shade trees in towns, wooded canyons, and streams.
Nest: In tree cavity or old woodpecker hole. Eggs (4–5) white.

FLAMMULATED OWL   *Otus flammeolus*   6½–7
(Flammulated Screech Owl)   p. 126
    Field marks: A rare little owl, smaller than Screech Owl, largely
    gray (and a touch of tawny), with inconspicuous ear-tufts (hard
    to see). *The only small owl with dark brown eyes.*
    Voice: A soft *hoot*, or *hoo-hoot*, low in pitch for so small an owl;
    repeated steadily at intervals of two or more seconds.
    Where found: S. British Columbia south to Guatemala. Winters
    Mexico, Guatemala. **Texas:** *Summers* in Trans-Pecos (Guada-
    lupe, Franklin, Chisos Mts., etc.). *Habitat:* High mt. forests
    above 6000 ft. **Nest:** In woodpecker hole. Eggs (3–4) white.

GREAT HORNED OWL   *Bubo virginianus*   18–25   p. 128
    Field marks: The "Cat Owl"; the only *large* owl with ear-tufts,
    or "horns." Heavily barred beneath; conspicuous white throat-
    collar. In flight the Horned Owl is as large as our largest hawks,
    is dark; looks neckless, large-headed.
    Similar species: The rare Long-eared Owl is much smaller (crow-
    sized in flight), with lengthwise streakings rather than crosswise
    barrings, beneath. "Ears" closer together.
    Voice: Hooting is deeper, more resonant than that of Barred
    Owl; three, five, or six uninflected hoots (Barred Owl, eight).
    Usually five, in this rhythm: *hoo, hoohoo, hoo, hoo.*
    Where found: Limit of trees in Arctic to Strait of Magellan.
    Texas: *Resident* throughout. *Habitat:* Woodlands, canyons,
    streamsides, deserts. **Nest:** In old tree nest of bird of prey,
    hollow tree, pothole, cliff or river bluff. Eggs (2–3) white.

SNOWY OWL   *Nyctea scandiaca*   20–26   p. 126
    Field marks: A large *white* owl with a round head, *yellow* eyes;
    more or less flecked or barred with dusky. Some birds are much
    whiter than others. Day-flying.
    Similar species: (1) Barn Owl is whitish on underparts only, has
    dark eyes. (2) Young owls of all species are whitish before
    feathers replace the down; are often miscalled "Snowy" Owls.
    Voice: Quite silent when in U.S.
    Where found: Arctic. Has cyclic migrations. **Texas:** Casual
    winter visitor (perhaps accidental today). In earlier years re-

FERRUGINOUS

ELF

FLAMMULATED

SAW-WHET

SPOTTED

BURROWING

SNOWY

OWLS

corded as far south as San Antonio, Austin, Port Arthur. *Habitat:* Open country, prairies, fields, marshes; to be looked for on dune, post, haystack, etc.

FERRUGINOUS OWL *Glaucidium brasilianum* 6½
Field marks: A very small earless owl, much smaller than Screech Owl; rusty brown with a striped breast and rather long barred tail. Has habit of jerking or flipping tail. Head proportionately smaller than that of most other owls. A *black patch* on each side of hind neck; suggests "eyes on back of head."
Similar species: None in lower Valley.
Voice: *Chook* or *took*, sometimes repeated 30–40 times at rate of once per second (G. M. Sutton). Often calls in daytime.
Where found: U.S.–Mexican border south to Strait of Magellan. **Texas:** Rare *resident* in lower Rio Grande delta (Brownsville upriver to Hidalgo Co.). *Habitat:* Woodlands. **Nest:** In woodpecker hole or tree cavity. Eggs (3–4) white.

ELF OWL *Micrathene whitneyi* 6
Field marks: A tiny earless owl about the size of a large sparrow, underparts striped with reddish brown, "eyebrows" white. Hides in hole in tree; more readily found at night, by calls.
Similar species: (1) Ferruginous Owl or (2) Pygmy Owl (both very unlikely but possible in w. Texas) would have a much longer tail and a large black patch on each side of hind-neck.
Voice: A rapid high pitched *whi-whi-whi-whi-whi-whi*, or *chewk-chewk-chewk-chewk*, etc., often becoming more excited, "puppylike," and chattering in middle of series.
Where found: U.S.–Mexican border south to cent. Mexico. Winters in Mexico. **Texas:** Rare *summer resident* in mts. of Big Bend. Formerly rare resident of lower Rio Grande. *Habitat:* Oak canyons (3000–5700 ft.). **Nest:** In tree cavity. Eggs (3) white.

BURROWING OWL *Speotyto cunicularia* 9
Field marks: A small brown owl of the prairies, often seen by day standing on the ground and on fence posts. About size of Screech Owl; round-headed, *very long legs* (for an owl), stubby tail. Bobs and bows when agitated.
Voice: A tremulous chuckling or chattering call, *quick-quick-quick;* at night a high mellow *coo-co-hoo coo-co-hoo*, like Mourning Dove's in quality but higher.
Where found: Sw. Canada and Florida south locally to Tierra del Fuego. Migrant in north. **Texas:** *Winters* (Dec.–Apr.) locally throughout state; more frequent westward. *Breeds* locally in Panhandle and w. Texas; very locally in cent. parts; south at least to San Antonio (rare), Rockport (irregular), Houston (occasional). *Habitat:* Open plains, prairies, fields. **Nest:** In burrow in open ground. Eggs (5–9) white.

OWLS

LONG-EARED OWL   p. 130
  Crow-sized; gray.
  Differs from Horned Owl by streaked belly, closer "ears";
  from gray Screech Owl by rusty face.

GREAT HORNED OWL   p. 125
  Large size; "ears," white throat.

SCREECH OWL   p. 124
  Gray phase: Small; gray, "eared."
  Red phase: Only rufous owl with "ears." In w. Texas only
  gray birds occur.

BARN OWL   p. 124
  Heart face or monkey face; pale breast.

BARRED OWL   p. 130
  Brown eyes, barred breast, streaked belly.

SHORT-EARED OWL   p. 131
  Buffy brown; streaked breast; marshes.

LONG-EARED OWL

HORNED OWL

Gray Phase

Red Phase

SCREECH OWL

BARN OWL

BARRED OWL

SHORT-EARED OWL

BOBWHITE

SCALED QUAIL

GAMBEL'S QUAIL

COTURNIX

CHUKAR

HARLEQUIN QUAIL

CHACHALACA

LESSER

GREATER

PRAIRIE CHICKENS

♀

♂

RING-NECKED PHEASANT

Plate 34   129

CHICKEN-LIKE BIRDS

Note: The birds on the page opposite are males
unless otherwise noted.

BOBWHITE   p. 75
Red-brown; striped head, white throat.
Female has buff throat.

SCALED QUAIL (BLUE QUAIL)   p. 75
Pale gray, scaly; "cotton top."

GAMBEL'S QUAIL   p. 75
Gray-brown; black face, head plume.
Female has light throat.

HARLEQUIN QUAIL   p. 76
Gray; spotted; harlequin face.
Female is brown, has white throat.

COTURNIX (MIGRATORY QUAIL)   p. 77
Very small; buff-brown; striped head.

CHUKAR   p. 76
Sandy; striped flanks, black "necklace," red legs.

GREATER PRAIRIE CHICKEN   p. 74
Barred; short dark tail; coastal prairie.
Male in display shows yellow-orange air-sacs on neck.

LESSER PRAIRIE CHICKEN   p. 74
Smaller, paler; northwestern counties.
Male in display shows purplish-red air-sacs on neck.

CHACHALACA   p. 73
Small head, long blackish, white-tipped tail; Rio Grande
delta only.

RING-NECKED PHEASANT   p. 76
Male: Highly colored; white neck-ring, long tail.
Female: Brown; long pointed tail.

BARRED OWL *Strix varia* 18–22 p. 128
Field marks: An owl with a puffy round head; the large, gray-brown, hornless owl of river woodlands. The large liquid brown eyes and the manner of streaking and barring — barred *crosswise* on puffy chest and streaked *lengthwise* on belly — identify it. Back spotted with white.
Similar species: In w. Texas see Spotted Owl.
Voice: Hooting is more emphatic than Great Horned Owl's but not so deep. May sound like barking of dog. Usually consists of *eight* accented hoots, in two groups of four: *hoohoo-hoohoo — hoohoo-hoohooaw.* The *aw* at the close is characteristic.
Where found: Canada (east of Rockies) to Honduras. **Texas:** *Resident* throughout e., n., and cent. Texas; west to Panhandle, Edwards Plateau; south to Corpus Christi. *Habitat:* Woodlands, wooded riverbottoms. **Nest:** In tree cavity or old nest of hawk. Eggs (2–3) white.

SPOTTED OWL *Strix occidentalis* 16½–19 p. 126
Field marks: Replaces the Barred Owl locally in w. Texas; a large dark brown earless owl with a puffy round head. *Dark eyes* and heavily *spotted* and barred underparts identify it.
Voice: A high-pitched hooting, like barking of a small dog; much higher than that of Horned Owl. Usually in groups of three: *hoo, hoo-hoo;* or four: *whowho-hoohoo.*
Where found: S. British Columbia south to cent. Mexico. **Texas:** Rare resident in Guadalupe Mts., of w. Texas. *Habitat:* Wooded canyons. **Nest:** In tree cavity, old nest of hawk, or hole in rocky ravine. Eggs (2–3) white.

LONG-EARED OWL *Asio otus* 13–16 p. 128
Field marks: A slender, crow-sized, grayish owl with long ear-tufts; much smaller than Horned Owl, streaked *lengthwise*, rather than barred crosswise, beneath. "Ears" closer together, toward center of forehead, giving a different aspect. Face dark rusty. Usually seen "frozen" close to trunk of dense tree.
Similar species: (1) Great Horned Owl is much larger, with ear-tufts more spread apart; seldom allows such a close approach. (2) Gray Screech Owl is smaller, has shorter ears, lacks rusty face. (3) In flight, Long-eared Owl's ear-tufts are pressed flat against head; then grayer color and habitat distinguish it from Short-eared Owl.
Voice: "A low moaning dove-like *hoo, hoo, hoo.* Also a catlike whine and a slurred whistle, *whee-you*" (Ludlow Griscom).
Where found: Cent. Canada to sw. and s.-cent. U.S.; also Eurasia, n. Africa. Partial migrant. **Texas:** Rare *winter visitor* locally in much of state. *Breeds* rarely or very locally in n. and w. parts. *Habitat:* Woodlands, thickets, cedar groves. **Nest:** In old tree nest of Crow or hawk. Eggs (3–6) white.

SHORT-EARED OWL *Asio flammeus* 13–17   p. 128
  Field marks: Nearly crow-sized; a day-flying owl of open coun-
try. The streaked tawny-brown color and irregular flopping
flight, like that of a Nighthawk, identify it. Large buffy wing-
patches show in flight, and on underwing, black patch at
carpal joint. The dark facial disks emphasize the yellow eyes.
  Similar species: Barn Owl has pale breast, white face, dark eyes.
  Voice: An emphatic sneezy bark, *kee-yow!*
  Where found: Nearly cosmopolitan. In N. America breeds from
Arctic south to cent. U.S. Winters to Gulf Coast. **Texas:**
Migrant throughout much of state, wintering locally (Oct.–Apr.).
Habitat: Prairies, marshes, coastal dunes.

SAW-WHET OWL *Aegolius acadicus* 7–8½   p. 126
  Field marks: A tiny, tame little owl; smaller than Screech Owl,
without ear-tufts. Brown with soft stripings on breast.
  Similar species: (1) Burrowing Owl has long legs, is barred
and spotted below. (2) See other small earless owls.
  Voice: "Song" a mellow whistled note repeated mechanically
in endless succession: *too, too, too, too, too, too,* etc.
  Where found: S. Alaska, Canada, south to ne. U.S. and mts. of
cent. Mexico. Winters south to s. U.S. **Texas:** Casual *winter
visitor.* Recorded Port Arthur, Liberty Co., Galveston area,
Franklin Mts., El Paso. *Habitat:* Woodlands, groves, conifers.

Goatsuckers: Caprimulgidae

NOCTURNAL birds with ample tails, large eyes, tiny bills, huge
gapes, and weak, tiny feet. During the day they rest horizontally
on a limb or on the ground, camouflaged by "dead-leaf" pattern.
Food: Mainly nocturnal insects. Nearly cosmopolitan. No. of
species: World, 67; N. America, 6; Texas, 6.

CHUCK-WILL'S-WIDOW
Caprimulgus carolinensis 11–13   p. 133
  Field marks: Like Whip-poor-will, but larger, very much buffier,
with brown throat (Whip-poor-will's *black*). Identify by size,
brownish look, more restricted white areas in male (see plate),
locality (when breeding), and voice.
  Voice: Call, *chuck-will'wid'ow*, less vigorous than efforts of
Whip-poor-will; distinctly 4-syllabled, *chuck* often inaudible;
accent on second and third syllables.
  Where found: Se. U.S. from Kansas, New Jersey, south to Gulf
States. Winters south to Colombia. **Texas:** *Migrant* (Apr.–
May, Aug.–Oct.) through e. half of state west to Edwards
Plateau. *Summers* in cent. and ne. Texas (not along coast); west

PIGEONS AND DOVES

The terms "pigeon" and "dove" are loosely used and often inter-
changeably, but for the most part "pigeon" refers to the larger
species, "dove" to the smaller. Sexes are similar.

MOURNING DOVE   p. 121
  Pointed tail.

WHITE-WINGED DOVE   p. 121
  White wing-patch.

WHITE-FRONTED DOVE   p. 122
  Light underparts, rounded tail, no wing-patches.

RED-BILLED PIGEON   p. 120
  Uniformly dark coloration.

BAND-TAILED PIGEON   p. 120
  White crescent on nape; light band at tail-tip.

ROCK DOVE or DOMESTIC PIGEON   p. 121
  Typical form: White rump; black band at tail-tip; black
  wing-bars.

GROUND DOVE   p. 121
  Short black tail; reddish wings.

INCA DOVE   p. 122
  Slender tail with white sides; reddish wings.

MOURNING
DOVE

WHITE-
WINGED
DOVE

WHITE-FRONTED
DOVE

RED-BILLED
PIGEON

BAND-TAILED
PIGEON

ROCK
DOVE

GROUND DOVE

INCA DOVE

YELLOW-BILLED
CUCKOO

BLACK-
BILLED
CUCKOO

GROOVE
BILLED
ANI

ROADRUNNER

WHIP-POOR-WILL

POOR-WILL

CHUCK-WILL'S-WIDOW

LESSER
NIGHTHAW

COMMON
NIGHTHAWK

PAURAQUE

Plate 36   133

CUCKOOS AND GOATSUCKERS

YELLOW-BILLED CUCKOO   p. 123
    Yellow bill, rufous wings, large tail-spots.

BLACK-BILLED CUCKOO   p. 123
    Black bill, red eye-ring, small tail-spots.

ROADRUNNER   p. 123
    Long tail; streaked; ragged crest.

GROOVE-BILLED ANI   p. 124
    Black; high-ridged bill, long loose-jointed tail.

WHIP-POOR-WILL   p. 134
    "Dead-leaf" pattern; wings shorter than tail. White tail-patches (male), blackish throat.
    Female has smaller buffy tail-patches.

CHUCK-WILL'S-WIDOW   p. 131
    Like Whip-poor-will but larger, browner; brown throat, buffier tail. See range.
    Female lacks white in buffy tail.

POOR-WILL   p. 134
    Small, gray; small white corners in tail (male). See text.

PAURAQUE   p. 134
    Patches in both wings and tail; rounded wings.

COMMON NIGHTHAWK   p. 135
    White wing-patches, pointed wings.
    At rest wings reach end of tail.

LESSER NIGHTHAWK   p. 135
    White bar nearer wing-tip.
    Flies lower than Common Nighthawk.

at least to Fort Worth, Coleman, Kerrville. *Habitat:* Pine forests, cedar hills and valleys, river woodlands, etc. **Nest:** Eggs (2) blotched; laid on leafy ground.

WHIP-POOR-WILL   *Caprimulgus vociferus*   9–10   p. 133
Field marks: Best known by its vigorous cry repeated in endless succession at night. When discovered by day, the bird springs from its hiding place and flits away on rounded wings like a large brown moth. If it is a male, white outer tail feathers flash out; if a female, it appears all brown.
Similar species: (1) Chuck-will's-widow, which breeds more widely in Texas, has a less vigorous, 4-syllabled cry, *chuck-will'wid'ow*. It is larger, browner, with a brown (not black) throat; male shows much less white in tail. Often called "Whip-poor-will" by country people. (2) Nighthawks show conspicuous white wing-patches, have long pointed wings.
Voice: At night, a vigorous oft-repeated *prrrip'-purr-rill'* or *whip'-poor-weel';* accent on first and last syllables.
Where found: Cent. and e. Canada south to Honduras. Winters mostly south of U.S. **Texas:** *Migrant* (Mar.–May, Sept.–Oct.) through e. and coastal parts; west to Fort Worth (rarely), Austin; also in Trans-Pecos. *Breeds* in Guadalupe and Chisos Mts. of w. Texas. Also said to summer in ne. corner of state. *Habitat:* Woodlands, oak thickets, wooded canyons (w. Texas). **Nest:** Eggs (2) blotched or unspotted (w. Texas); laid on dead leaves.

POOR-WILL   *Phalaenoptilus nuttallii*   7–8   p. 133
Field marks: Like a very small, short-tailed Whip-poor-will; grayer, with more white on throat and comparatively small white spots in tail-corners. Best known by its night call.
Similar species: Nighthawks are larger, have pointed (not rounded) wings with a conspicuous white bar near tip.
Voice: At night a loud, repeated *poor-will* or, more exactly, *poor-jill;* when close, *poor-will-low* or *poor-jill-ip.*
Where found: British Columbia south to cent. Mexico. Winters mostly south of U.S. **Texas:** *Summers* in w. half; east to San Antonio, Austin, Beeville, Edinburg. In migration occasionally east to Dallas, cent. coast. Winters occasionally in s. Texas. *Habitat:* Canyon mouths, dry open hillsides, arid country. **Nest:** Eggs (2) white; laid on bare ground or rock.

PAURAQUE   *Nyctidromus albicollis*   12   p. 133
Field marks: A large goatsucker of the Whip-poor-will type, best identified at night by voice. Whip-poor-will and Chuck-will's-widow migrate through its range, but it can be told from those species when discovered in daytime by bold black triangular marks on scapulars, and *white band* across primary

wing feathers (reduced in female). Separated from Nighthawk, which also has white in wing, by *large amount of white in tail*. Note shape of wings and tail.
Voice: At night a hoarse whistle, *pur-we'eeeer;* sometimes with preliminary notes (*pup-pup-pur-we'eeeer*). At a distance only *we'eeeer*, rolled out emphatically, can be heard.
Where found: S. Texas south to ne. Argentina, s. Brazil. **Texas:** *Resident* in s. Texas; north along lower Rio Grande to Starr Co.; on coastal plain to Rockport, Refugio Co., Beeville. Some winter throughout range; inactive in cold weather (hence thought to be absent). *Habitat:* Woodlands, brushy country, river thickets, coastal prairie. **Nest:** Eggs (2) pinkish, pale-spotted; laid on bare ground near bush.

COMMON NIGHTHAWK *Chordeiles minor* 8½–10   p. 133
Field marks: A slim-winged gray bird often seen high in the air, over the roofs of cities. Flies with easy strokes, "changing gear" to quicker erratic strokes. Prefers dusk but also flies abroad during midday. The *broad white bar* across the *pointed* wing is the nighthawk's mark. Male has white bar across notched tail, white throat.
Similar species: See Lesser Nighthawk.
Voice: A nasal *peent* or *pee-ik*. In aerial display, male cuts wings and dives earthward, then zooms up sharply with a sudden deep whir made by wings (sounds like Bronx cheer).
Where found: Canada south to s. Mexico. Winters in S. America. **Texas:** *Summers* (Apr.–Oct.) in all sections. *Habitat:* Varies from treeless country to mts. and open pine woods; most often seen in open air over countryside or towns. **Nest:** Eggs (2) speckled; laid on bare ground, sometimes on flat roof.

LESSER NIGHTHAWK *Chordeiles acutipennis* 8–9
(Texas Nighthawk, "Trilling Nighthawk")   p. 133
Field marks: Smaller than Common Nighthawk, with white bar (buffy in female) *closer to tip of wing*. More readily identified by its odd calls and manner of flight, *very low over ground*, never high.
Voice: Does not have characteristic *spee-ik* or *peent* of other nighthawk; instead a low *chuck chuck* and a soft purring or whinnying sound very like trilling of toad.
Where found: Sw. U.S. south to n. Chile and Brazil. Winters south of U.S. **Texas:** *Summers* (Apr.–Oct.) in w. and s. Texas; east to San Angelo, San Antonio, cent. coast; south to Rio Grande (entire length). Casual on upper coast. *Habitat:* Arid open country, sparse scrub, rocky slopes, canyons, prairie. **Nest:** Eggs (2) dotted; laid on open ground.

CHIMNEY SWIFT (left).   WHITE-THROATED SWIFT (right).

Swifts: Apodidae

SWALLOW-LIKE in appearance and behavior, but with slimmer, more scythe-like wings, short tails. Structurally distinct, with flat skulls, and all four toes pointing forward. Flight very rapid, sailing between spurts; wings often stiffly *bowed*. Food: Flying insects. Nearly cosmopolitan. No. of species: World, 79; N. America, 6; Texas, 2 (plus 1, possibly 2 accidentals).

CHIMNEY SWIFT *Chaetura pelagica* 5–5½
Field marks: The Chimney Swift has been called a "cigar with wings." It is a sooty swallow-like bird with long, slightly curved stiff wings and no apparent tail (occasionally it does spread its tail. It does *not appear* to beat its wings in unison, but alternately — such is the *illusion*, at least (slow-motion pictures to the contrary, notwithstanding). The narrow wings fairly twinkle, and it frequently sails between spurts, holding the wings *bowed like a crescent.*
Similar species: Swallows have gliding wingbeats; they frequently perch on wires and twigs; swifts never do. Swallows have forked, notched, or square tails.
Voice: Loud, rapid, ticking or chippering notes.
Where found: Canada to Gulf States. Winters in upper Amazon basin. **Texas:** *Migrant* through all parts except Trans-Pecos. *Summers* (Mar.–Oct.) in e., n., and cent. Texas, west to Fort Worth, San Angelo, Kerrville; south to Beeville, Corpus Christi; spreading. *Habitat:* Open sky. **Nest:** A bracket of twigs in chimney; rarely in hollow tree or old well. Eggs (4–5) white.

WHITE-THROATED SWIFT
Aeronautes saxatalis 6½–7

Field marks: Known as a swift by its long, narrow, stiff wings and characteristic twinkling and gliding flight; from other swifts by its contrasting black and white pattern (see drawing). Underparts white, with black side-patches.

Similar species: See Violet-green Swallow.

Voice: A shrill, excited *jejejejeje*, in descending scale.

Where found: Sw. Canada south to Cent. America. Winters from sw. U.S. south. **Texas:** *Summer resident* in mts. of Trans-Pecos (Guadalupe, Davis, and Chisos Mts., etc.). Casual transient to cent. Texas, and cent. coast (Rockport, Corpus Christi, Houston). Occasional in winter in Trans-Pecos. *Habitat:* Open sky in mt. country, canyons. **Nest:** A saliva-cemented bracket in crevice in cliff. Eggs (3–6) white.

Hummingbirds: Trochilidae

THE SMALLEST of all birds; iridescent, with needle-like bills for sipping from flowers. The wing motion is so rapid that the wings look gauze-like. The jewel-like throat feathers, or "gorgets," are the best aid in identifying males. Females lack these, and are mostly greenish above, whitish below, often presenting a very difficult identification problem. Some females and particularly young birds are not safely distinguishable in the field, even for experts. It is important to realize this.

There is a yearly clockwise movement of most hummingbirds in western United States and it is to be expected that most species would turn up occasionally in the Trans-Pecos. However, in recent years (Sept.–Oct.) nearly all of them have apparently been noted on the central Texas coast, especially at Rockport, a logical concentration point for migrant birds affected by wind drift. Some species have appeared in numbers but although observed by seasoned observers of unquestioned skill there should be further confirmation of two or three species, possibly by color movies or capture. Because of this development, a complete line-up of western hummingbirds is included on the color plate in this *Field Guide.* Food: Nectar, aphids, small insects. W. Hemisphere; majority in the tropics. No. of species: World, 319; N. America, 18; Texas, 9 (plus 4 to 6 accidentals; see pp. 272–73).

LUCIFER HUMMINGBIRD *Calothorax lucifer* 3½ p. 144

Field marks: The male of this rare hummer has a *purple* throat and *rusty* sides. No purple on forehead. The *decurved* bill is a sure mark. Tail deeply forked. *Female:* Distinguishable from

other female hummers by decurved bill, uniform buff underparts.
Similar species: Male Costa's Hummingbird (p. 272) also has
purple throat, but in addition has *purple forehead;* bill straighter,
sides green, tail not so deeply forked.
Where found: Mts. of cent., e., and s. Mexico. **Texas:** Rare
summer resident in vicinity of Chinati Peak and Chisos Mts.,
of w. Texas (probably breeds). Casual transient at Rockport
(sight records). *Habitat:* Arid country, agaves, etc. **Nest:** A
tiny lichen-covered cup in bush. Eggs (2) white.

RUBY-THROATED HUMMINGBIRD
Archilochus colubris 3–3¾   p. 144
Field marks: Hummingbirds are the tiniest of all birds; irides-
cent, with long needle-like bills for sipping from flowers. The
Ruby-throat is by far the most numerous hummingbird in the e.
half of Texas. Both sexes are bright shining green above; males
have *glowing red throats*, black forked tails; females have white
throats, rounded, white-tipped tails.
Similar species: Male Broad-tailed Hummingbird of mts. of
Trans-Pecos also has red throat (rose-red, not fire-red), is larger,
lacks strong fork in tail, and *trills* with wings as it flies.
Voice: Male in display swings like pendulum through the air in
a wide arc, each swing accompanied by a hum. Notes, high-
pitched, mouselike, petulant.
Where found: S. Canada south to Gulf States. Winters south to
Cent. America. **Texas:** *Migrant* (Mar.–May, Sept.–Dec.)
through e. two-thirds of state west to Pecos River and Panhandle. Casual in Trans-Pecos. *Winters* occasionally along
coast; regularly at Brownsville. *Breeds* in n., e., and cent. Texas;
west to Edwards Plateau (San Angelo); south to cent. coast,
Beeville. *Habitat:* Widespread; flowering plants. **Nest:** A tiny
lichen-covered cup saddled on horizontal branch. Eggs (2) white.

BLACK-CHINNED HUMMINGBIRD
Archilochus alexandri 3¾   p. 144
Field marks: *Male:* Identified by the *black throat* and conspicuous
white collar below it. The blue-violet band on lower throat
shows only in certain lights (but make certain you see it). *Female:* Greenish above, whitish below. Cannot safely be told in
field from female Ruby-throat.
Similar species: Throat of male Ruby-throat or that of almost
any other hummer may look black until it catches the light.
Voice: Male in display makes a *whirring* with wings as it swoops
back and forth in a shallow arc. Note, a thin excited chippering.
"Song," a thin high-pitched warble.
Where found: Sw. British Columbia south to n. Mexico. Winters in Mexico. **Texas:** *Summers* in w. and cent. parts; east to

Dallas, Austin, San Antonio. Also *migrant* (Mar.–May, Oct.–Nov.) through cent. coast and Brownsville. Accidental in winter. *Habitat:* Semi-arid country, cedar-oak canyonsides, streams, flowering plants, towns. **Nest:** A feltlike cup in shrub or tree, often near water. Eggs (2) white.

BROAD-TAILED HUMMINGBIRD
Selasphorus platycercus 4½   p. 144
Field marks: This mountain species can be identified at once by the sound of its wings, a *shrill trilling* as the male flies from place to place. The female produces scarcely any sound. *Male:* Back green; throat bright *rose-red*. *Female:* Similar to female Black-chin but larger; sides tinged with buffy; touch of rufous at sides of tail (near base when spread).
Similar species: (1) See Ruby-throated Hummingbird. Other red-throated hummers are: (2) male Rufous (rufous back); (3) male Anna's (red crown).
Voice: Note, a thin sharp chip. Male trills with wings.
Where found: Wyoming south to cent. Mexico. Winters in Mexico, Guatemala. **Texas:** *Summers* (Mar.–Oct.) in mts. of Trans-Pecos (Guadalupe, Davis, Chisos Mts., etc.). *Migrant* elsewhere through Trans-Pecos and in Panhandle. Apparently a rare *transient* (Sept.–Oct.) to cent. coast (Rockport, Sinton). *Habitat:* Open forests, glades, meadows in high mts. **Nest:** A lichen-covered cup in bush or small tree. Eggs (2) white.

RUFOUS HUMMINGBIRD *Selasphorus rufus* 3½   p. 144
Field marks: *Male:* Upper parts bright red-brown in full breeding plumage, throat flame-red. *No other hummingbird has a rufous back.* *Female:* Similar to other female hummingbirds but has considerable rufous at the base of the tail feathers.
Similar species: In autumn in Trans-Pecos, female Rufous is not safely distinguishable from female Broad-tailed Hummingbird, which also shows a touch of rufous at base of tail feathers. See Allen's Hummingbird (p. 272).
Voice: Note, a sharp, high *bzee;* also squeaks.
Where found: S. Alaska south to nw. California. Winters in Mexico. **Texas:** *Fall migrant* (July–Oct.) in w. Texas and Panhandle; a few go through cent. Texas. Frequent in fall and occasional in winter along Gulf Coast. *Habitat:* Mountain meadows, streamsides, flowering plants.

RIVOLI'S HUMMINGBIRD *Eugenes fulgens* 5   p. 144
Field marks: *Male:* A very large hummingbird with *blackish belly, bright green throat,* and *purple crown.* Looks all black at a distance. Wingbeats discernible, not buzzy as in smaller hummers; sometimes scales on set wings like a swift. *Female:* A large

SWALLOWS

PURPLE MARTIN   p. 167
  Male: Black breast.
  Female: Grayish breast.

CLIFF SWALLOW   p. 166
  Pale rump, square tail, dark throat.

CAVE SWALLOW   p. 166
  Like Cliff Swallow but throat pale, forehead dark.

BARN SWALLOW   p. 165
  Deeply forked tail.

ROUGH-WINGED SWALLOW   p. 165
  Brown back, dingy throat.

BANK SWALLOW   p. 165
  Brown back; dark breastband.

TREE SWALLOW   p. 164
  Back blue-black; breast snow-white.

VIOLET-GREEN SWALLOW   p. 164
  White patches on sides of rump. White around eye.

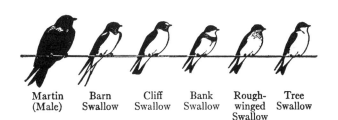

Martin	Barn	Cliff	Bank	Rough-	Tree
(Male)	Swallow	Swallow	Swallow	winged	Swallow
				Swallow	

SWALLOWS ON A WIRE

PURPLE MARTIN

CLIFF SWALLOW

CAVE SWALLOW

BARN SWALLOW

ROUGH-WINGED SWALLOW

BANK SWALLOW

TREE SWALLOW

VIOLET-GREEN SWALLOW

BLACK-CRESTED TITMOUSE

TUFTED TITMOUSE

PLAIN TITMOUSE

CAROLINA CHICKADEE

BLACK-CAPPED CHICKADEE

MOUNTAIN CHICKADEE

VERDIN

COMMON BUSHTIT

BLACK-EARED BUSHTIT

BROWN CREEPER

WHITE-BREASTED NUTHATCH

RED-BREASTED NUTHATCH

BROWN-HEADED NUTHATCH

PIGMY NUTHATCH

Plate 38   141

TITMICE, CREEPER, AND NUTHATCHES

BLACK-CRESTED TITMOUSE   p. 172
  Rusty flanks, black crest (gray in some individuals). Note
  light spot above bill. See range.

TUFTED TITMOUSE   p. 172
  Rusty flanks, gray crest. Note *black* spot above bill.
  See range.

PLAIN TITMOUSE   p. 173
  Very plain; small gray crest. W. Texas only. See text.

CAROLINA CHICKADEE   p. 172
  Black cap, black bib.

BLACK-CAPPED CHICKADEE   p. 171
  Casual visitor to w. Texas. "Northern frost" on wing.
  See text.

MOUNTAIN CHICKADEE   p. 172
  White eyebrow stripe.

VERDIN   p. 173
  Gray; yellowish head, rusty shoulder (not always visible).

COMMON BUSHTIT   p. 173
  Long tail, brownish cheek, gray crown.

BLACK-EARED BUSHTIT   p. 174
  Blackish ear-patch (male). See text.

BROWN CREEPER   p. 178
  Slender curved bill; creeping posture.

WHITE-BREASTED NUTHATCH   p. 174
  Black eye on white face.

RED-BREASTED NUTHATCH   p. 175
  Black line through eye.

BROWN-HEADED NUTHATCH   p. 175
  Brown cap to eye; pine forests, e. Texas.

PIGMY NUTHATCH   p. 175
  Gray-brown cap to eye; pine forests, w. Texas (local).

hummingbird, greenish above, heavily washed with greenish or
dusky below. Can be told from female Blue-throated by more
mottled underparts, heavily spotted throat, dark greenish tail,
obscure grayish tail-corners.
Similar species: Female Blue-throated Hummingbird has uniformly gray underparts and a blue-black tail with exceptionally
large white spots at corners.
Voice: Note, a thin sharp *chip.*
Where found: Mts. of U.S.–Mexican border south to Nicaragua.
Winters in Mexico. *Habitat:* High mt. forests. **Texas:** Rare
summer visitor to Chisos Mts. May nest.

BLUE-THROATED HUMMINGBIRD
Lampornis clemenciae 5   p. 144
   Field marks: *Male:* A very large hummingbird with black and
white streaks around the eye and a *bright blue throat.* Only U.S.
hummer in which *male* has *white tail-spots. Female:* Large, with
evenly gray underparts, white marks on face, and large blue-black
tail, which has *exceptionally large white spots* at corners. This big
tail with its prominent white patches is the best field mark in all
plumages.
   Similar species: See female Rivoli's Hummingbird.
   Voice: Note, a squeaking *seek.*
   Where found: U.S.–Mexican border south to s. Mexico. **Texas:**
Summers in Chisos Mts. of w. Texas (5000–7600 ft.). Casual at
El Paso and Rockport (sight records). *Habitat:* Wooded streamsides in mt. canyons. **Nest:** A feltlike cup fastened to slender
support along canyon stream. Eggs (2) white.

BUFF-BELLIED HUMMINGBIRD
Amazilia yucatanensis 4½   p. 144
   Field marks: *Male:* A rather large green hummer with a *green*
throat, *rufous* tail, buffy belly. Bill *coral-red* or pink with black
tip. *Female:* Similar to male. The only red-billed hummer in
Rio Grande delta and only one with green throat.
   Voice: Shrill squeaky notes.
   Where found: S. Texas south to Guatemala. **Texas:** *Summers* in
Rio Grande delta. Occasional in winter. A few wander in fall
to cent. coast (Corpus Christi, Rockport). *Habitat:* Woodlands,
thickets, flowering shrubs, citrus groves. **Nest:** A small cup
saddled in bush or small tree. Eggs (2) white.

BROAD-BILLED HUMMINGBIRD
Cynanthus latirostris 3¼   p. 144
   Field marks: *Male:* Green above and below with a metallic *blue
throat* (bird looks all-black in distance). Bill, *brilliant red* with a
black tip. *Female:* Identified by red bill and unmarked pearly-

gray throat and underparts. Females of most other humming-birds have some spotting on throat.

Similar species: Female White-eared Hummingbird (p. 273) has more white behind eye, spotted throat, mottled sides.

Voice: "A chatter like Ruby-crowned Kinglet" (J. Marshall).

Where found: U.S.–Mexican border to s. Mexico. **Texas:** Rare. *Summers* (has bred) in w. Texas (Big Bend to Alpine). *Habitat:* Desert canyons, gullies, mesquite oases. **Nest:** Similar to other hummingbirds'.

Kingfishers: Alcedinidae

SOLITARY fish-eaters with large heads, heron-like bills, small weak feet. They usually fish from a perch above water or may hover and plunge headlong. Food: Mainly fish; some species prefer insects, lizards. Almost cosmopolitan. No. of species: World, 87; N. America, 3; Texas, 3.

BELTED KINGFISHER *Megaceryle alcyon* 11–14   p. 176
Field marks: Hovering on rapidly beating wings in one spot in readiness for the headlong plunge, or flying with peculiar uneven wingbeats ("as if changing gear"), rattling as it goes, the Kingfisher is easily learned. Perched, it is big-headed and big-billed, larger than a Robin, blue-gray above, mostly white below, with a ragged, bushy crest and a broad gray breastband. Female has a second band (chestnut) below the gray one.

Voice: A loud high rattle.

Where found: Nw. Alaska, Canada south to s. U.S. Winters south to Panama. **Texas:** *Winters* throughout much of state. *Breeds* south to Pecos, Kerrville, Austin, Corpus Christi, but absent in summer from much of Staked Plains and arid w. sections. *Habitat:* Rivers, ponds, lakes, bays. **Nest:** In burrow in riverbank or sandbank. Eggs (5–7) white.

RINGED KINGFISHER *Megaceryle torquata* 15–16   p. 176
Field marks: Much larger than Belted Kingfisher; bill very large. Male has *chestnut breast and belly*. Female has broad bluish band across breast; separated by narrow white line from chestnut belly.

Similar species: Female Belted Kingfisher has a chestnut *band* across its white underparts.

Voice: A "rusty *cla-ack* or *wa-ak*" (Fred Webster).

Where found: Tropical Mexico south to Tierra del Fuego. **Texas:** Casual in s. Texas (at least 7 records). Reported Brownsville (twice), San Benito (twice), Laredo, Austin.

HUMMINGBIRDS

The plate opposite shows a complete line-up of western humming-birds, some of which are not normally to be seen in Texas. All, however, have been reported in the state either in the Trans-Pecos or at Rockport on the central coast, where a remarkable concentration of hummers often is reported in the fall. Two or three species require further substantiation (see Appendix I). Accidental species are indicated below by asterisks. Only males are described here. For the confusing females refer to the text.

BLACK-CHINNED HUMMINGBIRD   p. 138
    Black chin, blue-violet throat.

BUFF-BELLIED HUMMINGBIRD   p. 142
    Buff belly, green throat, red or pink bill.

WHITE-EARED HUMMINGBIRD*   p. 273
    Blue and green throat, white ear-stripe, red bill.

BROAD-BILLED HUMMINGBIRD   p. 142
    Blue throat, dark underparts, red bill.

CALLIOPE HUMMINGBIRD*   p. 272
    Gorget with red rays on white ground.

LUCIFER HUMMINGBIRD   p. 137
    Purple throat, green crown, decurved bill.

COSTA'S HUMMINGBIRD*   p. 272
    Purple throat, purple crown.

RIVOLI'S HUMMINGBIRD   p. 139
    Large, black; green throat.

BLUE-THROATED HUMMINGBIRD   p. 142
    Large; blue throat, large tail-spots.

ANNA'S HUMMINGBIRD*   p. 272
    Rose-red throat and crown.

BROAD-TAILED HUMMINGBIRD   p. 139
    Rose-red throat, green crown and back.

RUBY-THROATED HUMMINGBIRD   p. 138
    Fire-red throat, green crown and back.
    The common hummingbird of e. half of Texas.

ALLEN'S HUMMINGBIRD*   p. 272
    Like Rufous Hummingbird but upper back green.

RUFOUS HUMMINGBIRD   p. 139
    Fire-red throat, rufous back.

MALES

BLACK-CHINNED

BUFF-BELLIED

WHITE-EARED

BROAD-BILLED

LLIOPE

LUCIFER

COSTA'S

RIVOLI'S

BLUE-THROATED

ANNA'S

BROAD-TAILED

RUBY-THROATED

ALLEN'S

RUFOUS

FEMALES

LACK-CHINNED
UBY-THROATED
OSTA'S (similar)

LUCIFER

BROAD-TAILED

CALLIOPE

RUFOUS

ANNA'S

BROAD BILLED

RIVOLI'S

BLUE-THROATED

WHITE-EARED

YELLOW-SHAFTED
FLICKER

Juv.

RED-BELLIED

RED-SHAFTED
FLICKER

GOLDEN-
FRONTED

HAIRY

DOWNY

LADDER-
BACKED

Imm.

YELLOW-
BELLIED
SAPSUCKER

PILEATED

RED-COCKADE

Imm.

WILLIAMSON'S
SAPSUCKER

LEWIS'

ACORN

RED-HEADED

Plate 40   145

WOODPECKERS

YELLOW-SHAFTED FLICKER   p. 146
Brown back. Yellow wing- and tail-linings; black mustache
(male). Eastern.

RED-SHAFTED FLICKER   p. 147
Brown back. Red wing- and tail-linings; red mustache
(male). Western.

RED-BELLIED WOODPECKER   p. 147
Zebra back, red cap and nape (female, red nape).
Juvenal: Zebra back, brown head.

GOLDEN-FRONTED WOODPECKER   p. 148
Zebra back, yellow or orange nape (female has nape-patch
only).
Note black central tail feathers (Red-bellied, barred).

HAIRY WOODPECKER   p. 150
White back, large bill.

DOWNY WOODPECKER   p. 150
White back, small bill.

LADDER-BACKED WOODPECKER   p. 150
Zebra back, striped face. Female has black crown.

YELLOW-BELLIED SAPSUCKER   p. 149
Long white wing-stripe, barred back.
Adults with black breast-patch; male with red throat.

PILEATED WOODPECKER   p. 147
Very large; red crest.

RED-COCKADED WOODPECKER   p. 151
Zebra back, white cheek, black cap.

WILLIAMSON'S SAPSUCKER   p. 149
Male: Long white wing-patch, black back.
Female: Brown; zebra back, barred sides.

LEWIS' WOODPECKER   p. 149
Pink belly, black back.

ACORN WOODPECKER   p. 148
Clown face, black back.

RED-HEADED WOODPECKER   p. 148
Adult: Red head, broad wing-patch.
Immature: Brown head, broad wing-patch.

GREEN KINGFISHER *Chloroceryle americana* 7¼   p. 176
   Field marks: A very small kingfisher, not much larger than a large sparrow; upper parts greenish black, with white spots; collar and underparts white, sides spotted. The male has a broad *rusty breastband;* replaced by two greenish bands in female. (In Belted Kingfisher female wears rusty.) Its kingfisher shape when perched over the water and its small size will identify it. Flight, buzzy and direct.
   Voice: A clicking note; also a sharp squeak.
   Where found: Texas south to Argentina, Uruguay. **Texas:** Uncommon *resident* from Brownsville north to Kerrville, San Marcos, and along Rio Grande to Pecos River. Occasional north to Austin, Rockport; casual Panhandle. *Habitat:* Rivers, streams, resacas. **Nest:** In burrow in sandy bank. Eggs (4–6) white.

Woodpeckers: Picidae

CHISEL-BILLED wood-boring birds with powerful feet (usually two toes front, two rear), remarkably long tongues and stiff, spiny tails which act as props when climbing trees. Flight usually strong but undulating. Most males have some red on head. Food: Mainly tree-boring insects; some species eat ants, flying insects, berries, sap. Wooded parts of world except Madagascar. No. of species (including relatives): World, 210; N. America, 23; Texas, 14.

YELLOW-SHAFTED FLICKER
Colaptes auratus 13–14   p. 145
   Field marks: The *brown* back with its flashing *white rump*, visible as the bird flies, marks it as a flicker. Overhead this species flashes much yellow under the wings and tail. Close up, it shows a wide black crescent across the chest, numerous round black spots on underparts, a red nape-patch, and (male) black "whiskers." Often feeds on ground, hops awkwardly. Flight deeply undulating.
   Similar species: See Red-shafted Flicker.
   Voice: Song, a loud *wick wick wick wick wick*, etc.; notes, a loud *klee-yer* and a squeaky *flick-a, flick-a*, etc.
   Where found: Tree-limit in Alaska, Canada south to Gulf States, Cuba. Partial migrant. **Texas:** *Winters* (Sept.–Mar.) throughout most of state west to Panhandle, Edwards Plateau, Midland; casual to El Paso. *Breeds* in e. and n. Texas west to Commerce, Dallas (occasional), Waco; south to Austin (casual), upper coast. *Habitat:* Woodlands, groves, farms, towns, semi-open country. **Nest:** In excavated hole in tree, post. Eggs (6–8) white.

RED-SHAFTED FLICKER *Colaptes cafer* 13–14 p. 145
Field marks: Similar to Yellow-shafted Flicker but with the yellow of the wing- and tail-linings replaced by salmon-red. No red on nape. Male has *red* "whiskers" instead of black ones. Where the ranges of the two species overlap, hybrids sometimes occur, with *orange-yellow* wing-linings and spotted whiskers, or with one whisker black, the other red.
Similar species: See Yellow-shafted Flicker.
Voice: Similar to Yellow-shafted Flicker's.
Where found: Se. Alaska, sw. Canada south to s. Mexico. Partial migrant. **Texas:** *Winters* throughout much of state; rare in e. Texas and along coast. *Breeds* in Panhandle (local) and Trans-Pecos. *Habitat:* Varied: Groves, streamside woodlands, farms, towns, canyons. **Nest:** In hole in tree or post. Eggs (5–9) white.

PILEATED WOODPECKER
Dryocopus pileatus 17–19½ p. 145
Field marks: A spectacular, black *crow-sized* woodpecker with a conspicuous red *crest;* the only Texas woodpecker with a crest (except for the extirpated Ivory-bill). Female has black forehead, lacks red on "whisker" stripe. The great size, sweeping wingbeats, and flashing white underwing areas identify the Pileated in flight. The diggings, large *oval* or *oblong* holes, indicate its presence.
Voice: Call resembles flicker's but louder, more irregular: *kuk–kuk–kukkuk —— kuk–kuk,* etc. Also a more ringing and hurried call than flicker's; often rises or falls slightly in pitch.
Where found: Canada south to Gulf States. **Texas:** *Resident* in e. third of state west to Gainsville, Denton, Fort Worth (casual), Bastrop, Gonzales; south to Victoria, Goliad. *Habitat:* Woodlands. **Nest:** In hole in tree. Eggs (3–5) white.

RED-BELLIED WOODPECKER
Centurus carolinus 9–10½ p. 145
Field marks: A *"zebra-backed"* woodpecker with a white rump, pale underparts, *red cap.* Whole crown and nape are scarlet red in the male; female is red on nape only. Juvenal is patterned like adult but has a brown head, often devoid of red.
Similar species: See Golden-fronted Woodpecker.
Voice: Note, *churr* or *chaw;* also, *chiv, chiv.* Also a muffled flicker-like series.
Where found: Great Lakes area to Florida and Gulf Coast. **Texas:** *Resident* from e. Texas west to Panhandle (Canadian Breaks), San Angelo and Austin; south to cent. coast. *Habitat:* Woodlands, groves, towns. **Nest:** In hole in tree. Eggs (4–5) white.

GOLDEN-FRONTED WOODPECKER
Centurus aurifrons 9½–10½ p. 145
Field marks: *Male:* A *"zebra-backed"* woodpecker with light-colored underparts and a white rump. Shows a white wing-patch in flight. Head marked by separated patches of bright color: a touch of yellow near bill, poppy-red on crown, orange nape. *Female:* Similar to male, without red crown-patch; has yellow-orange nape-patch. Juvenal lacks head-patches.
Similar species: Male Red-bellied Woodpecker has red of crown "all in one piece." Female is *red* on nape, not orange. Red-bellied has central feathers of tail *barred* (solid black in Golden-fronted). Hybrids are said to occur. Immatures not separable.
Voice: A rolling *churr*. Notes similar to Red-bellied's; louder.
Where found: Sw. Oklahoma south to Nicaragua. **Texas:** *Resident* in mid-regions from e. Panhandle and Vernon south to Brownsville; west locally to Panhandle, San Angelo, Big Spring, Big Bend; east to Austin, cent. coast. *Habitat:* More arid than Red-bellied's, but ranges overlap; woodlands, groves, mesquite.
Nest: In hole in post, pole, or tree. Eggs (4–5) white.

RED-HEADED WOODPECKER
Melanerpes erythrocephalus 8½–9½ p. 145
Field marks: The only Texas woodpecker with the *entire* head red. Has a solid black back, white rump. Large square white patches on rear edge of wing are conspicuous; when perched, these patches make lower back look white. Sexes similar. Immature is dusky-headed; large white wing-patches identify it.
Similar species: Other woodpeckers have a *patch* of red on the head and are sometimes wrongly called "Red-heads."
Voice: A loud *queer* or *queeoh*, louder and higher-pitched than *churr* of Red-bellied Woodpecker.
Where found: S. Canada, east of Rockies south to Gulf States. Partial migrant. **Texas:** *Resident* in e. and cent. Texas; west to Panhandle (canyons), Vernon, Fort Worth, Waco, Austin; south to upper coast, Victoria; occasional wanderer to Corpus Christi, San Angelo. *Habitat:* Groves, farm country, towns, scattered trees. **Nest:** In hole in pole or tree. Eggs (4–6) white.

ACORN WOODPECKER *Melanerpes formicivorus* 9½
(California Woodpecker) p. 145
Field marks: A black-backed woodpecker with a large white rump and a white wing-patch in flight. The clownish black, white, and red head pattern is unique. Both male and female have red crowns (female has black forehead).
Voice: Most characteristic call, *whack-up, whack-up, whack-up* or *ja-cob, ja-cob, ja-cob.*
Where found: Se. Oregon, Arizona and w. Texas south to Panama. **Texas:** Local *resident* in Trans-Pecos; east occasion-

ally to Edwards Plateau. *Habitat:* Oak or oak-pine canyons. **Nest:** In hole in oak or pine. Eggs (4–5) white.

LEWIS' WOODPECKER *Asyndesmus lewis* 11   p. 145
Field marks: A large dark, black-backed woodpecker, with a rosy-red belly (the only woodpecker so marked), a wide gray collar around breast and back of neck; red face-patch. The reddish underparts, wide black wings are the best marks. Sexes similar. Has flycatcher habits, crow-like flight.
Voice: Usually silent. Occasionally a harsh *churr* or *chee-ur*.
Where found: Sw. Canada south to sw. U.S. Winters to n. Mexico. **Texas:** Rare *visitor*, mainly in winter, to w. Texas, east casually to Austin, Dallas. *Habitat:* Open forest, oaks, burns.

YELLOW-BELLIED SAPSUCKER *Sphyrapicus varius*
("Common Sapsucker") 8–8½   p. 145
Field marks: Adults are identified by the combination of *red forehead-patch* and *longitudinal white wing-patch* (shows well at rest). Male is the only woodpecker with a patch of red on both forehead and throat. Female has white throat. Young bird is sooty brown but the long white patch near shoulder identifies it. Drills orderly rows of small holes in trees.
Voice: A nasal mewing note, or squeal, *cheerrrr,* slurring downward. On nesting grounds distinctive drumming; several rapid thumps followed by several slow rhythmic ones.
Where found: Se. Alaska, cent. Canada, south to mts. of sw. U.S. and Georgia. Winters s. U.S. to Cent. America, West Indies. **Texas:** *Winters* (Oct.–Apr.) throughout. *Summers* locally in high mts. of Trans-Pecos (Davis Mts.). *Habitat:* Woodlands, groves. **Nest:** In hole in tree. Eggs (5–6) white.

WILLIAMSON'S SAPSUCKER
Sphyrapicus thyroideus 9½   p. 145
Field marks: *Male:* Identified by black crown, black back, long white shoulder-patch. The white face-stripes and narrow bright red throat-patch are also distinctive. Flying, looks black with white rump and shoulder-patches. *Female:* Very different, a brownish *"zebra-backed"* woodpecker with a white rump, *barred sides,* and *brown head.* Belly yellow in both sexes.
Similar species: Barred sides and brown head separate female from other zebra-backed woodpeckers.
Voice: A nasal *cheeer* or *que-yer,* suggestive of squeal of Red-tailed Hawk. Drumming distinctive; several rapid thumps followed by three or four slow, accented ones.
Where found: High mts., s. British Columbia south to sw. U.S. Winters to Mexico. **Texas:** Rare *migrant* and *winter visitor* to extreme w. parts; casual east to Edwards Plateau, Panhandle.

HAIRY WOODPECKER

Dendrocopos villosus　8½–10½　　　　　　　　p. 145

Field marks: Other woodpeckers have white rumps or white bars on the back, but the Downy and the Hairy are the only *white-backed* woodpeckers in Texas. They are almost identical in pattern, spotted with black and white on wings; *males* with a small red patch on back of head; *females*, without. Hairy is like a magnified Downy; bill is especially large, all out of size-relation to Downy's little "bark-sticker."

Similar species: (1) Downy at close range shows black bars on white outer tail feathers. The Hairy lacks this "ladder." The difference in bills is the quickest way to separate them. (2) Red-cockaded Woodpecker has *"zebra back," white cheeks*.

Voice: A kingfisher-like rattle, run together more than call of Downy. Note, a sharp *peek!*

Where found: Alaska, Canada south to Mexico. **Texas:** *Resident* of wooded sections of e., and n. Texas south at least to Waco, Bastrop, Houston. Casual in *winter* south to Rockport. Also *resident* in Guadalupe Mts. of w. Texas. *Habitat:* Woodlands, groves. **Nest:** In hole in tree. Eggs (3–5) white.

DOWNY WOODPECKER

Dendrocopos pubescens　6½–7　　　　　　　　p. 145

Field marks: See Hairy Woodpecker.

Similar species: See Hairy and Ladder-backed Woodpeckers.

Voice: A rapid whinny of notes, descending in pitch; not so run together as those of Hairy Woodpecker. Note, a flat *pick*, not as sharp as Hairy's note.

Where found: Se. Alaska, Canada south to Gulf States and sw. U.S. **Texas:** *Resident* in e., n., and cent. Texas; west to Panhandle, Coleman, Austin; south to upper coast (Matagorda Co.), Victoria, Austin. Occasional in *winter* in w. Texas (chiefly El Paso). *Habitat:* Woodlands, farm groves, towns. **Nest:** In hole in tree. Eggs (4–7) white.

LADDER-BACKED WOODPECKER　*Dendrocopos scalaris*　7½
("Mexican Woodpecker")　　　　　　　　p. 145

Field marks: A small black and white woodpecker known by its *"ladder back"* and *striped face*. Male has a red cap.

Similar species: Downy Woodpecker has white back. Ranges overlap in cent. Texas but Ladder-back prefers more arid country.

Voice: A rattling series, descending in pitch toward end (similar to Downy's). Note, a sharp *pick*, higher than Downy's.

Where found: Sw. U.S. south to British Honduras. **Texas:** *Resident* in w. two-thirds from Panhandle to Brownsville; east to Denton, Dallas, Waco, Mexia, College Station (occasional), and cent. coast. *Habitat:* Canyons, deserts, arid brushland, prairies. **Nest:** In excavated hole in tree, post, yucca, or agave. Eggs (4–5) white.

RED-COCKADED WOODPECKER
Dendrocopos borealis 8½   p. 145
  Field marks: A *"zebra-backed"* woodpecker with a black cap. The *white cheek* is the most conspicuous field mark. Male's red cockade is tiny, almost invisible.
  Similar species: (1) Red-bellied Woodpecker is zebra-backed but has a *red* cap. (2) Red-cockaded is more likely to be confused with Downy or Hairy but white cheek is a ready mark.
  Voice: A rough rasping *sripp* or *shilp*. Sometimes a higher *tsick*, but quite unlike notes of Downy or Hairy.
  Where found: Se. U.S. **Texas:** Local resident along e. edge of state; west to Tyler, Houston. *Habitat:* Pine forests. **Nest:** In hole in live pine with decayed heart. Eggs (3–5) white.

Cotingas: Cotingidae

A TROPICAL group, very varied in color, pattern, and behavior; omnivorous in food habits but our one species catches flying insects; eats berries. Cent. and S. America. No. of species: World, 90; N. America, 1; Texas, 1.

ROSE-THROATED BECARD   *Platypsaris aglaiae* 6½
(Xantus's Becard)   p. 161
  Field marks: A big-headed, thick-billed bird, somewhat resembling a flycatcher. *Male:* Gray above with *blackish cap and cheeks* and a lovely *rose-colored throat. Female:* Brown with rusty tail, *dark cap* and *light buffy collar* around nape. Underparts washed with buff.
  Voice: A thin slurred whistle *seeoo*, sometimes preceded by a weak chatter (Irby Davis).
  Where found: S. Arizona, s. Texas south to Costa Rica. **Texas:** Rare local *summer resident* in lower Rio Grande Valley (nests occasionally Hidalgo Co.). Casual winter. Accidental Galveston. *Habitat:* Woodlands, wooded resacas. **Nest:** A woven football-shaped mass suspended from forest tree. Eggs (4–6) white.

Tyrant Flycatchers: Tyrannidae

FLYCATCHERS usually perch upright on exposed twigs or branches and sally forth at intervals to snap up passing insects. They may sit quite motionless save for an occasional jerk of the tail. Bill flat, with bristles at base. Food: Mainly flying insects. N. and S. America; mainly tropical portions. No. of species: World, 365; N. America, 32; Texas, 25 (plus 5 accidentals).

EASTERN KINGBIRD *Tyrannus tyrannus* 8½–9 p. 160
Field marks: When this large black and white flycatcher flies, the *white band* at the *tip* of its fanlike tail leaves no doubt as to its identity. The red crown mark, sometimes emphasized in color plates, is concealed and rarely noticed. Often harasses hawks. Often seems to fly quiveringly on "tips of wings."
Voice: A rapid sputter of high nervous bickering notes: *dzee-dzee-dzee,* etc., and *kit-kit-kitter-kitter,* etc. Also a nasal *dzeeb.*
Where found: Cent. Canada south to Gulf of Mexico. Winters Peru to Bolivia. **Texas:** *Migrant* (Mar.–May, Aug.–Oct.) throughout, except Trans-Pecos (casual El Paso); most numerous along coast. *Breeds* in e. and n. Texas; west to e. Panhandle, Kerrville; south to Navasota, Houston, Kerrville. *Habitat:* Farmlands, orchards, roadsides. **Nest:** A twiggy, well-lined saucer on limb; occasionally on post. Eggs (3–4) blotched.

TROPICAL KINGBIRD *Tyrannus melancholicus* 9½
(Couch's Kingbird, "Olive-backed Kingbird") p. 160
Field marks: Back olive, head gray with dark mask through eye, belly *bright yellow.* Very similar to Western and Cassin's Kingbirds, but tail slightly *forked, dusky brown,* not black, *without white edgings.* Little or no gray across breast. The common kingbird of the lower Rio Grande.
Voice: A high nasal *queer* or *chi-queer,* resembling notes of Cassin's Kingbird but higher; described by E. Kincaid as *be-reeeeeeer* of police-whistle quality (suggesting Pauraque).
Where found: Se. Arizona, s. Texas to Argentina. **Texas:** *Resident* in s. Texas (south of a line from Falcon Dam to Raymondville). Occasional north to Laredo, Alice, Kingsville; straggler to Beeville and along coast to Galveston. Accidental Del Rio, El Paso. Irregular in winter. **Nest:** A saucer of twigs and Spanish moss on limb. Eggs (3–4) pinkish, spotted.

WESTERN KINGBIRD *Tyrannus verticalis* 8–9½
("Arkansas Kingbird") p. 160
Field marks: Smaller than Robin, with pale gray head and back, pale yellow underparts. The best index to the identity of the three yellow-bellied kingbirds is their tails. In this species the black tail is narrowly bordered on each side with white. Immature and worn birds do not always have white tail-margins but the grayish upper parts, lightest on the head, and yellowish underparts are enough to identify them.
Similar species: (1) Great and Wied's Crested Flycatchers have wing-bars, *rufous* tails. See (2) Cassin's and (3) Tropical Kingbirds.

Voice: Bickering calls; shrill twittering notes; a sharp *whit*.
Where found: Sw. Canada south to n. Mexico. Winters mainly from nw. Mexico to Nicaragua. **Texas:** *Migrant* (Mar.–May, Sept.–Oct.) throughout (less frequent east). *Breeds* from Panhandle and Trans-Pecos east to Denton, Dallas, Waco, Austin; south to Del Rio, San Marcos. *Habitat:* Semi-open country, scattered trees, farms, roadsides, towns. **Nest:** A saucer of twigs, grasses, on horizontal branch, post, pole. Eggs (3–5) boldly marked.

CASSIN'S KINGBIRD   *Tyrannus vociferans*   9   p. 160
Field marks: Like Western Kingbird but darker, with an *olive-gray* rather than pearly-gray back, and *no white sides* on black tail. (Tail is sometimes lightly *tipped* with white.) Cassin's appears to have *whiter chin* than the two similar kingbirds, owing to darker gray chest coloration.
Similar species: Immature Western Kingbird may lack white tail-margins, but grayer back, paler breast identify it. Although Cassin's prefers higher altitudes, Western and Cassin's are often found together. Calls, very different.
Voice: A low nasal *queer* or *chi-queer* or *chi-bew;* also an excited *ki-dear, ki-dear, ki-dear,* etc.
Where found: S. Montana south to s. Mexico. Winters in Mexico, Guatemala. **Texas:** *Breeds* in higher parts of w. Texas (mainly west of Pecos) and w. Panhandle. *Migrant* along upper Rio Grande. *Habitat:* Semi-open mt. country, scattered trees, ranches, towns. **Nest:** A saucer of twigs, grass, on limb of tree, pole, post, eaves, etc. Eggs (3–5) spotted.

SCISSOR-TAILED FLYCATCHER
Muscivora forficata   11½–15   p. 161
Field marks: A beautiful bird, pale pearly gray, with an extremely long scissor-like tail. Usually the "scissors" are folded. The sides and wing-linings are salmon-pink. No other land bird in its range has such streaming tail feathers (except the accidental Fork-tailed Flycatcher, p. 273).
Similar species: Young bird with short tail may resemble Western Kingbird, but has a touch of pinkish on lower belly instead of extensive pale yellow. Breast whiter, more white in tail.
Voice: A harsh *keck* or *kew;* a repeated *ka-leep;* also shrill, excited kingbird-like bickerings and stutterings.
Where found: Se. Colorado, s. Nebraska south to s. Texas. Winters s. Mexico to Panama. **Texas:** *Migrant and summer resident* (Mar.–Dec.); in all sections except extreme w. tip (casual at El Paso). *Habitat:* Roadsides, ranches, farms, mesquite, semi-open country. **Nest:** A twiggy, grass-lined cup in tree, on bush, telegraph pole, or other structure. Eggs (4–6) spotted.

KISKADEE FLYCATCHER　　*Pitangus sulphuratus*　　10½
(Derby Flycatcher)　　　　　　　　　　　　　　　　p. 160
　　Field marks: A very large big-headed flycatcher, near size of
Belted Kingfisher, and somewhat like that bird in actions, even
catching small fish. It has rufous wings and tail. The bright
yellow underparts and crown-patch, and *strikingly patterned
black and white face* identify it at once.
　　Voice: A loud *get-ter-heck* (I. Davis); also *wheep!*
　　Where found: S. Texas south to Argentina. **Texas:** *Resident* of
lower Rio Grande Valley. Occasional north to Laredo, Beeville,
Rockport. *Habitat:* Streamside thickets, groves, orchards,
towns. **Nest:** Football-shaped, with entrance in side; in acacia,
mesquite, palm, thorny tree. Eggs (2–5) dotted.

GREAT CRESTED FLYCATCHER　　*Myiarchus crinitus*　　8–9
(Crested Flycatcher)　　　　　　　　　　　　　　　p. 160
　　Field marks: A large woodland flycatcher with *cinnamon wings
and tail*, gray throat and breast, and yellow belly. Raises a slight
bushy crest when excited.
　　Similar species: See the other similar cinnamon-tailed flycatchers, (1) Wied's Crested Flycatcher (s. Texas) and (2) Ash-
throated Flycatcher (w. Texas). (3) The various kingbirds have
black or dusky tails.
　　Voice: Note, a loud whistled *wheeep!* with rising inflection; also
a throaty, rolling *prrrrrreet!*
　　Where found: S. Canada south to Gulf States. Winters from e.
Mexico to Colombia. **Texas:** *Summers* (Apr.–Sept.) throughout
much of state; west to ne. Panhandle and Edwards Plateau;
south at least to Beeville, Rockport. Migrant through Delta;
does not breed there; winters rarely. Casual Midland, El Paso.
Habitat: Woodlands, groves, orchards. **Nest:** In hole in tree
(sometimes bird box). Eggs (5–6) streaked with reddish.

WIED'S CRESTED FLYCATCHER
Myiarchus tyrannulus　　9–9½
(Mexican Crested Flycatcher, "Mexican Flycatcher")　　p. 160
　　Field marks: Like the Great Crested Flycatcher, which migrates
through its range in s. Texas, but can be distinguished by the
completely dark bill, somewhat paler coloration below and
different call notes.
　　Similar species: Great Crested has brown lower mandible.
　　Voice: A sharp *pwit;* a rolling throaty *purreeet.* A. C. Bent
describes a double-note *"come here"* accented on last syllable.
　　Where found: Sw. U.S. south to n. Argentina. **Texas:** *Summers*
(Mar.–Sept.) in s. Texas north to Beeville, Corpus Christi,
rarely to San Antonio; straggler to Big Bend. *Habitat:* Woodlands, semi-open country, ranches, streamside groves. **Nest:** In
cavity in tree or post. Eggs (3–5) streaked.

ASH-THROATED FLYCATCHER
Myiarchus cinerascens 8–8½   p. 160
Field marks: A medium-sized flycatcher, smaller than a king-bird, with two white wing-bars, white throat, *pale yellowish belly*, and *rufous tail*. Head slightly bushy. No other common flycatcher in western Texas has a rufous tail.
Similar species: (1) Some kingbirds have yellow bellies, but dusky or *blackish* tails. (2) In e. half of Texas see Great Crested Flycatcher; (3) in s. Texas see Wied's Crested.
Voice: *Pwit;* also a rolling *prrit* and *ke-wherr*.
Where found: E. Washington state south to s. Mexico. Winters from sw. U.S. south to Costa Rica. **Texas:** *Summers* (Mar.–Oct.) in Panhandle (local) and from w. Texas east through Edwards Plateau to Austin and Beeville and south along the Rio Grande to Laredo. In *migration* east to cent. coast. *Habitat:* Deserts, semi-arid country, brushland, mesquite. **Nest:** In hole in tree, post, mesquite, yucca. Eggs (4–5) streaked.

EASTERN PHOEBE *Sayornis phoebe* 6½–7   p. 161
Field marks: A sparrow-sized flycatcher, gray-brown above and whitish below. The only small flycatcher which has neither con-spicuous wing-bars nor an eye-ring. This lack of wing-bars, and the persistent tail-wagging habit are sure points. The bill is *black*. Young Phoebes sometimes have dull brownish wing-bars.
Similar species: Wood Pewees and other small flycatchers have conspicuous wing-bars. Their bills are yellowish or whitish on the lower mandible. They do not wag their tails.
Voice: Song, a well-enunciated *phoe-be*, or *fi-bree* (second note alternately higher or lower than first). Note, a *chip*.
Where found: Cent. Canada south to cent. Texas. Winters s. U.S. to s. Mexico. **Texas:** *Migrates* throughout except Trans-Pecos (casual El Paso). *Winters* (Sept.–May) except in Trans-Pecos and Panhandle. *Summers* in e., n., and cent. parts; west to Panhandle, Coleman, Kerrville; south to San Antonio. *Habitat:* Streamsides, farms, roadsides, towns. **Nest:** A cup of mud, moss, grass, on ledge, bridge, building. Eggs (4–5) white.

BLACK PHOEBE *Sayornis nigricans* 6½   p. 161
Field marks: The only *black-breasted* flycatcher. Upper parts, head, and breast *black;* belly *white*, in sharp contrast to black of sides and breast. Has phoebe tail-wagging habit.
Voice: Song, a thin, strident *fi-bee, fi-bee*, the first two notes rising, the last two dropping. Note, a sharp *tsip*.
Where found: Sw. U.S. south to n. Argentina. **Texas:** *Resident* in w. Texas; east to San Angelo and Del Rio (rarely Eagle Pass). Casual in winter in Panhandle and east to Fort Worth, Rock-port, Beeville, San Antonio, Delta. *Habitat:* Along streams and canyons. **Nest:** A bracket of mud, grass, on ledge or bridge near water. Eggs (3–6) white, sometimes dotted.

SAY'S PHOEBE *Sayornis saya* 7–8   p. 161
  Field marks: A large, pale phoebe with grayish back, head, and breast and pale *rusty-brown* belly and under tail-coverts. The *black tail* and rusty underparts give it the look of a small Robin, but has flycatcher habits. Flirts tail; often hovers.
  Similar species: See the various kingbirds.
  Voice: A plaintive *pee-ur* or *pee-ee;* also trilling note.
  Where found: Alaska, nw. Canada south to cent. Mexico. Partial migrant. **Texas:** *Resident* in Trans-Pecos. *Summers* also locally in Panhandle; *winters* in Trans-Pecos, s. Staked Plains, Edwards Plateau, eastward rarely to Dallas, Austin, San Antonio, Beeville, Rockport, Brownsville (uncommon). Casual Houston. *Habitat:* Brushy plains, desert edges, canyon mouths.
  Nest: A bracket of grass, wool, etc., on ledge, rock wall, bridge, etc. Eggs (4–5) white.

YELLOW-BELLIED FLYCATCHER
Empidonax flaviventris 5–5½   p. 161
  Field marks: The *Empidonax* flycatchers are a confusing lot, but they may be known as a group by their small size, eye-rings, and white wing-bars. The decidedly yellowish underparts simplify our difficulties with this *Empidonax*, at least in the spring. Others of this group have a tinge of yellow beneath, especially in fall, but none of the rest (in e. half of Texas) has yellow from throat to under tail-coverts. Eye-ring also yellow.
  Similar species: (1) Many Acadians look suspiciously like Yellow-bellies in the fall, and thus it is contended that these two cannot be safely distinguished in autumnal migration. (2) Any flycatcher looking like a Yellow-bellied in w. Texas would almost certainly be a Western Flycatcher.
  Voice: A simple, spiritless *per-wee* or *chu-wee*, rising on second syllable; a little like Wood Pewee's, but more suggestive of note of Semipalmated Plover. Also *killic*.
  Where found: Cent. Canada south to n. edge of cent. and e. U.S. Winters Mexico to Panama. **Texas:** *Migrant* (Apr.–May, Sept.–Nov.) through e. half (west to Fort Worth, Austin, Delta). Most frequent near coast. *Habitat:* Woodlands, thickets.

ACADIAN FLYCATCHER *Empidonax virescens* 5½–6¾   p. 161
  Field marks: A small flycatcher with a conspicuous light *eye-ring* and two white *wing-bars*. It is a greenish *Empidonax* with a yellowish wash on the sides, but is not safely identified except by habitat, range, and voice. It is the *only Empidonax* that breeds in the woodlands of the e. half of Texas.
  Similar species: (1) See other *Empidonax* flycatchers, especially when dealing with migrants. (2) Wood Pewee often shares same woods, is larger, lacks eye-ring. (3) White-eyed Vireo is sometimes mistaken for this species!

Voice: "Song" a sharp explosive *wee-see!* or *spit-chee!* (sharp upward inflection); also a thin *peet*.
Where found: South Dakota, s. New York south to Gulf States. Winters Costa Rica to Ecuador. **Texas:** *Migrant* (Apr.–May, Aug.–Oct.) through e. half; west to e. Panhandle and Edwards Plateau. *Summers* in forested parts of e. and cent. Texas; west locally to Gainesville, Edwards Plateau (Kerrville); south to Houston (rarely), College Station, Austin, Kerrville; casually Rio Grande delta. *Habitat:* Open woods, wooded streams. **Nest:** A woven cup suspended near end of branch. Eggs (2–4) dotted.

TRAILL'S FLYCATCHER *Empidonax traillii* 5½–6   p. 161
Field marks: A small flycatcher with a dark back and light breast, light *eye-ring* and two white *wing-bars*. Like Acadian Flycatcher, but browner and with a whiter throat (but these are not safe field characters). Rely only on habitat, voice. Nest is also determinative (usually in bush).
Voice: In some localities, the usual song is a 3-syllabled *fee-be'-o* with a hoarse burry quality, accent on the middle syllable. In other areas this is contracted into a sneezy *fitz-bew* or *witch-brew*. Common note, a low *pep* or *pit*.
Where found: Alaska, cent. Canada south to e.-cent. and sw. U.S. Winters Mexico to Argentina. **Texas:** *Migrant* (Apr.–May, Aug.–Oct.) probably throughout. *Summers* locally in Trans-Pecos; east rarely to Edwards Plateau (Kerrville); also locally in canyons of Panhandle. *Habitat:* Streamside thickets, bushy swamps; scrubby pastures in some areas. **Nest:** A loosely made cup of grass, stems, in shrub. Eggs (3–4) spotted.

LEAST FLYCATCHER
Empidonax minimus 5–5¾   p. 161
Field marks: A small flycatcher, smaller than Wood Pewee or Phoebe, dark above and light below, with a conspicuous white *eye-ring* and two white *wing-bars*. The Least Flycatcher is grayer above and whiter below than Acadian and Traill's Flycatchers. Its wing-bars are whiter, and its lower mandible brownish (in the others, whitish or flesh-colored). These are comparative characteristics of uncertain value in the field.
Similar species: Two other eastern *Empidonaces*, Traill's and Acadian, are almost identical. During a "wave" of these birds in May, we let most of them go as *"Empidonax"* flycatchers. Ludlow Griscom wrote: "Collecting has proved that it is *impossible* to be certain in separating Acadian, Traill's and Least Flycatchers by color characters even in spring. In fall, it is out of the question, the determination of museum skins often being very critical. The songs of all three are easily recognizable. However, in migration they seldom sing their names."

Voice: A sharply snapped dry *che-bek'*, accent on the second syllable; very emphatic. The *k* sound is distinctive.
Where found: Cent. Canada south to n.-cent. and ne. U.S. Winters from Mexico to Panama. **Texas:** *Migrant* (Apr.–May, Aug.-Oct.) throughout most of state, west to Big Bend and Panhandle. *Winters* rarely in Rio Grande delta. *Habitat:* Open woodlands, thickets, scattered trees, orchards.

HAMMOND'S FLYCATCHER
Empidonax hammondii 5–5½   p. 161
Field marks: Of the five similar western *Empidonax* flycatchers, the Dusky and the Hammond's have given field students the most headaches. It is a standing joke among western ornithologists that no one seems to have an infallible way of telling them apart in the field. Neither nest in Texas nor pass through the western part in migration. In fact, the advice given by Mr. Griscom (see Least Flycatcher) applies equally to the western complex of *Empidonaces*. On their breeding grounds farther north, Hammond's occurs higher in the mountains, in the taller firs; Dusky prefers chaparral or a mixture of chaparral and firs. As a rule, Hammond's is more olive, not so gray; the underparts are more yellowish, contrasting with a grayer chest. These points are so tricky as to be of almost no use.
Voice: Voice descriptions vary. The author can see no great difference in the songs of Dusky and Hammond's. Birds which he was assured were *hammondii* sang a thin colorless song: *se-lip*, *twur*, *tree-ip*. R. Hoffmann wrote that the low *twur* or *tsurp* note is always typical of *hammondii*. Dr. D. E. Davis interprets the song of the Dusky as *clip*, *whee*, *zee*, the last note highest.
Where found: S. Alaska, cent. w. Canada south to mts. of e. California, n. New Mexico. Winters Mexico to Nicaragua. **Texas:** *Migrant* (Mar.–May, Aug.–Oct.) mainly in Trans-Pecos. *Habitat:* In migration, woodlands, shady thickets, even brush.

DUSKY FLYCATCHER   *Empidonax oberholseri* 5¼–6
(Wright's Flycatcher)   p. 161
Field marks: See Hammond's Flycatcher.
Voice: See Hammond's Flycatcher.
Where found: W. Canada south to mts. of s. California and New Mexico. Winters in Mexico. **Texas:** *Migrant* (Apr.–May, Sept.–Oct.) through w. Texas, mainly west of Pecos River. *Habitat:* In migration, same as Hammond's.

GRAY FLYCATCHER   *Empidonax wrightii* 5½   p. 161
Field marks: Very similar to Dusky Flycatcher, but slightly larger, grayer on back, and with base of lower mandible more flesh-colored. Like most other *Empidonax* flycatchers, can hardly be safely identified except on breeding grounds, by habitat. In e. Oregon this is sagebrush. In Utah it is arid

piñon and juniper. In neither habitat would one expect to find Dusky or Hammond's Flycatcher (except possibly in migration).
Voice: R. Hoffmann states that the song is less varied than Dusky's or Hammond's, with only two elements, a vigorous *chiwip* and a fainter *cheep* on a higher pitch.
Where found: Sage country; cent. Oregon, sw. Wyoming south to California, w. New Mexico. Winters sw. U.S., Mexico.
Texas: Probably regular *migrant* (Apr.–May, Aug.–Sept.) in Trans-Pecos.

WESTERN FLYCATCHER *Empidonax difficilis* 5½–6 p. 161
Field marks: Upper parts olive-brown, underparts washed with yellowish, wing-bars whitish, eye-ring white. Very similar to the other small flycatchers of this group, but underparts usually more yellowish, *including the throat*. Some individuals of the other western species have a faint wash of yellow on the underparts, but their throats are white. It is the only *Empidonax* that breeds in the mountain forests of w. Texas and the one most likely to be encountered there in migration.
Similar species: Yellow-bellied Flycatcher migrates through e. half of Texas (has virtually the same appearance).
Voice: A sharp lisping *ps-seet*, with rising inflection, or *whea-tee* (E. Kincaid). Song, heard chiefly at daybreak, three thin colorless notes: *bzeek-trit-seet!*, last note highest.
Where found: Se. Alaska through w. N. America to Honduras. Winters Mexico to Honduras. **Texas:** *Migrant* (Apr.–May, Aug.–Sept.) through Trans-Pecos, s. Plains, and along Rio Grande; *summers* locally at 6000–8000 ft. in mts. of Trans-Pecos.
Habitat: Woodlands, groves. **Nest:** A cup of moss, rootlets, on ledge, stump, tree trunk, etc. Eggs (3–4) spotted.

EASTERN WOOD PEWEE *Contopus virens* 6–6½ p. 161
Field marks: A sparrow-sized flycatcher, dusky olive-brown above. It has *two conspicuous wing-bars* but *no* eye-ring. Lower mandible *yellow*. Wing much longer than that of Eastern Phoebe or other small flycatchers, reaching halfway down tail.
Similar species: (1) Phoebe lacks conspicuous wing-bars; wags tail. (2) The smaller and paler *Empidonax* flycatchers have conspicuous eye-rings. (3) In w. Texas see Western Wood Pewee.
Voice: A plaintive drawling whistle, *pee-a-wee*, slurring down, then up. Also *pee-ur*, slurring downward.
Where found: S. Canada south to Gulf States. Winters Costa Rica to Peru. **Texas:** *Migrant* (Apr.–May, Sept.–Oct.) throughout e. two-thirds of state, west to Panhandle, Edwards Plateau. *Summers* in e. and cent. Texas; west locally to Edwards Plateau (San Angelo, Kerrville); south to Victoria, San Antonio. *Winters* rarely in Delta. *Habitat:* Woodlands, groves. **Nest:** A neat, shallow cup saddled on horizontal branch. Eggs (3) spotted.

FLYCATCHERS

 Flycatchers perch in an upright attitude and often sit quite motionless. Sexes are similar.

GREAT CRESTED FLYCATCHER   p. 154
Yellow belly, rufous tail; brown lower mandible.
E. half of Texas.

WIED'S CRESTED FLYCATCHER   p. 154
Similar to Great Crested but somewhat paler breast; bill
wholly black. Different call notes. S. Texas.

ASH-THROATED FLYCATCHER   p. 155
Smaller, paler; whitish throat. W. Texas.

OLIVACEOUS FLYCATCHER   p. 273
Accidental in Texas.
Smaller than Ash-throated; throat gray.

WESTERN KINGBIRD   p. 152
Yellow belly, black tail with narrow white sides.

CASSIN'S KINGBIRD   p. 153
Whiter chin, darker breast; black tail, no white on sides.

TROPICAL KINGBIRD   p. 152
Tail forked, dusky brown, no white on sides. Upper breast
yellow, not gray.

EASTERN KINGBIRD   p. 152
Wide white band at tip of tail; white underparts.

KISKADEE FLYCATCHER   p. 154
Rufous wings and tail; striking head pattern.

SULPHUR-BELLIED FLYCATCHER   p. 273
Accidental in Texas.
Yellow underparts boldly *streaked;* rufous tail.

WIED'S CRESTED
FLYCATCHER

OLIVACEOUS
FLYCATCHER

GREAT CRESTED
FLYCATCHER

ASH-THROATED
FLYCATCHER

WESTERN
KINGBIRD

CASSIN'S
KINGBIRD

TROPICAL
KINGBIRD

EASTERN
KINGBIRD

KISKADEE
FLYCATCHER

SULPHUR-BELLIED
FLYCATCHER

SCISSOR-
TAILED
FLYCATCHER

ROSE-
THROATED
BECARD

COUES'
FLYC.

VERMILIC
FLYCATCH
♀

♂

SAY'S
PHOEBE

OLIVE-
SIDED
FLYC.

EASTERN
PHOEBE

EASTERN
WOOD PEWEE

WESTERN
WOOD PEWEE

TRAILL'S
EMPIDONAX FLYCATCHERS

WESTERN

BEARDLESS
FLYCATCHER

BLACK
PHOEBE

Plate 42

BECARD AND FLYCATCHERS

ROSE-THROATED BECARD p. 151
Male: Blackish cap, rose throat.
Female: Dark cap, buffy collar and underparts.

SCISSOR-TAILED FLYCATCHER p. 153
Very long forked tail.

VERMILION FLYCATCHER p. 162
Male: Vermilion underparts, crown; blackish back.
Female: Streaked pinkish or yellowish belly.

OLIVE-SIDED FLYCATCHER p. 162
Dark "vest" unbuttoned down front; white tufts.

COUES' FLYCATCHER p. 274
Accidental in Texas.
Similar to Olive-sided; more uniform gray; grayer throat.

SAY'S PHOEBE p. 156
Pale rusty underparts.

EASTERN WOOD PEWEE p. 159
Conspicuous wing-bars, no eye-ring. Song sweet, plaintive.
E. half of state.

WESTERN WOOD PEWEE p. 162
Darker on breast and sides than Eastern Wood Pewee.
Song nasal. W. parts of state.

EASTERN PHOEBE p. 155
No strong wing-bars (may have dull ones), no eye-ring;
wags tail.

EMPIDONAX FLYCATCHERS
Small; white wing-bars and eye-ring.
Traill's Flycatcher — Whitish underparts. p. 157
Other Empidonax Flycatchers, extremely close to
Traill's Flycatcher in appearance, are not illustrated
(for a full discussion see text, pp. 156–58). These are
Acadian and **Least Flycatchers** (e. half of Texas) and
Hammond's, Dusky, and **Gray Flycatchers** (w. Texas).
Western Flycatcher — Yellowish underparts. p. 159
Similar are: **Yellow-bellied Flycatcher** and some autumn
examples of **Acadian Flycatcher** (e. half of Texas).
p. 156

BEARDLESS FLYCATCHER p. 163
Very small; light brownish wing-bars. See text.

BLACK PHOEBE p. 155
The only black-breasted flycatcher.

WESTERN WOOD PEWEE *Contopus sordidulus* 6–6½ p. 161
Field marks: A sparrow-sized flycatcher, dusky gray-brown above, olive-gray on breast and sides. It has two narrow white wing-bars but *no* white eye-ring. The slightly larger size, much darker back, darker underparts, and lack of an eye-ring distinguish it from any of the smaller flycatchers, as do the much longer wings which extend halfway down the tail.
Similar species: Eastern Wood Pewee is not as strongly olive-gray on breast and sides; sings a very different song (sweet and plaintive, not nasal).
Voice: A nasal *peeyee* or *peecer*.
Where found: E. Alaska, to Cent. America. Winters Panama to Peru. **Texas:** *Summers* (Apr.–Oct.) in w. Texas east to Edwards Plateau (Kerrville). *Migrant* in Panhandle, Staked Plains and along Rio Grande (El Paso to Brownsville). *Habitat:* Woodlands, groves. **Nest:** A shallow cup saddled on limb. Eggs (3–4) spotted.

OLIVE-SIDED FLYCATCHER
Nuttallornis borealis 7¼–8   p. 161
Field marks: A rather large, stout bull-headed flycatcher, usually seen perched at the tip of a dead tree or exposed branch, from which it makes wide sallies after passing insects. Resembles the smaller Wood Pewee. Distinctive points are its large bill, white throat, *dark chest-patches* separated or nearly separated by a narrow strip of white (suggests a "dark jacket unbuttoned down front"). *Two cottony tufts of white* sometimes poke out from behind wings near the back.
Similar species: Wood Pewees are smaller, have light wing-bars.
Voice: Note, a trebled *pep-pep-pep*. Song, a spirited whistle: *quick-three-beers!*, middle note highest, last slurring down.
Where found: N. Alaska, cent. Canada south to mts. of sw. U.S. Winters in S. America. **Texas:** *Migrant* (Apr.–June, Aug.–Oct.) throughout. *Breeds* in Guadalupe Mts. of w. Texas. *Habitat:* In migration usually seen on tip of dead tree or dead branch; various country. **Nest:** A twiggy saucer well out on branch of conifer. **Eggs** (3) spotted.

VERMILION FLYCATCHER
Pyrocephalus rubinus 5½–6½   p. 161
Field marks: *Male: Crown, throat and underparts, flaming vermilion;* upper parts and tail blackish. Crown often raised in crest. *Female and immature:* Upper parts dark brown; breast white, narrowly streaked with dusky; lower belly and under tail-coverts washed with pinkish or yellow.
Similar species: Male Scarlet Tanager has scarlet back.
Voice: A slightly phoebe-like *p-p-pit-zeee* or *pit-a-zee;* elaborated during male's butterfly-like hovering display flight.

Where found: Sw. U.S. south locally to s. Argentina. **Texas:** *Resident* from w. Texas east through Edwards Plateau to Coleman, Austin, San Antonio; south to Rio Grande, Brownsville. Also *winters* along entire coast. Straggler to Panhandle (Amarillo, Canyon) and n. and e. sections (Fort Worth, Dallas, Nacogdoches, Tyler). *Habitat:* Near water in desert country; streamsides, fresh ponds, tanks. **Nest:** A flat twiggy saucer saddled on fork of limb. Eggs (2–3) blotched.

BEARDLESS FLYCATCHER *Camptostoma imberbe* 4½ p. 161
Field marks: A very small, nondescript flycatcher whose general appearance and behavior suggest a kinglet, a vireo, or an immature Verdin. Upper parts olive-gray; underparts dingy white; indistinct wing-bars and eye-ring; bill small and dark. Distinguished from *Empidonax* flycatchers by its smaller size, smaller head, different behavior, and very small bill.
Similar species: (1) Bell's Vireo is somewhat larger, slightly more yellowish on sides; wing-bars whitish or grayish (in many individuals of Beardless, wing-bars are buffy or even brownish). (2) Immature Verdin resembles Beardless Flycatcher very closely, but tends to be more pure gray above; no wing-bars. Does not live in woodlands; has different voice.
Voice: Call note, a thin *peeee-yuk*. Also a series of fine, rather gentle notes, *ee, ee, ee, ee, ee,* increasing in volume toward the middle of the series (G. M. Sutton).
Where found: S. Arizona, s. Texas south to Costa Rica. **Texas:** *Resident* mainly in Rio Grande delta; occasionally north to Norias. *Habitat:* Woodlands, thickets. **Nest:** Globular, entrance on side; in palmetto, tree tangle, or mistletoe. Eggs (3) speckled.

Larks: Alaudidae

STREAKED brown songbirds, mainly terrestrial. Hind claw elongated, almost straight. Voices musical; often sing high in display flight. Gregarious. Food: Mainly seeds; also insects. Mostly Old World except for our Horned Lark and introduced Skylark. No. of species: World, 75; N. America, 2; Texas, 1.

HORNED LARK *Eremophila alpestris* 7–8 p. 241
Field marks: A brown ground bird, larger than House Sparrow, with black "whiskers" and a contrasting head pattern. It has two small black *horns* (not always noticeable), and a black shield below the light throat; *walks,* does not hop; flying overhead, looks light-bellied with a *black* tail; folds wings tightly after each beat. Females and immatures are duller, but show Horned Lark pattern.

Similar species: See pipits, longspurs.
Voice: Song, tinkling, irregular, high-pitched, often long sustained; given from ground or very high in air in manner of European Skylark. Note, a clear *tsee-ee* or *tsee-titi.*
Where found: Breeds widely in N. Hemisphere; spreads in winter. **Texas:** Winters throughout. *Breeds* in w. Texas (local), Panhandle (the most abundant bird), and n. Texas (occasionally east to Tyler); also on coastal prairie from Galveston Bay to Brownsville (inland as far as Beeville); probably very locally in cent. Texas. *Habitat:* Plains, prairies, fields, golf courses, airports, dirt roads, shores. **Nest:** A grass-lined depression on ground. Eggs (3–4) spotted.

Swallows: Hirundinidae

SLIM streamlined form and graceful flight characterize these sparrow-sized birds. Tiny feet, long pointed wings, and short bills with very wide gapes. Food: Flying insects caught in flight. Nearly cosmopolitan, except polar regions. No. of species: World, 75; N. America, 11; Texas 8 (plus 1 accidental).

VIOLET-GREEN SWALLOW
Tachycineta thalassina   5½   p. 140
Field marks: Dark above, glossed with green and purple; clear white below. Separated from Tree Swallow by greener back and *white patches* that almost meet over base of tail. White of face more extensive, *partially encircling eye.*
Similar species: See (1) Tree Swallow, (2) White-throated Swift.
Voice: A rapid twitter; a thin *chip.* Dawn song, *"tsip tseet tsip"* (R. Hoffmann).
Where found: Yukon River south to n. Mexico. Winters Mexico, Cent. America. **Texas:** *Migrant* (Mar.–May, Sept.) in Trans-Pecos; occasional in Panhandle. Straggler to coast (Rockport, Sinton, Galveston Bay). *Breeds* in mts. of w. Texas (Guadalupe and Sacramento Mts.). *Habitat:* In migration widespread; when nesting, open pine forests, canyons. **Nest:** In hole in tree, bank of stream, bird box. Eggs (4–6) white.

TREE SWALLOW *Iridoprocne bicolor* 5–6   p. 140
Field marks: Steely blue-black or green-black above, *clear white* below. In e. half of Texas no other swallow has such immaculate white underparts. Immature is dusky brown above; has incomplete dusky collar on breast. Glides in circles, ending each glide with three or four quick flaps and a short climb.
Similar species: (1) In w. Texas see Violet-green Swallow. Immature Tree might be confused with (2) Rough-winged

Swallow (dusky throat) and (3) Bank Swallow (complete breast-band).

Voice: Note, *cheet* or *chi-veet*. A liquid twitter. Song, *weet, trit, weet*, repeated with variations.

Where found: Alaska, Canada, south to California and cent. U.S. Winters s. U.S. to Cent. America. **Texas:** *Migrant* (Feb.–May, July–Nov.) throughout. A few winter along coast. *Habitat:* In migration, open country near water: marshes, streams, lakes.

BANK SWALLOW *Riparia riparia* 5–5½   p. 140

Field marks: A small *brown-backed* swallow with a *distinct dark breastband* across the white underparts. Flight irregular, more fluttery than other swallows'; glides short, unstable (C. H. Blake).

Similar species: (1) Rough-winged Swallow is larger, lacks the band, has a *dusky throat*. Bank Swallow is colonial, Rough-wing more solitary. (2) In late summer brownish young Tree Swallows sometimes seem to have a faint breastband.

Voice: A short dry buzz or rattle, *brrt* or *bzzht*.

Where found: Breeds widely in N. Hemisphere. Winters in S. America, Africa, s. Asia. **Texas:** *Migrant* (Mar.–May, July–Oct.) throughout. *Breeds* very locally in e., n., and cent. Texas and Trans-Pecos (along Rio Grande). *Habitat:* Usually near water; over fields, marshes, streams, lakes. **Nest:** In hole in sand bank in colony. Eggs (3–6) white.

ROUGH-WINGED SWALLOW
Stelgidopteryx ruficollis 5–5¾   p. 140

Field marks: A *brown-backed* swallow, larger and lighter brown than Bank Swallow; *no breastband*. The light underparts shade into a *dingy color toward the throat*. Flight unlike Bank Swallow's, more like Barn Swallow's; direct; with wings folded back at end of stroke.

Similar species: (1) Bank Swallow has dark breastband. (2) Young Tree Swallow in late summer is brownish but darker than Rough-wing, has white throat, more snowy underparts.

Voice: A harsh *trrit;* rougher than Bank Swallow's.

Where found: S. Canada south to Argentina. Winters mostly south of U.S. **Texas:** *Summers* (Mar.–Nov.) locally throughout. A few *winter* along coast from Del Rio south along Rio Grande. *Habitat:* Usually near streams, lakes. **Nest:** In hole in bank, ledge or crevice in masonry. Eggs (3–6) white.

BARN SWALLOW *Hirundo rustica* 6–7½   p. 140

Field marks: The only native swallow that is truly "swallow-tailed"; the only one with white tail-spots. Blue-black above, cinnamon-buff below with darker throat. Immatures duller, with shorter tails. Flight direct, close to ground; wing-tips pulled back at end of stroke; not much gliding.

Voice: A soft *wit* or *kvik-kvik, wit-wit.* About nest, a harsh irritated *ee-tee* or *keet.* Song, a long musical twitter interspersed with gutturals.

Where found: Breeds widely in N. Hemisphere. Winters mainly in S. America, Africa, s. Asia. **Texas:** *Migrant* (Mar.–June, July–Nov.) throughout. *Winters* occasionally on coast. *Breeds* in w. Texas, locally in Panhandle and very locally in n. and e. Texas. *Habitat:* Open country, farms, fields, marshes, lakes, etc. **Nest:** An open mud cup lined with feathers, on ledge, bridge, beam, or building. Eggs (3–5) speckled.

CLIFF SWALLOW *Petrochelidon pyrrhonota* 5–6   p. 140

Field marks: Look for the pale rusty or *buffy* rump; it quickly marks the Cliff Swallow. Overhead it appears *square-tailed* with a *dark* throat-patch. Glides in a long ellipse, ending each glide with a much steeper climb than other swallows ("like a roller coaster" — C. H. Blake).

Similar species: (1) On Edwards Plateau see Cave Swallow. (2) When nesting on barns, Cliff Swallow builds gourdlike nest *outside*, beneath eaves; Barn Swallow builds open nest, *usually*, but not always, *inside* the barn.

Voice: A low *chur.* Alarm note, *keer.* Song, creaking notes followed by guttural gratings; harsher than Barn Swallow's song.

Where found: Cent. Alaska, cent. Canada south to cent. Mexico. Winters in S. America. **Texas:** *Migrant* (Mar.–June, July–Nov.) throughout. *Summers* locally except in e. Texas and upper coastal plain. Colonial. *Habitat:* Open country, farmland, cliffs, canyons, riversides, streams. **Nest:** A gourdlike jug of mud under bridge, eave, cliffside; in colony. Eggs (4–5) spotted.

CAVE SWALLOW *Petrochelidon fulva* 5–6
(Coahuila Cliff Swallow)   p. 140

Field marks: Like Cliff Swallow but throat and cheeks *pale* or *buffy*, forehead *dark chestnut.* Rump as in Cliff Swallow.

Similar species: Cliff Swallow has face colors reversed; forehead-patch pale, throat and cheeks dark chestnut. In the Big Bend (Brewster Co.) a race of the Cliff Swallow, *P. p. minima*, occurs very locally in which the forehead is dark; such birds would be dark on *both* forehead and throat.

Voice: A clear *weet* or *cheweet;* also a loud accented *chu, chu.* Song, "a series of squeaks blending into a complex melodic warble; ending in double-toned notes" (Selander and Baker).

Where found: Se. New Mexico, s.-cent. Texas, ne. Mexico, Yucatan, s. Mexico, West Indies. Winter range unknown. **Texas:** *Summer resident* (Feb.–Sept.) only of s. edge of Edwards Plateau. Colonial. Known to nest in about 16 limestone caves in w. Kerr, Edwards, n. Uvalde, n. Kinney, and e. Valverde Cos.

Nest: An open cup of mud in cave or sinkhole. Eggs (2–3) speckled.

PURPLE MARTIN *Progne subis* 7½–8½   p. 140
  Field marks: Our largest swallow. The male is uniformly blue-black *above and below*. No other swallow is black-bellied. Female light-bellied; throat and breast grayish, often a faint collar around neck. Glides in circles, alternating quick flaps and glides; spreads tail more often than other swallows.
  Similar species: Tree Swallow is much smaller than female Martin, is immaculate white, not gray on throat and breast. See Gray-breasted Martin (p. 274).
  Voice: Throaty and rich *tchew-wew*, etc., or *pew, pew*. Song, gurgling, running to a succession of low rich gutturals.
  Where found: S. Canada south to nw. Mexico and Gulf States. Winters in S. America. **Texas:** *Migrant* (Feb.–May, July–Oct.) through most of state; rare in w. Texas. *Breeds* locally except in w. and southernmost parts. *Habitat:* Towns, rural country; widespread in migration. **Nest:** A loose mass of debris in tree hollow, building, martin house. Eggs (3–5) white.

Jays, Magpies, and Crows: Corvidae

THE LARGEST of the perching birds — longish, powerful bills with nostrils covered by forward-pointing bristles. Crows and ravens are very large, black. Magpies have long tails. Jays are usually colorful (bright blue, green). Sexes look alike. Juveniles resemble adults. Food: Almost anything edible. Nearly cosmopolitan except polar regions, New Zealand, Polynesia. No. of species: World, 100; N. America, 16; Texas, 11 (plus 1 accidental).

BLUE JAY *Cyanocitta cristata* 11–12   p. 176
  Field marks: A large *bright blue* bird with a *crest;* white spots in wings and tail; dingy whitish on underparts; black "necklace."
  Similar species: Other "blue" jays lack white spots. Scrub and Mexican Jays lack crests. See Belted Kingfisher.
  Voice: A harsh slurring *jeeah* or *jay;* many other notes. Seems to imitate Red-shouldered and Red-tailed Hawks.
  Where found: S. Canada, e. of Rockies south to Gulf States. **Texas:** *Resident* in Panhandle and n. and e. Texas; west to e. edge of Edwards Plateau; south to Houston and nearly to San Antonio. Irregular in winter farther south; Straggler to Delta and Uvalde. *Habitat:* Woodlands, groves, towns. **Nest:** A bowl of twigs in tree. Eggs (3–5) variable, spotted.

STELLER'S JAY *Cyanocitta stelleri* 12–13½   p. 176
  Field marks: A *large dark black and blue bird with a long crest.* Foreparts blackish; wings, tail, and underparts deep blue. The

only jay with a crest found in mountains of w. Texas. Lives in conifers; other jays prefer oaks and scrub.

Similar species: (1) Blue Jay has white spots in wings and tail. (2) Scrub and (3) Mexican Jays are paler, lack crests.

Voice: A loud *shook-shook-shook* or *shack-shack-shack* or *wheck-wek-wek-wek-wek* or *kwesh-kwesh-kwesh;* many other notes.

Where found: S. Alaska south through w. N. America to Nicaragua. **Texas:** *Resident* (6000–8500 ft.) in Guadalupe and Davis Mts. of w. Texas. In winter to El Paso, Big Bend, Panhandle (rare). Casual Edwards Plateau. *Habitat:* Pine and Douglas fir forests. **Nest:** A twiggy bowl in tree. Eggs (3–5) greenish, spotted.

SCRUB JAY *Aphelocoma coerulescens* 11½
(Texas Jay; California Jay)　　　　　　　　　　　　　p. 176
　　Field marks: Look for this *crestless* Jay in the oak scrub. Head, wings and tail *blue;* back pale brownish. Underparts pale gray; dark band across breast. Often swoops in long shallow curves.
　　Similar species: (1) Steller's Jay has crest, black foreparts; prefers pines, firs. (2) In Chisos Mts. see Mexican Jay.
　　Voice: Rough rasping notes: *kwesh — kwesh.* Also a harsh *check-check-check-check* and a rasping *zhreek* or *zhrink.*
　　Where found: Sw. Washington and sw. Wyoming south through w. U.S. to s. Mexico. Also cent. Florida. **Texas:** *Resident* in w. Texas east to San Angelo; locally to cent. parts of Edwards Plateau (Kerrville, Boerne); in winter also to El Paso, Big Spring, Panhandle; casually to e. edge of Plateau. *Habitat:* Scrub oak, brush, cedars. **Nest:** A twiggy bowl in bush or low tree. Eggs (3–6) buff or green, spotted.

MEXICAN JAY *Aphelocoma ultramarina* 11½–13
(Arizona Jay)　　　　　　　　　　　　　　　　　　　p. 176
　　Field marks: A blue jay without a crest. Resembles Scrub Jay but *underparts more uniform,* pale gray, lacking the distinct whitish throat and dusky band across breast. Back grayer, not brownish like Scrub Jay's. Voice very different.
　　Voice: A rough querulous *drenk* or *jenk.*
　　Where found: Cent. Arizona, w. Texas to cent. Mexico. **Texas:** *Resident* only in Big Bend (Chisos Mts.). *Habitat:* Oak forests. **Nest:** A twiggy bowl in oak. Eggs (4) greenish, spotted.

GREEN JAY *Cyanocorax yncas* 11–12　　　　　　　　p. 176
　　Field marks: The only *green* jay. Throat-patch, *black;* top of head, bright blue, sides of tail, yellow. Unique.
　　Voice: *Cheh cheh cheh cheh;* also *cleep, cleep, cleep,* etc.; a dry throaty rattle like a cricket frog's; also other calls.
　　Where found: S. tip of Texas south to n. Honduras; also Venezuela to n. Bolivia. **Texas:** *Resident* only in s. tip of state, north to Norias and upriver to Laredo. Small colony at San Antonio.

Casual or occasional to Alice, Kingsville, cent. coast. *Habitat:* Brush, woodlands. **Nest:** A twiggy bowl in thicket or small tree. Eggs (3–5) spotted.

BLACK-BILLED MAGPIE *Pica pica* 17½–21½
(American Magpie)   p. 176
   Field marks: Tail 9½–12. Larger than a jay or a grackle; the only large *black and white* land bird with a long *wedge-shaped* tail. In flight the iridescent greenish-black tail streams behind; large white patches flash in the wings.
   Voice: A rapid *cheg cheg cheg cheg.* Also a nasal querulous *maaag?* or *maa–maa?*
   Where found: Coastal Alaska south through w. N. America to e. California and n. New Mexico; also Eurasia. **Texas:** Occasional fall or winter straggler to Panhandle and w. Texas.

COMMON RAVEN *Corvus corax* 21½–26½   p. 170
   Field marks: Although a Common Raven is much larger than a Crow, note the flight. Hawklike, the Raven alternates flapping with soaring. It soars on flat wings; the Crow with wings "bent upward." The ample tail, seen from below, is distinctly *wedge-shaped.* When bird perches at not too great a distance, shaggy throat feathers are evident. If the bird is undoubtedly a raven but near the size of a Crow, it is the next species.
   Similar species: See White-necked Raven.
   Voice: A croaking *cr-r-ruck* or *prruk;* a high metallic *tok.*
   Where found: Widespread in N. America, Eurasia, Africa. **Texas:** *Resident* in Trans-Pecos; a few eastward (Sonora; w. Kerr Co.). Casual east to San Antonio. Accidental cent. coast, Galveston. *Habitat:* Mts. and canyons. **Nest:** A mass of sticks usually on cliff. Eggs (4–5) greenish, spotted.

WHITE-NECKED RAVEN *Corvus cryptoleucus* 19–21   p. 170
   Field marks: A small raven, size of Crow. In w. Texas the larger Common Raven is most commonly seen in the mountains and steep canyons, while the White-neck prefers mesquite flats and yucca deserts. This species flies with the typical, flat-winged glide of the raven; has a somewhat wedge-shaped tail. The bases of the feathers on neck and breast are *white.* This shows only when the feathers are ruffled. Gregarious.
   Similar species: See (1) Common Raven and (2) Common Crow (latter is found in same range as White-neck locally but favors less arid situations, rivers, etc.).
   Voice: A hoarse *kraak,* flatter than croak of Common Raven.
   Where found: Deserts of sw. U.S. south to cent. Mexico. **Texas:** *Resident* in w. half; east to w. parts of Edwards Plateau and Coleman. Local in Panhandle. Also south along Rio Grande to Delta, mainly in winter. Casual on cent. coast.

Common Raven

Common Crow

Common Raven

Fish Crow

Common Crow

White-necked Raven
is similar in size but has
Raven's characteristics

SILHOUETTES OF CROWS AND RAVENS

Note the Raven's shaggy throat, heavy bill, wedge-shaped tail. The White-necked Raven has the Common Crow's size and the Raven's characteristics. Identify the Fish Crow by voice.

Habitat: Mainly arid country, rangeland, plains, deserts. **Nest:** A bulky platform of twigs on tree, mesquite, telegraph pole, etc. Eggs (3–7) greenish, spotted.

COMMON CROW *Corvus brachyrhynchos* 17–21
Field marks: This large chunky, ebony-hued bird needs little description. No other large birds save the ravens are so completely black. Glossed with purplish in strong sunlight. Bill and feet strong and black. Gregarious.
Similar species: White-necked Raven, Common Raven, Fish Crow. In s. and w. Texas White-necked Ravens are almost universally called "crows."
Voice: A loud *caw* or *cah* or *kahr*, easily imitated by voice.
Where found: Central Canada south to sw. U.S. and Gulf States. **Texas:** *Resident* in e. and n. Texas; west locally to Panhandle and Edwards Plateau; south to upper coast (Victoria) and on Plateau nearly to San Antonio and Uvalde. In winter to El Paso. Straggler to cent. coast. *Habitat:* Woodlands, farmlands, river groves. **Nest:** A well-made bowl of sticks in tree. Eggs (4–6) greenish, spotted.

FISH CROW *Corvus ossifragus* 16–20
Field marks: Along tidewater east of Galveston, listen for this small crow. Go by voice, not size (sizes overlap).

Voice: A short, nasal *car* or *ca*. Sometimes a 2-syllabled *ca-ha*. (Common Crows utter an honest-to-goodness *caw*.)
Where found: Coast from s. Rhode Island south to Florida and west along Gulf Coast. **Texas:** E. Texas along coast from Galveston Bay to Louisiana and up large rivers (San Jacinto, Trinity, Neches, etc.) for 100 miles. *Habitat:* Mainly coastal country, lower reaches of rivers. **Nest:** Bowl of sticks in tree. Eggs (4–5) greenish, spotted.

PIÑON JAY *Gymnorhinus cyanocephala* 9–11½   p. 176
Field marks: In appearance and actions like a small *dull blue* Crow, hardly larger than a Robin, with a long sharp bill. Easily told from Scrub Jay by its short tail, uniform coloration, and crow-like flight; from Steller's Jay by lack of crest (Steller's Jay depresses crest when flying). Often seen in large noisy flocks. Often walk about on ground like crows.
Voice: A high nasal cawing, *kaa-eh, karn-eh* (descending inflection); has mewing effect. Jaylike notes; chattering.
Where found: Oregon and Montana south to sw. U.S. **Texas:** *Resident* in or near Guadalupe Mts. Wanders to other parts of w. Texas (Davis Mts., Glass Mts., etc.) and Panhandle; occasionally to w. Edwards Plateau. Colonial. *Habitat:* Piñon pines, junipers ("cedars"). **Nest:** A bowl of twigs in piñon or juniper. Eggs (3–5) speckled.

Titmice, Verdins, and Bushtits: Paridae

SMALL, PLUMP, short-billed birds, very acrobatic when feeding. Sexes generally similar. Often roam in mixed bands. Food: Insects; also seeds, acorn mast, berries. Widespread in N. America, Eurasia, Africa. No. of species: World, 64; N. America, 14; Texas, 9 (plus 1 accidental).

BLACK-CAPPED CHICKADEE
Parus atricapillus 4¾–5½   p. 141
Field marks: Nearly identical with Carolina Chickadee, but noticeably larger with much more white ("northern frost") in the wing created by the white feather-edgings.
Similar species: See Carolina Chickadee. The differences in the wings may not always be reliable because of season, wear, angle of light, etc. Voice is quite distinctive.
Voice: A clearly enunciated *chick-a-dee-dee-dee* or *dee-dee-dee*, more deliberate than in Carolina Chickadee. In spring, a clear whistle, *fee-bee*, first note higher.
Where found: Cent. Alaska, cent. Canada south to n. half of U.S. Moves south some winters. **Texas:** Casual winter visitor to w. Texas and Panhandle.

CAROLINA CHICKADEE   *Parus carolinensis*   4¼–4¾   p. 141
Field marks: Chickadees are the only small birds with the combination of *black cap, black bib, white cheeks*. These small tame acrobats are smaller than sparrows.
Similar species: See Black-capped Chickadee (casual w. Texas).
Voice: A rapid, high-pitched *chick-a-dee-dee-dee* or *dee-dee-dee*. Song, usually a 4-syllabled whistle *fee-bee, fee-bay*.
Where found: Cent. U.S. south to Gulf States. **Texas:** *Resident* through e., n., and cent. Texas; west to ne. corner of Panhandle and cent. Edwards Plateau; south to San Antonio and upper coast; in winter to cent. coast. *Habitat:* Woods, groves, towns.
Nest: In hole in tree or stump. Eggs (6–8) speckled.

MOUNTAIN CHICKADEE   *Parus gambeli*   5–5¾   p. 141
Field marks: Similar to Carolina and Black-capped Chickadees but black of cap broken by *white line over each eye*.
Voice: Song, three high clear whistled notes, *fee-bee-bee*, first note highest, second two on same pitch; or three or four whistled notes going slightly down the scale in half-notes. "Chickadee" notes huskier than Carolina's: *chuck-a-zee-zee-zee*.
Where found: Sw. Canada south to mts. of sw. U.S. and Baja California. **Texas:** *Resident* in Guadalupe and Davis Mts. *Winters* El Paso; occasionally elsewhere in w. Texas. *Habitat:* Mt. woodlands. **Nest:** In tree cavity. Eggs (7–10) white.

TUFTED TITMOUSE   *Parus bicolor*   6–6½   p. 141
Field marks: The birds bearing the name titmouse are the only small gray-backed birds with conspicuous crests. This is the only species in the eastern parts of Texas. Often intergrades with the next so-called species, where ranges overlap in middle Texas. Both have rusty lower flanks; much alike but black-crested birds are the next species. Gray-crested birds may be either, but look for a *small black patch* immediately above bill in Tufted (Black-crested has light or brown patch).
Voice: A clear whistled chant: *peter, peter, peter* or *here, here, here, here;* other variants. Note, *tsee-eep*. Other notes suggest Chickadee's but more nasal, wheezy, complaining.
Where found: S. tip of Ontario south through e. U.S. to Gulf States. **Texas:** *Resident* in e. half; west to Decatur, Fort Worth, Coleman (not typical), Austin, cent. coast (Rockport). At west edge of range (Fort Worth, Austin, Victoria, etc.) overlaps with next species and hybrids are frequent. *Habitat:* Woodlands, shade trees, groves. **Nest:** In hole in tree, post, iron pipe, bird box, etc. Eggs (5–6) speckled.

BLACK-CRESTED TITMOUSE
Parus atricristatus   5–6   p. 141
Field marks: Similar to Tufted Titmouse, but with a *slender*

black crest (longer than crest of Tufted). Females may have some gray in crest. Young may be gray-crested. The sure point is a small light patch (either whitish or brown) on forehead, near bill. Some authorities would call this merely a black-crested subspecies of the Tufted Titmouse.

Voice: Similar to that of Tufted Titmouse. Also an abbreviated *pete, pete, pete, pete,* etc. (G. F. Simmons).

Where found: Texas and ne. Mexico. **Texas:** *Resident* in middle-w. Texas from Panhandle (Palo Duro and side canyons) south to Rio Grande delta; west to Trans-Pecos (Davis Mts. and mts. of Big Bend); east at least to Graham, Ranger, Killeen, Austin, and cent. coast (Rockport). *Habitat:* Woodlands, groves, towns. **Nest:** In hole in tree, post, bird box. Eggs (5–6) spotted.

PLAIN TITMOUSE   *Parus inornatus*   5–5½   p. 141
  Field marks: A small, drab titmouse with a relatively short crest, no rufous on flanks.
  Similar species: "Plain Titmice" frequently reported on Edwards Plateau are probably young Black-crests, which have short gray crests and are virtually indistinguishable.
  Voice: A rasping *tchick-a-dee-dee.* In spring a whistled *weety weety weety* or *tee-wit tee-wit tee-wit.*
  Where found: S. Oregon and sw. Wyoming south to Baja California and sw. U.S. **Texas:** *Winters* in El Paso, Guadalupe Mts., elsewhere in n. part of Trans-Pecos; irregular, local, in Panhandle (Palo Duro Canyon). *Habitat:* Oak scrub, cedars.

VERDIN   *Auriparus flaviceps*   4–4½   p. 141
  Field marks: A very small gray bird with a *yellowish head;* bend of wing *rufous* (not always visible).
  Similar species: Immature lacks the yellow and rusty; might be mistaken for Bushtit, but Bushtit is much longer-tailed and does not ordinarily inhabit desert valleys; prefers oak slopes.
  Voice: An insistent *see-lip* or *zee.* Song, *tsee, seesee.*
  Where found: Sw. U.S. south to cent. Mexico. **Texas:** *Resident* in Trans-Pecos, s. Staked Plains and east locally to Abilene, Coleman, Austin; south to the Rio Grande, cent. coast (irregular), and the Delta. *Habitat:* Brushy valleys in desert country and semi-arid savannahs. **Nest:** A ball of twigs in bush or tree. Eggs (3–5) greenish, dotted.

COMMON BUSHTIT   *Psaltriparus minimus*   4–4¼   p. 141
  Field marks: Very small plain gray-backed birds that move about from bush to tree in straggling flocks, constantly conversing in high-pitched notes. The nondescript appearance, gray-brown back, brownish cheeks, stubby bill, and rather long tail identify them. Females have light eyes, males dark.
  Similar species: (1) Males of Black-eared Bushtit (mts. of w.

Texas) have black cheeks or cheeks flecked with black. A light-faced bird with dark eyes would most likely be a male Common Bushtit. Females of the two are usually indistinguishable. (2) See also Blue-gray Gnatcatcher (p. 188).

Voice: Insistent light *tsits*, lisps, and *clenks* constantly uttered as flock moves about among the vegetation.

Where found: Se. British Columbia, nw. U.S. south to nw. Mexico. **Texas:** *Resident* in Trans-Pecos and east locally through Edwards Plateau to Kerrville; casually to Austin. Also local in canyons of Panhandle. *Habitat:* Oak scrub, cedars, brush. **Nest:** A long bag suspended in tree. Eggs (5–7) white.

BLACK-EARED BUSHTIT *Psaltriparus melanotis* 4½
(Lloyd's Bushtit) p. 141

Field marks: Similar to Common Bushtit but male has *black patch* on side of head or face flecked with black. Female, similar to female Common Bushtit but face may be grayer, occasionally with flecks of black; ordinarily not distinguishable. This species is more restricted to higher altitudes of mts.; Common Bushtit goes also to lower levels.

Where found: Se. New Mexico, w. Texas to Guatemala. **Texas:** *Resident* in Trans-Pecos (Davis Mts., Chisos Mts.). *Habitat:* Oaks, cedars, pines. **Nest:** As in preceding species.

Nuthatches: Sittidae

SMALL, STOUT tree-climbers with strong woodpecker-like bills, large powerful feet and stubby tails that are never braced against the tree, woodpecker-like, in climbing. The only tree-climbers that habitually go down tree trunks headfirst. Sexes similar. Food: Bark insects; also seeds, acorns, berries. Mostly N. Hemisphere but also Africa and Australia. No. of species: World, 29; N. America, 4; Texas, 4.

WHITE-BREASTED NUTHATCH
Sitta carolinensis 5–6 p. 141

Field marks: Nuthatches are the "upside-down birds." The White-breasted Nuthatch is known by its black cap and beady black eye on a white face. Chestnut under tail-coverts.

Similar species: Red-breasted Nuthatch has eye-stripe. Chickadees have black bibs.

Voice: Song, a series of low, nasal, whistled notes on same pitch: *whi, whi, whi, whi, whi, whi, whi,* or *who, who, who,* etc. Note, a nasal *yank;* also a nasal *tootoo.*

Where found: S. Canada south to s. Mexico. **Texas:** *Resident* in e. third (but not coastal prairie); west to Fort Worth, Bryan. Resident also in mts. of Trans-Pecos. Very local in Edwards Plateau (Kerrville, etc.). *Winters* also in Panhandle, upper coast, El Paso; casual Midland. *Habitat:* Woodlands, groves, shade trees. **Nest:** In hole in tree. Eggs (5–7) dotted.

RED-BREASTED NUTHATCH
Sitta canadensis 4½–4¾   p. 141
  Field marks: Smaller than the White-breast; rustier below. The only nuthatch with a *broad black line* through the eye.
  Similar species: White-breast has white cheeks, no eye-line.
  Voice: Call higher and more nasal than that of White-breast; *ank* or *enk*, like a "baby" Nuthatch or a "tiny tin horn."
  Where found: Conifer forests from se. Alaska, cent. Canada, south in mts. to sw. U.S. and w. North Carolina. Irregular migrant to s. U.S. **Texas:** Irregular *winter visitor* (Oct.–Apr.) to various sections; most frequent in e.; casual straggler in s. part. *Habitat:* Woodlands, groves, trees.

BROWN-HEADED NUTHATCH *Sitta pusilla* 4–5   p. 141
  Field marks: A dwarf, pine-loving nuthatch of e. Texas. As small as or smaller than the preceding species, with a *brown cap coming down to the eye;* white spot on nape.
  Similar species: (1) White-breast has *black cap;* (2) Red-breast, *black eye-stripe.* (3) Pigmy (*w. Texas*) also has brown cap.
  Voice: Un-nuthatch-like: a rapid, high *kit-kit-kit;* also a squeaky, piping *ki-day* or *ki-dee-dee,* constantly repeated, sometimes becoming an excited twitter or chatter.
  Where found: Se. U.S., n. Bahamas. **Texas:** *Resident* in e. Texas, upper coast; west to Tyler, Huntsville, Houston. *Habitat:* Pine forests. **Nest:** In hole in stub or tree. Eggs (5–6) spotted.

PIGMY NUTHATCH *Sitta pygmaea* 4½   p. 141
  Field marks: A very small conifer-loving nuthatch of w. Texas, usually smaller than either Red-breasted or White-breasted with a *gray-brown cap coming down to the eye.* A whitish spot is sometimes visible on the nape.
  Similar species: Very similar to Brown-head (e. Texas), but widely separated geographically; cap grayer.
  Voice: A piping *kit-kit-kit* and a high *ki-dee;* incessant, sometimes becoming an excited chatter.
  Where found: S. British Columbia, nw. U.S. south to s.-cent. Mexico. **Texas:** *Resident* in Guadalupe Mts. of w. Texas. In *winter* to El Paso and Panhandle (rare). *Habitat:* Conifers. **Nest:** In hole in stub or tree. Eggs (6–8) spotted.

JAYS, MAGPIE, AND KINGFISHERS

In the jays and magpies the sexes are alike in appearance. In the kingfishers there are differences in the sexes, usually in the presence or absence of rufous on the underparts, or its extent.

BLUE JAY p. 167
Crested; white spots in wings and tail, black "necklace."

STELLER'S JAY p. 167
Crested; dark; no white spots.

SCRUB JAY p. 168
Crestless; white throat; "necklace."

MEXICAN JAY p. 168
Crestless, gray throat, no "necklace."

PIÑON JAY p. 171
Dull blue throughout; short tail.

GREEN JAY p. 168
Green; black throat-patch.

BLACK-BILLED MAGPIE p. 169
Casual in w. Texas.
Long wedge-shaped tail; white wing-patches.

RINGED KINGFISHER p. 143
Casual in s. Texas.
Very large; chestnut belly.

BELTED KINGFISHER p. 143
Bushy crest, gray band across white breast (male).
Female has two bands (one rusty).

GREEN KINGFISHER p. 146
Small, green-backed; rusty breastband (male) or two greenish bands (female).

BLUE JAY

STELLER'S JAY

SCRUB JAY

MEXICAN JAY

PIÑON JAY

GREEN JAY

BLACK-BILLED MAGPIE

GREEN KINGFISHER
♂

RINGED
KINGFISHER
♀

BELTED
KINGFISHER
♀

LONG-BILLED
MARSH WREN

WINTER WREN

SHORT-BILLED
MARSH WREN

HOUSE WREN

BEWICK'S WREN

CAÑON WREN

CAROLINA
WREN

ROCK WREN

CACTUS WREN

♂

♀

♂ Spring

BLUE-GRAY
GNATCATCHER

BLACK-TAILED
GNATCATCHER

Plate 44

WRENS AND GNATCATCHERS

WINTER WREN p. 179
Dark; stubby tail, heavily barred flanks.

LONG-BILLED MARSH WREN p. 180
Strong eye-stripe; back stripes.

SHORT-BILLED MARSH WREN p. 180
Buffy; streaked crown, streaked back; buffy undertail-coverts.

HOUSE WREN p. 178
No facial striping; grayer.

BEWICK'S WREN p. 179
Whiter underparts; eye-stripe, white tail-corners.

CAROLINA WREN p. 179
Rusty coloration; strong eye-stripe.

CAÑON WREN p. 181
White throat, dark belly.

ROCK WREN p. 181
Grayish; narrowly streaked breast; buffy tail-corners.

CACTUS WREN p. 180
Large; heavily spotted breast.

BLUE-GRAY GNATCATCHER p. 188
Blue-gray, whitish below; long tail, white eye-ring.

BLACK-TAILED GNATCATCHER p. 188
Male in spring: Black cap.
Female: Very similar to Blue-gray Gnatcatcher (see text). Underside of tail largely black (largely white in Blue-gray Gnatcatcher).

Creepers: Certhiidae

SMALL, SLENDER, stiff-tailed birds with slender, slightly curved bills with which they probe the bark of trees. Food: Bark insects. Widespread in cooler parts of N. Hemisphere. No. of species: World, 6; N. America, 1; Texas, 1.

BROWN CREEPER *Certhia familiaris* 5–5¾   p. 141
    Field marks: A slim well-camouflaged brown bird, much smaller than a House Sparrow, with a slender curved bill and a stiff tail used as a brace when climbing. It ascends a tree in a spiral, then flies to the base of the next tree.
    Voice: Note, a single long thin *seee*, similar to quick trebled note (*see-see-see*) of Golden-crowned Kinglet. Song, weak, clear notes, *see-ti-wee-tu-wee* or *see-see-see-ti-ti-see*.
    Where found: Eurasia, se. Alaska, Canada to Nicaragua; in east to s. Appalachians; winters to Gulf States. **Texas:** *Winters* (Oct.–Apr.) throughout; rare in s. part. *Breeds* in Guadalupe Mts. *Habitat:* Woodlands, groves, trees. **Nest:** Behind strip of loose bark on tree trunk. Eggs (5–8) spotted.

Wrens: Troglodytidae

SMALL, energetic brown birds, plump and stumpy, with slender bills; tails often cocked over backs. Food: Mainly insects. New World; especially Cent. and S. America; only 1 species (Winter Wren) in Eurasia. No. of species: World, 63; N. America, 9; Texas, 9.

HOUSE WREN *Troglodytes aedon* 4½–5¼   p. 177
    Field marks: Recognized as a wren by its small size, brown coloration, energetic actions, and habit of cocking its tail over its back; distinguished from other wrens by its *lack of any evident facial stripings*.
    Similar species: See Bewick's Wren and Carolina Wren (all three nest in bird boxes). See also Winter Wren.
    Voice: Rapid churring note; a harsh scold; song, stuttering and gurgling, rising in a musical burst, falling at the end.
    Where found: Breeds from s. Canada south to sw. U.S. and cent. parts of e. U.S. Winters in s. U.S. and Mexico. **Texas:** *Migrant* throughout most of state; *winters* (Sept.–May) in all but Panhandle and colder northern counties. *Breeds* in Guadalupe Mts. of w. Texas. *Habitat:* Thickets, woodlands, brush, towns. **Nest:** In hole in tree, stub. Eggs (6–8) dotted.

WINTER WREN *Troglodytes troglodytes* 4–4¼   p. 177
Field marks: A very small round *dark* wren, smaller than House Wren; has a *much stubbier* tail, light line over the eye, and a *brownish, heavily barred belly;* often bobs and bows.
Similar species: House Wren is grayer, has longer tail.
Voice: Song, a rapid succession of high tinkling warbles, trills, long sustained; often ends on a *very high* light trill. Note, a hard 2-syllabled *kip kip;* suggests Song Sparrow's *chip.*
Where found: Breeds widely in cooler parts of N. Hemisphere. In W. Hemisphere winters south to s. U.S. **Texas:** *Winters* (Oct.–Apr.) throughout most of state; most frequent in n. parts; casual straggler in extreme south. *Habitat:* Dense tangles of underbrush, woodland undergrowth.

BEWICK'S WREN *Thryomanes bewickii* 5–5½   p. 177
Field marks: The white line over the eye and whitish tips of outer tail feathers (not always easy to see) distinguish this widespread species. Bewick's Wren (pronounced *Buick's*) is dark brown above and has whitish underparts, whiter than other wrens'. It wobbles its rather long tail from side to side.
Similar species: (1) House Wren lacks white eye-stripe and white tail-spots. Bewick's Wren sometimes nests in bird boxes and to some people it is their "House" Wren. (2) Carolina Wren is larger, bright rusty, lacks tail-spots. (3) Rock Wren is grayer, with buffy tail-tips, finely streaked breast.
Voice: Song variable; high opening notes, followed by lower burry notes, ending on a thin trill; sometimes suggests Song Sparrow. Another rendering is *sweee, sweee, cheeeeeeee* (first two notes high, last trilled). Note, a high *chit, chit.*
Where found: S. British Columbia, s. Ontario south through middle and w. U.S. to s.-cent. Mexico. **Texas:** *Resident* throughout except counties in e. part and upper coast. In e. Texas, found only in winter. *Habitat:* Thickets, undergrowth, towns, brush, deserts. **Nest:** In hole, crevice, bird box, etc. Eggs (5–7) spotted.

CAROLINA WREN *Thryothorus ludovicianus* 5½–6   p. 177
Field marks: A large, rusty wren; *rufous* above and buffy below, with a conspicuous *white stripe* over the eye.
Similar species: (1) Long-billed Marsh Wren has a white eye-line but is striped on the back; Carolina is unmarked. (2) Bewick's Wren is grayer, has white tail-corners on its longer tail.
Voice: A clear chanting whistle, *chirpity, chirpity, chirpity, chirpity, chirp* or *tea-kettle, tea-kettle, tea-kettle, tea.* Usually trisyllabic but sometimes 2-syllabled. Variable.
Where found: S. Ontario and s. New England south to ne. Mexico and Gulf States. **Texas:** *Resident* in e. two-thirds;

west to Edwards Plateau and Del Rio; south to Rio Grande delta. Rare visitor to Panhandle and s. Staked Plains. *Habitat:* Woodlands, thickets, undergrowth, towns. **Nest:** Usually in hole, bird box, brushpile, cranny. Eggs (4–6) spotted.

CACTUS WREN
Campylorhynchus brunneicapillum   7–8½   p. 177
   Field marks: A very large wren of the arid country. Distinguished from other wrens by its much larger size and heavy spotting, which in adults gathers into a heavy cluster on the upper breast. White stripe over the eye and white spots in outer tail.
   Similar species: Sage Thrasher (which also has spotted breast, white eye-line, and white spots in tail), is more thrasher-like in appearance, grayer, *without* white stripings on back.
   Voice: A monotonous *chuh-chuh-chuh-chuh*, etc., or *chug-chug-chug-chug-chug*, on one pitch, gaining rapidity; unbirdlike.
   Where found: Sw. U.S. south to cent. Mexico. **Texas:** *Resident* of Trans-Pecos and s. Staked Plains; east to San Angelo; locally to San Antonio, Beeville, Rockport; south to Rio Grande delta. *Habitat:* Cactus deserts, mesquite, arid brush. **Nest:** A football-shaped structure in top of cactus or thorny bush.

LONG-BILLED MARSH WREN
Telmatodytes palustris   4½–5½   p. 177
   Field marks: The wren of the cattail marsh; brown, with a conspicuous white line over the eye; known from other small wrens with white eye-stripes by the *black and white stripes on back.*
   Similar species: See Short-billed Marsh Wren. Several other wrens have eye-stripes but no marks on the back.
   Voice: Song, reedy, gurgling, ending in a guttural rattle: *cut-cut-turrrrrrrrr-ur;* sometimes heard at night. Note, a low *tsuck.*
   Where found: S. Canada south to Mexico, Gulf Coast. Winters to cent. Mexico. **Texas:** *Migrant* locally throughout; *winters* except in Panhandle and colder n. parts. *Breeds* locally in n. counties; also along Gulf, south to Corpus Christi; very locally in w. Texas (El Paso, Marathon). *Habitat:* Marshes, fresh and salt. **Nest:** Coconut-shaped; lashed to reeds or stems in marsh. Eggs (5–7) brown, dotted.

SHORT-BILLED MARSH WREN
Cistothorus platensis   4–4½   p. 177
   Field marks: A wren of wet meadows, *grassy* marshes. Underparts very *buffy; crown *streaked*.
   Similar species: Long-bill has more contrastingly marked upper parts, conspicuous white line over eye, solid unstreaked crown and, when tail is cocked, whiter under tail-coverts. The Long-

bill prefers reeds except where it lives in salt marshes.
Voice: Song, a dry staccato chattering: *chap chap chap chap chap
chap chap chapper-rrrrr.* Call note of same quality: *chap.*
Where found: S. Canada south to cent. U.S.; winters south to
Gulf States. Also local from Mexico to Tierra del Fuego. **Texas:**
Migrant in e. and cent. Texas; west rarely to Panhandle, Cole-
man, Austin. *Winters* (Oct.–Apr.) mainly along coast. *Habitat:*
Grassy marshes, sedge, cord-grass flats.

CAÑON WREN *Catherpes mexicanus* 5½–5¾   p. 177
Field marks: A reddish-brown wren, with *dark reddish-brown
belly,* contrasting with a *white breast and throat.* The conspicuous
white bib is the best field mark.
Similar species: Rock Wren is gray, with lightly streaked breast.
Voice: A gushing cadence of clear curved notes tripping down
the scale, sometimes picking up at the end: *te-you te-you te-you
tew tew tew tew* or *tee tee tee tee tew tew tew tew,* etc.
Where found: Sw. Canada south through w. U.S. to s. Mexico.
Texas: *Resident* in Panhandle, w. Texas, Edwards Plateau; east
locally to Waco, Austin. *Habitat:* Canyons, rocky slopes, buildings. **Nest:** A cup in crevice in rocks. Eggs (4–6) dotted.

ROCK WREN *Salpinctes obsoletus* 5¼–6¼   p. 177
Field marks: A rather *gray* wren with finely streaked breast
(streaks visible at close range). Shows conspicuous *light or buffy
patches* in tail-corners.
Similar species: (1) Bewick's has much darker back, white un-
streaked breast. (2) Cañon Wren has dark belly, white throat.
Voice: Song, a harsh mechanical chant, *tew, tew, tew, tew* or
chr-wee, chr-wee, chr-wee or *che-poo che-poo, che-poo,* etc. Call, a
loud dry trill on one pitch; also a clear *ti-keer.*
Where found: Sw. Canada south through w. North America to
Costa Rica. **Texas:** *Resident* in Panhandle, w. Texas, and
Edwards Plateau; east locally to Vernon, Austin; south to Eagle
Pass, San Antonio. *Winters* rarely east to Denton and south to
the Rio Grande delta. *Habitat:* Canyons, rocky places, rock
dams, etc. **Nest:** In crevice in rocks, walls, etc., often with path
of rock chips. Eggs (5–8) dotted.

Mockingbirds and Thrashers: Mimidae

"MIMIC-THRUSHES" are noted for their powers of mimicry. Longer-
tailed than true thrushes; bill more decurved. Food: Insects,
fruits. New World; most numerous in the tropics. No. of species:
World, 30; N. America, 10; Texas, 7 (plus 1 accidental).

MOCKINGBIRD *Mimus polyglottos* 9–11   p. 192
Field marks: More slender than Robin, with long mobile tail.
Gray above and whitish below, with *large white patches* on wings
and tail, conspicuous in flight. When on ground, bird often
periodically raises wings above body, displaying patches.
Similar species: (1) Loggerhead Shrike has black facial mask
and shows less white in wings and tail.
Voice: Song, a long continued succession of notes and phrases
of great variety. The Mockingbird rapidly repeats each phrase
a half-dozen times or more before going on to the next. (Brown
Thrasher usually repeats once; Catbird does not repeat.) Many
Mockingbirds are excellent mimics, mimicking a score or more
of the other species found in the neighborhood. Often sings at
night. Note, a loud *tchack;* also *tchair*.
Where found: S. Canada south to s. Mexico and West Indies.
Texas: *Resident* throughout. *Habitat:* Towns, farm country,
ranches, roadsides, mesquite, brush, etc. **Nest:** A loose twiggy
cup in bush or dense tree. Eggs (4–5) blue-green, spotted.

CATBIRD *Dumetella carolinensis* 8½–9¼   p. 192
Field marks: Smaller and slimmer than Robin; dark *slaty gray*
with a *black cap. Chestnut-red* under tail-coverts (seldom noticed). Flips tail about jauntily. Skulks in undergrowth.
Similar species: The other uniformly dark gray songbirds —
young Starling, female Cowbird, female Rusty and Brewer's
Blackbirds — are shorter-tailed, lack the black cap and rusty
under tail-coverts.
Voice: Catlike mewing note distinctive. Song, a disjointed suc-
cession of notes and phrases, some musical. Notes not repeated
as in songs of Brown Thrasher and Mockingbird.
Where found: S. Canada south to ne. New Mexico and Gulf
States. Winters s. U.S. to Panama, West Indies. **Texas:**
Migrant (Apr.–May, Sept.–Oct.) through e. two-thirds; west to
Panhandle, Edwards Plateau. Casual El Paso. *Winters* rarely
on coast. *Breeds* in ne. counties (west rarely to Denton, Dallas,
College Station). *Habitat:* Undergrowth, brush. **Nest:** A twiggy,
rootlet-lined cup in bush or tangle. Eggs (4–6) blue-green.

BROWN THRASHER *Toxostoma rufum* 10½–12   p. 192
Field marks: A slim rufous bird. Slightly longer than Robin;
bright *rufous* above, *heavily striped* below. Has *wing-bars*, a
slightly curved bill, a long tail, yellow eyes.
Similar species: (1) Long-billed Thrasher (s. Texas) is less
rufous, has blacker stripes. (2) Thrushes are shorter-tailed;
spotted, not striped, and lack wing-bars. Their eyes are brown.
Voice: Song, a succession of deliberate notes and short phrases,
resembling Catbird's song, but more musical, each phrase
usually in *pairs*. Note, a harsh *chack*.
Where found: S. Canada, e. of Rockies to Gulf States. Partial

migrant. **Texas:** *Winters* (Oct.–May) throughout except s. tip (south of Corpus Christi) and Trans-Pecos (but winters at El Paso). *Resident* in Panhandle and in n. and e. parts; south rarely to Waco, Houston (but not on coastal prairie). *Habitat:* Brushy places, thickets. **Nest:** A twiggy, rootlet-lined cup in bush or tangle. Eggs (4–5) dotted.

LONG-BILLED THRASHER *Toxostoma longirostre* 10½–12
(Sennett's Thrasher)   p. 192
    Field marks: Similar to Brown Thrasher but back darker, less rufous; breast-streaks *black* rather than brown. Cheeks grayer.
    Similar species: The other resident thrasher in the lower Valley, the Curve-billed, is grayish, lacks black stripes.
    Voice: Song, notes and phrases similar to other thrashers'; phrases not repeated as much. Call note, *too-ree.*
    Where found: S. Texas south to e. and s.-cent. Mexico. **Texas:** *Resident* in s. Texas north to Del Rio, San Antonio, Beeville, Corpus Christi. Casual to Big Springs, Victoria. Accidental Fort Worth. *Habitat:* Undergrowth, mesquite. **Nest:** A twiggy cup in thorny bush or thicket. Eggs (4) dotted.

CURVE-BILLED THRASHER
Toxostoma curvirostre 10½–11½   p. 192
    Field marks: A slim gray Robin-sized bird, dull gray or gray-brown above, with narrow wing-bars, a *deeply curved bill* and a *faintly spotted breast.* Eye orange or reddish.
    Similar species: Crissal Thrasher is browner, has *rusty* under tail-coverts, no breast-spotting, more deeply curved bill.
    Voice: Note, a sharp liquid *whit-wheet!* like a human whistle of attention. Song, a series of notes and phrases, Mockingbird-like in quality but without so much repetition.
    Where found: Sw. U.S. south to s. Mexico. **Texas:** *Resident* in w. half of Texas from Panhandle (rare) to Rio Grande delta (uncommon); east rarely to Austin, San Antonio, Beeville. *Habitat:* Deserts, arid brush. **Nest:** A twiggy cup in cactus or bush. Eggs (4–5) blue-green, dotted.

CRISSAL THRASHER *Toxostoma dorsale* 11½–12½   p. 192
    Field marks: A brownish desert Thrasher with a *deeply curved bill.* The *rusty under tail-patch* (or crissum, from which the bird gets its name) and the lack of breast-spotting identify it. Immature birds have whitish eyes, adults dark.
    Similar species: Curve-billed Thrasher is grayer, has a faintly spotted breast, lacks rufous under tail-coverts.
    Voice: Song sweeter, phrases less spasmodic than in other thrashers. Note, *pichoory* or *chideary.*
    Where found: Sw. U.S. south to s.-cent. Mexico. **Texas:** *Resident* in Trans-Pecos. *Habitat:* Dense brush along desert streams, mesquite thickets. **Nest:** A twiggy cup in bush or mesquite. Eggs (2–3) blue-green.

SAGE THRASHER   *Oreoscoptes montanus*   8–9   p. 192
   Field marks: Nearly size of Robin, similar in shape, actions.
A gray-backed bird with a straight slender bill, heavily streaked
breast, white spots at tip of tail, pale yellow eye. Small size,
shorter tail, shorter bill, striped breast distinguish it from other
western thrashers. Frequently jerks tail.
   Similar species: (1) See Cactus Wren. (2) Juvenal Mockingbird
also has spotted breast, but has white patches in wing and tail.
   Voice: Song, clear ecstatic warbled phrases, sometimes repeated
in thrasher fashion; more often continuous, suggestive of Black-
headed Grosbeak; more rapid and joyous than most thrashers.
   Where found: Sw. Canada (local) south to s. Nevada, n. New
Mexico, n. Texas. Winters from sw. U.S. to n. Mexico. **Texas:**
Winters (Aug.–May) throughout w. half; east irregularly to
Denton, Dallas, Waco, Austin, cent. coast. Casual upper coast.
Breeds in Panhandle in dry years. *Habitat:* Brushy plains.
Nest: A bulky twiggy cup in bush. Eggs (4–5) blue, spotted.

Thrushes, Bluebirds, Solitaires: Turdidae

RATHER long-legged, upstanding songbirds. Eyes rather large.
Bills slender, pointed. The five species that bear the name Thrush
are brown-backed birds with *spotted* breasts. Robins, Bluebirds,
Solitaires, etc., although unlike them in color, suggest relationship
through their speckle-breasted young. Among the finest bird
singers in the world. Food: Insects, worms, snails, berries, fruits.
Nearly cosmopolitan. No. of species: World, 304; N. America, 16;
Texas, 10 (plus 2 accidentals).

ROBIN   *Turdus migratorius*   8½–10½   p. 193
   Field marks: A very familiar bird; recognized by its gray back
and *brick-red* breast. In the male, the head and tail are blackish;
in the female, grayer. Bill *yellow*. Young Robin has speckled
breast, but gray back and rusty underparts identify it. Robins
walk on lawns with erect stance.
   Voice: Song, a clear caroling; short phrases, rising and falling,
often long continued. Notes, *tyeep* and *tut-tut-tut*.
   Where found: Limit of trees in Alaska, Canada south to s.
Mexico (mts.) and Gulf States. Migrates from n. sections.
Texas: *Winters* (Nov.–May) throughout. *Breeds* in e., n., and
cent. Texas; west at least to Fort Worth, Waco, Austin; south
to Bay City, Victoria, San Antonio. Also locally in mts. of w.
Texas, in w. Panhandle, and at Midland. *Habitat:* Farms, towns,
croplands, woodland borders, etc. **Nest:** A mud-walled, grass-
lined cup, usually in tree. Eggs (3–5) blue-green.

WOOD THRUSH *Hylocichla mustelina* 7½–8½ p. 193
Field marks: *Rusty-headed.* Smaller than Robin; breast and sides heavily spotted. Plumper than the other brown-backed thrushes; distinguished from them by the deepening redness *about the head* and the larger, more numerous *round* spots.
Similar species: (1) Brown Thrasher is longer-tailed, has wing-bars, yellow eyes, and is streaked, not spotted. (2) See Hermit Thrush, etc.
Voice: A very fine song; liquid, flutelike phrases with pauses. Listen for flutelike *ee-o-lay*, and occasional gutturals.
Where found: Se. South Dakota, se. Canada south to Gulf States. Winters Mexico to Panama. **Texas:** *Migrant* (Apr.–May, Sept.–Nov.) through e. half; west to e. Panhandle, Austin, San Antonio, lower Rio Grande. Casual Midland. *Breeds* in forested part of e. Texas; west to Dallas (occasionally), Hunts-ville, Houston. *Habitat:* Woodlands, shady thickets. **Nest:** A cup of leaves, mud, rootlets in bush or tree. Eggs (3–4) blue-green.

HERMIT THRUSH *Hylocichla guttata* 6½–7½ p. 193
Field marks: *Rusty-tailed.* Larger than House Sparrow; brown-backed with a slender bill and spotted breast. The *reddish tail* is the Hermit Thrush's mark. When perched it has a trick of cocking its tail at an angle and dropping it slowly.
Similar species: Three of the five brown thrushes are tinged with some rufous: (1) Veery is uniformly tawny brown above; (2) Wood Thrush is reddest *about head;* Hermit is reddest *on tail.* (3) Fox Sparrow is also reddish-tailed, but underparts are heavily streaked, not spotted.
Voice: Note, a low *chuck;* also a scolding *tuk-tuk-tuk* and a harsh *pay.* Song, clear, ethereal and flutelike. Three or four phrases on *different pitch levels,* each introduced by a *long introductory note.* A deliberate pause between each phrase.
Where found: Alaska, cent. Canada south in mts. to sw. U.S. and e. West Virginina. Winters from n. U.S. to Guatemala. **Texas:** *Migrates and winters* (Oct.–May) throughout but scarce in winter in Panhandle, Edwards Plateau, and colder sections. *Breeds* in Guadalupe Mts. of w. Texas. *Habitat:* Woodlands, thickets. **Nest:** A cup of leaves, moss, rootlets usually in small evergreen. Eggs (3–5) blue.

SWAINSON'S THRUSH *Hylocichla ustulata* 6½–7½
(Olive-backed Thrush, Russet-backed Thrush) p. 193
Field marks: A spotted thrush that lacks any warmth of color in its plumage and is uniformly gray-brown or olive-brown above is certainly one of two species. If the bird also has a conspicuous *buffy eye-ring* and *buffy cheeks,* it is Swainson's Thrush.
Similar species: If the cheeks are gray and the eye-ring indis-

tinct or lacking, then it is the Gray-cheek (but see it well and be cautious, especially in fall).

Voice: Song, melodious, breezy flutelike phrases; distinguished by tendency of each phrase to climb *upward* (like a Veery in reverse). Note, *whit*. Migrants at night, a short *heep*.

Where found: Alaska, cent. Canada south to California, Colorado, and in east to mts. of Virginia. Winters from Mexico to Peru. **Texas:** *Migrant* (Apr.–May, Sept.–Oct.) probably throughout; less frequent in w. parts. *Habitat:* Woodlands, shady thickets.

GRAY-CHEEKED THRUSH
Hylocichla minima   6¼–8   p. 193

Field marks: An olive-brown or gray-brown thrush. It is identified, when seen very well, by its *grayish cheeks* and lack of a conspicuous eye-ring.

Similar species: The only other olive-brown thrush without hint of rusty is Swainson's. It has *buffy cheeks* and a conspicuous *buffy eye-ring;* its breast is also suffused with buff. In fall migration the two are not always safely separated.

Voice: Note, *vee-a* or *quee-a*, higher and more nasal than Veery's note; uttered by migrants at night. Song, thin and nasal; suggests Veery, but often rises abruptly at close (Veery goes down): *whee-wheeoo-titi-whee*.

Where found: Ne. Siberia, Alaska, and across Canada to mts. of ne. U.S. Winters in S. America. **Texas:** *Migrant* (Apr.–May, Sept.–Oct.) probably throughout; rare or occasional in w. parts. *Habitat:* Woodlands, shady thickets.

VEERY   *Hylocichla fuscescens*   6½–7½   p. 193

Field marks: A thrush *uniformly* cinnamon-brown or tawny above is quite certainly a Veery. Of all the thrushes this is the least spotted on the breast; the spots are *indistinct*, often giving a clear-breasted appearance at a distance.

Similar species: (1) Gray-cheek and (2) Swainson's are *graybrown* above; (3) Wood Thrush is reddish *about head;* (4) Hermit reddish *on tail*.

Voice: Song, liquid, breezy, ethereal, wheeling downward: *vee-ur, vee-ur, veer, veer*. Note, a low *phew* or *view*.

Where found: Across s. Canada and south in mts. to ne. Arizona and n. Georgia. Winters in Cent. and S. America. **Texas:** *Migrant* (Apr.–May, Sept.–Oct.) mainly through e. and coastal parts of state; west rarely to Panhandle, Fort Worth, Austin. *Habitat:* Woodlands, shady thickets.

EASTERN BLUEBIRD   *Sialia sialis*   6½–7½   p. 193

Field marks: A little larger than a sparrow; a *blue-backed* bird with a *red* breast; appears dumpy, round-shouldered when perched. Females are paler and duller; young birds are speckle-

breasted, grayish, devoid of red, but there is always some telltale blue in the wings and tail.
Similar species: (1) Blue Jay is large, has *white* breast; (2) Indigo Bunting and (3) Blue Grosbeak have dark blue breasts. (4) See other bluebirds.
Voice: Note, a simple musical *chur-wi* or *purity.* Song, three or four soft gurgling notes.
Where found: S. Canada e. of Rockies south to Gulf States and from se. Arizona to Honduras. Partial migrant. **Texas:** *Winters* (Nov.–Apr.) throughout most of state except Trans-Pecos. *Breeds* throughout e. two-thirds from ne. Panhandle to lower Rio Grande Valley (occasionally); west to Edwards Plateau. *Habitat:* Farmlands, open country with scattering of trees. **Nest:** In hole in tree, stub, fence post, bird box. Eggs (3–6) light blue.

WESTERN BLUEBIRD   *Sialia mexicana*   6½–7
(Mexican Bluebird)   p. 193
Field marks: Similar to Eastern Bluebird, but throat *blue,* back *rusty red.* (In some individuals the back is partially or wholly blue.) Female paler and duller than male.
Similar species: (1) Except for Eastern Bluebird, the only other blue bird with a red breast is the male Lazuli Bunting, which has *white wing-bars.* (2) Male Mountain Bluebird has *blue* breast (see female Mountain Bluebird).
Voice: A short *pew* or *mew.* Also a hard chattering note.
Where found: Se. British Columbia through mts. of w. N. America to cent. Mexico. **Texas:** *Winters* (Nov.–May) in Trans-Pecos; rarely Panhandle. Irregular straggler to n. Texas, cent. coast. *Breeds* in Guadalupe Mts. *Habitat:* Open terrain, scattered trees. **Nest:** In hole in tree or stub. Eggs (4–6) pale blue.

MOUNTAIN BLUEBIRD   *Sialia currucoides*   6½–7¾   p. 193
Field marks: *Male: Turquoise-blue above* and *below,* belly whitish. *Female:* Dull brownish with bluish rump, tail, and wings. Distinguished from female Western Bluebird by straighter posture and lack of rusty wash on grayish-brown breast.
Similar species: (1) Other bluebirds have red breasts. Only other songbirds with blue breasts found in Texas are (2) male Blue Grosbeak, which has a thick bill and brown wing-bars, and (3) male Indigo Bunting, which is smaller, much darker.
Voice: A low *chur* or *phew.* Song, a short, subdued warble; not often heard. Sings mostly at daybreak (W. Weydemeyer).
Where found: Alaska, w. Canada to California, n. Arizona. Winters to n. Mexico. **Texas:** *Winters* (Sept.–May) in w. two-thirds of state from Panhandle to Brownsville; east to Dallas, Austin, San Antonio, and occasionally to cent. coast. Recorded in July in Davis Mts. *Habitat:* Open terrain, scattered trees.

TOWNSEND'S SOLITAIRE

Myadestes townsendi 8–9½   p. 193

Field marks: A slim gray-bodied bird, with a white *eye-ring,
white sides* of tail, and a *buffy patch* in the wing. The beginner
is likely to be confused, imagining it to be some sort of a thrasher,
flycatcher, or almost anything but a Solitaire.

Similar species: The white in the tail and the light wing-patches
give it a not too remote resemblance to a Mockingbird. The eye-
ring and darker breast at once distinguish it.

Voice: Song, long and warbled, suggesting Black-headed Grosbeak's, but more rapid. Note, a sharp *eek.*

Where found: Alaska, w. Canada, south to high mts. of n.
Mexico. Lower altitudes in winter. **Texas:** *Winters* (Sept.–May)
commonly in canyons of Panhandle, sparingly in w. parts of
state and Edwards Plateau east to Austin; casual Fort Worth.
Habitat: Chiefly canyons, brushy slopes.

Gnatcatchers and Kinglets: Sylviidae

TINY, ACTIVE, insectivorous birds with small slender bills. Gnat-
catchers have long mobile tails. Kinglets have bright crowns.
This family includes the numerous warblers of the Old World.
Food: Mainly insects, insect eggs, larvae. Most large forested land
areas of world except lower S. America. No. of species: World, 313;
N. America, 6; Texas, 4.

BLUE-GRAY GNATCATCHER *Polioptila caerulea* 4½ p. 177
Field marks: Looks like a miniature Mockingbird. A very tiny,
slender mite, even smaller than a chickadee, blue-gray above
and whitish below, with a narrow white eye-ring and a *long, contrastingly colored tail* (black in center, white on sides; often
cocked like a wren's tail, flipped about).

Similar species: (1) See Black-tailed Gnatcatcher. (2) Cerulean
Warbler lacks eye-ring, has *narrow black breastband.*

Voice: Note, a thin peevish *zpee.* Song, a thin, squeaky, wheezy
series of notes, easily overlooked.

Where found: S. Utah, Lake Erie south to Guatemala, Bahamas.
Winters from s. U.S. south. **Texas:** *Migrant* (Mar.–Apr., Sept.–
Oct.) throughout. *Winters* in s. half, north to upper coast,
Austin (rarely), Big Spring, El Paso. *Breeds* throughout much
of state except s. part (south of Del Rio, San Antonio, Beeville).
Habitat: Woodlands, thickets, brush. **Nest:** A small lichen-
covered cup saddled on limb of tree. Eggs (4–5) bluish, spotted.

BLACK-TAILED GNATCATCHER *Polioptila melanura* 4½
(Plumbeous Gnatcatcher)   p. 177
Field marks: Similar to Blue-gray Gnatcatcher but breeding

male has a *black cap* and much less white on sides of tail (outer web only). Winter male (without cap) and female are duller than Blue-gray; eye-ring less conspicuous; less white on tail.
Voice: Note, a thin *chee* repeated two or three times (Blue-gray Gnatcatcher usually gives single note).
Where found: Sw. U.S., n. Mexico. **Texas:** *Resident* locally in lowlands of Trans-Pecos; occasionally lower Rio Grande. Casual cent. coast. *Habitat:* Ravines, river thickets, mesquite. **Nest:** A small cup in bush or tree. Eggs (4–5) spotted.

GOLDEN-CROWNED KINGLET *Regulus satrapa* 3½–4 p. 208
  Field marks: Kinglets are tiny mites, smaller than Warblers. Their diminutive proportions and olive-gray backs often make them difficult to discern among the thick branches. The present species always shows a conspicuous bright crown-patch bordered by black; yellow in the female, orange-red in the male. There is also a *white stripe* over the eye.
  Similar species: See Ruby-crowned Kinglet.
  Voice: Call note, a high wiry *see-see-see*. Song, a series of high thin notes (like the ordinary call notes) ascending in pitch, then dropping into a chickadee-like chatter.
  Where found: S. Alaska, cent. Canada south in mts. (west) to Guatemala and (east) to North Carolina. Winters south to Gulf States. **Texas:** *Winters* (Oct.–Apr.) throughout. *Habitat:* Woodlands, thickets, groves.

RUBY-CROWNED KINGLET
Regulus calendula 3¾–4½   pp. 208, 220
  Field marks: A tiny short-tailed bird; olive-gray above with two pale wing-bars; male with a *scarlet* crown-patch (usually concealed; shows mostly when excited). Occasional males have yellow crowns. The best mark is the conspicuous *broken white eye-ring*, which gives the bird a big-eyed appearance. Any kinglet not showing a conspicuous crown-patch or eye-stripe is of this species. The stubbier tail distinguishes it from any of the warblers, as does the dark bar bordering the rear wing-bar. Kinglets have a habit of nervously flirting their wings.
  Similar species: (1) See Golden-crowned Kinglet. (2) In w. Texas see Hutton's Vireo (p. 196).
  Voice: Note, a husky *ji-dit*. Song, remarkable for so small a bird, starting with three or four high *tee*'s, then several low *tew*'s, and ending in a repetitious chant: *tee tee tee tew tew tew tew ti-dadee, ti-dadee, ti-dadee, ti-dadee.* Variable.
  Where found: Across Canada, Alaska; south in mts. to California, Arizona, New Mexico. Winters to Guatemala, Gulf States. **Texas:** *Migrant* throughout. *Winters* (Sept.–May) except in Panhandle. *Habitat:* Woodlands, thickets. The most common kinglet.

Pipits: Motacillidae

STREAKED brown ground birds with white outer tail feathers, long hind claws, thin bills. They walk briskly instead of hopping, and wag their tails constantly. Food: Insects, seeds. Nearly cosmopolitan. No. of species (including relatives): World, 48; N. America, 6; Texas, 2.

WATER PIPIT *Anthus spinoletta* 6–7
(American Pipit)   p. 241
  Field marks: A slender brown tail-wagging ground bird. Near size of sparrow, but with *slender* bill; underparts *buffy* with streakings; *outer tail feathers* white. On ground, walks; *constantly wags tail*. In flight, dips up and down. Learn the note — most Pipits are heard flying overhead.
  Similar species: (1) Vesper Sparrow (which also shows white outer tail feathers) has thicker bill, does not wag tail. (2) See Sprague's Pipit. (3) See Horned Lark (p. 163).
  Voice: Note, a thin *jeet* or *jee-eet* (can be interpreted *pi-pit*). In flapping song flight, *chwee chwee chwee chwee chwee chwee*.
  Where found: N. Eurasia, across American Arctic and south to high mts. of w. U.S. In N. America winters to Guatemala, Gulf States. **Texas:** *Migrant* throughout. *Winters* (Oct.–May) except in Panhandle. *Habitat:* Fields, prairies, marshes.

SPRAGUE'S PIPIT *Anthus spragueii* 6½–7   p. 241
  Field marks: A buffy sparrow-like bird with a striped back and white outer tail feathers (suggests a Vesper Sparrow with a thin warbler-like bill). Back *streaked* conspicuously with *buff* and *black*. Legs *pale*. More solitary than Water Pipit; when flushed often "towers" high in air, then drops.
  Similar species: (1) Water Pipit wags tail more, has a darker (not strongly striped) back, a deeper buff breast, and *darker* legs (light brown to black; Sprague's *pale flesh-* or *straw-colored*). (2) Longspurs and (3) Vesper Sparrow have finch bills. Vesper Sparrow hops (pipits walk).
  Voice: Sings high in air like Horned Lark, a series of sweet thin notes descending in pitch. Flight note, a soft *chur-r*.
  Where found: W. Canada south to Montana, South Dakota. Winters s. U.S. and Mexico. **Texas:** *Migrant* throughout except Trans-Pecos (casual). *Winters* (Sept.–Apr.) except in Panhandle and Trans-Pecos. *Habitat:* Plains, prairies, airports.

Waxwings: Bombycillidae

SLEEK crested birds, with red waxy tips on secondary wing feathers. Very gregarious. Food: Mainly berries; also insects. N. Hemisphere. No. of species: World, 3; N. America, 2; Texas, 2.

BOHEMIAN WAXWING *Bombycilla garrula* 7½–8½   p. 192
Field marks: Larger than Cedar Waxwing, grayer, especially on breast (no yellow); wings with conspicuous white and yellow markings (see plate). The surest mark is the *deep rusty* of the under tail-coverts (white in Cedar Waxwing).
Voice: A rough *zreee*, rougher than note of Cedar Waxwing.
Where found: N. Eurasia and nw. N. America. South in winter to sw. U.S., s. Eurasia. **Texas:** Casual or very rare winter visitor to Panhandle. Reported also at Midland, Fort Worth, College Station, cent. coast.

CEDAR WAXWING *Bombycilla cedrorum* 6½–8   p. 192
Field marks: A sleek, *crested*, brown bird, larger than a sparrow, with a *yellow band* at the tip of the tail. The only sleek *brown* bird with a long crest. Adults have minute waxy red droplets on tips of secondary wing feathers. The young bird (late summer) is gray, softly streaked with gray and white below. Gregarious; fly in compact flocks. Often have flycatching habits.
Voice: A high thin lisp or *zeee;* sometimes slightly trilled.
Where found: Se. Alaska, cent. Canada south to n. California, w. Oklahoma, and Georgia. Winters from s. Canada to Panama, West Indies. **Texas:** *Winters* (Oct.–June) throughout. *Habitat:* Various; semi-open, wooded, towns, etc.

Silky Flycatchers: Ptilogonatidae

SLIM, crested, waxwing-like birds found from southwestern United States to Panama. No. of species: World, 4; N. America, 1; Texas, 1.

PHAINOPEPLA *Phainopepla nitens* 7–7¾   p. 192
Field marks: Size of oriole. *Male:* A slim, *glossy, black* bird with a *slender crest* and conspicuous *white patches* in the wing. Unique. *Female:* Dark gray, with slender crest; wing-patches light gray, not conspicuous. Has flycatching habits.
Similar species: (1) Cedar Waxwing is much browner than female Phainopepla, has yellow tailband. (2) Mockingbird, like Phainopepla, has white wing-patches (but in addition, white in tail).

MIMIC THRUSHES, SHRIKES, WAXWINGS, AND PHAINOPEPLA

LOGGERHEAD SHRIKE   NORTHERN SHRIKE

BROWN THRASHER

LONG-BILLED THRASHER

CRISSAL THRASHER

CURVE-BILLED THRASHER

CATBIRD

SAGE THRASHER

MOCKINGBIRD

LOGGERHEAD SHRIKE

CEDAR WAXWING

BOHEMIAN WAXWING

PHAINOPEPLA

♂

♀

MOUNTAIN
BLUEBIRD

♀ ♂

WESTERN
BLUEBIRD

♀

Juve

♂

EASTERN
BLUEBIRD

VARIED THRUS

ROBIN

Juvenal

♂

VARIED THRUS

♂

TOWNSEND
SOLITAIR

VEERY

WOOD THRUSH

HERMIT
THRUSH

SWAINSON'S THRUSH

GRAY-CHEEKED THRUSH

Plate 46   193

THRUSHES

MOUNTAIN BLUEBIRD   p. 187
  Male: Turquoise-blue breast.
  Female: No rusty on gray-brown breast.

WESTERN BLUEBIRD   p. 187
  Male: Rusty patch on back (usually); blue throat.
  Female: Duller than male, throat whitish, rusty breast.

EASTERN BLUEBIRD   p. 186
  Male: Blue back, rusty breast, rusty throat.
  Female (not shown): Duller; whitish throat.
  Juvenal: Speckled breast, blue in wing and tail.

ROBIN   p. 184
  Brick-red breast, gray back.
  Juvenal: Speckled breast; trace of rusty.

VARIED THRUSH   p. 274
  Accidental in Texas. Similar to Robin but with black
  "necklace"; orange eye-stripe and wing-bars.

TOWNSEND'S SOLITAIRE   p. 188
  Gray; white eye-ring, white tail-sides; buffy wing-patch.

VEERY   p. 186
  Tawny from head to tail; little spotting.

HERMIT THRUSH   p. 185
  Rufous tail.

WOOD THRUSH   p. 185
  Rufous head; large spots.

SWAINSON'S (OLIVE-BACKED) THRUSH   p. 185
  Dull gray-brown above, no rusty. Buffy cheeks, conspicuous eye-ring.

GRAY-CHEEKED THRUSH   p. 186
  Dull gray-brown above, no rusty. Gray cheeks, inconspicuous eye-ring.

Voice: Note, a soft low *wurp*. Song, a weak, casual warble, wheezy and disconnected.

Where found: Sw. U.S. south to s.-cent. Mexico. **Texas:** *Resident* locally in Trans-Pecos from Big Bend to El Paso. Casual in winter at Midland and Rio Grande delta. *Habitat:* Desert scrub, mesquite. **Nest:** A shallow saucer of twigs on fork of limb. Eggs (2–3) speckled.

Shrikes: Laniidae

SONGBIRDS with hawklike behavior and hook-tipped bills. Perch watchfully on conspicuous vantage points. Prey often impaled on thorns or barbed wire. Often called "butcher birds." Food: Insects, lizards, mice, small birds. Widespread in Old World; only 2 in N. America. None in S. America. No. of species: World, 67; N. America, 2; Texas, 2.

NORTHERN SHRIKE *Lanius excubitor* 9–10½
(Northwestern Shrike)   p. 192
    Field marks: Very similar to the Loggerhead Shrike, but slightly larger; breast *finely barred*. At close range, the basal portion of the lower mandible is *pale-colored* (except in late spring). The Loggerhead's bill is solid black and the black mask meets above the base of the bill. Young Northern Shrikes are much browner and are recognizable by this alone; also by fine bars on the breast. The young Loggerhead is finely barred on the breast in late summer, but is *gray*, not brown.
    Voice: Note, *shek-shek;* also a grating *jaaeg.*
    Where found: Alaska, Canada, Eurasia, n. Africa. South in winter to middle U.S. **Texas:** Casual winter visitor. Recorded Waller Co., Decatur, Denton, College Station, San Angelo.

LOGGERHEAD SHRIKE *Lanius ludovicianus* 9   p. 192
    Field marks: This big-headed, slim-tailed bird, slightly smaller than a Robin, sits quietly on a wire or bush top in the open. Taking flight, it drops low and progresses with a rapid motion on a beeline course, rising to its next perch. It is gray above, white below, with a conspicuous *black mask* on its face.
    Similar species: (1) Mockingbird is slimmer, longer-tailed, has larger white wing-patches, and lacks the face mask. Perched on a wire the Shrike scans the ground; looks short-legged, heavy-headed (Mocker is longer-legged, alert-looking). Its flight is flickering; that of the Mockingbird more "like strokes of the oars of an old rowboat." (2) See also Northern Shrike.
    Voice: Song, halfhearted notes and phrases; repeated Mockingbird-like, but deliberate, with long pauses (*queedle, queedle;* over and over, or *tsurp-see, tsurp-see*). Note, *shack, shack.*

Where found: S. Canada south to s. Mexico and Gulf States. Partial migrant. **Texas:** *Winters* (Sept.–Apr.) throughout. *Breeds* in e. half (south locally to upper coast, Beeville; west to Austin); also throughout Panhandle, Staked Plains, Trans-Pecos. *Habitat:* Open country with scattered trees, roadsides, scrub, deserts, etc. **Nest:** A twiggy cup in bush or tree. Eggs (4–6) spotted.

Starlings: Sturnidae

SHORT-TAILED, blackbird-like birds with sharp bills. Food: Mostly insects; some berries, seeds. Widespread in Old World. Two species (Starling and Crested Mynah) introduced in N. America. No. of species: World, 103; N. America, 2; Texas, 1.

STARLING *Sturnus vulgaris* 7½–8½   p. 225
   Field marks: A very gregarious, garrulous, short-tailed "blackbird," with somewhat the shape of a Meadowlark. In flight, has a triangular look, and flies swiftly and directly, not rising and falling like most blackbirds. In spring, glossed with purple and green (visible at close range); bill *yellow*. In winter, heavily speckled with light dots; bill dark, changing to yellow as spring approaches. No other "blackbird" has a *yellow* bill. Young Starlings are dusky gray, a little like the female Cowbird, but the tail is shorter, and the bill longer and more spike-like.
   Similar species: The Starling is the *short-tailed* "blackbird"; the grackles are long-tailed; the Redwinged, Rusty, and Brewer's Blackbirds and Cowbird are the in-betweens.
   Voice: A harsh *tseeeer*, high-pitched and descending. Also clear whistles, clicks, rattles, and chuckles, woven into a rambling "song" delivered from housetop or tree. A good mimic.
   Where found: Eurasia, n. Africa. Introduced into N. America (1890) and elsewhere. Partially migratory. **Texas:** *Winters* (Oct.–Apr.) throughout. Now *breeds* at many points in state; west to Amarillo, Midland. *Habitat:* Towns, farms, open country, groves, fields, etc. **Nest:** In hole in tree, building. Eggs (4–6) pale bluish.

Vireos: Vireonidae

SMALL olive- or gray-backed birds; much like the warblers, but with somewhat heavier bills (with a more curved ridge); usually less active, slowly searching for insects under the leaves instead of flitting about. The eleven vireos in Texas are nearly equally divided between those species with conspicuous wing-bars and those without. Those without wing-bars generally have eye-stripes. Those possessing bars usually have eye-rings. Some of the latter might be confused with the small *Empidonax* flycatchers, but they do not sit in the typical upright flycatcher posture, and the eye-ring joins a light spot between the eye and bill, giving more the appearance of spectacles. Food: Mostly insects. Canada to Argentina. No. of species: World, 41; N. America, 12; Texas, 11.

BLACK-CAPPED VIREO *Vireo atricapilla* 4½–4¾   p. 208
Field marks: A small, sprightly vireo with *top and sides* of *head glossy black* in male, slaty gray in female. It has conspicuous white "spectacles" formed by the eye-ring and loral patch (between eye and bill) and two distinct wing-bars, which are pale yellow in male, white in female. Its custom of hanging head downward an instant before fluttering to a lower branch is characteristic (G. M. Sutton).
Voice: Song hurried, harsh; composed of phrases remarkable for variety and restless, almost angry quality. Alarm note, a harsh *chit-ah*, not unlike that of Ruby-crowned Kinglet.
Where found: Sw. Kansas south to Texas and Coahuila. Winters in w. Mexico. **Texas:** *Summers* (Mar.–Sept.) mainly on Edwards Plateau; north to Oklahoma; east to Dallas, Austin, San Antonio; west locally to Trans-Pecos (Brewster Co.). *Habitat:* Oak scrub, brushy canyons. **Nest:** A well-made cup in thick bush. Eggs (3–5) white.

WHITE-EYED VIREO *Vireo griseus* 4½–5½   p. 208
Field marks: A small vireo of the undergrowth; olive-backed, with wing-bars, yellowish sides, and *white eyes*. Know it by the combination of *yellowish "spectacles"* and *whitish throat.* Young birds have dark eyes.
Similar species: (1) Solitary Vireo has *white eye-ring,* dark eye. (2) The only other vireo with yellow spectacles is the easy-to-tell Yellow-throated. (3) Because of markings and un-vireo-like song, White-eye can be mistaken for a small flycatcher.
Voice: Song, un-vireo-like, an emphatic *chick'-a-perweeoo-chick'.* Variable; note the sharp *chick* at beginning or end.
Where found: Nebraska, Connecticut south to ne. Mexico, Gulf States. Winters Gulf States to Honduras, Cuba. **Texas:** *Migrant* (Mar.–May, Sept.–Oct.) throughout e. two-thirds; west to Panhandle, Edwards Plateau. *Breeds* in e., n., and middle Texas; west to Fort Worth, Austin, San Antonio; south to Delta. *Winters* in s. parts of state. *Habitat:* Thickets, dense shrubs. **Nest:** A shaggy cup in bush or tangle. Eggs (3–5) dotted.

HUTTON'S VIREO *Vireo huttoni* 4½–4¾   p. 208
Field marks: A small olive-brown vireo with two broad white

wing-bars, a *partial* eye-ring, and a large light loral spot (between eye and bill). The appearance of this light spot and the incomplete eye-ring *interrupted by a dark spot* above eye (see plate) distinguish it from other vireos with eye-rings.
Similar species: (1) It could be mistaken for one of the small *Empidonax* flycatchers, which, however, sit upright and have complete eye-rings. (2) The bird that most closely resembles it is the Ruby-crowned Kinglet. Hutton's Vireo has a heavier bill, is slightly larger; it is much more deliberate in its movements and does not flirt its wings.
Voice: A hoarse double-noted *zu-weep* with rising inflection, sometimes continuously repeated; vireo quality. Frequently a hoarse deliberate *day dee dee*, very different from the *ji-dit* of Ruby-crowned Kinglet (Laidlaw Williams).
Where found: Sw. British Columbia south to Guatemala. Partially migratory. **Texas:** *Summers* (and perhaps resident) in Chisos Mts. (6000–8000 ft.). Occasional transient elsewhere in Trans-Pecos. *Habitat:* Mostly oaks. **Nest:** A mossy cup hung from oak twigs. Eggs (3–4) dotted.

BELL'S VIREO   *Vireo bellii*   4¾–5   p. 208
   Field marks: A small grayish vireo with one or two light wing-bars and pale yellowish-washed sides; perhaps the most non-descript vireo. Distinguished from Warbling Vireo by the wing-bars and narrow light eye-ring. Most like White-eyed Vireo but has a *dark eye* and lacks yellow "spectacles."
   Similar species: Immature White-eye has dark eyes but always shows *yellow* in the loral spot and eye-ring. See Gray Vireo.
   Voice: Sings "as if through clenched teeth"; husky, unmusical phrases at short intervals; *cheedle cheedle chee? — cheedle cheedle chew!* First phrase ends in rising inflection; second phrase, given more frequently, has downward inflection and sounds as if bird were answering its own question.
   Where found: Middle-w. and sw. U.S., ne. Mexico. Winters from Mexico to Nicaragua. **Texas:** *Migrant* throughout most of state. *Summers* (Apr.–Oct.) except in upper coastal sections, extreme e. counties, and lower Rio Grande. *Habitat:* Willow thickets along streams, mesquite. **Nest:** A small cup hung from twig of bush. Eggs (3–5) dotted.

GRAY VIREO   *Vireo vicinior*   5½–5¾   p. 208
   Field marks: A plain, gray-backed vireo of arid mountains; has a *narrow white eye-ring* but differs from other vireos with eye-rings by having *no wing-bars* or one faint one. Though drab, it has much character, flopping its tail like a gnatcatcher.
   Similar species: Bell's Vireo is similar but usually has two wing-bars (sometimes one). Has a faint wash of yellow on sides and a different habitat.

Voice: Very similar to song of Solitary Vireo but more rapid and "patchy." (Solitary would not be in dry brush.)
Where found: Sw. U.S. and n. Mexico. Winters in n. Mexico. Texas: *Summers* locally in Trans-Pecos (Guadalupe, Davis, and Chisos Mts.). Rare and local in Panhandle (canyons). *Habitat:* Brushy mt. slopes, small oaks. Nest: A small cup in bush. Eggs (3–4) dotted.

YELLOW-THROATED VIREO
Vireo flavifrons   5–6   pp. 208, 220
Field marks: Olive-green above, with white wing-bars, yellow "spectacles," and *bright yellow throat and breast*. Other vireos are washed with yellowish on the sides but this is the only vireo possessing *bright* yellow.
Similar species: (1) Similarly-colored Yellow-breasted Chat is larger, has *no* wing-bars, has *white* "spectacles." (2) Pine Warbler has a more slender bill, dusky streaks on sides, and large white tail-spots. It lives mostly in pines.
Voice: Song, similar to Red-eyed Vireo's; more musical, lower-pitched, with a burr in the notes; longer pauses between phrases. One phrase sounds like *ee-yay* or *three-eight*.
Where found: S. Canada south to Gulf States. Winters from Mexico to n. S. America. Texas: *Migrant* (Mar.–May, Sept.–Oct.) in e. two-thirds of state, west rarely to Panhandle and s. Staked Plains. Casual El Paso. *Breeds* locally in wooded parts of e. Texas, cent. Texas (Bryan, Austin, San Antonio), and Edwards Plateau. *Habitat:* Woodlands, shade trees. Nest: A small basket-like cup hung from twig of tree. Eggs (3–4) spotted.

SOLITARY VIREO   *Vireo solitarius*   5–6
(Blue-headed Vireo)   p. 208
Field marks: A vireo with white wing-bars. Look for the *blue-gray* head, *white eye-ring*, and *snowy-white* throat. Migrants have a yellowish wash on sides, and show a contrast between gray head and olive back. Breeding birds of w. Texas, *V. s. plumbeus*, are gray, lacking contrast of gray head, olive back.
Similar species: The other two common eastern vireos with wing-bars are (1) White-eyed and (2) Yellow-throated Vireos. In w. Texas see (3) Bell's Vireo (inconspicuous eye-ring) and (4) Hutton's Vireo (dull throat).
Voice: Song, short whistled phrases, with rising and falling inflection, rendered with a short wait between phrases. Similar to Red-eyed Vireo's song, but sweeter, with sweeping slurs.
Where found: Canada south to El Salvador. Winters from s. U.S. to Nicaragua, Cuba. Texas: *Migrant* (Apr.–May, Sept.–Nov.) throughout. *Winters* in s. parts of state; occasionally to n. Texas. *Breeds* in Trans-Pecos (Guadalupe, Davis, and Chisos Mts.). *Habitat:* Woodlands, trees. Nest: A small basket-like cup hung from twig. Eggs (3–5) spotted.

YELLOW-GREEN VIREO   *Vireo flavoviridis*   6¼–6¾   p. 208
Field marks: A rare inhabitant of the Delta. Very similar to
Red-eyed Vireo, both in behavior and in voice, but with strong
yellow tones. Sides washed with greenish yellow, under tail-
coverts *yellow* (Red-eye, white). Head-stripes less distinct.
Similar species: See Philadelphia Vireo.
Voice: Song similar to Red-eye's; longer pauses between phrases.
Where found: S. tip of Texas to Panama. Winters in upper
Amazon Basin. **Texas:** Rare *summer resident* in Rio Grande
delta. Casual at Rockport. *Habitat:* Resaca woodlands, shade
trees. **Nest:** A small cup hung from twig. Eggs (3) spotted.

RED-EYED VIREO   *Vireo olivaceus*   5½–6½   p. 208
Field marks: Olive-green above, white below, *no wing-bars;*
characterized by the *gray cap* and the *black-bordered white "eyebrow"* stripe over the eye. Red eye is of little aid.
Similar species: Warbling Vireo is paler, more uniform above,
without black borders on eyebrow stripe. Songs unlike.
Voice: Song, short abrupt phrases of Robin-like character,
separated by deliberate pauses, repeated as often as forty times
in a minute. Monotonous. Note, a nasal whining *chway.*
Where found: Canada south to Gulf States. Winters in Amazon
Basin. **Texas:** *Migrant* (Mar.–May, Aug.–Oct.) throughout
most of state except Trans-Pecos. Casual El Paso. *Breeds* in e.,
n., and cent. Texas; locally on Edwards Plateau (w. to Kerrville);
south to upper coast and San Antonio (rarely). *Habitat:* Woodlands, shade trees, groves. **Nest:** A small basket-like cup hung
from twig of bush or tree. Eggs (3–4) dotted.

PHILADELPHIA VIREO
Vireo philadelphicus   4½–5   pp. 208, 221
Field marks: A vireo with the combination of *unbarred* wings
and *yellow-tinged* underparts (especially on breast).
Similar species: (1) Warbling Vireo is paler-backed, and usually
lacks the yellow, although some birds have a tinge on the sides.
A good mark at close range is a dark spot between eye and bill
(lores) in the Philadelphia. (2) Orange-crowned Warbler is
similar, but restless actions and dingier, more uniform coloration
help identify it. (3) Fall Tennessee Warbler is also similar but
has a more needle-like bill and usually clear-white under tail-
coverts. However, anyone unable to tell a vireo from a warbler
is hardly ready to recognize this species. Vireos are less trim,
usually less active; their bills are thicker.
Voice: Song similar to Red-eyed Vireo's, higher in pitch.
Where found: S. Canada and ne. edge of U.S. Winters Guatemala to Colombia. **Texas:** *Migrant* (Mar.–May, Aug.–Oct.)
through e. half of state; west occasionally to Panhandle and
s. Staked Plains. Accidental El Paso. *Habitat:* Woodlands,
trees.

WARBLING VIREO   *Vireo gilvus*   5–6   p. 208
  Field marks: Three species of vireos occurring widely in Texas
  have *no* wing-bars. If the head is *inconspicuously* striped and the
  breast is whitish, then it is this species. A pale vireo.
  Similar species: (1) Philadelphia Vireo (migrant only) is darker
  above, extensively tinged with yellow below (particularly breast).
  (2) Red-eyed Vireo has a more contrastingly striped head. In
  w. Texas, neither Red-eye nor Philadelphia normally occurs.
  Voice: Song, a languid warble, not broken into phrases as with
  other vireos; resembles slightly the Purple Finch's song but less
  spirited, and with burry undertone. Call note, a wheezy, querulous *twee.*
  Where found: Canada south to s. U.S., n. Mexico. Winters
  Mexico to Guatemala. **Texas:** *Migrant* (Mar.–May, Sept.–Oct.)
  throughout. *Breeds* locally in n. and e. parts and Panhandle;
  also in mts. of Trans-Pecos. *Habitat:* Woodlands, trees. **Nest:**
  A basket-like cup hung from twig of tree. Eggs (3–5) spotted.

Wood Warblers: Parulidae

THESE ARE the "butterflies" of the bird world — bright-colored,
smaller than sparrows (except the Chat), with thin bills. Vireos
are similar, but their bills are heavier, less needle-pointed; their
movements when foraging among the leaves are usually rather
sluggish, unlike the active flittings of the warblers.

   In the autumn there is a preponderance of olive-yellow species
— adults that have changed their plumage, immature birds, etc.
I have included two special color plates of these. One shows mostly
those species which either have *wing-bars* or are *streaked.* The other
plate depicts mostly those *devoid of both wing-bars and streaks.*

   These plates are titled "Confusing Fall Warblers." Such
obvious birds as Redstarts, Kentuckies, Yellow-throated Warblers,
Black-and-Whites, and others that are much the same in fall as
in spring are not included. However, I have added the Ruby-
crowned Kinglet, Philadelphia Vireo, and Yellow-throated Vireo,
which are often mistaken for fall warblers.

   These two plates show the difficult ones. Master the spring
warblers first. If at the end of ten years you can say you really
know the fall warblers you are doing very well.

   Food: Mostly insects. Alaska and Canada to Argentina. No.
of species: World, 109; N. America, 54; Texas, 48 (plus 6 accidentals and 2 hybrids).

BLACK-AND-WHITE WARBLER
Mniotilta varia   5–5½   p. 212
  Field marks: *Striped lengthwise with black and white; creeps*

along trunks and branches. Female has whiter underparts.
Similar species: (1) Blackpoll and (2) Black-throated Gray
Warblers somewhat resemble it but have *solid black caps;* Black-
and-White has a *striped* crown, white stripes on back.
Voice: Song, a thin *weesee weesee weesee weesee weesee weesee
weesee;* suggests one of Redstart's songs but higher-pitched and
longer (*weesee* repeated at least seven times). A second, more
sibilant song drops in pitch in middle.
Where found: Canada south to Gulf States. Winters from
Mexico, West Indies to n. S. America. **Texas:** *Migrant* (Mar.–
May, July–Oct.) throughout. A few *winter* in s. Texas (common
in Delta). *Breeds* locally in dry woodlands in ne., n., and cent.
Texas (south at least to Bryan, Austin), and Edwards Plateau.
Habitat: Woodlands, trees, undergrowth. **Nest:** A well-lined cup
on ground. Eggs (4–5) spotted.

PROTHONOTARY WARBLER
Protonotaria citrea 5½   pp. 213, 221
Field marks: A golden bird of wooded swamps. Entire head and
breast *deep yellow*, almost orange; wing *blue-gray* without bars;
sexes similar, but female duller.
Similar species: (1) Yellow Warbler has *yellowish* wings and
tail. (2) Blue-winged has *white wing-bars*, black eye mark.
Voice: Emphatic *tweet tweet tweet tweet tweet* on one pitch.
Where found: Great Lakes area south to Gulf States. Winters
Yucatan to Venezuela. **Texas:** *Migrant* (Mar.–May, Sept.–Oct.)
mainly through e. parts of state and along coast. *Breeds* locally
in e. and n. parts, west at least to Denton, Fort Worth, Houston.
Habitat: Wooded swamps. **Nest:** In hole in stub. Eggs (4–7)
spotted.

SWAINSON'S WARBLER *Limnothlypis swainsonii* 5   p. 209
Field marks: A skulker, seldom seen. Both sexes are olive-brown
above and plain buffy white below, with a *brown crown* and a
conspicuous *light stripe* over the eye.
Similar species: (1) Worm-eating Warbler has *black stripes* on
crown. (2) Waterthrushes have heavily *streaked* underparts.
Voice: Song suggests Louisiana Waterthrush; shorter (five notes)
— two slurred notes, two lower notes, and a higher one.
Where found: Ne. Oklahoma and se. Maryland south to e.
Texas, n. Florida. Winters from Yucatan, West Indies to
British Honduras. **Texas:** Rather rare *migrant* (Mar.–May,
Sept.–Oct.) in e. Texas and along coast. Recorded west to
Beeville. *Breeds* locally in e. Texas; west to Tyler, Houston.
Habitat: Swamps, bogs, streambottoms, heavy woodland under-
growth. **Nest:** A bulky, leafy cup in canebrake, bush, or tangle.
Eggs (3) white.

WORM-EATING WARBLER
Helmitheros vermivorus　5–5½　　　　　　　　　　　p. 209
Field marks: Dull olive, with *black stripes* on a *buffy head;* breast rich buff. Sexes similar. Forages on or near ground.
Voice: Song, a thin buzz; resembles rattle of Chipping Sparrow but thinner, more rapid and insect-like.
Where found: Kansas, Ohio, and s. New England south to ne. Texas and n. Georgia. Winters from Mexico, West Indies to Panama. **Texas:** Uncommon *migrant* (Apr.–May, Sept.–Oct.) through e. half; west rarely to Fort Worth, Austin. Casual Midland. Rare and local in *summer* in woodlands near ne. edge of state (Texarkana, Gainesville). *Habitat:* Woodlands, undergrowth. **Nest:** A leafy, moss-lined depression on ground. Eggs (4–5) spotted.

GOLDEN-WINGED WARBLER
Vermivora chrysoptera　5–5¼　　　　　　　　　　　p. 213
Field marks: The only warbler with the combined characters of *yellow wing-patch and black throat. Male:* Gray above and white below; yellow forehead-patch, yellow wing-patch, black patch through eye, black throat. In female, black is replaced by gray.
Voice: Song unlike that of any other warbler, except Blue-wing: *bee-bz-bz-bz* (one buzzy note followed by three in a lower pitch). Blue-wing *usually* has one lower buzz: *beee-bzzz.*
Where found: S. New England and Great Lakes states south to se. Iowa, nw. South Carolina. Winters from Guatemala to Colombia. **Texas:** *Migrant* (Apr.–May, Aug.–Oct.) mainly along coast. Recorded inland to Fort Worth, Austin, Beeville, *Habitat:* Open woodlands, brushy clearings, undergrowth.

BLUE-WINGED WARBLER　*Vermivora pinus*　4½–5　　p. 213
Field marks: Face and underparts yellow; *black mark through eye;* wings with two *white* bars. Sexes similar.
Similar species: Narrow black eye mark distinguishes it from other largely yellowish warblers (Yellow, Prothonotary, etc.).
Voice: Song, *beeee-bzzz* (inhale and exhale).
Where found: S. New England and Great Lakes states south to nw. Arkansas, n. Georgia. Winters from Mexico to Panama. **Texas:** *Migrant* (Apr.–May, July–Oct.) mainly along coast. Recorded inland to Denton, Fort Worth, Austin, Beeville. *Habitat:* Woodland openings, undergrowth, bushy edges.

TENNESSEE WARBLER
Vermivora peregrina　4½–5　　　　　　　　　　　pp. 209, 221
Field marks: *Male in spring:* Very plain; a *conspicuous white stripe over the eye;* head gray, contrasting with greenish back; underparts white. *Female in spring:* Similar, head less gray and underparts slightly yellowish. Eye-line is best mark.

Adults and immature in autumn: Greenish above, pale dingy yellow below; known by combined characters of *unstreaked* yellowish breast and *conspicuous* yellowish line over eye.

Similar species: (1) Red-eyed and (2) Warbling Vireos are larger with somewhat thicker bills, slower actions. (3) Autumn birds resemble Orange-crowned Warbler but differ as follows: (a) under tail-coverts are *white* in typical Tennessees (some immatures show a tinge of yellow); (b) Tennessee has more conspicuous eye-stripe; (c) is *greener*, has paler underparts, with no suggestion of faint streaking; (d) almost invariably shows *trace of a light wing-bar.* (4) See also Philadelphia Vireo.

Voice: Song, staccato, 2-parted (sometimes 3-parted): *tizip-tizip-tizip-tizip-tizip-tizip-zitzitzitzitzizizizizi.* The second part is like an emphatic Chipping Sparrow's but gets louder at the end. In pattern, suggests Nashville Warbler's song but very loud and more tirelessly repeated.

Where found: Across Canada and along ne. edge of U.S. Winters Mexico to Venezuela. **Texas:** *Migrant* (Apr.–May, Sept.–Nov.). Through e. half; west to Fort Worth, Austin, San Antonio. *Winters* rarely in Rio Grande delta. *Habitat:* Woodlands, groves, brush.

ORANGE-CROWNED WARBLER
Vermivora celata 5   pp. 209, 221
Field marks: The dingiest of all warblers. Has no wing-bars or other distinctive marks; olive-green above, greenish yellow below; *breast faintly streaked.* "Orange crown" seldom noticeable; sexes similar. The points to remember are greenish-yellow underparts, faint, blurry streakings, and lack of wing-bars. The *autumn immature* is greenish drab throughout — barely paler on underparts. Some birds are quite gray (see plate).

Similar species: (1) Autumn Tennessee Warbler has no faint breast-streakings, has a trace of a wing-bar, and usually (not always) has *white*, not yellow, under tail-coverts. (2) Philadelphia Vireo has a more noticeable light eye-stripe, thicker vireo bill, and lacks streakings. It is sluggish.

Voice: Song, a weak, colorless trill, dropping in energy at the end. Often changes pitch, rising, then dropping.

Where found: Alaska, w. and cent. Canada, and throughout most of w. U.S. Winters s. U.S. to Guatemala. **Texas:** *Migrant* throughout. *Winters* (Oct.–Apr.) in s. half; a few to n. and e. Texas. *Breeds* above 8000 ft. in Guadalupe Mts. of w. Texas. *Habitat:* Scattered trees, brush, undergrowth. **Nest:** A grassy cup on ground. Eggs (3–5) speckled.

NASHVILLE WARBLER
Vermivora ruficapilla 4½–5   pp. 213, 221
Field marks: The *white eye-ring* in conjunction with the bright

yellow throat is the best mark. Throat and underparts yellow; *head gray*, contrasting with the olive-green back; males may show a dull chestnut crown-patch.

Similar species: (1) Connecticut and (2) MacGillivray's Warblers have white eye-rings but their throats are *grayish*. In fall, the brownish or grayish hint of a hood sets them apart, as their size and sluggish actions do. (3) Immature Magnolia Warbler in fall has a yellow throat, gray head, and eye-ring, but it is known by the *wing-bars, yellow rump*, and *white tailband*.

Voice: Song, 2-parted: *seebit, seebit, seebit seebit, tititititititi* (first part measured; ends like Chipping Sparrow's).

Where found: S. Canada and south in mts. to cent. California and ne. West Virginia. Winters from s. Texas, s. Florida to Guatemala. **Texas:** *Migrant* (Mar.–May, Sept.–Nov.) throughout. A few winter in s. Texas and Rio Grande delta. *Habitat:* Woodland edges, thickets.

VIRGINIA'S WARBLER *Vermivora virginiae* 4   p. 224
Field marks: A small *gray-looking* warbler with a pale breast and *yellowish rump and under tail-coverts*. At close range a narrow white eye-ring, a rufous spot on the crown and a touch of yellow on the breast can be seen. Has tail-wagging habit. Immatures lack the colors on crown and breast but can be told by their gray color and touch of yellow at base of tail.

Similar species: (1) Near El Paso see Lucy's Warbler. (2) In Chisos Mts. see Colima Warbler.

Voice: Song, loose, colorless notes on nearly the same pitch; rises slightly at end: *chip-chlip-chlip-chlip-chlip-wick-wick.* Resembles song of Audubon's Warbler in quality.

Where found: Great Basin of w. U.S. from s. Idaho south to s. Arizona. Winters in Mexico. **Texas:** *Migrant* (Apr.–May, Aug.–Sept.) in Trans-Pecos. *Habitat:* Oak canyons, brushy desert.

COLIMA WARBLER *Vermivora crissalis* 5¼   p. 224
Field marks: Very similar to Virginia's Warbler, differing chiefly in lacking the yellowish wash on the breast; also a bit darker and distinctly larger. In the high Chisos Mts., a deliberate-acting, gray-looking warbler with a yellow rump and under tail-coverts is most likely this little-known species.

Similar species: Virginia's Warbler is migrant in w. Texas.

Voice: Song, "a simple trill, much like that of Chipping Sparrow but rather shorter and more musical and ending in two lower notes" (J. Van Tyne).

Where found: Sw. Texas and ne. Mexico. Winters in Mexico. *Breeds* in Chisos Mts. (6000–7000 ft.). *Habitat:* Small oaks, maples, madroñas, pines in canyons. **Nest:** A well-lined cup on ground among dead leaves. Eggs (4) spotted.

LUCY'S WARBLER *Vermivora luciae* 4   p. 224
Field marks: A little warbler of the desert; gray-backed, with a white breast and a small patch of chestnut on the crown. Its best field mark is a *chestnut rump-patch.* Immatures are largely gray, without distinctive marks.
Similar species: Virginia's Warbler has *yellowish* rump-patch.
Voice: Song, high and rapid *weeta weeta weeta che che che che che,* on two pitches (may end on lower pitch, or on higher).
Where found: Deserts of sw. U.S. and nw. Mexico. Winters in Mexico. **Texas:** *Breeds* in El Paso area but on New Mexico side of line (Radium Hot Springs). One bird recorded feeding young Cowbird at Sierra Blanca (June 8, 1958). *Winter* straggler at El Paso. *Habitat:* Cottonwoods and mesquite along desert streams. **Nest:** A well-lined cup in tree cavity, woodpecker hole, or under loose bark. Eggs (4–5) speckled.

PARULA WARBLER *Parula americana* 4¼–4¾ pp. 209, 220
Field marks: A small *bluish* warbler with a *yellow throat and breast.* Two white wing-bars and a white eye-ring are conspicuous. A greenish patch on the back is a clinching point. In the male, a *dark rusty band* crosses the yellow breast. In the female this band is indistinct or lacking. Identify it by the general blue and yellow color and white wing-bars.
Similar species: Male Olive-backed Warbler (Rio Grande delta) lacks the white eye-ring and dusky band across breast; front of face blacker. Female is very similar to female Parula, but eye-ring virtually absent; wing-bars shorter.
Voice: Song, a buzzy trill or rattle that climbs the scale and snaps over at the top, *zeeeeeeeee-up;* also buzzy notes that run into the familiar rising trill: *zh-zh-zh-zheeeeee.*
Where found: Se. Canada, e. U.S. to Gulf States. Winters Florida, Mexico to Cent. America. **Texas:** *Migrant* (Mar.– May, Sept.–Nov.) through e. two-thirds; rare in Staked Plains and Panhandle. *Breeds* in e., n.. and cent. Texas; west to Fort Worth, Austin, Kerrville; south to upper coast and George West (w. of Beeville). *Habitat:* Woodlands, groves, especially with Spanish moss. **Nest:** A purselike cup usually hung in Spanish moss. Eggs (4–5) spotted.

OLIVE-BACKED WARBLER *Parula pitiayumi* 4¼–4¾
(Sennett's Warbler, "Pitiayumi Warbler")   p. 224
Field marks: *Male:* A small bluish warbler with a *yellow* throat and breast; very similar to Parula Warbler, but *lacks* the white eye-ring and the dark band crossing the upper breast. The best field character is the *black face,* sharply separating the yellow throat from the blue crown. *Female:* Similar; face pattern not so contrasting. The general blue and yellow color is distinctive from everything except Parula. White wing-bars shorter.

Similar species: See Parula Warbler (migrant in lower Valley).
Voice: Nearly identical with Parula Warbler's.
Where found: S. tip of Texas and n. Mexico south to n. Argentina, Uruguay. **Texas:** *Resident* in lower Rio Grande Valley; upriver to Rio Grande City. *Habitat:* Woodlands with plenty of Spanish moss. **Nest:** Like Parula's. Eggs (3–4) spotted.

YELLOW WARBLER *Dendroica petechia* 5   pp. 213, 220
Field marks: No other small bird appears to be *all yellow*. Many other warblers are yellow below, but none is so yellow on the back, wings, and tail. Many have white spots in the tail; this is the only one with *yellow* spots (with exception of female Redstart). Male shows chestnut-red breast-streakings. In female these are faint or lacking. In fall, female and young might be mistaken for other warblers but this is the only species with *yellowish tail-spots*. There is also at least a trace of *yellow feather-edging in the wings.*
Similar species: (1) Female Wilson's Warbler has no tail-spots. (2) Some dull autumn Yellow Warblers, especially examples of the dark Alaskan race, *D. p. rubiginosa* look almost as greenish as Orange-crowns. *Look for the yellow tail-spots.* (3) Goldfinch has black wings and *black* tail.
Voice: Song, a cheerful, bright *tsee-tsee-tsee-tsee-ti-ti-wee* or *weet weet weet weet tsee tsee*, given rapidly. Variable.
Where found: Alaska, Canada south to West Indies, cent. Peru. Winters from Mexico, Bahamas, south. **Texas:** *Migrant* (Apr.–May, Aug.–Oct.) throughout. *Summers* locally along watercourses in ne. Texas, Panhandle, Edwards Plateau (local), and Trans-Pecos. *Habitat:* Willows, streamsides, shrubs. **Nest:** solidly built cup in upright crotch of shrub. Eggs (4–5) speckled.

MAGNOLIA WARBLER
Dendroica magnolia 4½–5   pp. 212, 220
Field marks: The old name, "Black-and-Yellow Warbler," well describes it. Upper parts blackish, with large white patches on wings and tail; underparts yellow with heavy black stripings. From below, the tail appears white with a *wide black terminal band*. In *fall*, Magnolias are olive above, yellow below, with stripings reduced to a few sparse marks on the flanks. The black tail, crossed midway by a *broad white band*, is the best mark.
Similar species: Four other spring warblers with yellow underparts are striped with black beneath — (1) Townsend's, (2) Canada, (3) Cape May, and (4) Prairie — but none has the black and white upper plumage. (5) Immature in fall may be taken for Nashville Warbler because of yellow throat, gray cap, and white eye-ring; but note the *wing-bars, yellow rump, white tail-band.*

Voice: Song suggests Yellow Warbler's, but shorter: *weeta weeta weetee* (last note rising) or *weeta weeta weeto* (last note dropping). See Hooded Warbler's song. Note, un-warbler-like *tizic*.
Where found: Cent. and e. Canada south to ne. U.S. and mts. of w. Virginia. Winters from Mexico, West Indies to Panama. **Texas:** *Migrant* (Mar.–May, Sept.–Nov.) throughout e. half; rare in Panhandle; casual in Trans-Pecos. *Habitat:* Woodlands, groves.

CAPE MAY WARBLER
Dendroica tigrina 5–5½   pp. 212, 220
Field marks: *Male: The only warbler with chestnut cheeks.* Pattern tiger-like; underparts yellow narrowly striped with black; rump yellow; crown black. *Female and immature* lack chestnut cheeks and are duller. Often very nondescript; breast often almost white, lined with dusky streaks. A good point is a dim, *suffused patch of yellow behind the ear.*
Similar species: Obscure autumn birds are perhaps the most heavily streaked of all the fall nondescripts. Some are peculiarly gray and the yellow spot behind ear is often absent. Similar birds are (1) female Myrtle Warbler, which has a white throat and a more *conspicuous* yellow rump-spot; (2) Palm Warbler, which is browner, has bright *yellow* under tail-coverts, and *wags its tail*. Both have streaked backs (Cape May plain).
Voice: Song, a very high thin *seet seet seet seet*, repeated four or more times. Most easily confused with Bay-breast.
Where found: Canada and along ne. edge of U.S. Winters in Caribbean area. **Texas:** Rare or occasional straggler. A handful of records, mostly in late April, early May, along cent. coast. Reported also at Galveston, and in Panhandle.

BLACK-THROATED BLUE WARBLER
Dendroica caerulescens 5–5½   pp. 209, 221
Field marks: *Male:* Very clean-cut; *blue, black, and white;* upper parts blue-gray; throat and sides black; breast and belly white. *Females* are very plain, brown-backed with a light line over eye and a small white wing-spot (not always visible).
Similar species: Fall immatures and females often lack the white wing-spot. They are buffy-breasted and dark-backed and suggest Philadelphia Vireo or Tennessee Warbler, but *the dark-cheeked look* is a good mark.
Voice: Song, a husky, lazy *zur, zur, zur, zree* or *I am la-zy* (rising inflection).
Where found: Canada and ne. U.S. south to ne. Georgia. Winters mainly in West Indies. **Texas:** Occasional, irregular *transient* (Mar.–May, Sept.–Oct.) in e. half; recorded west to Panhandle, Denton, Fort Worth, Coleman, Austin, San Antonio.

VIREOS AND KINGLETS

VIREOS WITHOUT WING-BARS
These have eyebrow stripes.

WARBLING VIREO   p. 200
Light eyebrow line, whitish breast.
RED-EYED VIREO   p. 199
Gray crown, black and white eyebrow stripes.
YELLOW-GREEN VIREO   p. 199
Like Red-eyed but yellower; yellow under tail-coverts.
Rio Grande delta.
PHILADELPHIA VIREO   p. 199
Light eyebrow line, yellowish breast.

VIREOS WITH ONE FAINT WING-BAR OR NONE

GRAY VIREO   p. 197
Very gray; light eye-ring. Mt. slopes of Trans-Pecos.
See text.

VIREOS WITH WING-BARS
These have eye-rings or "spectacles."

BELL'S VIREO   p. 197
Eye-ring and wing-bars not too prominent. See text.
Streamsides, willows.
SOLITARY VIREO   p. 198
Blue-headed form: Blue-gray head, olive back, white throat.
Plumbeous form: No contrast between head and back.
WHITE-EYED VIREO   p. 196
Yellow "spectacles," white eye, white throat.
YELLOW-THROATED VIREO   p. 198
Yellow "spectacles," yellow throat.
BLACK-CAPPED VIREO   p. 196
Black cap, very conspicuous "spectacles."
HUTTON'S VIREO   p. 196
Incomplete eye-ring; dingy underparts. Lacks strong
black bar of Ruby-crowned Kinglet's wing.

KINGLETS

GOLDEN-CROWNED KINGLET   p. 189
Male: Striped head, orange crown.
Female: Striped head, yellow crown.
RUBY-CROWNED KINGLET   p. 189
Male: Broken eye-ring, red crown-spot.
Female: Broken eye-ring, black wing-bar, stubby tail.
Note: Kinglets nervously twitch or flirt wings.

WARBLING
VIREO

RED-EYED
VIREO

YELLOW-GREEN
VIREO

PHILADELPHIA
VIREO

GRAY VIREO

BELL'S VIREO

Blue-headed
form

Plumbeous
form

SOLITARY VIREO

WHITE-EYED VIREO

YELLOW-THROATED VIREO

BLACK-CAPPED VIREO

HUTTON'S VIREO

♂ ♀

GOLDEN-CROWNED KINGLET

♂ ♀

RUBY-CROWNED KINGLET

WORM-EATING

SWAINSON'S

TENNESSEE ♂

ORANGE-CROWNED

YELLOW-BREASTED CHA

♀ ♂ PARULA

BLACK-THROATED
BLUE ♂ ♀

♀ ♂ CERULEAN

♀ ♂ BLACKBURNIAN

♀ ♂ REDSTART

OVEN-BIRD

LOUISIANA WATER-THRUSH

NORTHERN WATER-THRUSH

Plate 48   209

SPRING WARBLERS

WORM-EATING WARBLER   p. 202
  Black stripes on buffy head.

SWAINSON'S WARBLER   p. 201
  Brown crown, white stripe over eye.

TENNESSEE WARBLER   p. 202
  Gray head, white eye-stripe, white breast.

ORANGE-CROWNED WARBLER   p. 203
  Dingy greenish, faintly streaked; no wing-bars.

YELLOW-BREASTED CHAT   p. 223
  Large; white "spectacles," yellow breast.

PARULA WARBLER   p. 205
  Blue and yellow; white wing-bars. Male with dark breastband.

BLACK-THROATED BLUE WARBLER   p. 207
  Male: Blue-gray back, black throat.
  Female: White wing-spot.

CERULEAN WARBLER   p. 214
  Male: Blue back, black line across breast.
  Female: See text.

BLACKBURNIAN WARBLER   p. 214
  Male: Orange throat.
  Female: Paler.

AMERICAN REDSTART   p. 227
  Male: Orange tail-patches.
  Female: Yellow tail-patches.

OVENBIRD   p. 218
  Eye-ring, dull orange crown.

LOUISIANA WATERTHRUSH   p. 219
  White eye-stripe, unstreaked throat.

NORTHERN WATERTHRUSH   p. 218
  Yellowish eye-stripe, streaked throat.

MYRTLE WARBLER *Dendroica coronata* 5–6   pp. 212, 220
Field marks: The Myrtle Warbler in all plumages flashes a *bright yellow rump*. *Male in spring:* Blue-gray above; white below, with a *heavy inverted black U* on breast and sides; a patch of yellow on the crown and one in front of each wing. Throat *white*. *Female in spring:* Brown instead of bluish, pattern similar. *Winter adults and young:* Brownish above; white below, streaked with dark; rump yellow.
Similar species: (1) Audubon's Warbler has a *yellow* throat (Myrtle, *white*). (2) Cape May and (3) Magnolia Warblers, the only other species that possess contrasting yellow rump-patches, also have yellow throats.
Voice: Full song, a loose Chipping-Sparrow-like trill, but rising in pitch, or dropping. Usual spring song more primitive; weak, colorless, irregular. Note, a loud *check;* distinctive.
Where found: Alaska through Canada to ne. edge of U.S. Winters from s. New England to Panama. **Texas:** *Migrant* throughout but scarce in extreme w. Texas. *Winters* (Sept.– May) in most sections. *Habitat:* Varied; trees, brush, thickets.

AUDUBON'S WARBLER
Dendroica auduboni 4¾–5¼   pp. 212, 224
Field marks: *Male in spring:* Very similar to Myrtle Warbler but throat *yellow* instead of white. A large *white wing-patch* replaces the two white bars. *Female, young, autumn birds:* Resemble similar plumages of Myrtle, but throat always *yellow*.
Voice: Song, loose and Chipping-Sparrow-like in quality, but 2-parted, either rising or dropping in pitch at end, *seet-seet-seet-seet-seet, trrrrrrrr*. Note, a loud *tchip*.
Where found: Sw. Canada south through w. U.S. to nw. Mexico. Winters from w. U.S. to Costa Rica. **Texas:** *Migrates and winters* (Sept.–May) through w. parts east to Fort Worth (rare), Austin, cent. coast (rare), and Delta. Casual on upper coast. *Breeds* in Guadalupe Mts. of w. Texas. *Habitat:* Trees, brush, thickets. **Nest:** A small cup in conifer. Eggs (4) spotted.

BLACK-THROATED GRAY WARBLER
Dendroica nigrescens 4½–5   p. 224
Field marks: *Male:* Gray above and white below with *black throat, cheek, and crown*. A small yellow spot before eye (often difficult to see). Females lack the black throat but retain the black cheek- and crown-patches.
Similar species: (1) Townsend's Warbler has *yellow* on face and underparts instead of white. (2) Black-throated Sparrow has similar black and white head pattern. (3) Chickadees also have black caps and black bibs but have *white* cheeks. See also (4) Black-and-White and (5) Blackpoll Warblers.
Voice: Song, a buzzy chant, *zeedle zeedle zeedle zeet' che* (next to

last note higher). Song variable, sometimes ending on the higher note, but always recognizable by its drawly quality, which has been characterized as "full of z's."

Where found: Sw. British Columbia to Arizona, New Mexico. Winters mainly in Mexico. **Texas:** *Migrant* in w. half; occurs rarely east to Austin. Occasional in *winter* in s. Texas (north to Austin, Beeville, Rockport). *Habitat:* Oaks, cedars, brush.

TOWNSEND'S WARBLER *Dendroica townsendi* 4¼–5 p. 224
 Field marks: *Male:* Easily distinguished by the *black and yellow patterned head*, yellow underparts and striped sides. *Female:* Throat largely yellow instead of black, but may be known by dark cheek-patch on yellow face.
 Similar species: Golden-cheeked Warbler (Edwards Plateau) has a white belly and a more restricted dark mark on cheek.
 Voice: Song, similar to Black-throated Gray's: *"dzeer dzeer dzeer tseetsee.* The first three or four notes similar in pitch with a wheezy, buzzy quality, followed by two or more quick high-pitched sibilant notes" (H. H. Axtell).
 Where found: Fir forests from s. Alaska and s. Yukon south to nw. U.S. Winters California to Nicaragua. **Texas:** *Migrant* (Apr.–May, Aug.–Oct.) in Trans-Pecos, Panhandle (rare), and s. Staked Plains. *Habitat:* Oaks, conifers.

BLACK-THROATED GREEN WARBLER
Dendroica virens 4½–5¼   pp. 212, 220
 Field marks: *Male:* Bright *yellow face* framed by *black throat* and olive-green crown and back. *Female:* Much less black on throat and underparts; recognized by the yellow cheek-patch.
 Similar species: (1) On Edwards Plateau, see Golden-cheeked Warbler. (2) Young and female Black-throated Green in autumn have virtually no black on throat and upper breast. They suggest Pine Warbler or immature Blackburnian, but there is always enough dusky at edge of throat to act as a frame for the yellow cheeks.
 Voice: A lisping dreamy *zoo zee zoo zoo zee* or *zee zee zee zee zoo zee,* the *zee* notes on same pitch, the *zoo* notes lower.
 Where found: Canada and ne. U.S.; locally south to n. Georgia. Winters s. Texas to Panama. **Texas:** *Migrant* (Mar.–May, Sept.–Nov.) through e. two-thirds of state; west to Panhandle and s. Staked Plains. Casual El Paso. *Winters* in Rio Grande delta. *Habitat:* Woodlands, conifers.

GOLDEN-CHEEKED WARBLER
Dendroica chrysoparia 4¾   p. 224
 Field marks: Found only in the cedar-clad hills of the Edwards Plateau; the only warbler with yellow cheeks and black throat found in this area. *Male:* Similar to Black-throated Green

SPRING WARBLERS

(Most of these have streaked underparts.)

YELLOW-THROATED WARBLER p. 215
Gray back, yellow bib, striped sides.

MYRTLE WARBLER p. 210
Yellow rump, dark breast, yellow patches.

MAGNOLIA WARBLER p. 206
White tailband, heavy stripes.

GRACE'S WARBLER p. 215
Similar to Yellow-throated but no white on face; back striped; different range (Trans-Pecos).

CANADA WARBLER p. 226
"Necklace" of streaks; no wing-bars.

AUDUBON'S WARBLER p. 210
Like Myrtle but throat yellow; male has large white wing-patch. Mostly w. half of Texas.

BAY-BREASTED WARBLER p. 216
Chestnut breast, pale neck-spot.

CHESTNUT-SIDED WARBLER p. 215
Chestnut sides, yellow crown.

CAPE MAY WARBLER p. 207
Male: Chestnut cheek.
Female: Yellow neck-spot.

BLACK-AND-WHITE WARBLER p. 200
Black and white crown-stripes.

BLACKPOLL WARBLER p. 216
Male: Black cap, white cheek.
Female: See text.

BLACK-THROATED GREEN WARBLER p. 211
Black throat, yellow cheek.

PINE WARBLER p. 217
Yellow throat, dull streaks, wing-bars.

PALM WARBLER p. 218
Chestnut cap, wags tail.
(a) *Western form:* Whitish belly.
(b) *Eastern form:* Yellow belly.

PRAIRIE WARBLER p. 217
Striped face, striped sides; wags tail.

YELLOW-THROATED ♂

MYRTLE ♀ ♂

MAGNOLIA ♀ ♂

GRACE'S ♂

CANADA ♀ ♂

AUDUBON'S ♂

BAY-BREASTED ♀ ♂

CHESTNUT-SIDED ♂

CAPE MAY ♀ ♂

BLACK-AND-WHITE ♀ ♂

BLACKPOLL ♀ ♂

BLACK-THROATED GREEN ♂

PINE ♂

PALM b a

PRAIRIE ♂

MOURNING

♀ ♂

CONNECTICUT

NASHVILLE

♂

KENTUCKY

♂

HOODED

♀ ♂

WILSON'S

♀ ♂

YELLOW-THROAT

♀ ♂

LAWRENCE'S

♂

BACHMAN'S

♀ ♂

GOLDEN- WINGED

♂

BREWSTER'S

♂

BLUE- WINGED

♂

PROTHONOTARY

♀ ♂

YELLOW

♀ ♂

Plate 50   213

SPRING WARBLERS

(Most of these have unstreaked breasts.)

MOURNING WARBLER   p. 222
Gray hood, black throat (male).

CONNECTICUT WARBLER   p. 222
Gray hood, white eye-ring. See MacGillivray's Warbler
(Plate 53).

NASHVILLE WARBLER   p. 203
Yellow throat, white eye-ring.

KENTUCKY WARBLER   p. 219
Black "sideburns," yellow "spectacles."

HOODED WARBLER   p. 226
Male: Black hood, yellow face.
Female: See text.

WILSON'S WARBLER   p. 226
Male: Round black cap.
Female: See text.

YELLOWTHROAT   p. 223
Male: Black mask.
Female: Yellow throat, white belly.

LAWRENCE'S WARBLER (hybrid)   p. 275
Accidental (?) in Texas (needs substantiation).
Black bib, black cheek, yellow belly.

BACHMAN'S WARBLER   p. 275
Accidental or casual in Texas (needs substantiation).
Male: Black cap, black bib.
Female: See text.

GOLDEN-WINGED WARBLER   p. 202
Black bib, black cheek, white belly.

BREWSTER'S WARBLER (hybrid)   p. 275
Accidental (?) in Texas (needs substantiation).
Like Blue-wing with some white below. Yellow or white
wing-bars.

BLUE-WINGED WARBLER   p. 202
Black eye-line, yellow underparts.

PROTHONOTARY WARBLER   p. 201
Golden head, bluish wings.

YELLOW WARBLER   p. 206
Yellowish back, yellow tail-spots. Reddish breast-streaks
(male).

Warbler (which is seldom found on Edwards Plateau), but with a *black back* and stronger black mark through eye. *Female:* Similar to male but back olive-green.

Similar species: Migrant Black-throated Green Warblers, when in cent. Texas are nearly always in hardwoods and shade trees of lowlands; Golden-cheeks are usually in the cedar ridges.

Voice: Song, "a hurried *tweeah, tweeah, tweesy*" (H. P. Attwater) or "*bzzzz, layzee, dayzee*" (E. Kincaid). Has buzzy quality of Black-throated Green.

Where found: Edwards Plateau. Winters s. Mexico to Nicaragua. **Texas:** *Summer resident* (Mar.–Aug.) only in Edwards Plateau, from near San Angelo, Rocksprings, n. Uvalde Co., east locally to vicinity of Dallas, Waco, Austin, San Antonio. *Habitat:* Cedars, oaks; also streamside trees. **Nest:** A small cup in cedar or other tree. Eggs (4) speckled.

CERULEAN WARBLER *Dendroica cerulea* 4½   p. 209
Field marks: *Male:* Blue above, white below. It usually forages too high to reveal the blue back; then the *narrow black ring* crossing the upper breast is the best mark (only white-breasted warbler so marked). *Female:* Blue-gray and olive-green above, whitish below; two white wing-bars, white line over eye.
Similar species: (1) Female suggests Tennessee Warbler, but Tennessee has no wing-bars. (2) Female resembles closely the autumn Blackpoll but is greener above, whiter below, and has more of an eye-stripe. (3) See Blue-gray Gnatcatcher (p. 188).
Voice: Song suggests Parula Warbler's; rapid buzzy notes on same pitch followed by a longer note on a higher pitch: *zray zray zray zray zreeeee.*
Where found: Great Lakes states south to ne. Texas, Louisiana, and Virginia. Winters in S. America. **Texas:** *Migrant* (Mar.–May, Aug.–Sept.) mainly through e. and coastal Texas; west rarely to Dallas, Fort Worth, Austin. *Breeds* locally in Red River Valley in ne. Texas. *Habitat:* River woodlands. **Nest:** A shallow cup well up in forest tree. Eggs (3–5) spotted.

BLACKBURNIAN WARBLER
Dendroica fusca 5–5½   pp. 209, 220
Field marks: The "fire-throat." *Male in spring:* Black and white with *flaming orange* about head and throat. *Female:* Paler, but orange enough on throat to be recognized. *Autumn:* Pattern similar, but paler, orange more yellowish. The clean-cut yellow head-stripings are distinctive. The pale back stripes are helpful.
Similar species: (1) The differently patterned male Redstart is the only other small bird of similar color. (2) Young Blackburnians in autumn suggest young Black-throated Green Warblers except for: (a) strongly yellow throat, (b) dark ear-patch, (c) light stripes on back.

Voice: Song begins with several *zip* notes on same pitch and ends on a very high slurred note: *zip zip zip zip titi tseeeeee*. Wiry end note is diagnostic if you can hear it. Also a 2-parted song, more like Nashville's: *tizip tizip tizip tizip, zizizizizizizizizi*.
Where found: Canada and ne. U.S.; south in mts. to n. Georgia. Winters from Guatemala to Peru. **Texas:** *Migrant* (Mar.–May, Sept.–Oct.) through e. half; west to Panhandle (rare), Fort Worth, Austin, Beeville. *Habitat:* Woodlands, groves.

YELLOW-THROATED WARBLER
Dendroica dominica 5–5½   p. 212
Field marks: *A gray-backed warbler with a yellow bib.* White stripe over eye, two white wing-bars, and black stripes on sides; sexes similar; creeps about branches of trees.
Similar species: (1) Female Blackburnian (migrant) is slightly similar, but is *broadly striped with yellow* over eye and through center of crown. (2) In w. Texas see Grace's Warbler.
Voice: Song, a series of clear slurred notes dropping slightly, *tee-ew, tew, tew, tew, tew tew wi* (last note picking up).
Where found: S. Ohio and s. New Jersey south to Gulf States. Winters s. U.S. to Cent. America. **Texas:** *Migrant* (Mar.–May, Sept.–Oct.) in e. Texas and upper coast region; west rarely to Panhandle and Edwards Plateau (Uvalde and Junction). Casual Midland. *Winters* in s. Texas north to Austin region. *Breeds* in e. Texas and upper coast; very locally in n. and cent. Texas. *Habitat:* Open woodlands, river forests, groves. **Nest:** Well up in tree, often in tuft of Spanish moss. Eggs (3–5) spotted.

GRACE'S WARBLER *Dendroica graciae* 4½   pp. 212, 224
Field marks: *A gray-backed warbler with a yellow throat.* Belly white; two white wing-bars, yellowish line over eye, and black stripes on sides.
Similar species: Yellow-throated Warbler (e. half of Texas) is very similar, but has white patch on neck, *white* eye-stripe.
Voice: A repetitious *cheedle cheedle che che che che*, etc. ending in a Chipping-Sparrow-like trill.
Where found: S. Utah and s. Colorado south to n. Nicaragua. Winters from Mexico south. **Texas:** *Migrant* in w. Texas; reported east to Midland. *Summers* (Apr.–Aug.) in Guadalupe and Davis Mts. of w. Texas. *Habitat:* Mt. forests (pine and oak). **Nest:** A small cup high in pine or fir. Eggs (3–4) spotted.

CHESTNUT-SIDED WARBLER
Dendroica pensylvanica 5   pp. 212, 220
Field marks: *Adults in spring:* Easily identified by the combination of *yellow crown* and *chestnut sides*. *Autumn:* Greenish above, white below, with white eye-ring and two wing-bars. Adults usually retain some chestnut. The lemon-colored shade

of green, in connection with white underparts, is determinative.
Similar species: Bay-breast, in addition to chestnut sides, has chestnut throat and *dark crown* (appears dark-headed).
Voice: Song similar to one of Yellow Warbler's but more emphatic; can be interpreted *I wish to see Miss Beecher* or *please please pleased ta meetcha,* the last note dropping abruptly.
Where found: S. Canada and ne. U.S.; south in mts. to n. Georgia. Winters from Nicaragua to Panama. **Texas:** *Migrant* (Apr.–May, Aug.–Oct.) through e. half; west to Fort Worth, Austin, San Antonio, Uvalde; rare transient in Panhandle. *Habitat:* Shrubs, brush, open second-growth.

BAY-BREASTED WARBLER
Dendroica castanea 5–6   pp. 212, 220
Field marks: *Male in spring:* A dark-looking warbler with *chestnut throat, upper breast,* and sides, and a *large spot of pale buff* on side of neck. *Female in spring:* Similar, but paler and more washed out. *Autumn birds:* Totally different; olive-green above with two white wing-bars, dingy buff below. Some birds have traces of bay on sides.
Similar species: (1) Chestnut-sided Warbler is much paler than breeding Bay-breast; has a *yellow* crown and *white* throat. (2) One of the most challenging field problems is to distinguish the fall Bay-breast from the rarer fall Blackpoll: (a) Blackpoll is tinged with greenish yellow below and is noticeably streaked (Bay-breast is buffier; breast-streakings very indistinct or wanting); (b) Blackpoll has *white* under tail-coverts (Bay-breast *buff*); (c) some Bay-breasts have a touch of bay on flanks — these are easy; (d) Blackpoll has *pale yellowish legs* (Bay-breast, *blackish*). (3) See also Pine Warbler.
Voice: A high sibilant *teesi teesi teesi;* resembles song of Black-and-White but thinner, shorter, and more on one pitch.
Where found: Evergreen forests of e. Canada and ne. edge of U.S. Winters Panama to Venezuela. **Texas:** *Migrant* (Apr.–May, Sept.–Nov.) through e. half; west to Fort Worth, Waco, Austin, San Antonio, Brownsville. Recorded rarely in Panhandle and s. Staked Plains. *Habitat:* Woodlands, groves.

BLACKPOLL WARBLER *Dendroica striata* 5–5½ pp. 212, 220
Field marks: *Male in spring:* A striped gray warbler with a *solid black cap and white cheeks. Female in spring:* Less heavily streaked, lacking the black cap; a plain, black-streaked warbler, greenish gray above, white below. *Autumn birds:* Streaked, greenish-looking warblers, olive-green above; dingy yellow below, faintly streaked. Two white wing-bars.
Similar species: (1) Chickadee vaguely suggests spring male Blackpoll but has black throat. (2) Black-and-White Warbler has *striped crown.* (3) See fall Bay-breasted Warbler.

Voice: Song, a thin deliberate, mechanical *zi-zi-zi-zi-zi-zi-zi* on one pitch, becoming slightly louder and more emphatic in the middle, then diminishing (crescendo and diminuendo).

Where found: Alaska, across Canada to ne. U.S. Winters in S. America. **Texas:** Rare spring *migrant* (Apr.–May) in e. parts of state, mostly along coast. Casual west to Panhandle, Fort Worth, Austin. Accidental El Paso. *Habitat:* Trees, groves.

PINE WARBLER *Dendroica pinus* 5–5½ pp. 212, 220
Field marks: No other *bright* yellow-breasted warbler, lacking other conspicuous marks, has *white wing-bars*. Often creeps and clings on pine branches, trunks. *Male:* Olive-green above with two white wing-bars; underparts lemon-yellow, brightest on throat; breast dimly streaked. *Female:* Like a dull-colored male; rather nondescript. *Immature and autumn female:* Very obscure; grayish or brownish above, with *two white wing-bars;* underparts dull whitish, usually with a dull buffy wash across breast; best identified by "boiling-down" system (see following).
Similar species: (1) Yellow-throated Vireo has a thicker vireo bill, lacks breast-streaks, and does not show white tail-spots. (2) Autumn Blackpolls and (3) Bay-breasts are very similar to female and immature Pine Warblers — dingy, dull-colored, with white wing-bars. The plain, *unstreaked* back of the Pine Warbler eliminates the other two. In addition, Bay-breast has *buffy* under tail-coverts (Pine, *white*); Blackpoll has *pale yellowish legs* (Pine, *black*). Some female Pine Warblers can easily be told because the breast is strong yellow, but many immatures are plain grayish or brownish with a buffy wash across the breast; probably best identified by lack of back-streaking.
Voice: Song, a trill on one pitch like Chipping Sparrow's but looser, more musical; slower in tempo.
Where found: Se. Canada south to Gulf States, West Indies. Winters in s. part of range. **Texas:** *Migrant* (Mar.–Apr., Sept.–Nov.) through e. half of state. Casual Del Rio, El Paso. *Resident* in e. Texas, upper coast, and cent. Texas (local). *Winters* also in s. Texas and rest of coast. *Habitat:* Chiefly pinewoods.
Nest: A shallow cup in pine. Eggs (3–5) spotted.

PRAIRIE WARBLER *Dendroica discolor* 4½–5 pp. 212, 220
Field marks: This warbler *wags its tail* (so does Palm Warbler). Underparts yellow; black stripings *confined to the sides. Two black face marks,* one through eye and one below, are conclusive. At close range, in good light, *chestnut markings* may be seen on back of male (reduced in female; otherwise sexes are similar). Immatures nondescript (without wing-bars; pale yellow below, with indistinct streaking). Note *tail-wagging, dark neck mark.*
Voice: Song, a thin *zee zee zee zee zee zee zee zee,* going up the chromatic scale.

Where found: Cent. Ontario south to Gulf States. Winters Florida south to Nicaragua. **Texas:** *Migrant* in e. Texas and upper coast (rare). Casual west to Fort Worth, Austin, Beeville. *Summers* locally (Mar.–Sept.) in ne. corner of state (Texarkana, Tyler, Nacogdoches). *Habitat:* Semi-open brush, low pines, small sweetgums. **Nest:** A small cup in bush, low pine, or small sweetgum. Eggs (3–5) spotted.

PALM WARBLER *Dendroica palmarum* 5–5½   pp. 212, 220
Field marks: This tail-bobbing warbler spends most of its time on the ground. Brown above; yellowish or whitish below, narrowly streaked; yellow under tail-coverts, white spots in tail-corners. In spring, crown *chestnut* (obscure in fall, winter). *Constantly flicks tail up and down.* Sexes similar.
Similar species: (1) Prairie Warbler also wags tail. (2) Waterthrushes teeter, more like Spotted Sandpiper.
Voice: Song, a Chipping-Sparrow-like series of weak notes, *thi thi thi thi thi thi*, etc.
Where found: Canada and along n. edge of e. U.S. Winters in s. U.S., Caribbean area. **Texas:** Uncommon or rare *transient* in e. Texas, straggling occasionally to cent. Texas. Casual west to Fort Worth, Midland, Brownsville. *Winters* uncommonly (Oct.–Apr.) on coast. *Habitat:* Low vegetation, weedy ground.

OVENBIRD *Seiurus aurocapillus* 5½–6½   p. 209
Field marks: A sparrow-sized ground warbler; usually seen walking on pale *pinkish* legs over the dead leaves. Suggests a small thrush — olive-brown above, but striped rather than spotted beneath. *A light orange* patch on crown is visible at close range.
Voice: Song, an emphatic *teach′er*, TEACH′ER, *TEACH′ER*, etc., repeated rapidly, louder and louder, till the air rings with the vibrant accents (to be more exact the accent is really on the *second* syllable: *chertea′*, CHERTEA′, *CHERTEA′*, etc.).
Where found: S. Canada south to e. Colorado, Oklahoma, n. Georgia. Winters mainly in West Indies, Cent. America, n. S. America. **Texas:** *Migrant* (Apr.–May, Aug.–Nov.) in e. half; occasional west to Panhandle and s. Staked Plains. Casual El Paso. *Habitat:* Woodland undergrowth, thickets.

NORTHERN WATERTHRUSH
Seiurus noveboracensis 5–6   p. 209
Field marks: A brown-backed bird about the size of a sparrow, with a *conspicuous light eyebrow-stripe and heavily striped underparts.* Though a warbler it often walks along the water's edge and teeters in the manner of a Spotted Sandpiper. The under-

parts are strongly tinged with *yellowish* or buffy. Stripe over eye usually *yellowish*.

Similar species: Louisiana Waterthrush is larger, grayer, usually *whitish* below (sometimes slightly tinged with yellow). The eye-stripe is always *pure white*. Some Northern Waterthrushes in fall, particularly the northwestern race (*notabilis*), have eye-lines that are quite white. Know them by the small spots on throat (Louisiana has unspotted white throat).

Voice: Note, a sharp *chip*. Song, a vigorous, rapid *twit twit twit twee twee twee chew chew chew*, dropping in pitch at end. Variable, but *chew chew chew* at end is often diagnostic.

Where found: Alaska, Canada, to n. edge of U.S. Winters from Mexico, West Indies to S. America. **Texas:** *Migrant* (Mar.–May, Aug.–Oct.) through e. half of state, Panhandle, and Trans-Pecos. Apparently absent from most of Edwards Plateau, Staked Plains. *Habitat:* Swampy spots; streamsides, thickets.

LOUISIANA WATERTHRUSH *Seiurus motacilla* 6¼ p. 209
Field marks: See Northern Waterthrush.
Voice: Song musical and ringing; *three clear slurred whistles*, followed by jumble of twittering notes dropping in pitch.
Where found: Great Lakes and s. New England south to Gulf States. Winters from Mexico, West Indies to S. America. **Texas:** *Migrant* (Mar.–May, Aug.–Oct.) through e. half; west to e. Panhandle, Fort Worth, Austin, Rio Grande delta. *Breeds* locally in ne. part (Corsicana, Tyler, Silsbee). *Habitat:* Wooded swamps, streamsides, brooks, thickets. **Nest:** Of leaves, rootlets in overhang of bank, roots. Eggs (4–6) spotted.

KENTUCKY WARBLER *Oporornis formosus* 5½ p. 213
Field marks: The outstanding mark is the *broad black "side-burns,"* extending from the eye down the side of the yellow throat. Also a yellow eye-ring, or *"spectacles."* Sexes similar. Learn the song; ten Kentuckies are heard for every one seen.
Similar species: (1) Yellowthroat has a black face-patch but lacks yellow spectacles; is whitish on belly. (2) Canada Warbler also has spectacles but is gray above, not olive; usually shows trace of dark "necklace"; has *white* under tail-coverts.
Voice: Song, a rapid, rolling chant, *tory-tory-tory-tory* or *churry-churry-churry-churry*. Suggestive of song of Carolina Wren but less musical; 2-syllabled rather than trisyllabic.
Where found: Se. Nebraska, se. New York south to Gulf States. Winters Mexico to n. S. America. **Texas:** *Migrant* (Mar.–May, Sept.–Oct.) through e. half and Panhandle (rare). *Breeds* in wooded sections of e. and cent. Texas; west locally to Kerrville; south to Houston, San Antonio. *Habitat:* Woodland undergrowth. **Nest:** Of leaves, rootlets, on ground. Eggs (4–5) spotted.

CONFUSING FALL WARBLERS

(Migrants through e. half of Texas. Most of these
have streaks or wing-bars.)

RUBY-CROWNED KINGLET* p. 189
Broken eye-ring, dark wing-bar.

CHESTNUT-SIDED WARBLER p. 215
Immature: Yellow-green above, whitish below.

YELLOW-THROATED VIREO* p. 198
Bright yellow breast, yellow "spectacles."

BAY-BREASTED WARBLER p. 216
Dark legs, buffy under tail (see text).

BLACKPOLL WARBLER p. 216
Pale legs, white under tail (see text).

PINE WARBLER p. 217
Differs from preceding two by unstreaked back (see text).

PARULA WARBLER p. 205
Immature: Bluish and yellow; wing-bars.

MAGNOLIA WARBLER p. 209
Immature: White band across tail.

PRAIRIE WARBLER p. 217
Immature: Neck-spot, side-stripes; wags tail.

YELLOW WARBLER p. 206
Yellow tail-spots.

BLACKBURNIAN WARBLER p. 214
Immature: Yellow throat, dark cheek, striped back.

BLACK-THROATED GREEN WARBLER p. 211
Immature: Dusky streaks framing yellow cheek.

PALM WARBLER p. 218
Brownish back; wags tail.

MYRTLE WARBLER p. 210
Immature: Bright yellow rump.

CAPE MAY WARBLER p. 207
Immature: Heavy streaks, neck-spot (see text).

* Not a warbler, but often mistaken for one.

RUBY-CROWNED KINGLET

Immature

CHESTNUT-SIDED

YELLOW-THROATED
VIREO

Adult

mature

BLACKPOLL

Immature

BAY-BREASTED

♂ Adult

PINE

Immature

PARULA

Immature

MAGNOLIA

Immature

PRAIRIE

mmature
(Alaskan)

Immature

YELLOW

Immature

BLACKBURNIAN

Immature

BLACK-
THROATED
GREEN

Immature

PALM

Immature

MYRTLE

Immature

CAPE MAY

PHILADELPHIA
VIREO

TENNESSEE

Immature

ORANGE–CROWNED

Immature

BLACK–THROATED BLUE
♀

HOODED

Immature

Immature

WILSON'S

Immature

CONNECTICUT

MOURNING

Immature

NASHVILLE

YELLOW–THROAT
♀

PROTHONOTARY
♀

CANADA

Immature

Plate 52   221

CONFUSING FALL WARBLERS

(Migrants through e. half of Texas. Most of these
have no streaks or wing-bars.)

* Not a warbler, but often mistaken for one.

CONNECTICUT WARBLER
Oporornis agilis 5¼–6   pp. 213, 221
Field marks: This species, like the Mourning Warbler, possesses a gray *hood*, contrasting with the yellow and olive of its body. It is at once recognized by the *round white eye-ring*. *Fall females and young* are duller, with no gray, but there is always a suggestion of a hood (like a *brownish* stain across the upper breast). The eye-ring is always present.
Similar species: (1) Nashville Warbler is of similar color scheme, white eye-ring and all, but throat is *yellow* not gray. (2) Mourning Warbler in breeding plumage *lacks* eye-ring, but in fall often has a broken one. The yellow under tail-coverts reach nearly to end of tail in Connecticut, halfway in Mourning. (3) In w. Texas see MacGillivray's Warbler.
Voice: Song, an Ovenbird-like *beecher beecher beecher beecher beech* without the change of emphasis.
Where found: Cent.-s. Canada south to n. Minnesota, n. Wisconsin, n. Michigan. Winters in S. America. Texas: Rare *migrant* (Mar.–May, Sept.–Oct.) in e. and n. Texas and Panhandle; more frequent along coast. *Habitat:* Thickets, undergrowth.

MOURNING WARBLER
Oporornis philadelphia 5–5¾   pp. 213, 221
Field marks: Olive above, yellow below, with a *gray hood* completely encircling the head and neck; *male* with an apron of *black crape* on upper breast where hood meets yellow.
Similar species: (1) Connecticut Warbler has a conspicuous white eye-ring; male lacks the black crape. *Female and immature* Mourning Warblers in fall often have an eye-ring, but it is broken in front of eye, *not complete*. Mourning is brighter yellow below and smaller. (2) On Edwards Plateau see also MacGillivray's Warbler.
Voice: Song, *chirry chirry, chorry chorry*, voice falling on last two notes; considerable variation.
Where found: Canada and ne. U.S.; south in mts. to Virginia. Winters in Cent. and S. America. Texas: *Migrant* (Apr.–May, Sept.–Oct.) throughout e. half of state; west at least to Fort Worth, cent. Edwards Plateau, San Antonio, Rio Grande delta. Casual Midland. *Habitat:* Undergrowth, thickets.

MacGILLIVRAY'S WARBLER
Oporornis tolmiei 4¾–5¼   p. 224
Field marks: *Male:* Olive above, yellow below, with a *slate-gray hood* completely encircling the head and neck, and a conspicuous white *eye-ring*, broken fore and aft.
Similar species: (1) The only remotely similar *western* warbler with a white eye-ring is Nashville, which has *yellow* throat. (2) Connecticut Warbler also has hood and eye-ring (although lores

of MacGillivray's are blacker and eye-ring is broken fore and aft; also, there is some obscure black spotting on throat). However, the ranges are quite separate (MacGillivray's is western). (3) Mourning Warbler, which may meet MacGillivray's on cent. Edwards Plateau, lacks eye-ring (except in some autumn birds). **Voice:** Song, a rolling chant, *chiddle-chiddle-chiddle, turtle-turtle*, voice dropping on last two notes; one popular interpretation is *sweeter-sweeter-sweeter, sugar-sugar*. **Where found:** S. Alaska, w. Canada south to sw. U.S. Winters in Mexico and Guatemala. **Texas:** *Migrant* (Apr.–June, Sept.–Oct.) in w. Texas and Panhandle; east to Edwards Plateau (Uvalde, Kerrville), Rio Grande delta (rare). Casual east to Gainesville, Austin, Beeville. *Habitat:* Undergrowth, thickets.

YELLOWTHROAT *Geothlypis trichas* 4½–5½ pp. 213, 221
Field marks: A wrenlike warbler, *male* with a yellow throat and black *mask*, or "domino." *Females and immatures* are olive-brown with a rich yellow throat, buffy yellow breast, and *white belly;* no black mask. Distinguished from similar warblers by *whitish belly* (others are solid yellow below) and by habitat.
Similar species: See Kentucky Warbler (p. 219).
Voice: Song, very distinctive; rapid, well-enunciated *witchity-witchity-witchity-witch* or *witchity-ta-witchity-ta-witchity-ta-witch*. Note, a husky *tchep*, distinctive.
Where found: Se. Alaska, Canada, south to s. Mexico, Gulf Coast. Winters from s. U.S. to Canal Zone. **Texas:** *Migrant* (Apr.–May, Sept.–Oct.) throughout. *Winters* except in colder n. and w. areas. *Breeds* in e., n., and cent. Texas; south locally to Houston, Austin; also in Panhandle (Canadian Breaks), Trans-Pecos and Rio Grande delta. *Habitat:* Swamps, thickets, streamsides. **Nest:** A loose cup on or near ground. Eggs (3–5) spotted.

YELLOW-BREASTED CHAT *Icteria virens* 7–7½
(Long-tailed Chat) p. 209
Field marks: Except for its color, the Chat seems more like a Catbird or a Mockingbird than a warbler. Its superior size (larger than a sparrow), its *rather long tail*, eccentric song and actions, and brushy habitat all suggest those larger birds. Both sexes are olive-green above, with white "spectacles"; bright yellow throat and breast, white belly.
Similar species: Yellow-throated Vireo is smaller, with two white wing-bars, *yellow* spectacles.
Voice: Song, clear repeated whistles, alternated with harsh notes and soft crow-like *caw*'s. Occasionally gives imitations, suggests Mockingbird, but repertoire more limited; much longer pauses between phrases. Single notes, such as *whoit* or *kook*, are distinctive. The Chat often sings on the wing, with dangling legs, and like the Mockingbird frequently sings at night.

WESTERN WARBLERS AND SOME TEXAS SPECIALTIES

Several of these (Red-faced, Hermit, Lucy's, and Golden-crowned Warblers and Ground-Chat) are accidental or casual in Texas.

BLACK-THROATED GRAY WARBLER   p. 210
  Male: Black crown, cheek-patch, and throat.
  Female: Blackish crown and cheek-patch.
RED-FACED WARBLER   p. 276
  Accidental in Texas. Bright red on face and upper breast.
  Sexes similar.
PAINTED REDSTART   p. 227
  Bright red lower breast; white wing- and tail-patches.
  Sexes similar.
TOWNSEND'S WARBLER   p. 211
  Like Black-throated Gray, but with yellow.
GOLDEN-CHEEKED WARBLER   p. 211
  Yellow cheek, black throat (male), white underparts,
  dark back. Edwards Plateau only. See Black-throated
  Green Warbler (Plate 49).
HERMIT WARBLER   p. 275
  Accidental in Texas. Yellow head (including crown), black
  throat. Female duller.
VIRGINIA'S WARBLER   p. 204
  Gray; yellowish rump, yellowish breast.
COLIMA WARBLER   p. 204
  Like Virginia's but larger; deeper yellow under tail-coverts;
  lacks yellow on breast. Chisos Mts. only.
LUCY'S WARBLER   p. 205
  Casual in w. Texas. Gray; white below, rusty rump.
GRACE'S WARBLER   p. 215
  Yellow throat and breast, striped sides. Sexes similar.
  See Yellow-throated Warbler (e. half of Texas), Plate 49.
AUDUBON'S WARBLER   p. 210
  Distinguished from Myrtle Warbler (Plate 49) by yellow
  throat. Spring male usually has large white wing-patch.
MacGILLIVRAY'S WARBLER   p. 222
  Gray hood, incomplete white eye-ring. See Mourning and
  Connecticut Warblers (Plate 50).
OLIVE-BACKED WARBLER   p. 205
  Bluish and yellow; wing-bars, black face (male). Rio
  Grande delta. See Parula Warbler (Plate 48).
GOLDEN-CROWNED WARBLER   p. 276
  Accidental in Delta. Yellow crown bordered by black.
GROUND-CHAT   p. 276
  Casual in Rio Grande delta (formerly, at least). Male has
  gray cap, broken white eye-ring, black lores. Both sexes
  yellow on lower belly (Yellowthroat is white).

LACK-THROATED GRAY ♀ ♂

RED-FACED

PAINTED REDSTART

TOWNSEND'S ♀ ♂

GOLDEN-CHEEKED ♀ ♂

HERMIT ♂

VIRGINIA'S ♂ Spring

COLIMA ♂

LUCY'S ♂ Spring

GRACE'S ♀

AUDUBON'S Winter ♀ Spring ♂

MacGILLIVRAY'S ♀ ♂

OLIVE-BACKED ♀ ♂

GOLDEN-CROWNED ♂

GROUND-CHAT ♂

BREWER'S
BLACKBIRD

Spring ♂
Spring ♀
Winter

RUSTY
BLACKBIRD

Spring ♂
Spr ♀
Winter

BROWN-HEADED
COWBIRD

♂
♀

Adult
Spring

Juvenal

Winter

STARLING

BRONZED
COWBIRD

♂

COMMON
GRACKLE

♂

BOAT-TAILED
GRACKLE

♂
♀

YELLOW-HEADED BLACKBIRD

♂
♀

REDWINGED BLACKBIRD

♂
♀

Plate 54   225

BLACKBIRDS AND STARLING

BREWER'S BLACKBIRD   p. 233
  Male in spring: Purplish head, yellow eye, medium tail.
  Female in spring: Grayish; dark eye.
  Winter: Slight barring of rusty. See text.

RUSTY BLACKBIRD   p. 233
  Male in spring: Differs from Brewer's by lack of iridescence.
  Female in spring: Grayish; yellow eye.
  Winter: Rusty; barred breast.

BROWN-HEADED COWBIRD   p. 234
  Male: Brown head, short bill.
  Female: Grayish; short bill.

BRONZED COWBIRD   p. 235
  Male: Blackish throughout; ruff on neck.
  Female (not shown): Blackish; smaller ruff.

STARLING   p. 195
  Spring: Iridescent; sharp yellow bill, short tail. Sexes
  similar.
  Winter: Finely spotted; sharp black bill.
  Juvenal: Gray or gray-brown; short tail, sharp bill.

COMMON GRACKLE   p. 234
  Male: Bronzy back, purple head; creased tail.
  Female (not shown): Smaller; less iridescent.

BOAT-TAILED GRACKLE   p. 233
  Male: Very large; long creased tail.
  Female: Smaller; brown.

YELLOW-HEADED BLACKBIRD   p. 229
  Male: Yellow head.
  Female: Yellow throat and breast.

REDWINGED BLACKBIRD   p. 230
  Male: Red "epaulets."
  Female: Heavily striped.

Where found: S. Canada to cent. Mexico, Gulf Coast. Winters Mexico to Panama. **Texas:** *Migrant* (Mar.–May, Sept.–Oct.) throughout, except Staked Plains. *Breeds* from Panhandle (Canadian Breaks) to Rio Grande delta and from El Paso to e. Texas, but absent from most of coastal area and Staked Plains. Casual in winter on coast. *Habitat:* Brushy tangles, briars, thickets. **Nest:** A bulky cup in bush. Eggs (3–5) spotted.

HOODED WARBLER *Wilsonia citrina* 5–5¾   pp. 213, 221
Field marks: The black "hood" of the *male* completely encircles the yellow face and forehead, which stand out as a bright spot. *Females and young* are plain olive above and bright yellow on *forehead* and underparts. Aside from white tail-spots they are *without streaks, wing-bars, or distinctive marks.*
Similar species: Female Wilson's is almost identical with female Hooded except for its smaller size. Wilson's has no white in tail, whereas *white tail-spots* show plainly in Hooded.
Voice: Song, a loud whistled *weeta wee-tee-o.* Other arrangements but slurred *tee-o* is a clue. Note, a metallic *chink.*
Where found: Great Lakes and s. New England south to Gulf States. Winters from Mexico to Panama. **Texas:** *Migrant* (Mar.–May, Sept.–Oct.) through e. and coastal Texas; sparingly in n. and cent. Texas (Fort Worth, Dallas, Austin). Casual Panhandle, El Paso, Midland. *Breeds* locally in woodlands, wooded swamps, in e. Texas. *Habitat:* Woodland undergrowth. **Nest:** A leafy cup in upright crotch in shrub. Eggs (3–4) spotted.

WILSON'S WARBLER *Wilsonia pusilla* 4½–5
(Pileolated Warbler)   pp. 213, 221
Field marks: *Male:* A yellow warbler with a *round black cap.* *Females* sometimes do, and *immatures* do not, show traces of the cap. They appear as small, very active warblers, olive above and bright yellow below, with no streaks or wing-bars; golden-looking with a yellow stripe above the beady eye.
Similar species: (1) Female Hooded has white spots in tail; (2) Yellow Warbler, yellow spots. Wilson's has no tail-spots.
Voice: Song, a thin rapid little chatter dropping in pitch at the end: *chi chi chi chi chi chet chet.*
Where found: Alaska, Canada south to California, New Mexico; in east to n. New England. Winters Mexico to Panama. **Texas:** *Migrant* (Apr.–May, Aug.–Oct.) throughout. A few *winter* along coast and in lower Valley. *Habitat:* Low shrubs, thickets.

CANADA WARBLER *Wilsonia canadensis* 5–5¾ pp. 212, 221
Field marks: The "necklaced warbler." Plain gray above, bright yellow below; male with a *necklace of short black stripes* across breast. *Females and immatures* similar, but necklace fainter, sometimes nearly wanting. All have *yellow "spectacles."* In any plumage gray upper parts in connection with *total lack of white in wings and tail* is conclusive.

Voice: Song, a jumble of clear emphatic musical notes, irregularly arranged. Variable. Note, a loud *tchack*.
Where found: Canada and ne. U.S.; south in mts. to n. Georgia. Winters in S. America. **Texas:** *Migrant* (Apr.–May, Aug.–Oct.) through e. half of state; west to Fort Worth, San Angelo, Uvalde. *Habitat:* Shady thickets, woodland undergrowth.

AMERICAN REDSTART
Setophaga ruticilla   4½–5½   p. 209
Field marks: One of the most butterfly-like of birds, constantly flitting about, drooping wings, and spreading its tail. Has flycatching habits. *Male:* Largely black with *bright orange patches on wings and tail;* belly white. *Female:* Olive-brown above, white below; large yellow flash-patches on wings and tail. *Immature male:* Variable; much like female; yellow often tinged with orange. The Redstart pattern is always obvious.
Similar species: Male Blackburnian Warbler has orange confined to head, throat, and upper breast (none on wings, tail).
Voice: Three commonest songs, *tsee tsee tsee tsee tseet* (last note higher), *tsee tsee tsee tsee tsee-o* (drop on last syllable), and *teetsa teetsa teeetsa teetsa teet* (double-noted). Songs often alternated; an excellent field aid. Note, a clear *tseet*.
Where found: Se. Alaska, Canada south to ne. Texas, Louisiana, n. Georgia. Winters from Mexico, West Indies to S. America. **Texas:** *Migrant* (Mar.–May, Aug.–Oct.) throughout; less frequent in w. parts. *Breeds* in woodlands in ne. part of state (Tyler, etc.). *Habitat:* Woodlands, groves. **Nest:** A neat cup in upright crotch in sapling. Eggs (3–4) spotted.

PAINTED REDSTART   *Setophaga picta* 5   p. 224
Field marks: A beautiful bird; postures with half-spread wings and tail in redstart fashion. Black head and upper parts; *large white patches* in wings and on sides of tail; *large bright red patch* on breast. Sexes similar.
Voice: Song, a repetitious *weeta weeta weeta wee* or *weeta weeta chilp chilp chilp*. Note, a ringing *clee-ip* or *che-ilp*.
Where found: U.S.–Mexican border to Nicaragua. Winters largely south of U.S. **Texas:** *Breeds* irregularly in Chisos Mts. in w. Texas. Casual El Paso. *Habitat:* High oak canyons. **Nest:** A grassy cup on ground or on steep bank. Eggs (3–4) speckled.

Weaver Finches: Ploceidae

A WIDESPREAD, varied group of which the introduced House Sparrow (not related to our native sparrows) is the best-known example. Food: Mainly insects, seeds. Widespread in Old World; most species in Africa. No. of species: World, 263 (of which the sparrow-weavers are 35); N. America, 2; Texas, 1.

HOUSE SPARROW   *Passer domesticus*   5–6¼
("English Sparrow")   p. 244
   Field marks: A species with which everybody is familiar. City
   birds are often so sooty that they bear a poor resemblance to
   a clean country male with its black throat, white cheeks, and
   chestnut nape. Females and young lack the black throat, are
   dull brown above and dingy whitish below; dull eye-stripe.
   Voice: Garrulous and varied. A loud *cheep;* also *chissis* and
   various grating, twittering, and chirping notes.
   Where found: Native to Eurasia, n. Africa. Introduced into N.
   America, S. America, S. Africa, Australia, etc. **Texas:** *Resident* in all settled parts of state. *Habitat:* Cities, towns, farms.
   Nest: A bulky mass, usually in cavity or in building; sometimes
   in branches of tree. Eggs (5–6) speckled.

Meadowlarks, Blackbirds, and Orioles: Icteridae

A VARIED group difficult to generalize about except that they have
conical, sharp-pointed bills and rather flat profiles. Food: Insects,
small fruits, seeds, waste grain, small aquatic life. Widespread
throughout New World; most species in tropics. No. of species:
World, 88; N. America, 22; Texas, 18.

BOBOLINK   *Dolichonyx oryzivorus*   6½–8   p. 241
   Field marks: *Male in spring:* The only songbird that is *black
   below and largely white above*, like a dress suit backwards. *Female
   and autumn:* Somewhat larger than House Sparrow, yellowish
   buff with dark stripings on crown and upper parts.
   Similar species: (1) Male Lark Bunting is black with white
   confined to wings. (2) Female Redwinged Blackbird is duskier,
   has a longer bill and heavy stripings on breast.
   Voice: Song, in hovering flight and quivering descent, ecstatic
   and bubbling, starting with low reedy notes and rollicking upward. Flight note, a clear *pink*.
   Where found: N. U.S. and s. Canada. Winters in S. America.
   Texas: Irregular *transient* (Apr.–May, Aug.–Oct.) through e.
   and n. Texas and e. Panhandle. Occasional or casual on cent.
   and s. coast. *Habitat:* Fields, marshes.

EASTERN MEADOWLARK   *Sturnella magna*   9–11   p. 241
   Field marks: As we cross the grass country a chunky brown bird
   flushes, showing a conspicuous patch of *white* on each side of its
   short, wide tail. Its flight is distinctive — several short, rapid
   wingbeats alternating with short periods of sailing. Should it

perch on a fence post, our glass reveals a bright yellow breast crossed by a black V, or gorget. When walking, it nervously flicks its tail open and shut.

Similar species: Western Meadowlark is paler, but in field can be recognized only by song. Other ground birds that show white outer tail feathers (pipits, longspurs, Vesper Sparrow, and juncos) all are very much smaller, slimmer.

Voice: Song, two clear slurred whistles, musical and pulled out: *tee-yah tee-yair* (last note "skewy" and descending). Notes, *tchuck* and a guttural chatter.

Where found: Se. Canada south through e. U.S. to Gulf States, Cuba and from sw. U.S. to Brazil. Partial migrant. **Texas:** *Resident* in e. half of state; west locally to e. Panhandle, Mineral Wells, Austin (rare), Rio Grande delta; also Trans-Pecos (Big Bend to El Paso). *Habitat:* Fields, meadows, prairies. **Nest:** A grassy saucer, partially domed, among grass, weeds.

WESTERN MEADOWLARK *Sturnella neglecta* 8–10 p. 241
Similar species: Nearly identical with Eastern Meadowlark, but paler, yellow of throat nearly touching cheek; but in the field can only be recognized by song.
Voice: A variable song of seven to ten notes, flutelike, gurgling, and double-noted; very unlike clear slurred whistles of Eastern Meadowlark.
Where found: Sw. Canada south through w. U.S. to cent. Mexico. **Texas:** *Winters* throughout, but rare on e. edge. *Breeds* locally in nw. portion of state (Trans-Pecos, Staked Plains, and Panhandle; east to Fort Worth; not on Edwards Plateau). Said to breed locally near cent. coast (needs further clarification). *Habitat:* Fields, meadows, prairies. **Nest:** Like Eastern Meadowlark's. Eggs (4–6) spotted.

YELLOW-HEADED BLACKBIRD
Xanthocephalus xanthocephalus 9–11 p. 225
Field marks: *Male:* A Robin-sized marsh blackbird with an *orange-yellow* head and breast; shows a conspicuous white wing-patch in flight. Females are smaller and browner, with most of the yellow confined to the throat and chest; lower breast streaked with white. Very gregarious.
Voice: Note, a low *kruck* or *kack.* Song, low hoarse rasping notes produced with much effort; "like very rusty hinges."
Where found: Canada to nw. Mexico. Winters sw. U.S., Mexico. **Texas:** *Migrant* (Apr.–May, July–Oct.) through w. three-quarters; east to Commerce, Tyler, Bryan, Galveston, Corpus Christi. *Winters* sparingly along Rio Grande from El Paso to Brownsville. *Summers* n. Panhandle and w. Texas (Big Bend to El Paso); may possibly breed. *Habitat:* Fields, ranches, marshes.

REDWINGED BLACKBIRD   *Agelaius phoeniceus*   7½–9½
(Red-wing)   p. 225
  Field marks: *Male:* Black, with red *epaulets* or shoulder-patches.
  Often the scarlet is concealed, only the yellowish margin is then
  visible. *Immature male:* Dusky-brown, but with red shoulder-
  patches. *Female and young:* Brownish; identified by the sharp-
  pointed bill, blackbird appearance, and *well-defined black stripings* below (the only blackbird with such stripings). Very
  gregarious.
  Voice: A loud *check* and a high, slurred *tee-err.* Song, a liquid
  gurgling *kɵnk-la-ree* or *o-ka-leeee.*
  Where found: Canada to West Indies, Costa Rica. Partial
  migrant. **Texas:** *Resident* throughout; breeding locally in
  marshes. *Habitat:* Marshes, swamps, fields, streams, lakes.
  Nest: A woven cup fastened to reeds, grass, bush. Eggs (3–5)
  bluish, scrawled.

ORCHARD ORIOLE   *Icterus spurius*   6–7¼   p. 240
  Field marks: Smaller than a Robin. *Adult male:* The only *dark*
  oriole; *chestnut and black.* Head, neck, back, wings, and tail
  black; rump and underparts deep chestnut. *Immature male:*
  Greenish above, yellow below, with a *black throat.* (Some
  plumages of other orioles have black throats, but such birds
  appear more orange or yellow than green.) *Female and young:*
  Olive above, yellow below, with two white wing-bars.
  Similar species: (1) Males of other orioles are fiery orange or
  yellow and black. Female and young of other orioles are not as
  green-looking as this species. (2) See female tanagers.
  Voice: Song, a fast-moving joyous outburst interspersed with
  piping whistles and guttural notes; unlike abrupt piping of most
  other orioles. A strident slurred *what-cheeer!* or *wheeer!* at or near
  end is distinctive. Suggests Blue Grosbeak's song.
  Where found: Se. Canada south through e. U.S. to Gulf States
  and cent. Mexico. Winters from Mexico to n. S. America.
  Texas: *Summers* (Apr.–Sept.) in most parts of state from Panhandle (Canadian Breaks) to Rio Grande delta; west to Trans-
  Pecos. Casual El Paso. *Habitat:* Towns, farms, orchards, edges.
  Nest: A pouch hung from branch. Eggs (4–6) scrawled.

BLACK-HEADED ORIOLE   *Icterus graduacauda*   8–9¼
(Audubon's Oriole)   p. 240
  Field marks: A *yellow* oriole with black head, wings, and tail.
  The *yellowish back* is conclusive. All other male orioles have
  black backs. Sexes are similar.
  Similar species: The only other black-headed, *yellow* oriole,
  Scott's, is not found in the range of this species (s. Texas).
  Voice: Song, low whistled notes of a human quality, disjointed,
  with half-tones; suggests a boy learning to whistle.

Where found: S. Texas south to nw. Guatemala. **Texas:** *Resident* in lower Rio Grande Valley; occasional north to Beeville and upriver to Eagle Pass. Casual, San Antonio, cent. coast. *Habitat:* Woodlands, thickets. **Nest:** A pouch of green grass hung in tree. Eggs (4) scrawled.

HOODED ORIOLE *Icterus cucullatus* 7–7¾   p. 240
Field marks: *Male:* Orange and black with a black throat and *orange crown,* or "hood." The only *common* oriole with an orange crown. *Female:* Back olive-gray, head and tail dull yellowish, underparts yellowish, wings with two white bars. Similar to female Bullock's Oriole, but underparts entirely yellow. *Immature male:* Resembles female but has *black throat.*
Similar species: (1) Female and immature Bullock's have whitish on belly; bill shorter, less curved. (2) Immature male Orchard Oriole is more greenish than immature male Hooded.
Voice: Song, throaty notes and piping whistles, *chut chut chut whew whew,* opening notes throaty. Note, a sharp *eek.*
Where found: Sw. U.S. south to s. Mexico. **Texas:** *Resident* (rare in winter) in Rio Grande Valley; occurs upriver and breeds locally to Trans-Pecos (Terrell and Brewster Cos.). Also along lower coast to Corpus Christi (rare). *Habitat:* Woodlands, thickets, palms, shade trees. **Nest:** A pouch sewn under old palm fronds, yucca, or Spanish moss. Eggs (4) scrawled.

LICHTENSTEIN'S ORIOLE *Icterus gularis* 8¼–9¼
(Alta Mira Oriole)   p. 240
Field marks: Very similar to Hooded Oriole, but larger, thicker-billed, and more orange (does not shade off to yellow on rump and belly). The point to look for is the upper wing-bar, which is *yellow* or *orange* instead of white. Sexes similar.
Voice: A harsh rasping "fuss" note, *ike-ike-ike* (E. Kincaid). Song, disjointed whistled notes.
Where found: S. tip of Texas south to Nicaragua. **Texas:** Rare resident in Rio Grande delta. Has bred in Cameron and Hidalgo Cos. *Habitat:* Woodlands. **Nest:** A swinging stocking, 2 ft. long, suspended from high branch. Eggs (3–4) scrawled.

SCOTT'S ORIOLE *Icterus parisorum* 7¼–8¼   p. 240
Field marks: *Male:* A lemon-yellow oriole with black head, back, wings, and tail. The *solid black head* and pale *yellow* underparts distinguish it from other orioles in its range. *Female:* Similar to other female orioles but of a more greenish-yellow cast beneath. *Immature male:* Has a black throat similar to that of young male Hooded and Orchard Oriole's; dingier underparts, grayer back, and more extensive black on face help identify it.
Similar species: (1) Female Orchard Oriole is also greenish but

is smaller, with shorter bill. (2) Female Hooded has warmer-yellow underparts; (3) female Bullock's, whitish belly.
Voice: Song, rich whistled notes; suggests Western Meadowlark.
Where found: Sw. U.S. to n. Mexico. Winters in Mexico.
Texas: *Summer resident* (Mar.–Oct.) in Trans-Pecos; east locally to s. Staked Plains. Accidental near Beaumont. *Habitat:* Rocky yucca deserts, oak slopes of mts., piñons. **Nest:** A grassy pouch in yucca; occasionally in small tree. Eggs (2–4) blotched.

BALTIMORE ORIOLE *Icterus galbula* 7–8   p. 240
Field marks: Smaller than Robin. *Male: Fiery orange and black* with *solid black head. Female:* Olive-brown above, yellow below, often with some black around head, thereby resembling males. *Young:* Orange-yellow; olive-brown above, white wing-bars.
Similar species: (1) Male Bullock's Oriole (w. half of state) has orange face, large white wing-patches. Female Bullock's has grayer back, whiter belly. (2) Female Orchard Oriole is greener (not orange-yellow). (3) Female tanagers have more swollen bills and show no wing-bars (except Western Tanager).
Voice: Song, a series of rich, piping whistled notes. Note, a low whistled *hew-li.*
Where found: Canada through e. U.S. to ne. Texas, n. Georgia. Winters Mexico to n. S. America. **Texas:** *Migrant* (Apr.–May, Aug.–Sept.) throughout e. half. *Breeds* locally in e. edge of Texas, rarely in n. Texas (Dallas) and n. Panhandle (Canadian Breaks). *Habitat:* Woodlands, groves, shade trees. **Nest:** A deep pouch hung from tip of high branch. Eggs (4–6) scrawled.

BULLOCK'S ORIOLE *Icterus bullockii* 7½–8½   p. 240
Field marks: The western counterpart of the Baltimore. *Male:* Fiery orange and black, with *orange cheeks,* and large *white wing-patches. Female:* Olive-gray above, yellowish on tail and underparts; belly *whitish;* two white wing-bars. *Immature males:* Similar to female but with black throat.
Similar species: (1) Male Baltimore has a *solid black head* and less white in wing. Where breeding ranges meet (ne. Panhandle) puzzling hybrids sometimes occur. (2) Male Hooded Oriole has orange crown. Female and young Bullock's have grayer backs and *whiter bellies* than Baltimore or Hooded Orioles.
Voice: A series of accented double notes with one or two piping notes thrown in. Call note, a sharp *skip;* also a chatter.
Where found: Sw. Canada south through w. U.S. to n. Mexico. Winters from w. Mexico to Costa Rica. **Texas:** *Summer resident* (Apr.–Oct.) of w. half of Texas (but avoids most of Edwards Plateau) east to Vernon, Coleman, Austin, cent. coast, and Rio Grande delta. Occasional migrant farther east; rarely to e. Texas. Casual in winter. *Habitat:* River groves, towns, ranches. **Nest:** A pouch hung from branch. Eggs (5) scrawled.

RUSTY BLACKBIRD *Euphagus carolinus* 8½–9½   p. 225
Field marks: The Rusty Blackbird is "rusty" only in fall. *Male in spring:* A Robin-sized blackbird with a whitish eye. Very similar to male Brewer's Blackbird, but at close range shows dull greenish instead of purplish head reflections. The iridescence is almost lacking, not noticeable as in Brewer's Blackbird or Common Grackle. *Female in spring:* Slate-colored; resembles female Brewer's but eyes *yellow*, not dark. *Adults and young in winter:* Tinged with rusty; closely *barred* on back and underparts.
Similar species: (1) See Brewer's Blackbird. (2) Grackles are the long-tailed blackbirds, Starlings the short; the other blackbirds (including Rusty and Brewer's) are of more average proportions. Grackles are larger, have ample *rounded* or *keel-shaped* tails, and in strong light brighter iridescence. (3) Cowbirds are smaller, *dark-eyed, short-billed.*
Voice: Note, a loud *chack.* The "song" is a split creak like a rusty hinge (*koo-a-lee*); penetrating.
Where found: Alaska through Canada to ne. edge of U.S. Winters to Gulf Coast. **Texas:** *Winters* (Oct.–Apr.) in e. half; south to cent. coast; west to Fort Worth, Coleman, Austin (rare). Casual in Trans-Pecos. *Habitat:* River groves, wooded swamps.

BREWER'S BLACKBIRD
Euphagus cyanocephalus 8–9½   p. 225
Field marks: *Male:* A blackbird with white eyes; shows *purplish* reflections on head and greenish on body in strong light. Usually looks quite black. *Female:* Grayish with *dark* eyes.
Similar species: Male Rusty Blackbird has *dull greenish* head reflections, and the iridescence is almost lacking. Female Rusty has *light* eyes, not dark. In winter, Brewer's Blackbird may have some rusty barring, but note the light-eyed females. Where both birds occur, they tend to separate out, Brewer's preferring fields and farms; Rusty, river groves and swamps.
Voice: Note, a harsh *check.* Song, a harsh wheezy *que-ee* or *ksh-eee,* like the creaking of a rusty hinge.
Where found: Sw. Canada south to sw. U.S. Winters to Mexico. **Texas:** *Winters* (Oct.–Apr.) throughout. *Breeds* locally in Panhandle (Canyon), n. Texas (Vernon), Trans-Pecos (Marathon), and perhaps elsewhere in n. and w. Texas. Colonial. *Habitat:* Open country, fields, ranches, farms, towns. **Nest:** A twiggy grass-lined cup, on ground, in bush or tree. Eggs (3–7) spotted.

BOAT-TAILED GRACKLE *Cassidix mexicanus*
(Great-tailed Grackle)   ♂ 16–17; ♀ 12–13 p. 225
Field marks: A very large iridescent blackbird, *well over a foot long*, with a long, wide *keel-shaped* tail. Females are brown, not black, and are *much* smaller than males.

Similar species: Common Grackle is much smaller, and is less frequent around salt water. Female Boat-tails are much browner than female Common Grackles and have pale breasts.

Voice: A harsh *check check check;* a loud *may-ree, may-ree!* Also a variety of harsh whistles and clucks.

Where found: New Jersey coast south to Texas and through Mexico to n. Peru. **Texas:** *Resident* widely in state but usually avoids e. Texas forest, Edwards Plateau (except big rivers near edges), Panhandle (straggler), and mts. and waterless deserts west of Pecos. *Habitat:* Riversides, swamps, groves, wet thickets, towns. **Nest:** A bulky grass-lined cup in reeds, bush or tree. Eggs (3–4) bluish, scrawled.

COMMON GRACKLE *Quiscalus quiscula* 11–13
(Bronzed Grackle)   p. 225

Field marks: A large iridescent blackbird, larger than a Robin, with a long wedge-shaped tail. A crease in the center often gives the tail a keel-shaped appearance, particularly in spring. The flight is more even, not as undulating as that of other blackbirds. Males are glossed with iridescent purple on the head, deep bronze on the back. Females smaller, less iridescent.

Similar species: (1) Brewer's Blackbird and (2) Rusty Blackbird are smaller (size of Redwinged Blackbird), with less heavy bills and shorter tails. (2) Boat-tailed Grackle is considerably larger, with longer tail, less iridescence; female is brown.

Voice: Note, *chuck* or *chack;* "song," a split rasping note that is both husky and squeaky.

Where found: S. Canada, e. of Rockies, south to Gulf States. Partially migratory. **Texas:** *Resident* in e. and n. parts of state; west to Fort Worth, Coleman; south to upper Coast and Austin. In *winter* a few wander west to Del Rio and Sabinal and south to San Antonio. *Habitat:* Croplands, towns, streamsides. **Nest:** (often in colony) A deep bulky cup, usually in tree. Eggs (4–5) blotched, scrawled.

BROWN-HEADED COWBIRD *Molothrus ater* 7–8
(Common Cowbird)   p. 225

Field marks: A rather small blackbird with a short, *conical sparrow-like bill. Male:* The only black bird with a *brown* head. *Female:* Uniformly gray; the finchlike bill is a good mark. *Juvenal:* Paler than female, buffy gray with soft breast-streakings; often seen fed by smaller birds. When with other blackbirds, cowbirds are smallest and walk with tails lifted high.

Similar species: (1) In s. Texas see Bronzed Cowbird. Gray female Cowbird can be told from (2) female Rusty and (3) female Brewer's Blackbirds by *shorter bill*, smaller size. Other all-gray birds are (4) Catbird (darker, *chestnut* under tail-coverts) and (5) young Starling (shorter-tailed, longer-billed).

Voice: Note, *chuck.* Also a chatter. Flight note, *weee-titi* (a high whistle, two lower notes). Song, bubbly and creaky, *glug–glug–gleeee* (last note thin, on high pitch).
Where found: S. Canada south to n. Mexico. Partially migratory. **Texas:** *Resident* throughout; some withdrawal in winter. *Habitat:* Croplands, pastures, wood edges, groves, brush. *Parasitic:* Lays speckled eggs in nests of other species.

BRONZED COWBIRD *Tangavius aeneus* 6½–8¾
(Red-eyed Cowbird)   p. 225
    Field marks: *Male:* Larger than Brown-headed Cowbird (does not have brown head). Bill longer. Red eye can be seen only at close range. In breeding season, a conspicuous *ruff* on back of neck. *Female:* Smaller, with smaller neck ruff; dull blackish, much like male, not gray like female of other cowbird.
    Voice: High-pitched mechanical creakings (E. Kincaid).
    Where found: U.S.–Mexican border to w. Panama. **Texas:** *Resident* in s. Texas north to Eagle Pass, San Antonio (rare), cent. coast (Rockport). Casual Houston. *Habitat:* Croplands, farms, brush, semi-open country. *Parasitic:* Lays its blue-green eggs in nests of various species; most often in those of orioles.

Tanagers: Thraupidae

MALE tanagers are brilliantly colored, the United States species exhibiting more or less bright red. Females are dull green above and yellow below, a little like very large warblers or vireos. They are most likely to be confused with female orioles, but are less active, have shorter, thicker bills, darker cheeks, and (except for Western Tanager) lack wing-bars. Food: Insects, small fruits. New World; most species in tropics. No. of species: World, 196; N. America, 4; Texas, 4.

WESTERN TANAGER *Piranga ludoviciana* 6¼–7   p. 240
    Field marks: *Male:* Yellow, with black wings, yellow wing-bars, and *red face.* Very distinctive. Males in autumn lose most of red. *Female:* Dull greenish above, yellowish below; the only female tanager with conspicuous white or yellowish wing-bars.
    Similar species: (1) Female resembles a female oriole but tail and sides of face darker; bill more swollen, not so sharply pointed. (2) Females of other tanagers lack wing-bars.
    Voice: Note, a dry *pi-tic* or *pit-i-tic.* Song, short phrases; similar to Robin's in form, but less sustained, hoarser.
    Where found: S. Alaska, w. Canada, south to w. U.S. Winters Mexico to Costa Rica. **Texas:** *Migrant* (Apr.–June, Aug.–Sept.) through w. half; straggler east to n. and cent. Texas; occasional

along coast. *Winters* rarely in Rio Grande delta. *Breeds* locally in mts. of Trans-Pecos. *Habitat:* Open woodlands. **Nest:** A loose cup in pine or oak. Eggs (3–4) blue, spotted.

SCARLET TANAGER *Piranga olivacea* 6½–7½ p. 240
Field marks: *Male: Bright scarlet* with *black* wings and tail. *Female, immature,* and *winter male:* Dull green above, yellowish below, with brownish or blackish wings. Males in changing plumage may be patched with scarlet, yellowish, green.
Similar species: (1) Male Summer Tanager and (2) Cardinal are more extensively red, wings and tail included. (3) Sluggish actions and large size (larger than House Sparrow) distinguish female and young Scarlet Tanagers from warblers and vireos; (4) greener back and lack of wing-bars, from female orioles.
Voice: Note, a low *chip-burr*. Song, four or five short phrases, Robin-like but hoarse (like Robin with sore throat).
Where found: Se. Canada south to Oklahoma, Tennessee, n. Georgia. Winters in S. America. **Texas:** *Migrant* (Apr.–May, Sept.–Oct.) mainly through e. Texas and along coast; west rarely to Panhandle, Fort Worth, Austin (uncommon), San Antonio. Casual Midland. *Habitat:* Forest and shade trees, especially oaks.

HEPATIC TANAGER *Piranga flava* 7–7¾ p. 240
Field marks: *Male:* Darker than the Summer Tanager (orange-red); *dark ear-patch, blackish bill. Female:* Dusky above, yellowish below; can be told from female orioles by shorter bill, lack of wing-bars; from female Summer Tanager by more orange-yellow throat and *blackish* lower mandible.
Similar species: Male Summer Tanager is rosier, has *yellowish* bill. Females, see above. Hepatic Tanager prefers mountain woodlands; the Summer, low streambottoms.
Voice: Song, similar to that of Summer Tanager, but call note quite different, a single *chuck*.
Where found: Sw. U.S. south to Argentina. Migrant in n. part. **Texas:** *Migrant* in Trans-Pecos; occasional (Apr.–May) along lower coast (Brownsville to Rockport). *Breeds* in Chisos, Davis, Guadalupe Mts. Also occurs in summer on Edwards Plateau (San Marcos, Kerrville). *Habitat:* Open mt. forests, oaks. **Nest:** A shallow saucer in tree. Eggs (3–4) blue, spotted.

SUMMER TANAGER *Piranga rubra* 7–7½
(Cooper's Tanager) p. 240
Field marks: *Male: Rose-red all over* with yellowish bill; no crest. *Female:* Olive above, deep yellow below. Young male acquiring adult plumage may be patched with red and green.
Similar species: (1) Cardinal has a *crest* and a black face. (2) Male Scarlet Tanager has black wings and tail. (3) Female

Scarlet has dusky or blackish wings; the yellow underparts lack orange cast. In w. Texas see (4) Hepatic Tanager (darker color, blackish bill) and (5) female Western Tanager (wing-bars).
Voice: Note, a staccato *pi-tuck* or *pik-i-tuck-i-tuck;* song, Robin-like phrases, less nasal and resonant than those of Scarlet or Western Tanagers.
Where found: S. Iowa, Ohio, Maryland, south to Gulf States and from sw. U.S. to cent. Mexico. Winters Mexico to Brazil. **Texas:** *Migrant* throughout. *Summers* (Mar.–Oct.) throughout except in treeless areas and most of Panhandle. *Winters* rarely in Rio Grande delta. *Habitat:* Woodlands, river groves, towns. **Nest:** A loose shallow cup in tree. Eggs (3–4) bluish, spotted.

Grosbeaks, Finches, Sparrows, and Buntings: Fringillidae

THE BEST character by which this family can be recognized is the bill, short and stout, adapted for seed-cracking. There are three types of bills: that of the grosbeaks, extremely large, thick, and rounded in outline; the more canary-like bill of the finches, sparrows, and buntings; and that of the crossbills, the mandibles of which are crossed at the tips. Many of the family are highly colored; the sparrows are brown and streaked. Food: Seeds, insects, small fruits. World-wide. No. of species: World, 425; N. America, 85; Texas, 60 (plus 3 accidentals).

CARDINAL *Richmondena cardinalis* 8–9   p. 244
Field marks: *Male:* The only all-red bird with a crest; black patch at base of bill. *Female:* Yellowish brown, with a touch of red; recognizable by its crest and heavy red bill.
Similar species: (1) Male Summer Tanager has no crest. (2) Male Scarlet Tanager has black wings. (3) Female Pyrrhuloxia has gray back, yellow bill.
Voice: Song, clear, slurred whistles diminishing in pitch. Several variations: *what-cheer cheer cheer*, etc.; *whoit whoit whoit; birdy, birdy, birdy*, etc. Note, a short thin chip.
Where found: S. Ontario south to Gulf States; also sw. U.S. to British Honduras. Introduced Bermuda, Hawaii. **Texas:** *Resident* throughout most of state (local in w. Texas and Panhandle). *Habitat:* Woodland edges, thickets, towns. **Nest:** A loose cup in bush or thicket. Eggs (3–4) spotted.

PYRRHULOXIA *Pyrrhuloxia sinuata* 7½–8¼   p. 244
Field marks: *Male:* A slender *gray and red finch with a crest*, and a small stubby, almost parrot-like bill. The rose-colored

breast and crest suggest the male Cardinal, but the gray back and *yellow* bill set it apart. *Female:* Gray-backed and yellow-breasted, with a touch of red in wings and crest. Resembles female Cardinal but has *yellow* bill.

Similar species: Female Cardinal is brown, has reddish bill.

Voice: Song, a clear *quink quink quink quink quink,* all on one pitch; also a slurred whistled *what-cheer, what-cheer,* etc., thinner and shorter than Cardinal's song.

Where found: Sw. U.S. south to cent. Mexico. **Texas:** *Resident* of w. Texas; north to Panhandle (rare); east locally to San Angelo, San Antonio, Sinton, Rockport; south to Rio Grande delta. Not on Edwards Plateau. *Habitat:* Mesquite, deserts.

Nest: A loose cup in mesquite or bush. Eggs (3–4) speckled.

ROSE-BREASTED GROSBEAK
Pheucticus ludovicianus   7–8½   p. 245

Field marks: *Male:* Black and white, with a large triangle of *rose-red* on breast, large pale bill. In flight, a ring of white flashes across black upper plumage. *Female:* Streaked, like a large sparrow; recognized by large grosbeak bill, broad white wing-bars, conspicuous white line over eye.

Similar species: (1) Female resembles in pattern the much smaller female Purple Finch. (2) Female Black-headed Grosbeak is similar but breast is browner, with light streaks on sides only.

Voice: Song resembles Robin's but mellower, given with more feeling; note, a sharp metallic *kick,* or *eek.*

Where found: Canada, east of Rockies south to e. Kansas, Missouri, n. Georgia (mts.). **Texas:** *Migrant* (Apr.–May, Sept.–Oct.) through e. and coastal Texas, less frequent in cent. parts; west occasionally to Panhandle and s. Staked Plains. Casual at El Paso. *Habitat:* Woodlands, thickets.

BLACK-HEADED GROSBEAK
Pheucticus melanocephalus   6½–7¾   p. 245

Field marks: *Male: Rusty* breast, *black* head, and boldly marked black and white wings make it a striking bird. In flight shows black and white wing and tail pattern, cinnamon rump. *Female:* Largely brown; easily recognized by *light brown* breast (light streaks on sides), *striped head,* and heavy pale bill.

Similar species: (1) Two birds whose coloration remotely resembles the male are Robin, Rufous-sided Towhee. (2) Female Rose-breasted Grosbeak has a whiter, more streaked breast.

Voice: Song, very similar to Rose-breasted Grosbeak's; rising and falling passages; resembles Robin's song but more fluent and mellow. Note, a sharp *ik* or *eek.*

Where found: Sw. Canada through w. U.S. to s. Mexico.

Winters in Mexico. **Texas:** *Migrant* (Apr.–May, Sept.–Oct.) through w. Texas and Panhandle; east rarely to Edwards Plateau. Occasional strays to cent. Texas and coast (recorded in winter). *Breeds* in mts. of Trans-Pecos. *Habitat:* Oaks in mts.; streamside groves. **Nest:** A loose saucer in tree or bush. Eggs (3–4) spotted.

BLUE GROSBEAK *Guiraca caerulea* 6½–7½ p. 245
Field marks: *Male:* Deep dull blue, with a thick bill and two *rusty* wing-bars. *Female:* About size of Cowbird; warm brown, lighter below, with two *buffy* wing-bars; rump tinged with blue. Immature males are a mixture of brown and blue.
Similar species: (1) The male appears black at a distance, then resembling a Cowbird. (2) Indigo Bunting is smaller (Chipping-Sparrow-sized) with a much smaller bill; lacks the tan wing-bars. See immature male Indigo Bunting.
Voice: Song, a rapid warble; short phrases rising and falling; suggests Orchard Oriole but lower and more guttural, without the clear whistled notes. Note, a sharp *chink.*
Where found: California across U.S. to s. New Jersey and south to Costa Rica and Gulf States. Winters Mexico to Panama. **Texas:** Migrant and *summer resident* (Apr.–Oct.) in most sections. *Habitat:* Brushy places, roadsides, thickets. **Nest:** A loose cup in bush or low tree. Eggs (3–5) pale blue.

INDIGO BUNTING *Passerina cyanea* 5¼–5¾ p. 245
Field marks: *Male:* A small finch; deep, rich blue *all over.* In autumn the male becomes more like the brown female, but there is usually some blue in the wings and tail. *Female:* Plain brown; breast paler, with indistinct streakings; a small brown finch devoid of obvious stripings, wing-bars, or other marks. Hybridizes with Lazuli Bunting where ranges overlap.
Similar species: Blue Grosbeak is much larger, with heavy bill, tan wing-bars.
Voice: Song, lively, high, and strident, with well-measured phrases at different pitches, notes usually paired: *sweet-sweet, chew-chew,* etc. Call note, a sharp thin *spit.*
Where found: Se. Canada to Gulf States. Winters Mexico to Panama. **Texas:** *Migrant* (Mar.–May, Aug.–Nov.) through most of state; abundant coastwise; casual in Trans-Pecos. *Breeds* in e., n., and cent. Texas; west to ne. Panhandle, Fort Worth, Kerrville, south to San Antonio, Bryan. *Habitat:* Brushy places, edges. **Nest:** A cup in crotch of bush. Eggs (3–4) pale blue.

ORIOLES AND TANAGERS

Note: Female orioles differ from female tanagers by
their sharper bills, and from all but the female Western
Tanager by their white wing-bars.

SCOTT'S ORIOLE   p. 231
    Male: Yellow and black; black back.
    Female: Greenish yellow; wing-bars. See text.
    Immature male: Extensive black on throat. See text.

ORCHARD ORIOLE   p. 230
    Adult male: Deep chestnut breast and rump.
    Female: Yellow-green; wing-bars.
    Immature male: Yellow-green; black throat-patch.

BLACK-HEADED ORIOLE   p. 230
    Dull yellow and black; yellow back. Female duller.

BULLOCK'S ORIOLE   p. 232
    Male: Black crown, orange cheeks; large wing-patch.
    Female: Grayish back; whitish belly.

BALTIMORE ORIOLE   p. 232
    Male: Orange below, black head.
    Female: Yellow-orange breast.

HOODED ORIOLE   p. 231
    Male: Orange crown, black throat.
    Female: Similar to Bullock's but belly yellow.
    Immature male: Black throat. See text.

LICHTENSTEIN'S ORIOLE   p. 231
    Much larger than Hooded Oriole; thick bill. Upper wing-
    bar yellow or orange (not always visible). Sexes similar.
    Rio Grande delta only.

WESTERN TANAGER   p. 235
    Male: Red face, black back.
    Female: Wing-bars, tanager bill.

SUMMER TANAGER   p. 236
    Male: Rose-red all over; light bill.
    Female: Deeper yellow than Scarlet Tanager; wings not as
    dusky.

HEPATIC TANAGER   p. 236
    Male: Deep dull red; blackish bill; w. Texas.
    Female: Resembles female Summer but has blackish bill;
    gray cheek.

SCARLET TANAGER   p. 236
    Male: Scarlet, with black wings.
    Female: Yellow-green; dusky wings.

♂ Adult

Immature ♂

♂ Immature

♂ Adult

SCOTT'S
ORIOLE

♀

ORCHARD ORIOLE

BLACK-HEADED
ORIOLE

♀

BULLOCK'S
ORIOLE

♀

♂

♂

♂ Adult

Immature

BALTIMORE
ORIOLE

♀

HOODED
ORIOLE

♀

LICHTENSTEIN'S
ORIOLE

♂₁

♂

WESTERN
TANAGER

♀

SUMMER
TANAGER

♀

♂

♀

SCARLET
TANAGER

♀

♂

HEPATIC TANAGER

BOBOLINK

♀

♂

Breeding

DICKCISSEL

♂

♀

WESTERN
MEADOWLARK

LARK BUNTING

Breeding

♂

♀

HORNED LARK

Immature

WATER PIPIT

SPRAGUE'S
PIPIT

LAPLAND LONGSPUR

♂
Breeding

♂
Winter

McCOWN'S
LONGSPUR

♂
Breeding

♀
Breeding

SMITH'S LONGSPUR

♂
Breeding

♂
Winter

CHESTNUT-COLLARED LONGSPUR

♂
Breeding

♀

Plate 56 241

BIRDS OF FIELDS, PRAIRIES, PLAINS

BOBOLINK p. 228
Male, breeding: Black below; white patches above.
Female: Striped crown; buffy breast.
Autumn male is similar to female.

DICKCISSEL p. 243
Male: "Like a little Meadowlark."
Female: Sparrow-like. See text.

WESTERN MEADOWLARK p. 229
Black V; short tail, white outer feathers.

EASTERN MEADOWLARK (not illustrated) p. 228
Different song. See text.

LARK BUNTING p. 250
Male, breeding: Black body, white wing-patch.
Female: Streaked; some white in wing.

HORNED LARK p. 163
Adult: "Horns," face-patch, breast-splotch.
Immature: Suggestion of adult pattern.

WATER PIPIT p. 190
SPRAGUE'S PIPIT p. 190
Both pipits: Thin bill, white outer tail feathers.
Water Pipit: Dark back, dark legs (usually).
Sprague's Pipit: Striped back, yellowish legs.

LAPLAND LONGSPUR p. 264
Male, breeding: Black throat, rusty collar.
Winter: Smudge on breast, rusty nape (male).
Tail pattern below (No. 1).

SMITH'S LONGSPUR p. 265
Male, breeding: Buffy; black and white ear-patch.
Winter: Buffy; tail pattern below (No. 2). Adult male may
show white patch near shoulder.

McCOWN'S LONGSPUR p. 264
Male, breeding: Black breast-splotch, black cap.
Female and winter: Rusty shoulder; tail pattern below
(No. 4).

CHESTNUT-COLLARED LONGSPUR p. 265
Male, breeding: Black breast and belly; rusty collar.
Female and winter: Tail pattern below (No. 3).

TAILS OF LONGSPURS

LAZULI BUNTING *Passerina amoena* 5–5½ p. 245
Field marks: *Male:* A small bright blue finch. Head and upper parts *turquoise*-blue; band across breast and sides *cinnamon;* belly and wing-bars white. *Female:* Nondescript; *brownish,* whitening on throat and belly; whitish wing-bars. At close range a trace of gray-blue in wings and tail. Lack of streakings on back or breast distinguishes it from sparrows.
Similar species: (1) Bluebird is larger, has more slender bill, *lacks wing-bars.* (2) Female Blue Grosbeak is larger than female Lazuli, is darker, has larger bill, *tan wing-bars.* (3) Female Indigo Bunting lacks strong wing-bars.
Voice: Song, very similar to Indigo Bunting's; high and strident phrases at varying pitches. Introductory notes usually paired: *sweet-sweet, chew-chew,* etc. Call note, a sharp *tsip.*
Where found: S. Canada south to sw. U.S. Winters in Mexico. **Texas:** *Migrant* (Apr.–May, Aug.–Sept.) in w. parts; east rarely to Fort Worth, Austin, San Antonio, cent. coast, Rio Grande delta. *Summers* rarely in Panhandle. *Habitat:* Open brushy country. **Nest:** A loose cup in bush. Eggs (3–4) pale blue.

VARIED BUNTING *Passerina versicolor* 4½–5½ p. 245
Field marks: *Male:* A small dark finch with a plum-purple body (looks black at a distance); crown blue with a *bright red patch on the nape;* "colored like an Easter egg." *Female:* A small plain *gray-brown* finch with lighter underparts. *No wing-bars, stripes, or distinctive marks of any kind.*
Similar species: (1) Male Painted Bunting has a bright red breast. (2) Female Seedeater is smaller and browner than female Varied Bunting and has wing-bars. (3) Female Indigo is browner, with a trace of wing-bars and faint blurry breast-streakings.
Voice: Song, a thin bright finch song, more distinctly phrased and less warbled than Painted Bunting's; notes not so distinctly paired as in song of Lazuli Bunting.
Where found: S. Arizona and Texas to Guatemala. Winters south of U.S. **Texas:** *Summers* (Apr.–Sept.) from w. Texas (Presidio Co. and Big Bend) south along Rio Grande locally to Brownsville (rare). Casual cent. coast. *Habitat:* Streamside thickets, brush. **Nest:** A grassy cup in bush. Eggs (3–4) bluish white.

PAINTED BUNTING *Passerina ciris* 5¼ p. 245
Field marks: The most gaudily colored American bird. *Male:* A little Chipping-Sparrow-sized finch, a patchwork of *bright red, green, and indigo.* Red on rump and underparts, green on back, blue-violet on head. *Female:* Very plain greenish above, paling to lemon-green below; no wing-bars or streaks.
Similar species: The only other small greenish finch, the female Lesser Goldfinch, has blackish wings, white bars.

Voice: Song, a bright pleasing warble; resembles song of Warbling Vireo, but more wiry. Note, a sharp *chip.*
Where found: Across s. U.S. to ne. Mexico. Winters Mexico and Florida to Panama. **Texas:** *Summers* (Apr.–Oct.) throughout much of state. *Habitat:* Woodland edges, roadsides, brush, stream edges. **Nest:** A woven cup in crotch of bush. Eggs (3–4) spotted.

DICKCISSEL   *Spiza americana*   6–7   p. 241
Field marks: Near size of House Sparrow. *Male:* Suggestive of a tiny Meadowlark, with yellow breast and black bib. In the fall the black bib is obscured or lacking. *Female:* Very much like female House Sparrow; paler, with much whiter stripe over eye, touch of yellow on breast, bluish bill. Chestnut band of wing is also an aid. Often travels in large flocks.
Similar species: (1) Female often looks much like House Sparrow (see above). (2) It might also be confused with female Bobolink.
Voice: Song, a staccato rendition of its name: *Dick-ciss-ciss-ciss* or *chup-chup-klip-klip-klip.* Also a short electric buzzer or "raspberry" call; often heard at night in migration.
Where found: W. Montana, s. Ontario to Louisiana, Texas. **Texas:** *Migrates and summers* (Apr.–Oct.) through e. two-thirds of state; west to Panhandle, Edwards Plateau. Occasional migrant in Trans-Pecos. *Habitat:* Fields, meadows, prairies. **Nest:** A bulky cup on or near ground. Eggs (3–5) blue.

EVENING GROSBEAK *Hesperiphona vespertina* 7½–8½ p. 244
Field marks: A large, chunky, short-tailed finch, near size of Starling; has an extremely large, conical, whitish bill. In the air it is recognized as a finch by the undulating flight and as this species by its stocky shape, large white wing-patches. *Male:* Dull yellow, with dark head, yellow eye-stripe, and black and white wings; suggests an overgrown American Goldfinch. *Female:* Silvery gray, with just enough of the yellow, black, and white to be recognizable.
Voice: Note, a ringing chirp: *cleer* or *clee-ip.*
Where found: Across Canada to ne. edge of U.S. and south in w. mts. to s. Mexico. Winters irregularly to s. U.S. **Texas:** Irregular *winter visitor* to Panhandle and w. Texas. Casual or occasional east to Edwards Plateau, Coleman, Austin. Accidental near upper coast. *Habitat:* Box elders, maples, fruiting shrubs.

PURPLE FINCH *Carpodacus purpureus* 5½–6¼ p. 244
Field marks: Size of House Sparrow. *Male:* Dull rose-red, brightest on head and rump ("like a sparrow dipped in raspberry juice"). *Female and immature:* Heavily striped, brown, sparrow-like. Broad whitish line behind eye; heavy dark jaw-stripe. The large, stout bill distinguishes them from sparrows.

FINCHES AND HOUSE SPARROW

PURPLE FINCH p. 243
Male: Rosy; size of House Sparrow.
Female: Light eye-stripe, dark jaw-stripe.

CASSIN'S FINCH p. 246
The Trans-Pecos counterpart of Purple Finch. See text.
Male: Paler rose than House Finch, red cap, larger bill.
Female: Distinguished from House Finch by face pattern, larger bill.

HOUSE FINCH p. 246
Male: Striped belly and sides.
Female: Face without strong pattern. Bill stubbier than preceding two.

RED CROSSBILL p. 248
Male: Dull red; blackish wings, crossed bill.
Female: Dull olive; dark wings.

WHITE-COLLARED SEEDEATER p. 247
Male: Dark cap, incomplete collar.
Female: Small, buffy; light wing-bars, stubby bill.

EVENING GROSBEAK p. 243
Male: Dull yellow; black and white wings, large pale bill.
Female: Silver-gray and yellow; large bill.

CARDINAL p. 237
Male: Red; crested, black patch on face.
Female: Brownish; red bill and crest.

PYRRHULOXIA p. 237
Male: Gray; red down front, red crest; yellow bill.
Female: Gray-brown; yellow bill.

PINE SISKIN p. 247
Streaked; touch of yellow in wings and tail (not always evident).

HOUSE SPARROW p. 228
Male: Black throat, gray crown.
Female: Plain dingy breast, dull eye-stripe.

AMERICAN GOLDFINCH p. 247
Male in spring: Yellow body, black wings.
Male in winter: Yellow-olive; black wings, whitish rump.
Female (not shown): Similar to winter male.

LESSER GOLDFINCH p. 248
Male: Black above, yellow below.
Female: Greener than American Goldfinch; dark rump.

LAWRENCE'S GOLDFINCH p. 248
Male: Black face, gray head; yellow wing-bars.
Female: Gray head, yellow wing-bars.

PURPLE FINCH

CASSIN'S FINCH

HOUSE FINCH

RED CROSSBILL

WHITE-COLLARED SEEDEATER

EVENING GROSBEAK

CARDINAL

PYRRHULOXIA

PINE SISKIN

HOUSE SPARROW

Breeding

Winter

AMERICAN GOLDFINCH

LESSER GOLDFINCH

LAWRENCE'S GOLDFINCH

INDIGO BUNTING

LAZULI BUNTING

BLUE GROSBEAK

♂

♀

PAINTED
BUNTING

♀

♂

♀

♂

VARIED BUNTING

ROSE-BREASTED
GROSBEAK

♀

♂

♀

♂

BLACK-HEADED
GROSBEAK

RUFOUS-
SIDED
TOWHEE

♀

Eastern
type

♂

Western type

♂

BROWN
TOWHEE

GREEN-TAILED
TOWHEE

OLIVE SPARROW

SLATE-COLORED
JUNCO

♂

♀

dorsalis
form

caniceps form
GRAY-HEADED
JUNCO

"Pink-sided"
form
(mearn

OREGON
JUNCO

Plate 58   245

FINCHES

BLUE GROSBEAK p. 239
Male: Blue; tan wing-bars, large bill.
Female: Brown; tan wing-bars, large bill.

INDIGO BUNTING p. 239
Male: Blue all over; no wing-bars.
Female: Brown; faint streakings. See text.

LAZULI BUNTING p. 242
Male: Blue back, reddish breast; white wing-bars.
Female: Brownish; wing-bars but no streaks. See text.

PAINTED BUNTING p. 242
Male: Red underparts, violet head, green back.
Female: A small all-green finch; no wing-bars.

VARIED BUNTING p. 242
Male: Dark; red patch on nape.
Female: See text.

ROSE-BREASTED GROSBEAK p. 238
Male: Rose breast-patch.
Female: Striped head, large bill; streaked breast.

BLACK-HEADED GROSBEAK p. 238
Male: Black head, rusty breast; white wing-spots.
Female: Similar to Rose-breast; breast with few streaks.

RUFOUS-SIDED TOWHEE p. 249
Eastern type, male: Rusty sides, white tail-spots; black back.
Eastern type, female: Similar but back brown.
Western type: White spots on back.

BROWN TOWHEE p. 250
Brown; rusty cap, buff throat with short streaks.

GREEN-TAILED TOWHEE p. 249
Greenish; rusty cap, white throat.

OLIVE SPARROW p. 249
Olive; striped crown.

SLATE-COLORED JUNCO p. 258
Gray sides, gray back; white outer tail feathers. Male has blacker head.

GRAY-HEADED JUNCO p. 259
Gray sides, rusty back.
Caniceps form: Entire bill pale.
Dorsalis form: Upper mandible dark.

OREGON JUNCO p. 258
Rusty or buffy sides; brown back; black head (male).
"Pink-sided" form: Clear gray hood (male); dull brown back.

Similar species: (1) Male House Finch has sharp streaks on flanks. Female House Finch is paler, lacks strong white marks outlining cheek-patch. (2) In w. Texas see Cassin's Finch. Voice: Song, a fast, lively warble; resembles song of House Finch, but lower in pitch, shorter, less disjointed. Note, a dull metallic *tick*, unlike any note of House Finch.

Where found: Canada and n. U.S., and south through Pacific states to Baja California. Winters to s. U.S. Texas: *Winter visitor* (Nov.–Apr.) to e., n., and cent. Texas and Panhandle; south rarely to Corpus Christi, San Antonio, and Del Rio. *Habitat:* Woodlands, groves.

CASSIN'S FINCH *Carpodacus cassinii* 6–6½
(Cassin's Purple Finch)   p. 244

Field marks: The west Texas counterpart of the Purple Finch. *Male:* Similar to House Finch but larger, red of breast, paler; *squarish red crown-patch* contrasts abruptly with brown neck and back. *Lacks* dark stripes on flank and belly. *Female:* Sparrow-like; back gray-brown streaked with black; underparts whitish, narrowly streaked. Sharper stripings, strong face pattern, whitish stripe over eye distinguish it from female House Finch.

Similar species: (1) Purple Finch does not normally occur in Trans-Pecos. (2) See House Finch.

Voice: Song, a lively warble, similar to Purple Finch's, but not so closely knit; between songs of House Finch and Purple Finch.

Where found: British Columbia south to high mts. of sw. U.S. Winters to mts. of Mexico. Texas: *Winter visitor* (Oct.–Mar.) to Trans-Pecos; east casually to s. Staked Plains (Midland), Big Bend. *Habitat:* Conifers, mt. forests.

HOUSE FINCH *Carpodacus mexicanus* 5½   p. 244

Field marks: *Male:* Near size of House Sparrow, brownish with bright *red breast*, forehead, stripe over eye, and rump. Resembles males of Purple and Cassin's Finches (which do not nest about buildings); is brighter red. Some individuals are almost orange. *Narrow dark stripes* on flanks and belly are best distinction. *Female:* Sparrow-like; gray-brown above; underparts whitish streaked with dusky; face without strong stripings.

Similar species: See (1) Purple Finch (east) and (2) Cassin's Finch (west).

Voice: A bright lengthy song, loose and disjointed; frequently ends in a harsh nasal *wheer* or *che-urr*. Notes, finchlike; some suggest chirping of House Sparrow but are more musical.

Where found: S. British Columbia, w. U.S. to s. Mexico. Texas: *Resident* through w. half; east to Coleman, Austin, San Antonio, Beeville. Straggler to Fort Worth, cent. coast. *Habitat:* Towns, ranches, canyons, deserts. Nest: Compact; in bush, tree, cactus, building, etc. Eggs (4–5) blue, spotted.

WHITE-COLLARED SEEDEATER
Sporophila torqueola 3¾–4¼
(Sharpe's Seedeater, "Morrelet Seedeater") p. 244
Field marks: *Male:* A tiny finch with whitish or buffy underparts and blackish cap and upper parts. Much white in wing; bill very stubby and swollen; a narrow, dark breastband (usually incomplete in Texas birds) and a broad *light collar* around neck. *Female:* The small size, buffy underparts, and very stubby bill are good marks; light wing-bars.
Similar species: (1) American Goldfinch in winter plumage resembles female somewhat but has blacker wings, white rump. (2) See also female Varied Bunting.
Voice: A sweet loud song; begins on several high repeated notes and drops to several notes on a lower pitch: *sweet sweet sweet sweet, cheer cheer cheer cheer* (often only two *cheer*'s).
Where found: S. Texas to Costa Rica. **Texas:** *Resident* in Rio Grande delta. *Habitat:* Weedy places, tall grass, brush. **Nest:** A compact cup in bush. Eggs (4–5) blue-green, spotted.

PINE SISKIN *Spinus pinus* 4½–5 p. 244
Field marks: A small dark, *heavily streaked* finch with a deeply notched tail. A *touch of yellow* in wings and tail (does not often show well). In size and actions resembles American Goldfinch. Learn the calls; most Siskins are noted as they fly overhead.
Similar species: (1) Winter goldfinches are unstreaked; (2) female Purple Finch is larger (size of House Sparrow), with a larger bill. Neither shows any yellow in wings or tail, nor has the Siskin's very pointed face and bill.
Voice: Song, similar to American Goldfinch's; more coarse and wheezy; call, a loud *clee-ip* or *chlee-ip*, also a light *tit-i-tit* and a long buzzy *shreeeee* — latter unique.
Where found: Alaska, Canada, ne. U.S.; south in w. mts. to Guatemala. Winters Canada to Gulf States. **Texas:** *Winters* (Nov.–May) irregularly throughout; rare in s. part. *Summers* in Guadalupe Mts. *Habitat:* Woodlands, groves, conifers.

AMERICAN GOLDFINCH *Spinus tristis* 5–5½
(Common Goldfinch) p. 244
Field marks: *Male in summer: The only small yellow bird with black wings;* forehead and tail also black. *Female in summer:* Dull olive-yellow with blackish wings and conspicuous wing-bars; distinguished from other small olive-yellow birds (warblers, etc.) by its conical finch bill. *Winter birds:* Much like summer females, but grayer. Flight deeply undulating.
Similar species: (1) Yellow Warbler is yellowish all over, including wings and tail. (2) Female Lesser Goldfinch differs from female American by greener back; lacks whitish rump.

Voice: Song, sustained, clear, light, Canary-like. In flight, each dip is often punctuated by *ti-dee-di-di*.
Where found: S. Canada to n. Baja California, s. U.S. Winters s. Canada to n. Mexico. Texas: *Winters* (Oct.–June) throughout. *Breeds* locally in ne. corner of state. *Habitat:* Weedy places, edges, groves. Nest: A compact cup in upright fork of bush or tree. Eggs (4–5) pale blue.

LESSER GOLDFINCH *Spinus psaltria* 4
(Arkansas Goldfinch, "Dark-backed Goldfinch")   p. 244
Field marks: *Male:* A very small finch with *black* upper parts and *bright yellow* underparts; bold white marks on wings. *Female:* Very similar to female or winter male of American Goldfinch, but smaller; lacks white near rump; back more greenish. *Immature male:* Dark greenish back, black cap, *blackish* rump.
Similar species: All plumages of American Goldfinch show white near rump; summer males have yellow backs.
Voice: Sweet plaintive notes: *tee-yee* (rising inflection) and *tee-yer* (dropping). Song, Canary-like, more phrased, less sustained than American Goldfinch's.
Where found: From w. U.S. south to Peru. Texas: *Resident* in w. half of state; east to Coleman, Austin, Beeville. *Winters* east to Fort Worth, Beeville, Brownsville; casual on cent. coast. *Habitat:* Semi-open or brushy country. Nest: A loose cup in bush or tree. Eggs (4–5) pale blue.

LAWRENCE'S GOLDFINCH *Spinus lawrencei* 4–4½ p. 244
Field marks: *Male:* A *gray-headed* goldfinch with a touch of yellow on throat and rump; *broad yellow wing-bars*. Black face (forehead and chin). No other male goldfinch has a *black chin*. No seasonal change. *Female:* Similar to male without black face. Grayer color and *broad yellow wing-bars* distinguish it from other female goldfinches.
Voice: Song similar to that of American Goldfinch. Call note distinctive: *tink-oo*, syllables emphasized equally.
Where found: California and n. Baja California. Texas: Irregular *winter visitor* to El Paso.

RED CROSSBILL *Loxia curvirostra* 5¼–6½   p. 244
Field marks: Size of House Sparrow; heavy head, short tail. They act like small parrots as they dangle around evergreen cones, the cracking of which often betrays their presence. Their *crossed* mandibles are distinctive. *Male: Brick-red*, brighter on rump; wings and tail dusky. Young males are more orange. *Female:* Dull olive-gray; yellowish on rump and underparts.
Similar species: In w. Texas mts., see Hepatic Tanager (p. 240).
Voice: Note, a hard *jip-jip* or *pip-pip-pip*. Song, finchlike warbled passages: *chip-chip-chip-jee-jee*.

Where found: Eurasia, nw. Africa, se. Alaska, Canada; in mts. south to North Carolina and n. Nicaragua. Irregular wanderer. **Texas:** Rare, erratic wanderer to Panhandle and n. and w. Texas, reported south to Galveston, Waco. May breed in Trans-Pecos (Chisos and Guadalupe Mts.). *Habitat:* Chiefly conifers.

OLIVE SPARROW *Arremonops rufivirgata* 5½–6
(Texas Sparrow) p. 245
Field marks: A plain *olive-backed* finch with *two broad dull brown stripes* on crown. No wing-bars or stripes on back. Underparts lighter; dingy buffish wash across breast and sides.
Similar species: Green-tailed Towhee is larger, with a gray breast, clear-cut white throat, and solid rufous crown.
Voice: Song, a series of dry notes on one pitch, starting deliberately and trailing into a Chippy-like rattle.
Where found: S. Texas to s. Mexico; w. Costa Rica. **Texas:** *Resident* in s. tip; a few noted north to Del Rio, Sabinal, Beeville, Rockport. *Habitat:* Brush, undergrowth, weedy thickets.
Nest: Round, domed; in bush or cactus. Eggs (3–4) white.

GREEN-TAILED TOWHEE *Chlorura chlorura* 6¼–7 p. 245
Field marks: Slightly larger than House Sparrow, a ground-dwelling finch with a plain *olive-green* back, *rufous crown*, and conspicuous *white* throat; breast gray. The rufous cap and white throat are the best marks.
Similar species: Brown Towhee has a buffy throat.
Voice: Kitten-like mewing notes, and a *chink* like Brown Towhee. Song, variable; opening with one or two sweet notes and ending in long burry notes: *weet-chur — cheeeeeee — churrr.*
Where found: High mts. of w. U.S. Winters sw. U.S. to cent. Mexico. **Texas:** *Winter visitor* through w. half of state; east irregularly to Fort Worth, Austin, Brownsville. Occasional on coast. Casual e. Texas (Tyler). *Habitat:* Brush, thickets.

RUFOUS-SIDED TOWHEE *Pipilo erythrophthalmus* 7–8¾
(including Eastern and Spotted Towhees) p. 245
Field marks: Smaller and more slender than Robin; *reddish confined to sides.* Often detected by noisy rummaging among dead leaves. *Male:* Entire head and upper parts black; *sides robinred;* belly white. Large white spots show toward outer tips of ample tail. In the e. half of Texas most birds are of the typical eastern race, *P. e. erythrophthalmus,* and have unspotted backs. In the w. half, two or three western races are represented in which the back is marked with rows of white spots. *Female:* Similar, but dusky brown where male is black. Young birds in summer are streaked below like large slender sparrows but have the telltale Towhee wing and tail pattern.

Voice: Song of eastern bird, *drink your teeeeee*, last syllable higher, wavering. Call, a loud *chewink!* or *shrink* or *zreee*. Western birds sing a buzzy trill, *chweeeeee*, or *chup chup chup zeeeeeeee*. Call sounds more like *shrank* or *wank*.
Where found: S. Canada south to Guatemala, e. Gulf Coast. Migrant in North. **Texas:** *Winters* (Oct.–Apr.) throughout. *Breeds* in mts. of Trans-Pecos. *Habitat:* Brush, thickets, edges. **Nest:** A loose cup on ground or in bush. Eggs (4–6) spotted.

BROWN TOWHEE *Pipilo fuscus* 8¼–9½ p. 245
Field marks: A rather large dull gray-brown bird with a moderately long dark tail; suggests a very plain overgrown sparrow. The only distinctive marks on this somber finch are the *pale rusty* under tail-coverts, *rusty crown*, *buffy throat*, edged with short streaks, and a central breast-spot.
Similar species: (1) See Green-tailed Towhee. (2) The desert thrashers are larger, with thin curved bills.
Voice: Note, a sharp metallic *chink*. Song, a rapid *chink-chink-ink-ink-ink-ink-ink-ink*. Often ends in a trill. Some songs sound more like *chilp-chilp-chilp-chilp-chilp-chilp*.
Where found: Sw. U.S. to s. Mexico. **Texas:** *Resident* in w. Texas and Edwards Plateau; east to San Angelo and w. Kerr Co. Rare migrant in Panhandle. *Habitat:* Brushy, stony areas; dry canyons. **Nest:** A grassy cup in bush. Eggs (3–4) spotted.

LARK BUNTING *Calamospiza melanocorys* 5½–7½ p. 241
Field marks: *Male in spring:* Like a small blackbird (House Sparrow size) *with large white wing-patches. Females, young, and winter males* are brown with striped breast; usually some members of the flock show white or buffy wing-patches. Gregarious.
Similar species: (1) Male Bobolink has white *on back* as well as on wings. (2) Striped brown Lark Buntings slightly resemble female Purple Finches except for whitish wing-patches.
Voice: Song, "Cardinal-like slurs, chatlike (unmusical) *chugs*, clear piping notes and trills; each note repeated 3–11 times" (Norma Stillwell). Note, a soft *hoo-ee*.
Where found: Prairies of s. Canada, south to n. Texas. Winters sw. U.S. to cent. Mexico. **Texas:** *Migrant* through w. half, *wintering* (Oct.–Apr.) except in Panhandle; east irregularly to Denton, Dallas, Austin, cent. coast, Rio Grande delta. *Breeds* irregularly in Panhandle. *Habitat:* Plains, prairies, fields. **Nest:** A loose cup on ground. Eggs (4–5) pale blue.

SAVANNAH SPARROW
Passerculus sandwichensis 4¾–6 p. 252
Field marks: A streaked open-country sparrow; suggests a Song Sparrow with a *yellowish stripe* over the eye, whitish stripe

through crown, short, slightly forked tail, pinker legs.
Similar species: (1) Song Sparrow's tail is rounded (not forked). (2) The obvious notch is also an aid when flushing sparrows from meadows and marshes where both Savannahs and "sharptailed" types are common. (3) See Baird's Sparrow.
Voice: Song, a dreamy lisping *tsit-tsit-tsit, tseeee-tsaaay* (last note lower). Note, a slight *tsip.*
Where found: N. Alaska, across Canada to n. U.S. and south locally in West to Guatemala. Winters n. U.S. to El Salvador, West Indies. **Texas:** *Winters* (Sept.–May) throughout. *Habitat:* Prairies, fields, marshes, open country.

GRASSHOPPER SPARROW
Ammodramus savannarum 5–5¼   p. 252
Field marks: A *short-tailed,* flat-headed little sparrow with a feeble flight. Crown with a pale stripe through center; back striped with chestnut and black. Differs from other sparrows of open country in having an *unstreaked* buffy breast. The conspicuously striped back and short, sharp tail are also good marks. Young birds in late summer have streaked breasts. They resemble adult Henslow's Sparrow, but are not so reddish on wings.
Similar species: Savannah has streaked breast, notched tail.
Voice: Two songs: (1) a long, sizzling insect-like tumble of notes; (2) two low introductory notes and a thin dry buzz, *pi-tup zeeeeeeeeeee* (introductory notes usually inaudible).
Where found: S. Canada south locally to s. U.S., West Indies; also s. Mexico to Ecuador. Winters from s. U.S. south. **Texas:** *Migrant* throughout (rare in w. parts). *Winters* (Oct.–May) in s. half, mostly on coast. *Breeds* locally in Panhandle and n. Texas south to upper coast. *Habitat:* Fields, prairies. **Nest:** A grassy cup in grass. Eggs (4–5) speckled.

BAIRD'S SPARROW *Ammodramus bairdii* 5–5½   p. 252
Field marks: A prairie sparrow with a light breast crossed by a *narrow band of fine black streaks.* Head yellow-brown streaked with black. The best mark is the very broad *center stripe on the crown,* which is conspicuously *ocher.*
Similar species: Savannah Sparrow has more extensive streakings on underparts, tail is strongly notched and the light stripe through crown is much narrower (whitish, not yellow-brown).
Voice: Song begins with 3 or 4 musical *zip*'s and ends with a trill on a lower pitch; more musical than Savannah's.
Where found: Sw. Canada (e. of Rockies) to n. prairie states. Winters sw. U.S., n. Mexico. **Texas:** Local *winter resident* (Oct.–Apr.) in w. half; east occasionally or rarely to Commerce, Dallas, Waco; casual along coast. *Habitat:* Prairies.

SPARROWS

(A majority of these have *streaked* breasts.)

FOX SPARROW   p. 263
Rufous tail, heavily striped breast.
Western form: Gray; dull rusty tail.

SONG SPARROW   p. 264
Streaked breast, with large central spot.

VESPER SPARROW   p. 255
White outer tail feathers.

LINCOLN'S SPARROW   p. 263
Like Song, but buffy breast, fine black streaks.

SAVANNAH SPARROW   p. 250
Like Song, but striped crown, short notched tail.

SEASIDE SPARROW   p. 255
Dingy; yellow eye-spot, white jaw-line, and black "whisker."

LE CONTE'S SPARROW   p. 254
Buffy breast, streaked sides, white crown-stripe, pinkish-
brown nape.

BAIRD'S SPARROW   p. 251
Ocher crown-stripe, "necklace" of short streaks.

SHARP-TAILED SPARROW   p. 254
Ocher face pattern, gray ear-patch.

HENSLOW'S SPARROW   p. 254
Olive head, rufous wings.

GRASSHOPPER SPARROW   p. 251
Clear buffy breast, striped crown.

BACHMAN'S SPARROW   p. 256
Dull unstriped breast, brown back-stripes. Pinewoods, etc.

CASSIN'S SPARROW   p. 257
Streaked crown with no center stripe; dull unmarked
breast; "skylarking" song. See text.

BOTTERI'S SPARROW   p. 256
Very similar to Cassin's but browner, with brown tail.
See text. Rio Grande delta.

Typical form
FOX

SONG

VESPER

Western form
FOX

LINCOLN'S

SAVANNAH

SEASIDE

LE CONTE'S

BAIRD'S

SHARP-TAILED

HENSLOW'S

GRASSHOPPER

BACHMAN'S

CASSIN'S

BOTTERI'S

BLACK
THROATED

Immature

Adult
HARRIS'

BLACK-CHINNED

Immature

WHITE-
CROWNED

Adult

Immature

Adult
WHITE-
THROATED

Immature

Adult
GOLDEN-CROWNED

SAGE

LARK

FIELD

TREE

RUFOUS-
CROWNED

Immature

Adult
Spring
SWAMP

Immature

Adult
Spring
CHIPPING

Immature

Adult
Spring
CLAY-COLORED

BREWER'S

Plate 60   253

SPARROWS

(Most of these have unstreaked breasts.)

LE CONTE'S SPARROW

Passerherbulus caudacutus 5   p. 252

Field marks: A sharp-tailed sparrow of prairie marshes, characterized by the *bright buffy-ocher* eye-line, throat, and breast, and the wide *pinkish-brown* collar on nape. White stripe through crown. Back very strongly striped; sides streaked.

Similar species: (1) Ocher of underparts distinguishes it from Henslow's Sparrow; (2) streaked sides, from Grasshopper Sparrow; (3) *white stripe* through crown, from Sharp-tail.

Voice: Song, two extremely thin grasshopper-like hisses, first note barely audible.

Where found: S. cent. Canada south to n. prairie states. Winters in Gulf States. Texas: *Winters* (Oct.–Apr.) in e. half of state. Rare transient in Panhandle. *Habitat:* Grassy, weedy places.

HENSLOW'S SPARROW

Passerherbulus henslowii 4¾–5¼   p. 252

Field marks: Short-tailed and flat-headed, with a big pale bill; finely striped across breast. The striped *olive-colored head* in conjunction with *reddish wings* identify it. Flies low and jerkily with a twisting motion of tail.

Similar species: Other "sharp-tailed" sparrows of grass country are: (1) Grasshopper Sparrow, which is clear-breasted. Summer juvenals are streaked and resemble adult Henslow's except for Henslow's olive and russet tones. Young Henslow's is practically without breast-streakings, thus resembling adult Grasshopper Sparrow. (2) Baird's Sparrow (ocher crown-stripe). (3) Le Conte's Sparrow (buffy face and breast, "pinkish" collar).

Voice: Song, one of the poorest vocal efforts of any bird; throwing back its head, it ejects a hiccoughing *tsi-lick*.

Where found: Cent. and ne. U.S. Winters in se. U.S. Texas: *Winters* (Oct.–Apr.) in e. third; west rarely to Austin; south to cent. coast. Has summered in n. Texas (Wichita Falls); also se. of Houston (Deer Park). *Habitat:* Weedy fields.

SHARP-TAILED SPARROW

Ammospiza caudacuta 5–6   p. 252

Field marks: Sharp-tails are marsh sparrows. They are identified by the *ocher-yellow of the face*, which completely surrounds the gray ear-patch. Most Sharp-tails that come to the Texas coast are of the inland race *A. c. nelsoni* and are very buffy on the breast, almost devoid of streaking. Birds with sharply defined breast-streakings are occasionally recorded.

Similar species: (1) Savannah Sparrow, often seen in the salt marsh, has a notched tail, evident when the bird flies ahead. It also has a striped crown. (2) See also Seaside Sparrow.

Voice: Song, a gasping buzz, *tuptup-sheeeeeeeee;* more hissing than husky, accented song of Seaside Sparrow.

Where found: Prairies of Canada; along Atlantic Coast from

e. Canada to North Carolina. Winters along coast from New York to Texas. **Texas:** *Winters* (Nov.–Apr.) along coast. Occasional inland in e. Texas. *Habitat:* Mainly salt marshes.

SEASIDE SPARROW *Ammospiza maritima* 5½–6½ p. 252
Field marks: Very dingy-looking. A dark, streaky, olive-gray, "sharp-tailed" sparrow of the salt marsh, with a short yellow line *before the eye* and a white streak *along the jaw*.
Similar species: Sharp-tailed Sparrow has conspicuous ocher head-markings, buffy breast.
Voice: Song, *cutcut, zhe'-eeeeeeee*. Note, *chack*.
Where found: Coast; Massachusetts to Texas. **Texas:** *Resident* locally along coast south to Corpus Christi. In *winter* to mouth of Rio Grande. *Habitat:* Salt marshes. **Nest:** A grassy cup in marsh grass. Eggs (4–6) spotted.

VESPER SPARROW *Pooecetes gramineus* 5½–6½ p. 252
Field marks: The *white outer tail feathers* flashing conspicuously as the bird flies make the best mark. Looks like a grayish Song Sparrow, but often seems to have a *whitish eye-ring*. A *chestnut patch* at bend of wing is determinative.
Similar species: Other open-country birds with white tail feathers: (1) meadowlarks, much larger, chunkier; (2) juncos, largely slate-gray; (3) longspurs (which see); (4) pipits, thin-billed, *walk* instead of hop, *bob tails;* (5) Lark Sparrow, large white spots in *corners of tail*, in addition to white edges.
Voice: Song, throatier and more minor in quality than that of Song Sparrow, and beginning with *two* low clear whistled notes followed by two higher ones.
Where found: Canada, south to sw. states, Missouri, North Carolina. Winters to Mexico, Gulf States. **Texas:** *Migrant* throughout; *winters* (Oct.–Apr.) except in Panhandle. Has been seen in summer in n. Panhandle. *Habitat:* Fields, open country.

LARK SPARROW *Chondestes grammacus* 5½–6½ p. 253
Field marks: The best mark is the *black tail with much white in the corners* (as in Rufous-sided Towhee, not as in Vesper Sparrow). *Chestnut* ear-patches, striped crown, and white breast with a *single central spot*. Young birds are finely streaked below and lack the central button; otherwise recognizable.
Similar species: See Vesper Sparrow.
Voice: A broken song; clear notes and trills with pauses in between; best characterized by buzzing and churring passages.
Where found: S. Canada (w. of Appalachians) south to n. Mexico, Louisiana. Winters s. U.S. to El Salvador. **Texas:** *Summers* throughout; *winters* except in Panhandle. *Habitat:* Open country, brush, farms, edges. **Nest:** A well-built cup on ground, in bush or small tree. Eggs (4–5) spotted.

RUFOUS-CROWNED SPARROW

Aimophila ruficeps 5–5¾   p. 253

Field marks: A dark sparrow with an unstreaked breast and *rufous cap.* A black *"whisker"* bordering the throat is the best mark.

Similar species: Chipping Sparrow has conspicuous eye-stripes, notched tail, black back-stripes (Rufous-crown has *rounded* tail, brown back-stripes, black whisker).

Voice: A stuttering and gurgling song, first part ascending slightly, last notes descending; suggests House Wren. Note, a nasal *chur, chur, chur, chur* or *dear, dear, dear.*

Where found: Sw. U.S. to s. Mexico. **Texas:** *Resident* in Trans-Pecos and Edwards Plateau; east to Fort Worth, Austin. *Habitat:* Rocky, brushy slopes. **Nest:** A grass-lined cup on ground. Eggs (3–4) white.

BACHMAN'S SPARROW   *Aimophila aestivalis*   5¾

(Pine Woods Sparrow)   p. 252

Field marks: In dry open woods, this shy sparrow flushes reluctantly, and drops back into the brush, where it plays hide-and-seek. A glimpse shows it to be striped with reddish brown above and washed with *dingy buff* across its unstreaked breast.

Similar species: (1) Resembles the better-known Field Sparrow, but less rusty, with a larger bill, which is *not pink.* (2) Also suggests Grasshopper Sparrow, which lives in meadows, has a light crown-stripe, and a tail only half as long. (3) Summer young have eye-rings and buffy breasts with streaks. They suggest Lincoln's Sparrow, which has a distinctly striped crown and of course would not be found in Texas in summer.

Voice: Variable; usually a clear liquid whistle followed by a loose trill or warble on a different pitch. For example, *seeeee, slipslipslipslipslip.*

Where found: Ohio, Maryland south to Gulf States. Winters mainly in Gulf States. **Texas:** *Resident* in e. Texas; south to upper coastal area. *Habitat:* Open pine or oak woods, bushy pastures. **Nest:** An arched cup on ground. Eggs (3–4) white.

BOTTERI'S SPARROW   *Aimophila botterii*   5¼–6¼   p. 252

Field marks: A plain-breasted sparrow of the coastal prairies near Brownsville. Very nondescript, best told by its unstreaked grayish-white breast. Cassin's, the only other sparrow breeding in the same habitat, is almost identical, but grayer above. Botteri's has a much browner tail. Best told by their very different songs (see below).

Similar species: (1) See Cassin's Sparrow. (2) In winter, Grasshopper Sparrow invades the same area. It is browner, has conspicuous light stripes on the back, and a stripe through the crown. Botteri's is apparently not present in winter.

Voice: Song, a constant tinkling and "pitting," sometimes run-

ning into a dry rattle. Very unlike song of Cassin's.
Where found: Se. Arizona and s. Texas south to s. Mexico. Winters south of U.S. **Texas:** *Summer* resident in s. tip of state (Cameron and Willacy Cos.); north to Raymondville. Casual in May on cent. coast. *Habitat:* Brushy coastal prairies. **Nest:** On ground. Eggs (3–5) white.

CASSIN'S SPARROW   *Aimophila cassinii*   5¼–5¾   p. 252
   Field marks: A plain grayish sparrow of open country; underparts dingy white or buffy white without markings, or with a touch of streaking on the lower sides. Its dull grayish upper parts obscurely marked with brown and the unmarked breast are the best clues. "Skylarking" song is very distinctive.
   Similar species: Other obscure, clear-breasted sparrows of open country: (1) Grasshopper, browner, more contrastingly marked on back; buffier breast, light stripe through crown. (2) Brewer's, smaller-headed, Chippy-like (notched tail), distinctly striped with buff and black above. (3) Botteri's (Rio Grande delta only) does not "skylark."
   Voice: Song, quite sweet; one or two short opening notes, a high sweet trill and two lower notes: *ti ti tseeeeeee tay tay;* vaguely suggestive of Savannah Sparrow. Often "skylarks" or flutters into the air, giving the high trill at the climax.
   Where found: Nevada, Kansas south to ne. Mexico. Winters mostly in Mexico. **Texas:** *Summers* (Apr.–Sept.) in w. two-thirds; east to Dallas (rare), Austin, cent. coast, Delta. *Winters* in s. and w. parts. *Habitat:* Arid grassy country with some bushes. **Nest:** A deep cup on or near ground. Eggs (3–4) white.

BLACK-THROATED SPARROW *Amphispiza bilineata* 4¾–5¼
(Desert Sparrow)   p. 253
   Field marks: A pretty, gray-backed desert sparrow with white underparts, *white face-stripes* and *jet-black throat.* Face pattern is distinctive. Sexes similar. Young birds lack black throat but have cheek pattern; breast finely streaked.
   Similar species: (1) Only other bird with similar face pattern is Black-throated Gray Warbler, which has broad white wing-bars. (2) Young birds somewhat resemble Sage Sparrow.
   Voice: Song, a sweet *cheet cheet cheeeeeeee* (two short, clear opening notes and a fine trill on a lower or higher pitch).
   Where found: Ne. California, sw. Wyoming to n. Mexico. Migrant in n. part. **Texas:** *Resident* in w. parts; east to Coleman, Austin, Beeville, Kingsville, Delta. Occasional in Panhandle. Irregular cent. coast. *Habitat:* Deserts, arid country. **Nest:** A loose cup in bush or cactus. Eggs (3–4) white.

SAGE SPARROW *Amphispiza belli* 5–6¼   p. 253
   Field marks: A gray sparrow of arid brush; identified by a *single dark breast-spot* and *dark* "whisker" *marks on side of throat.* Has dark cheek, eye-ring, and whitish line over eye.

Similar species: Lark Sparrow resembles this species slightly because of the breast-spot and whisker marks, but is known by its rusty head-stripes and large white tail-patches.

Voice: A simple song of set pattern, suggestive of Song Sparrow in quality: *tsit-tsoo-tseee-tsay*, third note highest.

Where found: Washington, Wyoming south to Baja California, nw. New Mexico. Winters sw. U.S., n. Mexico. **Texas:** *Winters* locally (Nov.–Mar.) in Trans-Pecos. Rare visitor to Panhandle, s. Staked Plains. *Habitat:* Desert scrub, brush.

JUNCOS   *Junco*

Juncos are unstriped, sparrow-shaped birds characterized by *conspicuous white outer tail feathers* and gray or black heads. Some species show areas of rusty red on the back or sides. In identifying juncos, the three points of major importance are the *head* (whether black or gray), *sides* (whether "pinkish" or gray), and *back* (rusty or gray). Females are duller than males. There is sometimes hybridization or intergradation between species, so it is therefore impossible to identify all individuals.

Species with gray sides:
  Slate-colored Junco (fairly uniform gray)
  Gray-headed Junco (rusty back)
Species with rusty or "pinkish" sides:
  Oregon Junco

SLATE-COLORED JUNCO   *Junco hyemalis*   6–6½   p. 245
Field marks: Smaller than House Sparrow; dark slate-gray above with a hood and *conspicuous white outer tail feathers;* belly white. The uniformly gray upper parts, without red or brown areas, separate this from other juncos. Immatures often have a trace of buff or brownish on the sides, but it blends and is not sharply separated from the hood as in Oregon Junco.
Similar species: (1) Vesper Sparrow and pipits also show conspicuous white outer tail feathers, but those birds are brown and streaked. (2) Oregon Junco has a red-brown back, "pinkish" sides. (3) Gray-headed Junco has a rusty back, gray sides.
Voice: Song, a loose trill suggestive of Chipping Sparrow's; more musical; note a light smack; twittering notes.
Where found: Cold forests; Alaska, Canada, and south in mts. to n. Georgia. Winters s. Canada to Gulf Coast, n. Mexico. **Texas:** *Winters* (Oct.–Apr.) throughout; rare or casual in Trans-Pecos and in s. tip. *Habitat:* Woodlands, edges, brushland.

OREGON JUNCO   *Junco oreganus*   5–6
(including Pink-sided Junco)   p. 245
Field marks: A *rusty-backed* junco. Typical males have a contrasting *black hood.* The *yellowish or rusty sides* distinguish it from all other juncos. Females have grayer heads, and the rusty

of the back is not so sharply defined, but the "pink" or brownish sides are always sharply separated from the gray of the hood. The race *J. o. mearnsi* (Pink-sided Junco), which visits w. Texas in winter, is often recognizable. Males have a paler *gray* head and a *dull brown* back. The combination of clear gray hood and bright "pink" sides is quite certainly this race, which until recently was regarded as a distinct species.

Similar species: Gray-headed and Slate-colored Juncos have gray sides, gray wings.

Voice: Similar to Slate-colored Junco's.

Where found: Se. Alaska, sw. Canada, nw. U.S., Pacific States, Baja California. Winters se. Alaska to n. Mexico. **Texas:** *Winters* (Oct.–Apr.) throughout w. half; rarely to e. Texas; casually to Delta. *Habitat:* Woodlands, edges, brush.

GRAY-HEADED JUNCO   *Junco caniceps*   5½–6
(including Red-backed Junco)   p. 245

Field marks: The combination of *ashy-gray* sides and wings and *bright rufous* back distinguishes this species from other Texas juncos. The head is also ashy gray, even in males. Two races are distinguishable: (1) *J. c. caniceps* has the entire bill pale. (2) *J. c. dorsalis*, which breeds in the Guadalupe Mts. (the only breeding junco in Texas), has a *dark upper mandible* and a paler hood. Until recently the latter was regarded as a dark-eyed race of the Mexican Junco, *J. phaeonotus*.

Similar species: Oregon Junco has rusty or pinkish-buff sides, rusty wings. Males have a blackish hood.

Voice: Similar to other juncos'.

Where found: Nevada, Wyoming south to Arizona, w. Texas. Winters Wyoming to n. Mexico. **Texas:** *Winters* (Nov.–May) in Panhandle and Trans-Pecos. Casual east to Tyler, Houston, Austin, Beeville. *Breeds* in Guadalupe Mts. *Habitat:* Like other juncos'. **Nest:** A grassy cup on ground. Eggs (4–5) speckled.

TREE SPARROW   *Spizella arborea*   6–6½   p. 253

Field marks: The single *round black spot* or "stickpin" in the center of the breast and the solid *red-brown cap* are the marks that identify the rare "winter Chippy." Two white wing-bars are also characteristic. Bill dark above, yellow below.

Similar species: See (1) Field Sparrow, (2) Chipping Sparrow.

Voice: Song, sweet, variable; opening on one or two high, clear notes. Note, *tseet;* feeding note a musical *teelwit.*

Where found: Alaska, n. Canada. Winters s. Canada to cent. U.S. **Texas:** Irregular *winter visitor* (Oct.–Apr.) in Panhandle, n. and w. Texas. *Habitat:* Weedy fields, brushy open country.

CHIPPING SPARROW   *Spizella passerina*   5–5½   p. 253

Field marks: A small clear gray-breasted sparrow with a bright *rufous cap*, a *black line* through the eye, and a *white line* over it.

Winter adults are browner, not so gray-breasted. *Young* in summer are finely streaked below, but are recognized by their small size and appearance. Immatures in winter look like adults, but are buffier, with a striped crown.

Similar species: See (1) Field, (2) Rufous-crowned, and (3) Clay-colored Sparrows.

Voice: Song, a dry chipping rattle or trill on one pitch. (Birds with similar songs are juncos, Pine Warbler, Worm-eating Warbler.) Note, a short *chip*.

Where found: Canada to Nicaragua. Migrates from n. part. **Texas:** *Migrant* (Oct.–Dec., Mar.–May) throughout; *winters* except in n. Texas and Panhandle. *Breeds* in mts. of w. Texas and Edwards Plateau east to Austin; locally in e. Texas. *Habitat:* Open woodlands, farmland, orchards, towns. **Nest:** A small hair-lined cup in bush or tree. Eggs (3–5) blue, speckled.

CLAY-COLORED SPARROW *Spizella pallida* 5–5½ p. 253

Field marks: A small pale sparrow, clear-breasted like Field Sparrow and Chipping, but with a *light stripe* through center of crown and a *sharply outlined brown ear-patch*.

Similar species: (1) Somehow the idea got started that Chippings with brown ear-patches are Clay-colored Sparrows. Both birds possess them in fall and winter. The patch in the Clay-colored adult is *outlined* above and below by black lines; the fall Chipping lacks them. The only sure point in most birds is the rump, which is buffy brown; that of the Chipping is gray. (2) See also Brewer's Sparrow. (3) Immature White-crowned (larger) has a superficial resemblance.

Voice: Song, unbirdlike; three or four low flat buzzes, *bzzzz, bzzzz, bzzzz* (slow tempo).

Where found: W. Canada to n.-cent. U.S. Winters s. Texas, Mexico. **Texas:** *Migrant* (Mar.–May, Aug.–Nov.) through w. half; rare in e. half. *Winters* mostly along Rio Grande, from Delta to El Paso. *Habitat:* Open brush, fields. **Nest:** A hair-lined cup in grass or bush. Eggs (3–5) blue, spotted.

BREWER'S SPARROW *Spizella breweri* 5 p. 253

Field marks: A small pale sparrow of the brush. Clear-breasted; resembles Chipping Sparrow or Clay-color but sandier in color; *crown finely streaked*, no hint of rufous or median line.

Similar species: Young (1) Chipping and (2) Clay-colored Sparrows in fall or winter might be confused with it, but their crowns are usually browner and often divided by a pale median line.

Voice: Song, long musical buzzy trills on different pitches; suggests trilling and chopping of Canary, but weaker; sounds like a Chipping Sparrow trying to sing like a Canary.

Where found: Sw. Canada, w. U.S. Winters sw. U.S., n.

Mexico. **Texas:** *Winters* (Sept.–May) in w. Texas east to Midland, Del Rio. Migrant in Panhandle. *Habitat:* Open brush.

FIELD SPARROW *Spizella pusilla* 5¼–6   p. 253
Field marks: The *pink bill* marks this rusty-capped sparrow. It has reddish upper parts and a clear breast; less noticeable facial striping than the other red-capped sparrows. An *eye-ring* gives it a big-eyed expression. Young birds in summer are finely streaked like young Chippings, but have a pinkish bill.
Similar species: (1) Chipping Sparrow has well-defined eye-stripings, blackish bill. (2) See Rufous-crowned Sparrow.
Voice: Song, opening on deliberate, sweet slurring notes and speeding into a trill (which ascends, descends, or stays on same pitch). Note, *tseee;* has querulous quality.
Where found: Se. Canada through U.S., east of Rockies, to Gulf States. Winters to n. Mexico. **Texas:** *Winters* (Oct.–Apr.) except in Panhandle and extreme w. part. *Breeds* in Panhandle (Canadian Breaks), Edwards Plateau; locally in n., cent., and e. parts of state. *Habitat:* Brushy, semi-open country. **Nest:** Hair-lined cup in grass or low bush. Eggs (4–5) spotted.

BLACK-CHINNED SPARROW
Spizella atrogularis 5–5½   p. 253
Field marks: A very different, somewhat junco-like, sparrow; has a streaked brown back, but *head and underparts gray*, with a *black chin-patch.* The *flesh-colored bill* is set off conspicuously by the black that encircles it. Immatures lack the black patch; can be told by the *unmarked gray head and breast.*
Voice: Song, a series of notes on about same pitch, or descending slightly; starts with several high, thin, clear notes and ends in a rough trill, *sweet, sweet, sweet, weet trrrrrr.*
Where found: Sw. U.S. to s. Mexico. **Texas:** *Resident* locally in Trans-Pecos (Chisos, Davis, Guadalupe, and Franklin Mts.). Casual at El Paso. *Habitat:* Brushy mt. slopes. **Nest:** A compact cup in low bush. Eggs (3–4) plain or spotted.

HARRIS' SPARROW *Zonotrichia querula* 7–7¾   p. 253
Field marks: A sturdy sparrow, longer than Fox Sparrow. Sexes alike. In breeding plumage recognizable instantly by *black crown, face, and bib encircling pink bill.* In winter adults, black crown is veiled with gray. Young birds in first winter are *white on throat*, less black on crown, buffy brown on rest of head, and blotched and streaked on breast. Birds in second winter plumage are black *on the chin* (G. M. Sutton).
Similar species: In breeding plumage wholly unlike other species (save possibly male House Sparrow). In behavior like White-crowned and White-throated Sparrow, but when disturbed flies into trees rather than down into underbrush.

Voice: Song has quavering quality of White-throated Sparrow's; clear whistles, all on same pitch, or first one or two at one pitch, rest at a slightly higher or lower pitch, *general effect being minor*. Winter songs interspersed with chuckling sounds. Alarm note, a loud *weenk* or *wink* (G. M. Sutton).

Where found: N.-cent. Canada. Winters in s.-cent. U.S. **Texas:** *Winters* (Nov.–May) mainly in e., n., and cent. Texas; west to Panhandle (rare), Edwards Plateau; south to coast and (occasionally) Delta. *Habitat:* Brush, edges, open woodlands.

WHITE-CROWNED SPARROW
Zonotrichia leucophrys 6½–7½   p. 253

Field marks: *Adult:* A clear pearly-gray breast and a puffy crown *striped with black and white* make this one of the handsomest of all sparrows. *Immature:* Browner, with head-stripings of dark red-brown and light buffy; *bill bright pinkish.* The race *Z. l. gambelii* (Gambel's White-crown), which occurs commonly in the w. parts of the state, can be separated from the nominate race, *Z. l. leucophrys*, by the white eye-stripe which starts *from the bill* instead of from the eye.

Similar species: White-throated Sparrow is also striped on crown, but has (a) conspicuous white throat, (b) yellow spot before eye, (c) black bill. It is, on the whole, much browner. Young White-throats, though duller, always look like White-throats (dark bill, white throat-patch, etc.).

Voice: Song, one or more clear plaintive whistles (suggesting White-throat) followed by husky trilled whistles. Variable.

Where found: Alaska and across Canada; south through w. U.S. to California, Arizona, New Mexico. Winters w. and s. U.S., Mexico, Cuba. **Texas:** *Migrant and winter resident* (Oct.–May) throughout. *Habitat:* Brushy places, edges, towns.

WHITE-THROATED SPARROW
Zonotrichia albicollis 6½–7   p. 253

Field marks: *Adult:* Gray-breasted with *white throat-patch*, *striped black and white crown*, and *yellow* spot between bill and eye. Bill blackish. *Immature:* Duller; head-stripes brown and buffy, but same essential pattern; bill dark.

Similar species: White-crowned Sparrow lacks clean-cut white throat and yellow loral spot; has a bright pink or flesh bill.

Voice: Song, several clear, pensive whistles easily imitated; one or two clear notes, followed with three quavering notes on a different pitch. Note, a hard *chink*, also a slurred *tseet*.

Where found: Across Canada to ne. U.S. Winters New England to Gulf Coast, ne. Mexico. **Texas:** *Winters* (Oct.–Apr.) in e. two-thirds of state; west to Coleman, Edwards Plateau. Rare transient in Panhandle. Casual in s. Staked Plains and at El Paso. *Habitat:* Woodland undergrowth, thickets.

FOX SPARROW *Passerella iliaca* 6¾–7¼ p. 252
Field marks: Larger than House Sparrow, with a *rufous tail*, noticeable when the bird flies. The rich rusty combined with gray about the neck gives the bird its "foxy" look. Its breast is more heavily streaked than that of any other sparrow. Actions towhee-like; rustles among dry leaves. In w. Texas a gray type from the Northwest occurs. It may be known by its dull rusty tail.
Similar species: Hermit Thrush has a reddish tail, but is unstreaked on back, thin-billed, and spotted rather than striped.
Voice: Song, brilliant and musical; a variable arrangement of short clear notes and sliding whistles.
Where found: Alaska and across Canada; south in w. mts. to California, Colorado. In winter to s. U.S. **Texas:** *Winters* (Oct.–Apr.) in e., n., and cent. Texas; west to Coleman, Austin; south to upper coast, San Antonio; rarely to cent. coast, Beeville, Del Rio. Occasional in Trans-Pecos and Panhandle. *Habitat:* Wooded undergrowth, thickets.

LINCOLN'S SPARROW *Melospiza lincolnii* 5½–6 p. 252
Field marks: Lincoln's Sparrow is a skulker, "afraid of its shadow." It is like a Song Sparrow, but trimmer, side of face grayer, and breast-streakings *much finer* and often not aggregated into a central spot; best identified by a broad band of *creamy buff* across breast. It has a narrow eye-ring.
Similar species: (1) The buffy breast and fine streakings distinguish it from most sparrows except young Swamp and Song Sparrows. It is grayer-backed than either, with a more contrastingly striped crown (rusty brown on light gray). The narrow *eye-ring* is characteristic. (2) Immature Swamp Sparrow is continually misidentified as Lincoln's, but its breast is duller, with dull blurry streaks. (3) See Juvenal Bachman's Sparrow.
Voice: Song, sweet and gurgling; suggests both House Wren and Purple Finch; starts with low passages, rises abruptly, drops.
Where found: Alaska, across Canada to ne. U.S.; south in high w. mts. to sw. U.S. In winter, s. U.S. to Guatemala. **Texas:** *Migrant* throughout. *Winters* (Sept.–May) except in Panhandle. *Habitat:* Thickets, pastures, edges, tangles.

SWAMP SPARROW *Melospiza georgiana* 5–5¾ p. 253
Field marks: A rather stout, dark rusty sparrow, with clear gray breast, white throat, and *reddish cap;* frequents marshes, swamps. *Immature* birds in the first winter resemble adults but are streaked and have no red on the crown.
Similar species: (1) Chipping Sparrow is less robust and shows a white or buffy stripe over the eye. (2) Field and (3) Tree Sparrows both show prominent wing-bars. (4) Rufous-crowned Sparrow has different habitat.

Voice: Song, a trill, similar to Chipping Sparrow's but slower, sweeter, and stronger (sometimes on two pitches simultaneously). Note, a hard *chink*, similar to White-throat's.
Where found: Canada and ne. U.S. Winters s. New England to Gulf Coast. **Texas:** *Winters* (Oct.–May) in e. half. Casual in Big Bend. *Habitat:* Fresh marshes, sedgy swamps.

SONG SPARROW *Melospiza melodia* 5–6¾ p. 252
Field marks: Breast heavily streaked, streaks confluent into a *large central spot.* Pumps its tail as it flies.
Similar species: (1) Savannah Sparrow (more of a field bird) usually shows yellowish over the eye, and has a shorter, *notched* tail. (2) See also Lincoln's Sparrow.
Voice: Song, a brisk outpouring of notes, some musical, some buzzy; usually starting with three or four bright repetitious notes, *cheet cheet cheet*, etc. Variable. Call note, a low nasal *tchuk;* also a light *tseet.*
Where found: Alaska, Canada; south through w. U.S. to mts. of cent. Mexico; in e. U.S. to mts. of Georgia. Winters n. U.S. to Gulf Coast and Mexico. **Texas:** *Winters* (Sept.–Apr.) throughout. *Habitat:* Brush, thickets, edges, streamsides.

McCOWN'S LONGSPUR *Rhynchophanes mccownii* 6 p. 241
Field marks: *Spring male:* Forehead and patch on breast black; tail largely white. Hind neck *gray*, not brown or chestnut as in other longspurs. *Female and winter:* See Chestnut-collared Longspur. Note tail pattern in diagram (p. 241).
Similar species: (1) Male Chestnut-collared Longspur in spring has chestnut collar and black belly. (2) Horned Lark has similar breast-splotch but has thin bill, black face-patch.
Voice: Flight song, clear sweet warbles, suggesting Lark Bunting (R. J. Niedrach). Note, a dry rattle.
Where found: Plains of s.-cent. Canada and n.-cent. U.S. Winters sw. U.S., n. Mexico. **Texas:** *Winters* (Sept.–Apr.) locally in w. two-thirds; east to Commerce, Dallas, Houston, Austin. Occasional in s. Texas. *Habitat:* Open plains, fields.

LAPLAND LONGSPUR *Calcarius lapponicus* 6–7 p. 241
Field marks: Longspurs, like Horned Larks and pipits, are birds of open country; like those birds they often *run* (but occasionally take big hops). This species, which is rare or casual in Texas, appears a trifle like a House Sparrow. Two white wing-bars, some black streakings on the sides, and a varying amount of reddish on the nape (in males) are distinctive points. There is often a smudge of streaks across the upper breast. In spring both sexes acquire black throats. Much less white on outer tail feathers than in other longspurs.
Similar species: See other longspurs (see tail diagram, p. 241).

Voice: Note, a musical *teew* or a rattle and a whistle, *ticky-tick-tew*. Song (in flight) vigorous and musical.
Where found: Arctic. Winters s. Canada to s. U.S.; cent. Eurasia. **Texas:** Rare *winter visitor* (Nov.–Mar.) in Panhandle and locally in n. and e. Texas; south irregularly to upper coast area, Houston. *Habitat:* Fields, prairies.

SMITH'S LONGSPUR *Calcarius pictus* 6½ p. 241
Field marks: A *buffy* longspur; with warm buff on entire underparts. The tail is edged with white as in Vesper Sparrow (no terminal band). Male in spring is deeper buff and is marked on cheek with a white spot strikingly outlined with a triangle of black (black ear-patch with white spot in center); unique. In winter the breast is finely streaked.
Similar species: (1) See Vesper Sparrow, (2) Sprague's Pipit, (3) other longspurs (study tail diagram, p. 241).
Voice: Note, a weak *whit*. Also rattling or clicking notes in flight (suggest winding of cheap watch).
Where found: Alaska, Canada. Winters in s. U.S. **Texas:** *Winters* (Nov.–Apr.) locally in e. and middle parts (east of Edwards Plateau). *Habitat:* Fields, prairies, airports.

CHESTNUT-COLLARED LONGSPUR
Calcarius ornatus 5½–6½ p. 241
Field marks: The smallest longspur — smaller than House Sparrow. *Male in breeding plumage: Solid black below* except on throat; nape chestnut. *Female and winter male:* Sparrow-like, known from other longspurs (except McCown's) by large amount of white on sides of tail.
Similar species: Vesper Sparrow and the pipits have straight white sides of tail to tip; Chestnut-collared and McCown's Longspurs have a *dark band across end of tail*. In Chestnut-collar the dark central tail feathers *curve* into the terminal band, fanwise; in McCown's the band is more angular, forming a T with the dark central feathers (see tail diagram, p. 241). This is about the only way to distinguish females and winter birds.
Voice: Song, short, feeble, but musical, "suggestive of Western Meadowlark" (R. J. Neidrach). Note, a finchlike *ji-jiv*.
Where found: Plains of s.-cent. Canada, n.-cent. U.S. Winters sw. U.S., n. Mexico. **Texas:** *Winters* (Oct.–Apr.) locally throughout except e. edge and s. tip. *Habitat:* Plains, prairies.

Texas Accidentals

(including hypothetical species)

Accidentals are here defined as species recorded *five* times or less in the state of Texas. Undoubtedly, as qualified observers increase, more new species will be added to the list. More birds will also pass the arbitrary figure of five and be transferred to the casual category. For the sake of flexibility I have treated in both the main text and in this appendix those birds for which I am aware of precisely five records.

Many of these rarities are very distinctive, while others are more obscure and are unlikely to be identified by the casual observer. By far the most rewarding localities for rare stragglers are in the corners of Texas or on the perimeter of the state: the Rio Grande delta for Mexican rarities; Rockport and the central coast for wind-drifted strays; the Beaumont–Big Thicket–Port Arthur section for stragglers from eastern forests, swamps, and shores; the canyons of the Panhandle for northern items; El Paso for western waifs along the river; the mountain ranges of western Texas, especially the Guadalupes and the Chisos, for mountain species reaching their southern or northern limits.

Hypotheticals are those species which have been recorded in the state but which have not been substantiated by a specimen, capture, or by good photography. I have indicated these with an asterisk (*) after the name. I have not included those hypotheticals which have been discredited or are suspect or were reported by relatively inexperienced observers, nor those which offer subtle field problems. For example, sight reports of Barnacle Goose, Common Eider, Short-tailed Hawk, Arctic Tern, Sutton's Warbler, White-winged Junco, and others have come to my attention but I have not included them, although it is just possible that some may have been authentic. In nearly all cases the accepted observations have been carefully and critically made by experienced observers and have been substantiated by at least one other person. (In the case of two Sulphur-bellied Flycatchers, listed here tentatively, neither individual was seen by a second person.) When the existence of a bird in the state list hangs on a hypothetical sight record, I have named the principal observer or observers (but not necessarily everyone who saw the bird). In the case of collected birds I have given localities (and dates when I could) but not the collector. A number of so-called specimen records (Black Catbird, Mexican Chickadee, Abert's Towhee, Ipswich Sparrow, Worthen's Sparrow, and others) are ignored because of reasonable doubts as to the existence of the specimen, its validity, origin, etc.

The following brief notes give the salient field marks of 61 birds accidental to Texas. Of these, 27 are hypothetical (including 2 hypothetical hybrids).

For illustrations of the following birds see either *A Field Guide to the Birds* (Eastern) or *A Field Guide to Western Birds*. A field guide to Mexican birds is in preparation.

ARCTIC LOON* *Gavia arctica.* In breeding plumage, resembles Common Loon, but smaller (23), top of head and hind neck *pale smoke-gray;* squarish white spots on back arranged in *four distinct patches,* two on each side. Winter plumage difficult; dark as Common Loon, bill as slender as Red-throat's but not upturned. (Alaska, nw. Canada, n. Eurasia. Winters on Pacific and European coasts.) Sight record, Rockport, Mar. 29–Apr., 1958 (F. Weston, B. Monroe, Jr., C. Hagar). See plate, p. 4.

SOOTY SHEARWATER *Puffinus griseus.* See p. 6. (Oceanic; breeds in S. Hemisphere; ranges to N. Hemisphere.) Specimen, Port Aransas, June 19, 1952; reported also from Rockport (several times) and Padre I.

AUDUBON'S SHEARWATER *Puffinus lherminieri.* See p. 7. (Oceanic; breeds on tropical islands in Atlantic, Pacific, and Indian Oceans.) Casual along Texas coast; dead birds picked up at Brazos I., Jan. 28, 1947, and Port Aransas, Apr. 29, 1955; reported also from Sabine Pass and mouth of Rio Grande.

HARCOURT'S PETREL (Madeira Petrel) *Oceanodroma castro.* Larger than Wilson's Petrel (7–8); tail distinctly forked. Very similar to Leach's Petrel of N. Atlantic but white in even band across rump; more white on flanks and under tail-coverts. (Breeds in Azores, Ascension I., St. Helena, Hawaiian, and Galápagos Is.) Specimen picked up (one of three exhausted birds) at Edinburg (s. Texas), June 25, 1954, after tropical hurricane.

WILSON'S PETREL *Oceanites oceanicus.* Smaller than Purple Martin (7). A tiny black swallow-like sea bird with conspicuous white rump-patch; tail even at end. Feet (with yellow webs) extend beyond tail's tip. (Breeds on Antarctic mainland and islands near Antarctic; migrates to N. Atlantic, Pacific, and Indian Oceans.) Bird taken June 5, 1912, San Jacinto Bay, Harris Co.

WHITE-TAILED TROPIC-BIRD (Yellow-billed Tropic-bird) *Phaethon lepturus.* See p. 7. (Breeds in West Indies and elsewhere in tropical oceans.) Casual (June–Dec.) off Texas coast (Matagorda I., Sabine, Cove, Rockport).

BROWN BOOBY (White-bellied Booby)* *Sula leucogaster* 28–30. A dark brown, blackish-looking booby with a *clear white belly,* in clean-cut contrast to a dark breast. Immature resembles young Gannet closely, but is much blacker, with yellow feet. See immature Blue-faced Booby. (Breeds on islands in tropical oceans; ranges widely in warm seas.) Has been observed off Rockport, June and Sept. (C. Hagar and F. M. Packard). No Texas specimen.

RED-FOOTED BOOBY *Sula sula.* Resembles Blue-faced Booby but adults distinguished by *bright red feet,* white tail. Black in wings restricted to primaries. Like a small Gannet with red feet. (Tropical oceans.) Specimen taken near Rockport, prior to 1910 (U.S. Fish and Wildlife Service).

GANNET *Morus bassanus.* See p. 9. (N. Atlantic coasts and islands; winters south to Gulf of Mexico.) Casual straggler (perhaps regular); reported Jefferson Co., Galveston, Rockport (captured May 1, 1944).

SCARLET IBIS *Eudocimus ruber.* Size, shape, pattern (including black wing-tips) of White Ibis, but white replaced by scarlet. (Venezuela to Brazil.) Said to have been a straggler, formerly, to Texas coast. No recent records.

AMERICAN FLAMINGO *Phoenicopterus ruber.* An extremely slender vermilion-pink wading bird, with a grotesque down-bent bill; as tall as Great Blue Heron. In flight shows large black wing-areas; its extremely long neck extends in front and its long legs trail behind. Pale washed-out birds are likely to be escaped captives. (Bahamas to Yucatan, Venezuela; Galápagos.) At least three or four records along Texas coast.

BLACK BRANT *Branta nigricans.* Like Brant but underparts blackish to under tail-coverts; lacks sharp contrast between black breast and light belly. (Ne. Siberia, coastal Alaska; winters on Pacific Coast.) One shot near San Angelo, 1884. Sight record, Brownsville, Nov. 18, 1936 (E. R. Ford).

BARROW'S GOLDENEYE* *Bucephala islandica.* Male has a *crescent-shaped* white patch before eye instead of round spot as in Common Goldeneye. Head glossed with *purple* (not green); shows more black on body (row of white spots on sides of black back). Females not safely separable. (S. Alaska, Canada, nw. U.S., s. Greenland, Iceland. Winters to California, ne. U.S.) Sight records: Chambers Co., Apr. 20, 1957 (A. K. McKay); Rockport, Dec., 1957 (C. Hagar). See plate, p. 48.

HARLEQUIN DUCK* *Histrionicus histrionicus* 15–17½. *Adult male:* A rather small dark blue-gray duck (blackish at a distance) with reddish-brown flanks; white crescent before eye, white spots on cheek and neck and scattered white bars and spots on body. *Female:* Dusky brown with two or three round white spots on side of head; no wing-patch. Has pattern of female Surf Scoter, but shape and stubby bill of Bufflehead. (Mts. of Alaska, Canada, nw. U.S., Iceland, Greenland, n. Asia. Winters south to n. U.S., Japan.) Sight record at Rockport (2 birds), Jan. 14, 1945 (Hagar and Friedmann). See plate, p. 45.

SURFBIRD *Aphriza virgata* 10. A stocky gray sandpiper-like wader that shows a conspicuous *white tail tipped with a broad black band.* Legs yellowish. (Mts. of s.-cent. Alaska. Winters Pacific Coast south to Strait of Magellan.) Sight record on stone jetty at Port Aransas, Texas, Apr. 1–12, 1951 (F. Watson, J. L. Edwards, C. D. Brown, C. Hagar). Substantiated by photographs.

PURPLE SANDPIPER *Erolia maritima* 8–9½. Rock-feeding habits, portly build, and rather junco-like coloration, with slate-gray back and breast, white belly, are good field marks. Important points are short yellow legs, whitish eye-ring, yellow base of bill. Very tame. (Arctic. Winters along coasts of N. Atlantic.) Bird photographed in color by R. Bentley and C. E. Hall, Galveston, Dec. 4, 5, 1953. Possible sight records at Lake Dallas, Tyler. See plates, pp. 93, 113.

SHARP-TAILED SANDPIPER* *Erolia acuminata* 8½. Like Pectoral Sandpiper, but in winter plumage, breast rich buffy (young) or pale gray-buff (adult), spotted lightly on sides of breast only. No sharp contrast between white belly, dark breast as in Pectoral Sandpiper. (N. Siberia. Winters south to Australia.) Careful sight record, Galveston, Mar. 21, 1948 (G. Williams).

CURLEW SANDPIPER* *Erolia ferruginea* 7–9. Characterized by slim, *down-curved*, slightly curlew-like bill and *whitish rump*. In breeding plumage, reddish-breasted (darker than spring dowitcher). In winter similar to winter Dunlin, but longer-legged, less streaked on breast; bill *curved slightly throughout length*, not drooped only at tip. The most obvious difference is the *whitish rump;* Dunlin's is whitish along sides only. (N. Siberia. Winters south to Africa, Australia.) Careful sight record, Galveston I., Apr. 13, 1947 (G. Williams). Also possible sight record at Bayside. See plates, pp. 93, 112, 113.

RUFF, REEVE *Philomachus pugnax* 10–12½. In fall or winter, a nondescript brownish wader; male larger than Lesser Yellowlegs, female smaller. Known by buffy wash on breast and sides, *dark tail with conspicuous oval white patch at each side*. Legs and base of bill yellowish or greenish. See Eastern or European Field Guides for illustration, further details. (Eurasia.) Accidental on Padre I., Dec. 12, 1902. See plate, p. 112.

PARASITIC JAEGER *Stercorarius parasiticus* 16–21. A dark hawk-like sea bird, size of Laughing Gull; chases terns and gulls. Known by *pointed* central tail feathers (projecting ½ to 3½ inches) and flash of white in wings. Immatures almost inseparable from Pomarine Jaeger. (Arctic. Winters at sea to S. Hemisphere.) Specimens taken at Galveston (1909) and Corpus Christi Pass (Apr., 1958). Perhaps regular on waters of continental shelf.

GLAUCOUS GULL *Larus hyperboreus* 26–32. A large pale gull *without dark wing-tips;* larger than Herring Gull. First winter birds are pale buffy, with *"frosty"* primaries. Second-year birds are *extremely white* throughout. Adults have a pale gray mantle but *unmarked white primaries*. (Arctic. Winters to n. U.S., coasts of Eurasia.) Accidental in Panhandle (Muleshoe Refuge) and n.-cent. Texas. (Specimen, Clay Co., Dec. 17, 1880, and Gainesville, date unknown.) Reported at Rockport, Apr. 1949; wintered, 1952–53.

GREAT BLACK-BACKED GULL* *Larus marinus* 28–31. Much larger than Herring Gull. *Adult:* Dark slaty back and wings contrasting with snow-white underparts. Legs pale flesh. Young birds resemble corresponding stages of Herring Gull, but are less brown, more two-toned, paler on head and underparts; "saddle-back" pattern is evident; head and bill noticeably larger. (E. Canada, New England, Greenland, nw. Europe. Winters south to ne. U.S., Mediterranean.) Careful sight record at Rockport, Feb. 23, 1952 (J. L. Edwards, C. D. Brown).

LESSER BLACK-BACKED GULL* *Larus fuscus.* Adult may be told from Great Black-backed Gull by smaller size (size of Herring Gull) and *yellow* instead of pink feet. Young bird not safely identifiable in field. (Europe. Winters to Africa.) Adult studied at Port Aransas on Mar. 28, 1952, by three experienced observers (R. H. Herbert, J. L. Edwards, C. D. Brown).

BLACK-LEGGED KITTIWAKE *Rissa tridactyla* 16–18. Smaller than Ring-bill Gull. In adult Kittiwake, wing-tips are *solid black* (without white spots) and cut *straight across*, as if dipped in ink. Legs *black;* bill pale yellow, unmarked. Young resembles young Bonaparte's Gull, but has dark bar on back of neck, instead of dark spot behind eye; has more black on outer primaries and *fore border* of wing. (Circumpolar, breeding on islands in northern seas. Winters south to n. U.S., Mediterranean, Japan.) Immature bird observed on Dec. 30, 1956, at Woodlawn Lake, San Antonio, and found dead on Jan. 1, 1957.

SABINE'S GULL *Xema sabini* 13–14. The only gull with a strongly *forked tail.* Jet-black outer primaries and white triangle on rear edge of wing make an unmistakable pattern. Dark head in breeding plumage. Bill black with yellow tip. Juvenile has similar wing pattern, but tail tipped with black. (Arctic. Winters to Peru, also in Atlantic.) Recorded Corpus Christi and Anahuac.

ELEGANT TERN *Thalasseus elegans* 16–17. Similar to Royal Tern, but much smaller (larger than Forster's Tern); bill deep yellow, proportionately much longer and more slender than bill of Royal. (Pacific Coast of nw. Mexico. Winters south to Chile.) Recorded at Corpus Christi, July, 1889.

NODDY TERN *Anous stolidus* 15. The only brown tern (except immature Sooty) and the only tern with a rounded tail. The whitish cap on a dark bird gives this tern a "negative" effect. (Tropical oceans.) May have nested formerly on Texas coast (St. Joseph I.). One record for Rockport area.

RUDDY GROUND DOVE* *Columbigallina talpacoti* 6–7. A tiny cinnamon-backed dove; Common Ground Dove is red on wings only. (Tropical Mexico to Argentina.) Sight record, Rio Grande delta, Dec. 23, 24, 1950; Jan., 1951 (Irby Davis, Luther Goldman, William Jennings).

PYGMY OWL *Glaucidium gnoma* 7–7½. Very similar to Ferruginous Owl but a bird of mountains. Grayer, with *blackish* (not brown) streaks on breast; light dots on crown. (Conifer forests from se. Alaska south to Guatemala.) Taken at El Paso, Apr. 26, 1918.

BLACK SWIFT* *Cypseloides niger* 7¼. A large *black* swift with a slightly forked tail which it sometimes fans wide in flight. At close range shows a touch of white on forehead. Known from Purple Martin by its longer, scythe-like wings and style of flight. (Se. Alaska south to Costa Rica; Cuba to British Guiana. Winters in tropics.) No Texas specimen. Sight records at Cove, Chambers Co., Oct. 4, 1949 (A. K. McKay), and Chisos Mts. (4 or 5 over Blue Canyon, July 22, 1951; A. Sprunt and J. H. Dick).

VAUX'S SWIFT* *Chaetura vauxi*. Like Chimney Swift but smaller (4½); paler beneath, especially on throat. Probably not safely distinguishable unless in the hand, but any small mid-winter swift on the Gulf Coast would probably be this western species. (Se. Alaska south to Cent. America, n. Venezuela. Winters Mexico to Panama.) Not definitely recorded from Texas (possible sight records at Corpus Christi, May 6, 7, 8, 1946; F. M. Packard). Undoubtedly a casual transient as it sometimes winters at Baton Rouge, Louisiana.

COSTA'S HUMMINGBIRD* *Calypte costae* 3¼. *Male: Throat and forehead violet-purple or amethyst.* Feathers of "gorget" are longer and stand out more from sides of throat than in other hummers. Male Lucifer Hummingbird is very similar but has *curved* bill, rusty sides, and *no purple on forehead.* Male Anna's is larger and has throat and forehead rose-red, not purple. *Female:* Impossible to distinguish in field from female Black-chin. (Cent. California, s. Nevada south to Sonora, Sinaloa; winters in Mexico.) No Texas specimen. Recent sight records in Sept.–Oct. at Rockport (C. Hagar and others). Substantiation by capture or color photography desirable. See plate, p. 144.

ANNA'S HUMMINGBIRD *Calypte anna* 4. *Male:* A rather large hummingbird; has a rose-red throat and a rose-red crown. *Female:* Similar to females of other hummingbirds, but is larger than most and darker green above; has grayer underparts and more heavily spotted throat, often forming a central patch or scattering of red spots; immature male Ruby-throat may have such spots. (California, Baja California. Spreads in winter.) Specimen, Brewster Co., Oct., 1936. Many recent sight records, Sept.–Oct., at Rockport (C. Hagar, E. W. Teale, and others) but needs further confirmation by capture or photography. See plate, p. 144.

ALLEN'S HUMMINGBIRD* *Selasphorus sasin* 3⅛. *Male: Green back, rufous rump* and cheeks, flame-red throat. The only similar hummingbird, the male Rufous, has entire back rufous. Easily confused if not scrutinized carefully; be sure to see middle of back. *Female:* Not distinguishable in field from female Rufous; in hand, female Allen's has narrower tail feathers. (Coast region of s. Oregon to Ventura Co., California. Winters in nw. Mexico.) Possible record at San Antonio but specimen not preserved. Sight records of probable birds in fall at Rockport, Sinton, Houston (C. Hagar, Mrs. Clarence Cottam, and others). Substantiation by capture or color photography advisable. See plate, p. 144.

CALLIOPE HUMMINGBIRD* *Stellula calliope* 3. The smallest U.S. hummer. *Male:* Throat with *lavender-red rays on a white ground,* the only hummingbird with this effect. *Female:* A half-sized edition of female Broad-tail — buffy sides, rusty at base of tail feathers. (Mts. from sw.

Canada south to n. Baja California. Winters in Mexico.) Occasional at
El Paso (specimen 1851; also sight records, Aug., 1951, and Aug., 1956).
See plate, p. 144.

RIEFFER'S HUMMINGBIRD *Amazilia tzacatl.* Similar to Buff-
bellied Hummingbird but belly *grayish.* (Tropical e. Mexico south to
n. S. America.) Accidental at Brownsville (Fort Brown, 2 specimens,
June and July, 1876).

WHITE-EARED HUMMINGBIRD *Hylocharis leucotis* 3¼. *Male:*
Underparts greenish, throat blue and green, forehead purple, *bill red* with
black tip, *broad white stripe behind eye. Female:* Lacks metallic forehead
and throat-patches but easily identified by red bill and white stripe
behind eye similar to those of male; see Broad-billed Hummingbird.
(S. Arizona south to Nicaragua.) Female collected in Chisos Mts.,
July 7, 1937. See plate, p. 144.

COPPERY-TAILED TROGON *Trogon elegans* 11½. Erect posture,
parrot-like profile and bright red and green color identify this Mexican species. *Male:* Underparts *bright geranium-red,* separated by a
white band from the dark head. Head and upper parts dark glossy
green; tail moderately long; bill stout and pale. Female similar but head
and upper parts brown; white spot on cheek. (U.S.–Mexican border to
Costa Rica. Winters south of U.S.) Straggler to lower Valley; recorded
Brownsville, San Benito, Las Cuevas, Rio Grande City.

GRAY KINGBIRD* *Tyrannus dominicensis* 9–9½. Resembles Eastern Kingbird, but larger; of a *pale* washed-out gray color. Tail *notched,*
no white band. The *very large bill* gives a bull-headed look. Call, a rolling
pi-teer-rrry. (Coast of S. Carolina through West Indies and Netherlands
Antilles. Leaves U.S. in winter.) Sight record, Rockport, Aug. 31, 1951
(C. Hagar, G. and S. Williams).

FORK-TAILED FLYCATCHER* *Muscivora tyrannus.* Similar to
Scissor-tailed Flycatcher but *black-capped;* no crimson on sides. (S.
Mexico south to Argentina.) Sight records: Rio Grande delta, Nov. 19,
1946 (M. and T. Gill); also north of Uvalde, Aug. 10, 1946 (S. G.
Williams).

SULPHUR-BELLIED FLYCATCHER* *Myiodynastes luteiventris* 8.
A large *streaked* flycatcher with a bright rufous tail, black stripe through
eye; underparts pale yellow with black streakings; back also streaked.
No other flycatcher has a streaked yellow breast. (Se. Arizona south to
Costa Rica. Winters in Peru and Bolivia.) No verified record for Texas.
Two sight reports: Rio Grande delta (A. T. Hale) and Big Bend (P. Koch);
but in neither case was the bird corroborated by a second observer. See
plate, p. 160.

OLIVACEOUS FLYCATCHER *Myiarchus tuberculifer* 7¼. Of the
same type as Ash-throated Flycatcher, rufous-tailed and yellow-bellied,
but considerably smaller, with a gray instead of white throat. Voice,
a mournful drawling *peeur* slurring downward. (Se. Arizona, sw. New
Mexico to nw. Argentina.) Female collected in Chisos Mts., June 17,

1932. Also two specimens collected near El Paso in May and June (U.S. Fish and Wildlife Service). See plate, p. 160.

COUES' FLYCATCHER *Contopus pertinax* 7¾. Size of Olive-sided Flycatcher but underparts more uniformly gray, throat *grayer*, lower mandible yellow; no narrow white strip up center of breast separating gray into two side-patches. Voice, a plaintive whistled *ho-say, re-ah.* (S. Arizona and se. New Mexico to Nicaragua.) Specimen taken in Davis Mts., Sept. 12, 1916. See plate, p. 161.

GRAY-BREASTED MARTIN *Progne chalybea.* Both sexes resemble female Purple Martin, but are noticeably smaller (6½) and possess a *darker forehead* (pale in female Purple Martin). (Tropical Mexico south to cent. Argentina.) Accidental wanderer to lower Rio Grande Valley (Rio Grande City, Hidalgo). Also a recent sight record of a possible breeding pair at Brownsville (F. Nye).

CLARK'S NUTCRACKER* *Nucifraga columbiana* 12–13. Built like a small Crow, with a *light gray* body and conspicuous *white patches* in black wings and tail. (High mts. from sw. Canada south to n. Baja California, New Mexico.) Straggler in winter to w. Texas (Davis and Chisos Mts.) and Panhandle.

BRIDLED TITMOUSE* *Parus wollweberi* 4½–5. The crest and black and white face (white cheek, black throat and "bridle") identify this species. (Se. Arizona, sw. N. Mexico to Oaxaca.) The species was described by Cassin from a specimen collected by J. W. Audubon supposedly on the Rio Grande. Source of specimen in doubt. Sight record, Big Bend, 1937 (Mrs. J. F. Dobie, Mrs. W. S. Randall). Also unconfirmed sight record for Big Bend (L. M. Whitaker).

DIPPER (Water Ouzel)* *Cinclus mexicanus* 7–8½. Shaped like a large chunky wren (size of a fat thrush) with a short tail. *Slate-colored;* legs pale; eyelids *white.* Bobbing motions, slaty color, and shape are distinctive. (Mt. streams from w. Canada, Alaska to w. Panama.) Sight records: Kimble Co., Kerr Co. (Mrs. B. Reid); Vernon, May 14, 1939 (R. More, G. Maxon).

BENDIRE'S THRASHER* *Toxostoma bendirei* 9½–10½. Similar to Curve-billed Thrasher but has a shorter, straighter, more Robin-like bill. Sight record near Amarillo, Apr. 14, 1955 (J. and G. Creager, Bess Smith). Also unsubstantiated sight records near Eagle Pass.

CLAY-COLORED ROBIN (Tamaulipas Thrush, Gray's Robin)* *Turdus grayi.* Very much like Robin in appearance, voice, and actions, but grayish brown above with slight olive wash; below, pale buffy or clay color. Chin and throat striped with thin dark lines. (Ne. Mexico to n. Colombia.) Careful sight record, Brownsville, Mar. 10–17, 1940 (Irby Davis).

VARIED THRUSH *Ixoreus naevius* 9–10. Similar to Robin but with *orange eye-stripe, orange wing-bars,* and *black band* across rusty breast. *Female:* Breastband gray. (Se. Alaska south to n. California.) Accidental at El Paso, Feb. 12 to Mar. 21, 1956. Photographed in color movies. Also a sight record at Cove (e. Texas), Nov. 4, 6, 1935 (A. McKay). See plate, p. 193.

BREWSTER'S WARBLER* *Vermivora chrysoptera* × *V. pinus*. The Golden-winged and Blue-winged Warbler frequently hybridize. Two distinct types are produced, Lawrence's Warbler and Brewster's, which occurs more frequently. Typical Brewster's are like Golden-wings without the black throat. Some individuals have white wing-bars, others yellow, and some are tinged with yellow below. The thin black eye-mark, as in Blue-wing, and white or largely white, instead of solid yellow, underparts are diagnostic. Although virtually unrecorded away from nesting grounds, the hybrids must follow their parents' migration routes and therefore should occasionally occur in Texas. Mrs. C. Hagar reports one observed at Rockport, Mar. 9, 1945. See plate, p. 213.

LAWRENCE'S WARBLER* *Vermivora chrysoptera* × *V. pinus*. The recessive hybrid of the Blue-wing–Golden-wing combination. Yellowish with white wing-bars as in Blue-wing, but with black face pattern of Golden-wing. The only other yellow-bellied warbler with both a *black bib* and *black ear-patch* is Townsend's, which shows black side-stripes and a black crown. The very rare Bachman's Warbler has a black crown-patch and lacks the black cheek-patch and white wing-bars. Both Lawrence's and Bachman's would be real finds in Texas and require substantiation for a definite place on the state list. Like Brewster's Warbler, this hybrid undoubtedly occurs in Texas occasionally. Mrs. C. Hagar reports one seen at Rockport (undated) and F. M. Packard reports another at Corpus Christi, Apr. 30, 1946. See plate, p. 213.

BACHMAN'S WARBLER* *Vermivora bachmanii* 4¼. The rarest North American songbird. *Male:* Olive-green above; face and underparts yellow; *throat-patch and crown-patch black. Female:* Lacks black throat; upper parts olive-green; forehead and underparts yellow; crown grayish. Male Lawrence's Warbler (also extremely rare) has black bib, yellow underparts, but is recognized by two *white wing-bars*, broad black patch through eye, and *none* on crown. Female Hooded and female Wilson's are also solid yellow below, olive-green above and lack wing-bars. All have yellowish foreheads, but female Bachman's has a *blue-gray crown and cheeks set off by a yellow eye-ring.* Yellowish bend in wing is an aid. Female Hooded is much larger, with white tail-spots. Song of Bachman's, a wiry buzzing trill; resembles Parula's but rendered on one pitch. (Se. U.S. Very rare, local. Winters Cuba.) Said to have been noted in timbered swamps of e. Texas (Miner, 1946). Needs substantiation. Possible sight record, Fort Worth, Oct. 3, 1945. See plate, p. 213.

LUCY'S WARBLER *Vermivora luciae* 4. See p. 205. (Deserts of sw. U.S. and nw. Mexico; winters in Mexico.) Recorded as breeding near El Paso, but north of Texas border. One bird recorded feeding young Cowbird at Sierra Blanca, June 8, 1958 (Mr. and Mrs. D. T. Johnson). Winter straggler at El Paso.

HERMIT WARBLER *Dendroica occidentalis* 4½–4¾. *Male:* Similar to Black-throated Green Warbler but gray-backed; yellow of face more extensive (includes forehead); black of throat more restricted, not extending across breast and sides. In female, black of throat is much reduced or wanting. (Se. Washington to California. Winters s. Mexico to Nicaragua.) Specimen, Chisos Mts., May 3, 1935; observed at El Paso, May 1, 1954, Sept. 7, 1956. See plate, p. 224.

GROUND-CHAT (Rio Grande Yellowthroat) *Chamaethlypis poliocephala* 5½. Larger than Yellowthroat with a more vireo-like bill. Male recognized by *restricted black face-patch between eye and bill* (unlike extensive mask of Yellowthroat); gray cap, partial white eye-ring. Female lacks black; is larger than female Yellowthroat and lacks whitish on belly. Song, cheerful, bunting-like, not like Yellowthroat's. (Ne. Mexico south to w. Panama.) Formerly an occasional summer resident in Rio Grande delta. No recent records. See plate, p. 224.

RED-FACED WARBLER* *Cardellina rubrifrons* 5¼. A gray-backed warbler with an unmistakable *bright red face and breast;* black patch on head, white nape, and white belly. Sexes similar. (Breeds s. Arizona, sw. New Mexico to se. Chihuahua, Durango.) Sight record, Midland, April 5, 1956 (Mrs. J. W. LeSassier). Six seen at El Paso by four good observers, Aug. 1, 1956. See plate, p. 224.

GOLDEN-CROWNED WARBLER (Brasher's Warbler)* *Basileuterus culicivorus.* Slate-gray above (no wing-bars), bright yellow underparts; crown with two black stripes enclosing a *yellow center stripe;* cheeks dark gray, light line over eye. (Mexico to Argentina.) Careful sight record near Harlingen, Rio Grande delta, Sept. 5, 1943 (Irby Davis). See plate, p. 224.

PINE GROSBEAK *Pinicola enucleator* 9–9¾. The largest finch. *Male:* Rose-red with a black tail; blackish wings with two white bars. *Female:* Gray with two wing-bars; head and rump tinged with dull yellow. *Immature male:* Similar to female but with touch of reddish on head and rump. Call, a clear whistle: *tee-tee-tew,* suggesting Greater Yellowlegs. (Conifers from n. New England across Canada to Alaska; also high mts. of w. U.S.; n. Eurasia. In winter irregularly to cent. U.S.) Straggler to Panhandle; Pampa, Gray Co., Dec., 1933 (specimen); sight record, Amarillo, Oct. 10, 1953 (Acord and Dupree).

COMMON REDPOLL* *Acanthis flammea* 5–5½. Goldfinch-sized, gray-brown; *bright red cap* on forehead; *black chin,* dark streaks on sides. *Males* pink-breasted; Purple Finches and House Finches are larger, redder. (Arctic and Subarctic. Winters irregularly to n. U.S.) Four sight records (some questionable?), Corsicana, Houston, Rockport (files of U.S. Fish and Wildlife Service).

GOLDEN-CROWNED SPARROW *Zonotrichia atricapilla* 6–7. *Adult:* Size of White-crowned Sparrow; darker; "Chinese gold" patch through crown. Immature looks like female House Sparrow, but is darker, grayer on head and breast; sometimes has dull yellowish suffusion on crown. (Alaska, w. Canada. Winters s. British Columbia to nw. Mexico.) Two collected in Orange Co., by F. B. Armstrong (Mar. 15, Apr. 4, 1887). Observed near El Paso over New Mexico line by L. McBee and M. Keefer. Sight records, Amarillo: Jan. 17, 1954 (J. and B. Bailey); Jan. 2, 1955 (Christmas Count); also Muleshoe Refuge. See plate, p. 253.

Extinct and Unsuccessful Birds

THE following list of 15 species embraces three categories:

1. Birds that are extinct or very close to extinction: Eskimo Curlew (?), Passenger Pigeon, Carolina Parakeet, Ivory-billed Woodpecker (?).

2. Birds that formerly lived in or visited Texas but no longer do so: Trumpeter Swan, California Condor, Sharp-tailed Grouse. The Ground-chat and one or two other accidentals perhaps also fit this category.

3. Introduced exotic game species that have not become established: Sage Grouse, Red-legged Partridge, Chukar, Gray (Hungarian) Partridge, See See Partridge, Gray Francolin, Coturnix, Guinea-fowl. These might be released from time to time in further attempts. In the case of the Coturnix and Chukar, listed both here and in the main text, it is anyone's guess what the final results will be. It is possible that wealthy landowners have turned loose California Quail and other exotics, but these are not on record. Two other species, the Mute Swan, *Cygnus olor* (orange bill with black knob), and Ringed Turtle Dove, *Streptopelia risoria* (cream-colored with partial black ring on nape), are borderline cases. They are common in captivity and frequently escape. The Mute Swan is perhaps the swan most likely to be seen in Texas. The dove is sometimes seen in city shade trees.

TRUMPETER SWAN *Olor buccinator.* Larger than Whistling Swan (65), without the small yellow spot at base of bill (some Whistlers lack this spot). Voice lower pitched, more bugle-like. (S. Alaska, w. Canada, and nw. U.S.) Formerly occasional winter visitor to Texas. Not recorded in recent years.

CALIFORNIA CONDOR *Gymnogyps californianus.* Much larger than Turkey Vulture (spread 8½–10½ ft.); adults with extensive *pure white wing-linings*. Head yellow or orange. (California.) The fossil record indicates that this bird was present in the Big Bend 2000 years ago.

SHARP-TAILED GROUSE *Pedioecetes phasianellus* 17½. A pale prairie grouse with a short, *pointed whitish* tail. (Alaska, nw. Canada to n. New Mexico.) Formerly resident in extreme nw. Panhandle of Texas. Extirpated about 1906.

SAGE GROUSE *Centrocercus urophasianus.* As large as a small Turkey (♂ 28, ♀ 22); gray-brown with contrasting *black belly* and spike-like tail feathers. (Se. Alberta, s. Saskatchewan south to w. Colorado.) Birds from Montana introduced unsuccessfully in w. Texas (1955) by Texas Game and Fish Commission.

RED-LEGGED PARTRIDGE *Alectoris rufa* 13½. Like a large quail; brown with *bright red* legs and bill; whitish throat heavily bordered by black; light stripe over eye. Flanks *heavily barred* chestnut, black, white. (Sw. Europe.) Nearly 400 birds from Spain released in n. Texas and Panhandle in 1955, 1956, 1957 by Texas Game and Fish Commission. Status questionable; some young raised.

CHUKAR (Rock Partridge) *Alectoris graeca* 13. See p. 76. (Asia and e. Europe. Introduced successfully locally in w. U.S.) Birds from India released in Moore Co. in 1940 by Texas Game and Fish Commission. They did not survive. In Sept., 1958, 500 Nevada wild-trapped birds were released in w. Texas (Brewster Co.). There is a fair chance these might survive.

SEE SEE PARTRIDGE *Ammoperdix griseigularis*. Smaller than Gray (Hungarian) Partridge or near size of Bobwhite. Gray and sandy-colored with orange-yellow legs and bill. Double whistling call gives bird its name; wings produce a peculiar whistling sound. (Asia.) 260 birds from West Pakistan released in Panhandle (Palo Duro Canyon) in 1956, 1957. Unsuccessful.

GRAY PARTRIDGE (Hungarian Partridge) *Perdix perdix*. In flight this rotund grayish partridge shows a *short rufous tail*. It is larger than a quail (12–14), has a dark splotch on belly, rusty face, and broad *chestnut-colored bars* on flanks. (Eurasia.) Introduced at Wichita Falls, 70 birds (1927), and in Deaf Smith and Oldham Cos. 200 birds (1943). Unsuccessful.

COTURNIX (Migratory Quail) *Coturnix coturnix*. See p. 77. (Eurasia.) Birds of Mediterranean or Japanese origin introduced in 1957, 1958, in w., cent., s., and n. Texas by Texas Game and Fish Commission. It is too early at this time (1959) to assess results. Reproduction has been recorded.

GRAY FRANCOLIN (Gray Partridge) *Francolinus pondicerianus* 12. A brown partridge, *thickly barred* above and below; rusty tail, *red throat-patch*. Legs dull red. (Asia.) 20 birds from Pakistan released in Panhandle (Palo Duro Canyon) in 1956. Unsuccessful.

GUINEA-FOWL *Numida meleagris*. A large henlike bird with large body, small tail, small head with reddish bony crest. Slate-gray, completely speckled with small white spots. (Africa.) 200 birds of Cuban origin introduced in s. Texas (Kenedy and Hidalgo Cos.) in 1940. Unsuccessful.

ESKIMO CURLEW *Numenius borealis*. See p. 98. (Arctic America; winters in S. America.) May not be extinct. Formerly migrated through prairies of e. and middle Texas. Recent sight records: Galveston, Apr. 20, 1945 (J. M. Heiser, Jr.); Galveston I., Apr. 5–26, 1959 (Feltner, G. Williams, E. Edwards, and others), and recorded there in succeeding Aprils.

PASSENGER PIGEON *Ectopistes migratorius*. Larger than Mourning Dove, with longer tail, longer wings; bluer on upper parts, redder below. Head blue-gray. (E. N. America; extinct.) Formerly abundant in migration in e. and cent. Texas. Last authentic Texas record in 1896.

CAROLINA PARAKEET *Conuropsis carolinensis* 13. Size of Mourning Dove, with pointed tail; bright green, adults with yellow head deepening into orange about base of bill. (Extinct. Formerly e. U.S.) Once ranged to e. and cent. Texas. Last reported appearance, Corpus Christi (about 1895).

IVORY-BILLED WOODPECKER *Campephilus principalis* 20. Larger than Pileated Woodpecker; *male* with flaming crest; *female* with black crest. Known by superior size, *ivory-white bill*, and large white wing-patches *visible when bird is at rest*. In flight overhead, whole *rear* edge of Ivory-bill's wing is white; in Pileated white is on *front edge*. Voice, very different; a single loud tooting note. (Se. U.S. Possibly extinct. Related form in Cuba.) Formerly resident in river forests of e. Texas, west to Trinity and Brazos Rivers. Last Texas specimen record, Tarkington, Texas (2), Nov. 26, 1904.

APPENDIX III

ROADSIDE SILHOUETTES

1. Kingfisher
2. Lark Sparrow
3. House Sparrow
4. Purple Martin
5. Barn Swallow
6. Tree Swallow
7. Cliff Swallow
8. Bluebird

9. Grackle
10. Blackbird
11. Starling
12. Cowbird
13. Hummingbird
14. Kingbird
15. Robin
16. Shrike

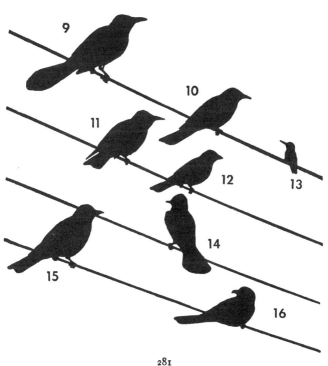

WESTERN SILHOUETTES

(Typical of the western parts of the state. Magpie
is only an occasional straggler to Texas.)

1. Sparrow Hawk
2. Red-tailed Hawk
3. Turkey Vulture
4. Burrowing Owl
5. Steller's Jay (Pines)

6. Scrub Jay (Oaks)
7. Nighthawk
8. Scissor-tailed Flycatcher
9. Magpie
10. Gambel's Quail

11. Roadrunner

SHORE SILHOUETTES

1. Great Blue Heron
2. Night Heron
3. Green Heron
4. Clapper Rail
5. Marbled Godwit
6. Dowitcher
7. Whimbrel
8. Yellowlegs
9. Black Skimmer
10. Herring Gull
11. Forster's Tern
12. Semipalmated Sandpiper
13. Sanderling
14. Spotted Sandpiper
15. Black-bellied Plover
16. Semipalmated Plover
17. Ruddy Turnstone
18. Killdeer

WATER SILHOUETTES

1. Cormorant
2. Loon
3. Herring Gull
4. Black Skimmer
5. Phalarope (Northern)
6. Merganser (Red-breasted)
7. Coot
8. Forster's Tern
9. Black Tern
10. Mottled Duck
11. Canada Goose
12. Pintail
13. Pied-billed Grebe
14. Common Gallinule

DUSK SILHOUETTES

1. Bat (not a bird)
2. Nighthawk
3. Chuck-will's-widow
4. Night Heron
5. Great Horned Owl
6. Screech Owl
7. Woodcock

Index

IN THE FIELD, the reader will find it most practical to go directly to the illustration. In most cases his problem will be settled there without the necessity of referring to the text.

Page numbers in boldface type refer to the plate illustrations. They are placed only after the common English names of species. They are not used after the scientific names.

The names of all birds are those officially designated in the 5th edition of the A.O.U. *Check-list* (1957). Common names that were in use in the 4th edition of the *Check-list* (1931) and have been changed are also listed. If a common name appears in quotes the name has never been officially sanctioned by the Committee on Classification and Nomenclature of the American Ornithologists' Union, but has attained wide popular use either because of its adoption in Richard Pough's Audubon Bird Guides or because of very widespread gunner's use. Obsolete or little-used vernacular names are not listed.

Flight Silhouettes

1 BARN SWALLOW
2 CLIFF SWALLOW
3 PURPLE MARTIN
4 CHIMNEY SWIFT
5 STARLING
6 GRACKLE
7 RED-WINGED BLACKBIRD
8 BLUEBIRD
9 ROBIN
10 GOLDFINCH
11 HOUSE SPARROW
12 KINGFISHER
13 BLUE JAY
14 FLICKER
15 MOURNING DOVE
16 MEADOWLARK
17 BOBWHITE
18 RUFFED GROUSE
19 PHEASANT
20 NIGHTHAWK
21 CROW
22 SHARP-SHINNED HAWK
23 KESTREL
24 KILLDEER
25 COMMON SNIPE
26 WOODCOCK